Education and Religion in Late Antique Christianity

This book studies the complex attitude of late ancient Christians towards classical education. In recent years, the different theoretical positions that can be found among the Church Fathers have received particular attention. Their statements ranged from enthusiastic assimilation to outright rejection, the latter sometimes masking implicit adoption. Shifting attention away from such explicit statements, this volume focuses on a series of lesser-known texts in order to study the impact of specific literary and social contexts on late ancient educational views and practices. By moving attention from statements to strategies this volume wishes to enrich our understanding of the creative engagement with classical ideals of education.

The multi-faceted approach adopted here illuminates the close connection between specific educational purposes on the one hand, and the possibilities and limitations offered by specific genres and contexts on the other. Instead of seeing attitudes towards education in late antique texts as applications of theoretical positions, it reads them as complex negotiations between authorial intent, the limitations of genre and the context of performance.

Peter Gemeinhardt is Professor of Church History at Göttingen University, Germany. He is director of the DFG-funded Collaborative Research Centre 'Education and Religion in Cultures of the Mediterranean and Its Environment from Ancient to Medieval Times and to the Classical Islam' at the University of Göttingen. Recent publications include: *Antonius: Der erste Mönch* and *Die Kirche und ihre Heiligen. Studien zu Ekklesiologie und Hagiographie in der Spätantike.*

Lieve Van Hoof is a Postdoctoral Research Fellow at Ghent University, Belgium. Trained as a classicist, historian and political scientist, she studies the interplay between literature and politics, culture and power. She is the author of *Plutarch's Practical Ethics: The Social Dynamics of Philosophy*, and editor of *Libanius: A Critical Introduction.*

Peter Van Nuffelen is Professor of Ancient History at Ghent University, Belgium. His main research interests are the religious history of the ancient world and Late Antiquity. He has recently published *Orosius and the Rhetoric of History*. Another book, entitled *Penser la tolérance durant l'Antiquité tardive*, will appear shortly.

Education and Religion in Late Antique Christianity

Reflections, Social Contexts and Genres

Edited by
Peter Gemeinhardt,
Lieve Van Hoof and
Peter Van Nuffelen

LONDON AND NEW YORK

First published 2016
by Routledge
2 Park Square, Milton Park, Abingdon, Oxon OX14 4RN

and by Routledge
711 Third Avenue, New York, NY 10017

Routledge is an imprint of the Taylor & Francis Group, an informa business

© 2016 selection and editorial matter, Peter Gemeinhardt, Lieve Van Hoof and Peter Van Nuffelen; individual chapters, the contributors

The right of Peter Gemeinhardt, Lieve Van Hoof and Peter Van Nuffelen to be identified as the author of the editorial material, and of the authors for their individual chapters, has been asserted in accordance with sections 77 and 78 of the Copyright, Designs and Patents Act 1988.

All rights reserved. No part of this book may be reprinted or reproduced or utilised in any form or by any electronic, mechanical, or other means, now known or hereafter invented, including photocopying and recording, or in any information storage or retrieval system, without permission in writing from the publishers.

Trademark notice: Product or corporate names may be trademarks or registered trademarks, and are used only for identification and explanation without intent to infringe.

British Library Cataloguing in Publication Data
A catalogue record for this book is available from the British Library

Library of Congress Cataloging-in-Publication Data
A catalog record for this book has been requested

ISBN: 978-1-4724-3476-0 (hbk)
ISBN: 978-1-315-57881-1 (ebk)

Typeset in Bembo
By Apex CoVantage, LLC

Contents

List of Figures	vii
Acknowledgements	viii
List of Abbreviations	ix
List of Contributors	x

Education and Religion in Late Antiquity: An Introduction   1
PETER GEMEINHARDT, LIEVE VAN HOOF AND PETER VAN NUFFELEN

PART I
Monastic Education   11

1   **Early Monasticism and the Rhetorical Tradition:**
    Sayings and Stories as School Texts   13
    LILLIAN I. LARSEN

2   **The Education of Shenoute and Other Cenobitic Leaders:**
    Inside and Outside of the Monastery   34
    JANET TIMBIE

3   **Teaching the New Classics: Bible and Biography**
    in a Pachomian Monastery   47
    EDWARD WATTS

PART II
Gnomic Knowledge   59

4   **An Education through Gnomic Wisdom: The *Pandect* of**
    Antiochus as *Bibliotheksersatz*   61
    YANNIS PAPADOGIANNAKIS

vi *Contents*

5 **Syriac Translations of Plutarch, Lucian and Themistius: A Gnomic Format for an Instructional Purpose?** 73
ALBERTO RIGOLIO

6 **Athens and/or Jerusalem? Basil's and Chrysostom's Views on the Didactic Use of Literature and Stories** 86
JAN R. STENGER

PART III
Protreptic 101

7 **Christian Hagiography and the Rhetorical Tradition: Victricius of Rouen, *In Praise of the Saints*** 103
PETER GEMEINHARDT

8 **Falsification as a Protreptic to Truth: The Force of the Forged Epistolary Exchange between Basil and Libanius** 116
LIEVE VAN HOOF

9 **Scripture and Liturgy in the *Life of Mary of Egypt*** 131
DEREK KRUEGER

PART IV
Secular and Religious Learning 143

10 **How Shall We Plead? The Conference of Carthage (411) on Styles of Argument** 145
PETER VAN NUFFELEN

11 **Victor of Vita and Secular Education** 159
KONRAD VÖSSING

12 **Education in the Syriac World of Late Antiquity** 171
DANIEL KING

Bibliography 187
Index 211

Figures

1.1 Letters of the Alphabet. Pottery fragment with ink inscription. Rogers Fund, 1914 (14.1.188). Image copyright: © The Metropolitan Museum of Art. Image source: Art Resource, NY   17

1.2 Alphabet followed by 'θεοφιλεστατοι μοναχοι'. Pottery fragment with ink inscription. Rogers Fund, 1912 (12.180.107). Image copyright: © The Metropolitan Museum of Art. Image source: Art Resource, NY   18

1.3 Alphabets and Syllabary. *Source:* Newberry 1893 (Plate XXV)   18

1.4 *Iliad* 1.1–2. Limestone with ink inscription. Rogers Fund, 1914 (14.1.139). Image copyright: © The Metropolitan Museum of Art. Image source: Art Resource, NY   19

1.5 Sentences of Menander. Wood with ink inscription. Rogers Fund, 1914 (14.1.210). Image copyright: © The Metropolitan Museum of Art. Image source: Art Resource, NY   20

1.6 Χαλινός Wood with ink inscription. Rogers Fund, 1914 (14.1.219). Image copyright: © The Metropolitan Museum of Art. Image source: Art Resource, NY   20

Images are published with permission of The Metropolitan Museum of Art

Acknowledgements

The editors would like to thank the following persons and institutions: the authors of the present volume for accepting to contribute to the present investigation of education and religion in Late Antiquity; the Lichtenberg-Kolleg of the Georg-August-Universität Göttingen for hosting the workshop in June 2013 during which some of the chapters were first presented; the Deutsche Forschungsgemeinschaft (DFG), the Lichtenberg-Kolleg and the Georg-August-Universität for supporting the research stay of Lieve Van Hoof and Peter Van Nuffelen at the Lichtenberg-Kolleg in 2012–13; Ashgate Publishers and Michael Greenwood for accepting this volume and tolerating repeated delays; the anonymous reviewer for helping to improve the coherence of the volume; and finally to Lorenzo Focanti at Ghent as well as to Friederike Magaard at Göttingen for formatting the chapters and preparing the index. Lieve Van Hoof and Peter Van Nuffelen also thank the European Research Council for funding their research under the European Union's Seventh Framework Programme (FP/2007–2013/ ERC Grant Agreement n. 313153).

Abbreviations

AugL	*Augustinus-Lexikon*
CCG	*Corpus Christianorum, Series Graeca*
CCL	*Corpus Christianorum, Series Latina*
CSCO	*Corpus Scriptorum Christianorum Orientalium*
CSEL	*Corpus Scriptorum Ecclesiasticorum Latinorum*
GCS	*Die griechischen christlichen Schriftsteller der ersten drei Jahrhunderte*
MS	Manuscript
OCA	*Orientalia Christiana Analecta*
PAC	Mandouze, A., 1982. *Prosopographie de l'Afrique chrétienne (303–533)* (Prosopographie chrétienne du Bas-Empire 1). Paris: Centre national de la recherche scientifique.
PG	*Patrologia Graeca*
PL	*Patrologia Latina*
PLRE	Jones, A.H.M., Martindale, J.R. and Morris, J. eds, 1971–92. *The Prosopography of the Later Roman Empire*, 3 vols. Cambridge: Cambridge University Press.
SChr	*Sources chrétiennes*

Contributors

Peter Gemeinhardt took his doctoral degree at Marburg University in 2001 (*Die Filioque-Kontroverse zwischen Ost- und Westkirche im Frühmittelalter*) and received his habilitation from Jena University in 2006 (*Das lateinische Christentum und die antike pagane Bildung*). Since 2007 he has been Professor of Church History at Göttingen University. From 2010 to 2014 he directed the Courant Research Centre *Education and Religion from Early Imperial Roman Times to the Classical Period of Islam* (EDRIS), and in 2011 and 2013 he was associate fellow at the Lichtenberg-Kolleg at Göttingen. Current research focuses on education and religion in Late Antiquity and the Middle Ages, on Christian hagiography and on the doctrine of the Trinity. Recent publications include: *Athanasius Handbuch* (ed., 2011); *Von Rom nach Bagdad* (ed. with Sebastian Günther, 2013); and *Die Kirche und ihre Heiligen: Studien zu Ekklesiologie und Hagiographie in der Spätantike* (2014).

Daniel King is Lecturer in Syriac Studies at Cardiff University. His research has focused on the interface of the Greek and Syriac worlds, publishing on the subjects of Greek/Syriac translations and also on Syriac philosophical traditions. He edited the *Earliest Syriac Translation of Aristotle's Categories* (2011) and published various articles on the transmission of Greek ideas to the Syriac and Arabic worlds. He is concerned with cross-cultural translation of religious and philosophical ideas in all contexts, and is now extending his research further into the Bantu cultures of East Africa.

Derek Krueger is the Joe Rosenthal Excellence Professor of Religious Studies at the University of North Carolina at Greensboro. He is the author of three monographs: *Symeon the Holy Fool: Leontius's Life and the Late Antique City* (1996); *Writing and Holiness: The Practice of Authorship in the Early Christian East* (2004); and *Liturgical Subjects: Christian Ritual, Biblical Narrative, and the Formation of the Self in Byzantium* (2014). He also edited *Byzantine Christianity*, the third volume in the series *A People's History of Christianity* (2006). Current projects include essays on the cultivation of emotions in Byzantine Christian rituals and a book that explores how the culture of monasticism in Byzantium produced ideas about masculinity, gender, sexuality and friendship.

Lillian I. Larsen is Professor of Early Christianity at the University of Redlands in Southern California, and a founding Research Fellow in the *Early Monasticism and Classical Paideia* project at Lund University in Sweden. Her main research interest is the history and historiography of monastic education. Her publications include a recent spate of articles treating discrete aspects of monastic pedagogy and a co-edited volume aimed at 'rethinking monastic education', currently under review. Presently, she is completing a monograph focused on re-reading monastic literary sources in light of the material record of monastic education in Egypt, while continuing work on an accompanying catalogue to be submitted for publication.

Yannis Papadogiannakis is a lecturer at King's College London and specialises in Late Antique and Byzantine intellectual and religious history. He is currently leading a team of research associates involved in a multilingual and multidisciplinary ERC-funded project (DEBIDEM) on the role of debate in the definition of belief and identities in the Eastern Mediterranean (sixth–eighth centuries AD). His publications include *Christianity and Hellenism in the Fifth-Century Roman Empire: The Apologetics of Theodoret of Cyrrhus against the Greeks* (2012) and *Defining Identities, Defining Beliefs in the Eastern Mediterranean* (2015).

Alberto Rigolio is a Stipendiary Lecturer in Classics at Merton College, Oxford. His recently defended doctoral dissertation, which is being converted into a monograph, has used both Greek and Syriac sources to study the developments in the provision of literate education within Roman Syria between the fourth and fifth centuries AD. Syriac translations of Greek secular literature in particular have provided a mostly unexplored corpus of texts that offer rich evidence for cultural life in the region during Late Antiquity. His research interests lie in the developments of rhetorical and philosophical education in the later Roman world; on the afterlife and uses of classical literature in early Christianity; and on intercultural and interlinguistic interactions throughout antiquity. As a side project, he has been working on the dialogue form in early Christianity in Greek, Latin and Syriac.

Jan R. Stenger is MacDowell Professor of Greek at the University of Glasgow. His main research interests are Greek lyric poetry and Greek oratory and literature of Late Antiquity. He focuses particularly on the relationship between education and religion in the fourth to sixth centuries. Stenger's publications include *Poetische Argumentation: Die Funktion der Gnomik in den Epinikien des Bakchylides* (2004) and *Hellenische Identität in der Spätantike* (2009). He is currently preparing a monograph on the rhetoric of urban space in John Chrysostom's homilies and writings.

Janet Timbie teaches Coptic language and literature, as well as the history of the Christian Near East, in the Department of Semitic and Egyptian Languages and Literatures at the Catholic University of America, Washington. Her main area of interest is Coptic monastic texts, especially those

xii *Contributors*

representing communal monasticism (Pachomian Koinonia and the White Monastery Federation). In her study of these works, she often focuses on their use of scripture in monastic guidance, both in the way the monastic texts borrow linguistic patterns from the Coptic Bible and in the way biblical role models (patriarchs, prophets and apostles) are selected for emulation by male and female monastics who live in community.

Lieve Van Hoof is a Postdoctoral Research Fellow at Ghent University, Belgium. Trained as a classicist, historian and political scientist, she studies the interplay between literature and politics, culture and power. After publishing a monograph entitled *Plutarch's Practical Ethics: The Social Dynamics of Philosophy* (2010), she turned her attention to Late Antiquity. She has published several articles on Greek literature in the fourth century AD, edited *Libanius: A Critical Introduction* (2014) and is currently preparing a monograph on the letters of Libanius.

Peter Van Nuffelen is Professor of Ancient History at Ghent University, Belgium. His main research interests are the religious history of the ancient world and Late Antiquity. He currently directs a research group on late ancient historiography, co-funded by the ERC, the FWO and the FWO/NWO. He has recently published *Orosius and the Rhetoric of History* (2012) and a book entitled *Penser la tolérance durant l'Antiquité tardive* will appear shortly.

Konrad Vössing is Professor of Ancient History at the Rheinische Friedrich-Wilhelms-Universität in Bonn. Since 2012 he has been a member of the Nordrhein-Westfälische Akademie der Wissenschaften in Düsseldorf. His field of research includes the cultural history of antiquity (notably schools and education, banquets and eating culture, and the history of dress and habitus); the representation of the ruler in antiquity; the imperial cult; Roman North Africa; and the history of the Germanic peoples in Roman Late Antiquity, especially the Vandals.

Edward Watts is the Alkiviadis Vassiliadis Chair and Professor of History at the University of California, San Diego. His research treats the cultural and religious history of Late Antiquity, with a particular focus on the changes caused by the rise of Christianity. His latest book, *The Final Pagan Generation* (2015), details the experiences of men and women born in the 310s as they learned to function in and respond to an increasingly Christian imperial order.

Education and Religion in Late Antiquity

An Introduction

Peter Gemeinhardt, Lieve Van Hoof and Peter Van Nuffelen

Jerome and Caesarius

In a famous passage in his *Letter 22* to the virgin Eustochium, written in 384, Jerome reports how he once dreamed that he was brought to trial, Christ himself being the judge. When he declared to be a Christian, Christ replied: 'You are lying! You are a Ciceronian, not a Christian, for wherever your treasure is, there will be your heart.' Utterly shocked, young Jerome swore that he would never again dare to possess or even read pagan writings – 'and if I ever do so, I have denied you';[1] that is, he would have acted like Peter disowning Jesus during the trial at Pilate's court. Addressing Eustochium, Jerome pointed out that a Christian virgin should avoid any contact with and contamination by the texts commonly used at the grammar and rhetorical schools, and instead acquire a genuinely Christian education, for 'what has Horace to do with the Psalter? what Virgil with the Gospels? what Cicero with the Apostle?'[2] To put it simply: away with all the pagan stuff!

As is well known, this was by no means Jerome's last word concerning the rejection, reception or appropriation of pagan education by pious Christians. It is less well known that this story is re-enacted in the mid-sixth century in the *Life of Caesarius of Arles*, one of the most influential bishops in early Merovingian Gaul. In his youth, Caesarius went to the Isle of Lérins in order to live an ascetic life. Neglecting the admonitions of his fellow monks to moderate his ascetic efforts, he fell ill due to overexertion and was rescued by his family to the city of Arles. Here, Caesarius was supposed to acquire a solid education by studying with the famous teacher of rhetoric, Julianus Pomerius. Like Jerome, however, Caesarius soon experienced a terrifying dream. Tired by the endless study of classical school texts, Caesarius fell asleep, using the book as a pillow for his shoulder. Suddenly he became aware that a dragon had appeared and was about to devour his shoulder and arm. Deeply threatened by this dream, Caesarius – like Jerome – immediately chose to despise any secular skills, knowledge and glory. Or, more precisely, he despised acquiring such competences at school, while he did not deny their usefulness for a Christian preacher: 'He knew well that the jewellery of perfect oratory will not be wanting in those who have gained their insights in a spiritual manner.'[3]

2   *Peter Gemeinhardt, Lieve Van Hoof and Peter Van Nuffelen*

Both texts aim at digging a gap between secular education and Christian teaching, that is, between the wisdom of the world and the wisdom of God, tacitly referring to the 1 Corinthians 1.2 and representing a long-standing inner-Christian discourse concerning values and threats of secular education to religious conduct. And yet, there are significant differences with respect to genre, context and audience: Jerome, in the last quarter of the fourth century, uses the classical epistolographical style with its rhetorical features in order to persuade Eustochium (or in fact her mother, Paula) to acquire a Christian education. He thus employs the literary code of written communication. Therefore, as was already registered by Rufinus, the form of his letter consciously contradicts the content of the narration. And of course Jerome did not at all cease to make use of his ample knowledge of classical literature! When Rufinus accused him of still quoting Horace, Cicero and Virgil, Jerome indignantly replied that already the Old Testament prophets had warned against taking dreams too seriously.[4] What is more important, Jerome claims that if he still remembered and quoted the classics, this would not testify to his continuous reading but to the deep and indelible impregnation by such knowledge acquired at school: 'Shall I drink from the river Lethe – according to the fables of the poets – in order to avoid the accusation of knowing what I have learnt?'[5]

The addressees of Jerome's letters were noble men and women in Rome and other cities of the empire, longing for ascetic instruction while being eager to maintain their education as part of their Christian life. The *Life of Caesarius*, in contrast, was written for an audience that was still capable of written communication but confronted with the disintegration of Roman administration and educational institutions under 'barbarian' rule. The *Life* of their venerated bishop aimed at advocating a Christian way of life within a radically changed world, without any hope to restore ancient ideals of *Romanitas* in Gaul, including a thorough instruction in the *artes liberales*. Thus, it is no longer an epistolographical but instead a hagiographical discourse within which the anonymous authors situate their writing. Caesarius, however, was placed on the threshold of the Roman and the barbarian epoch. Himself a man of letters, Caesarius embodied the uselessness of such educational values in post-Roman society and thus represented change, while Jerome argued for the coexistence of classical and Christian education, the former functioning as propaedeutic for the latter (a model already crucial to the philosophical and theological instruction by Origen in Alexandria and Caesarea).[6]

Jerome's *Letter 22* and the *Life of Caesarius of Arles* thus bear witness to continuities and changes in the perception of education and religion during the fourth to sixth centuries. This period to which we refer as Late Antiquity has famously been declared a period of 'decline and fall' in general by Edward Gibbon and in particular, concerning education, by Henri-Irénée Marrou (although Marrou later came to view this epoch from a more nuanced perspective).[7] It has been denounced as a time of 'décadence', the contemporaries not being able to live up to the values of their forefathers, at best only incompetently reproducing them.[8] In recent times, however, the focus has shifted to Late Antiquity as an epoch *sui generis*, that is, a period in which classical Hellenistic and Roman educational values were merged with a new approach to education from a religious perspective. Peter Brown has highlighted how classical rhetoric was fundamental to the imperial discourse even under the auspices of the Christianisation of empire;[9] Averil Cameron has pointed to the fact that Christian discourse depended on the learning acquired at school even when such learning was rejected outright, terming this phenomenon 'the rhetoric of paradox'.[10] All in all, with 'Late Antiquity' we face a time of intensified debate about classical texts and skills, and of astonishing innovations in combining such learning with the demands of the day. To this debate, the relationship of education and religion was fundamental.

Scope of the Present Volume

As the texts quoted above indicate, the attitude of late ancient Christians towards classical education was complex – and becomes even more complex when looking beyond the Latin part of the empire to Greek Patristic and Christian Oriental literature and, moreover, to non-Christian texts and traditions. In recent years this field has been extensively studied, with particular attention for the different theoretical positions that can be found among the Church Fathers, a development to be observed not only in Christianity but also in Neoplatonic philosophy and paralleled in Jewish religion and early Islam.[11] The respective attitudes ranged, generally speaking, from enthusiastic assimilation to outright rejection, which sometimes covered up implicit adoption. The present volume seeks to shift attention away from such explicit statements that have been used to construct 'the' Christian attitude towards education. It argues that there is no simple way to define this attitude, for at least three reasons.

First, the Christian position towards teaching and classical learning was, as said, complex at any given time, due to the fact that the Christian practice is always accompanied by a reflection on that very practice. In other words, teaching could never be an unreflective practice for Christians in Late Antiquity, as they were acutely aware of its non-Christian origins. This did not necessarily imply immediate rejection, but the reflection on the practice could raise doubts about one's own training (as it did with Jerome) or be exploited in protreptic and polemic.[12] This necessitated, in turn, Christian adaptations that by and large kept the classical form but substituted Christian content.[13] Instead of identifying any of these as 'the' Christian attitude, they should be understood as *cas de figure* generated by the Christian second-order reflection on education.

Second, social contexts produce particular forms of learning, obviously relying on existing models. Late Antiquity was a time of tremendous social change, and we can thus expect substantial differences across time and the Mediterranean. In this volume, this change is present in many ways:

- the rise to prominence of languages such as Coptic and Syriac;[14]
- the decline of traditional social classes in North Africa, defusing the traditional identification of secular learning with paganism;[15]

- the continued presence of a civic elite in the Syriac realm, expressing demand for education;[16]
- as a mirror image of the decline of traditional schools, the rise of learning in specific social contexts, such as the church and liturgy, monasteries and episcopal, legal and rhetorical practice.[17]

This last development, in turn, may have meant that it was possible to reach out to lower social classes that traditionally received little education.[18] This, however, takes place against a background in which the ideal of classical education as exemplified in the traditional teacher of rhetoric remains strong.[19]

Third, the form in which education is practised or opinions about it are expressed shapes the argument itself. Genre (however defined) is thus an important factor in shaping positions on education. As we have seen, there is a difference between a letter to noble Roman ascetics and the life of a saintly bishop written for other Gaulish bishops, and there is an analogous difference between hidden combination and overt rejection of classical education by Christians. In both cases, the subtext may lead to the conclusion drawn by Augustine in *On Christian Doctrine* that grammatical and rhetorical skills are simply necessary for interpreting the Bible and Christian preaching. The precious little treatise of Basil of Caesarea – *Address to Young People on the Right Use of Greek Literature* – witnesses to another approach to classical learning informed by critical reflection from a Christian point of view.[20] Many texts may seem to draw strict lines of separation between secular and Christian learning. Yet, if we look more closely at specific texts, we shall see more nuanced perspectives crop up which are as much part of the Christian discourse on education as the more strident rejections. Conversely, pedagogical concepts could strongly impact on the production of religious literature and determine the choice of genre: processes of selection, condensation, rhetorical elaboration and forgery turn out to be driven by specific protreptic aims.[21] This process may become most tangible in translations: the translator had to make a series of conscious choices ranging from which text to translate, what parts of it to omit or change, to how to translate specific words.[22]

By highlighting these three factors, this volume wishes to shift attention from statements to strategies, so as to enrich our understanding of the creative Christian engagement with classical ideals of education. In order to provide a more diversified sample than is often brought together, the chapters study texts in Latin, Greek, Coptic and Syriac, and usually focus on little-studied texts and examples (letters, historiography, sayings, orations and sermons, acts of councils, philosophical texts, hagiography, translated works from classical antiquity, papyri). The volume thus illuminates the close connection between specific educational purposes on the one hand, and the possibilities and limitations offered by specific genres and contexts on the other. Instead of seeing attitudes towards education in late antique texts as applications of theoretical positions, it reads them as complex negotiations between authorial intent, the limitations of genre and the context of performance. The volume covers over three centuries, from the fourth to the seventh, a period of momentous change in the Mediterranean. Change is indeed prominently present in all chapters, for it is a consciousness of change and difference that shapes many of the debates this volume chronicles. Yet we do not wish to offer a history of attitudes towards education from the fourth to the seventh century. Rather, the thematic organisation of the four parts invites the reader to notice how similar queries and responses would emerge in very different circumstances. In thus shifting attention to specific texts and themes, we hope to heighten our awareness of the richness and complexity of the way late ancient Christianity grappled with education.

Summary of the Chapters

So far we have focused on the overarching questions and arguments of the present volume. Its 12 chapters have been divided into four parts, according to their thematic coherence. The first part contains three chapters on monastic education, and hence focuses on Egypt. The second part highlights one particular and widespread form assumed by education: gnomic sayings. The third collects three chapters on three very different constructions of Christian protreptic, whereas the last focuses on the relationship between secular and religious learning and the perception of that distinction.

Part I, entitled *Monastic Education*, addresses the *locus classicus* supposed to demonstrate how Christians turned away from classical education: the uncouth Egyptian monks. It contributes to a re-evaluation of monastic education, in terms of both its fundamental continuity with classical education and its distinct features due to the peculiar type of community that monasteries constituted. In the first chapter, 'Early Monasticism and the Rhetorical Tradition: Sayings and Stories as School Texts', Lillian Larsen adduces descriptive and documentary evidence to show that classical rhetoric continued to frame monastic education. Given the integral role accorded to gnomic sentences and maxims in ancient education, it argues for the particular merits of reading collections of monastic *apophthegmata* in light of ancient pedagogical models. They incorporate traditional rhetorical prescriptions, and as such may have served the same purposes as ancient maxims, that is, to progress in virtue and in literacy. The next chapter, by Janet Timbie, tackles a similar problem, but with an even greater acuity: the training of Coptic-speaking monastic leaders. The monastic leaders of late ancient Egypt are mainly known to us through their writings in Coptic. This raises the question as to the kind of education they received (Coptic or Greek) and where they were instructed (inside or outside of the monastery). She argues that monasteries were literate communities and that monks were expected to acquire a modicum of reading and writing skills. This could be acquired in the monastery itself, but higher education was probably not institutionalised in monasteries, even if many would learn in practice from listening to educated brothers and reading their works. Most monastic leaders, however, had acquired some training in Greek before embarking on an ascetic life, and when writing in Coptic they applied the rules taught then, in particular the following of established models (increasingly, but not exclusively, the Bible). We witness thus a transfer of rules developed in Greek education to Coptic writing, without proper higher education in Coptic being developed. In the third and last chapter of this section, Edward Watts looks more closely at the social structures underpinning monastic education. Individual monks were put under the guidance of a mentor, who in turn obeyed superiors. Teaching and the affirmation of authority therefore went hand in hand. Personal authority was crucial, as the pupil–mentor relationship was individual and direct. At the same time, this authority was affirmed in the nature of the Pachomian community as a hierarchical community that expressed the continuity between Apostolic preaching and Pachomian communities. This self-understanding was instilled through oral exegesis of biblical passages as well as through the circulation of anecdotes about past leaders. This happened both in formal settings such as house meetings and in individual encounters. The structure of the community thus favoured teaching, and such teaching reinforced the identity and cohesion of the community.

The second part, *Gnomic Knowledge*, concentrates on a certain kind of didactic tool employed in philosophical and religious literature. It already surfaced in the chapter by Larsen, and is now explored through evidence from outside Egypt. Yannis Papadogiannakis ('An Education through Gnomic Wisdom: The *Pandect* of Antiochus as *Bibliotheksersatz*') reassesses the nature of the *Pandect* of Antiochus, the seventh-century author of a set of moralising homilies. Approaching them with a modern spirit searching for systematic exposition, scholarship has tended to dismiss them as derivative and superficial. By situating them in the rhetorical and philosophical tradition of the ancient world, Papadogiannakis shows that they offer condensed instruction which served the needs of meditation and memorisation of a monastic community. Interiorised, the gnomic morality became a guidance for action in real life. In his chapter, Alberto Rigolio asks whether Syriac translations of Greek secular literature might represent 'a gnomic format for an instructional purpose'. A series of Syriac translations of Greek moral treatises – in particular works by Plutarch, Lucian and Themistius – were made in the fifth and sixth centuries. The close analysis of the modifications the texts underwent in the process of translating shows a clear influence from wisdom literature; for example, how through the use of aphorisms, moral expansions and other literary tools, the knowledge transmitted acquires a gnomic nature. Rigolio draws attention to parallels with the *Dialogues* of John of Apamea and the didactic situation they presuppose; namely, how in order to convey his message to an audience that had received little instruction, the interlocutors use tools such as stories and moral sentences. The translations, so Rigolio suggests, may have functioned in a similar educational context. In the final contribution to this part, Jan Stenger tackles the question of 'Athens and/or Jerusalem' – prominent already in Tertullian – with respect to Basil's and Chrysostom's views on the didactic use of literature and stories. His chapter provides some background to the approaches to education witnessed in Antiochus and the Syriac translations. John Chrysostom and Basil of Caesarea set out very different conceptions of Christian education. John expects the complete Christianisation of the household and the abandonment of classical learning, he identifies the elite habitus of *paideia* as one of the causes of their lack of moral virtue and hopes that the Christian household can become the place of a Christian education. Basil, by contrast, accepts the value of traditional education, even towards virtue, but sees Christianity as capping the achievement. Both, thus, insist on the moral value of education but judge the role of traditional education differently. Both, however, insist on the use of stories and quotations to make the education they have to offer accessible to their audiences.

The third part, *Protreptic*, shifts attention away from precise educational context towards broader didactic uses of texts. It focuses on how texts function as protreptic and how they therefore reflect and presuppose social conditions and a certain valuation of education. The chapter by Peter Gemeinhardt – 'Christian Hagiography and the Rhetorical Tradition: Victricius of Rouen, *In Praise of the Saints*' – analyses the use of rhetoric for establishing a 'community of saints' formed by relics of deceased martyrs, on the one hand, and by the Christian people of Rouen, on the other hand. Victricius employs the rhetorical devices of an imperial 'adventus' in order to welcome the saints in his town. Moreover, he develops a perception of holiness as preserved even in the tiniest parts of bodily remains of the martyrs, so that their holiness may be materially present all over the world; but, finally, Victricius goes on to argue that saints are not only to be venerated but also imitated. Thus, by teaching that imitation of Christ is fundamental to the veneration of relics, and by preaching as well as by performing the present panegyric, the bishop functions as spiritual teacher of his flock. The next chapter, by Lieve Van Hoof, shifts attention to the genre of letters. Twenty-six letters document an exchange of views between Libanius, the famous pagan teacher of rhetoric from Antioch, and Basil of Caesarea, the equally famous Father of the Church. Besides providing additional proof that this is a forged collection, a close reading of the letters shows how the forger subtly shapes the collection as a protreptic for aspiring members of the elite. They are invited to reconsider the role played in their life by rhetoric – identified as a pagan practice and associated with pride – and to assimilate themselves with Basil, who not only surpasses Libanius in rhetoric and virtue, but also decided to embrace an ascetic life. A subtle hierarchy is thus evoked, whereby Christian rhetoric surpasses its pagan counterpart, but is itself overcome by a higher way of life. The third part concludes with a chapter by Derek Krueger on the use of biblical references in the seventh-century *Life of Mary of Egypt*. The text presupposes that Mary learns in church about Scripture. This reveals, in turn, that many biblical echoes in contemporary texts reflect attendance at the liturgy, which functions as the main conduit for the transmission of knowledge. An allusion to a hymn by Romanus the Melodist confirms this. The *Life* itself, finally, also partakes in that process; that is, it was itself read in a liturgical context and thus provided instruction in a liturgical setting.

The contributions by Gemeinhardt and Van Hoof already touch on the religious valuation of education as pagan or Christian. The third part tackles this theme explicitly. Peter Van Nuffelen takes the Conference of Carthage (411), convoked by the Emperor Honorius to allow Catholics and Donatists to settle their differences through debate, as a springboard to highlight how Christian use of education was usually accompanied by a second-order reflection on that use. Indeed, one of the issues debated at Carthage was what the issue at stake was. If it was a legal issue, the bishops would plead according to the rules of forensic (that is, secular) rhetoric; if the argument was theological, they would revert to an ecclesiastical mode of arguing, which relied on the Bible. Such an opposition was not neutral. The former was negatively characterised, allowing the latter to emerge as the proper way to settle the issue. If shown with particular clarity at the conference, such distinctions can be found elsewhere.

Besides demonstrating the well-known preference for ecclesiastical learning, they also demonstrate an awareness that different types of argument and learning were appropriate in different social contexts and for different subjects, and that they should, at any rate, not be misconstrued as wholesale rejections of secular learning or debate. Rather, the normative views attached to certain practices and types of learning were used as part of the argument itself, and the sometimes heated debates about education in Christian circles can be understood, so Van Nuffelen argues, as deriving from the Christian integration of a first-order use and a second-order reflection on this use.

In the history of the Vandal persecution, written by Victor of Vita towards the end of the fifth century, Konrad Vössing notes less of a need to distinguish secular from ecclesiastical learning. Victor, a clearly ecclesiastical author, praises classical authors without feeling the need to introduce the qualifications or caution that was standard in the age of Augustine. Rather than seeing this as a feature typical for Victor, Vössing argues that this attitude reflects a general shift in attitudes due to the social changes brought about by the Vandal conquest. Whereas before the conquest power was held by the provincial elite for which classical learning was a second nature, the Vandal kings established their power on faithfulness to Arianism and to a Vandal, non-Roman, identity. Traditional elite and Catholic Church now faced the same enemy. This led to an integration of both groups, but also removed much of the social tension that underpinned earlier debates about education. Thus, classical learning in fifth-century Africa is not only marked by a gradual erosion but also by a wider social acceptance.

Finally, Daniel King shows how the Syriac world engaged with the same issues surrounding the heritage of classical education as the Greek- and Latin-speaking regions. One reason for this is that the Syriac world remained for a long time bilingual Greek-Syriac and thus had direct access to Greek texts and the debates surrounding them. At the same time, Syriac texts and education rapidly gained prestige. Emphasising how Syriac authors adopted the standards and contents of Greek education, for example in grammar and rhetoric, and how the same aspiration of a rise in social status was attached to it, he demonstrates that this content and assessment survived the decline of urban structures and the transferral of education towards monasteries, which became from the sixth century onwards centres of intellectual activities. Yet learning also survived outside formal institutions: philosophy, for example, never seems to have been taught at schools, but was rather associated with the practice and teaching of medicine (as it was in the Greek-speaking world too).

Notes

1 Jerome, *Letter* 22.30.4–5 (CSEL 54, 190.5–191.7 Hilberg): *Interrogatus condicionem Christianum me esse respondi. Et ille, qui residebat: 'mentiris, ait, Ciceronianus es, non Christianus; ubi thesaurus tuus, ibi et cor tuum' . . . Domine, si umquam habuero codices saeculares, si legero, te negaui.*

2 Jerome, *Letter* 22.29.7 (CSEL 54, 189.2–4 Hilberg): *quid facit cum psalterio Horatius? cum euangeliis Maro? cum apostolo Cicero? nonne scandalizatur frater, si te uiderit in idolio recumbentem?*

3 *Life of Caesarius of Arles* 1.9 (SChr 536, 160.18–20 Delage): *Igitur contempsit haec protinus, sciens quia non deesset illis perfectae loquutionis ornatus, quibus spiritalis eminet intellectus.*

4 Jerome, *Apology against Rufinus* 1.31 (CCL 79, 31.5–8 Lardet).

5 Jerome, *Apology against Rufinus* 1.31 (CCL 79, 30.52–3 Lardet): *Bibendum igitur mihi erit de lethaeo gurgite, iuxta fabulas poetarum, ne arguar scire quod didici?*

6 See Origen's *Letter* to Gregory Thaumaturgus.

7 Cf. Marrou 1938 and 1978.

8 For a new approach to the 'décadence' paradigm see now Formisano/Fuhrer 2014.

9 Brown 1992.

10 Cameron 1991.

11 Gemeinhardt/Günther 2013.

12 This is discussed in the contributions by Gemeinhardt, Van Hoof, Van Nuffelen and Vössing.

13 See, in particular, Larsen and Rigolio.

14 See Timbie, Rigolio and King.

15 See Vössing.

16 See King.

17 Respectively Krueger, Timbie and Watts, Van Nuffelen.

18 See Timbie and Rigolio.

19 See Van Hoof.

20 See Stenger.

21 See Larsen, Papadogiannakis, Rigolio, Van Hoof.

22 See Rigolio, King.

Part I
Monastic Education

1 Early Monasticism and the Rhetorical Tradition

Sayings and Stories as School Texts

Lillian I. Larsen

One would be hard put to find even one reader of early monastic texts who is unfamiliar with the Athanasian portrayal of Antony, 'founder' of the *anchoretic* strain of early Egyptian monasticism, as not only 'unlettered', but also explicitly uninterested in becoming otherwise.[1] Many could recite the pertinent lines of Athanasius' *Vita* by heart:

> Καὶ παιδίον μὲν ὢν, ἐτρέφετο παρὰ τοῖς γονεῦσι, πλέον αὐτῶν καὶ τοῦ οἴκου μηδὲν ἕτερον γινώσκων· ἐπειδὴ δὲ καὶ αὐξήσας ἐγένετο παῖς, καὶ προέκοπτε τῇ ἡλικίᾳ, γράμματα μὲν μαθεῖν οὐκ ἠνέσχετο, βουλόμενος ἐκτὸς εἶναι καὶ τῆς πρὸς τοὺς παῖδας συνηθείας· τὴν δὲ ἐπιθυμίαν πᾶσαν εἶχε ... ὡς ἄπλαστος οἰκεῖν ἐν τῇ οἰκίᾳ αὐτοῦ.
>
> [Antony was] cognizant of little else besides [his parents] and his home. As he grew and became a boy, and was advancing in years, he could not bear to learn letters, wishing also to stand apart from friendship with other children. All his yearning . . . was for living, an unaffected person, in his home.[2]

Conjoined with Antony's studied a-literacy, two apophthegms featuring the famously literate monks Arsenius and Evagrius are as familiar.[3] In one well-rehearsed exchange, Evagrius queries Arsenius:

> *Quomodo nos excitati eruditione et scientia nullas virtutes habemus, hi autem rustici in Aegypto habitantes tantas virtutes possident?*
>
> How is it that we educated and learned men have no goodness, and the Egyptian peasants have a great deal?

Arsenius responds:

> *Nos quia mundanae eruditionis disciplinis intenti sumus, nihil habemus; hi autem rustici Aegyptii ex propriis laboribus acquisierunt virtutes.*
>
> We have nothing because we go chasing after worldly knowledge. These Egyptian peasants have got their goodness by hard work.[4]

14   *Lillian I. Larsen*

In a second account, Arsenius is challenged while consulting an Egyptian γέρων about his thoughts. Here an unidentified interlocutor queries:

> Ἀββᾶ Ἀρσένιε, πῶς τοσαύτην παίδευσιν Ῥωμαϊκὴν καὶ Ἑλληνικὴν ἐπιστάμενος, τοῦτον τὸν ἀγροῖκον περὶ τῶν σῶν λογισμῶν ἐρωτᾷς;
>
> Abba Arsenius, how is it that you with such a good Latin and Greek education, ask this peasant about your thoughts?

Arsenius replies:

> Τὴν μὲν Ῥωμαϊκὴν καὶ Ἑλληνικὴν ἐπίσταμαι παίδευσιν· τὸν δὲ ἀλφάβητον τοῦ ἀγροίκου τούτου οὔπω μεμάθηκα.
>
> I have indeed been taught Latin and Greek, but I do not know even the alphabet of this peasant.[5]

Numerous narrative allusions to early monks reading, writing and commenting on scripture overtly challenge these well-worn depictions.[6] However, in subsequent scholarship, it is the caricatured binaries of 'a-' and 'exceptional' literacy, assigned to Antony, Evagrius and Arsenius, that have routinely shaped representation of early monastic investment in education and literate pursuits.[7]

The scholarly trajectory that attends Henri Marrou's *History of Education in Antiquity* offers a particularly compelling example of the puzzling problematics posed by such selective citation. In this epic work, Marrou deems resistance to literate pursuits 'one of the most characteristic features of "Eastern" monasticism'.[8] Naming as evidence Athanasius' caricature of Antony's studied a-literacy, Marrou introduces his discussion of 'the monastic school in the East' with the premise that the earliest monks would have received 'a kind of training that was ascetic and moral, spiritual rather than intellectual'. Obliquely alluding to the apophthegmatic exchanges of Arsenius and Evagrius noted above, he names a 'fundamental feature of Eastern monasticism', its emphasis not on 'learning . . . [but] forgetting . . . poetry and secular knowledge'.[9]

Affirming the scope of Marrou's particular influence,[10] in a recent anthology explicitly devoted to re-thinking Marrou's 'totalizing narrative',[11] an included re-analysis of monastic investment in literate pursuits begins with immediate reference to Antony, and to the well-worn apophthegmatic exchanges between Evagrius and Arsenius. Evagrius is astutely named 'one of the most original thinkers . . . in the tradition', and his teaching 'a kind of absent chapter' in the history of education. However, consonant with the well-rehearsed caricature of a-literate, rustic monks, he is pictured 'pitted against the fathers'; an urban intellectual 'facing off' with 'desert wisdom'.[12]

Encountering pedagogical binaries, supported solely by uninterrogated caricature that spans generations of increasingly critical surveys of ancient education,[13] must give pause. However, having sparked imaginations for well over a millennium, perhaps it should not surprise that the larger than life personas assigned to Antony, Evagrius and Arsenius continue to catch the reader's eye. Rhetorically, this is exactly the point. Ironically, it is a measure of the literary acumen of late ancient writers that these depictions remain operative. Painted in compelling shades, the personas that populate these sayings and stories are intended to capture attention, and so shape a civic ethos.[14] There is, nonetheless, much to be gained by resisting their persuasive appeal. Although narrative snapshots of Antony, Evagrius and Arsenius have persistently been framed as authentic portrayals, it is important to register the constructed character of the caricatured figures being deployed. In reading such hagiographical figures historically, this chapter argues that long-standing emphasis on monastic resistance to pedagogical pursuits merits re-assessment: (a) relative to descriptive discussions of the role accorded education in early monastic life; (b) in conversation with extant material remains that derive from monastic pedagogical settings; and perhaps most importantly, (c) in light of the literary genre to which such texts belong.[15]

Descriptive Evidence

If one truly aims to 're-think' monasticism as an 'absent chapter' in the history of education, pairing narrative depictions of 'a-' or 'exceptionally' literate monks with the uniform patterns that characterise descriptive discussions of early monastic education is instructive. As geographically disparate refrains reflect routine pedagogical practice across a spectrum of monastic settings, common strains of literate investment challenge conventional caricature in productive ways.

Basil (AD 329–79)

Albeit compiled in Caesarea, far from the deserts of Egypt, Basil's lengthy fourth-century *Asketikon* (*Reg. Fus.*) mandates that children held in common by the community be educated according to a monastic 'ideal'.[16] He recommends that both children and adults meet together for prayer, but that the groups be kept separate with respect to houses and meals, to ensure that 'the house of the monks . . . not be disturbed by . . . repetition of lessons necessary for the young'.[17] Conceiving what may be most accurately regarded as an emergent monastic curriculum, he suggests lessons include the 'language of Scripture' and 'maxims drawn from the Proverbs'.[18] In place of 'myths', he advises that instruction incorporate stories of wonderful deeds 'so [that] . . . [children's] soul[s] may be led to [practice] good immediately and from the outset, while [they are] still plastic and soft, pliable as wax, and easily moulded by the shapes pressed upon [them]'.[19] This will assure that 'when [with maturity] reason is added, and the power of discrimination, [early training will] run its course . . . [and] habit will make success easy'.[20]

Jerome (AD 347–419)

Relatively contemporary writing, originating from a Palestinian context, is still more explicit. In a letter to one Laeta, about the education of her daughter,[21] Jerome recommends that Laeta have 'a set of letters made . . . of boxwood or of ivory', so that young Paula may learn to call

16 *Lillian I. Larsen*

each by its proper name.[22] In order to know them by sight as well as by sound, he suggests that the child be made to grasp 'not only . . . the right order of the letters and remember their names in a simple song, but also frequently upset their order and mix the last letters with the middle ones, the middle with the first'.[23]

Moving from letters to syllables to words, Jerome advises that the very names (*ipsa nomina*) Paula uses in forming sentences not be assigned haphazardly, but 'chosen and arranged on purpose'. To aid in training both tongue and memory, he suggests wordlists include 'the names of the prophets and the apostles, and the whole list of patriarchs from Adam downward, as [given by] Matthew and Luke'.[24] Progressing to sentences and short passages, Jerome advises that Paula recite portions of scripture as a fixed daily task, noting that these 'verses' should be learned first in Greek, then in Latin. With Basil, he recommends that young Paula begin 'with the sweet music of the Psalms',[25] then turn to 'lessons of life [found] in the proverbs of Solomon'.[26]

After outlining his ideal curriculum, Jerome concludes by emphasising the difficulties implicit in Laeta's tackling such lofty instructional goals amidst her busy duties in Rome. He urges, instead, that young Paula be sent to Bethlehem, to be educated in a monastery. Here, in an establishment run by the child's grandmother, the elder Paula and her aunt Eustochium, he offers his own services as tutor. As Paula's ideal instructor, a man of 'approved years, life, and learning', he likens his role to that of Aristotle – teaching Alexander 'his first letters'.[27]

Pachomius (AD 320–40/340–404)

While, per caricatured depictions of Antony, Arsenius and Evagrius, Egyptian monasticism has traditionally been framed as anomalously 'rustic', texts hailing from a Pachomian milieu also portray training in basic literary skills as part of the community's daily rhythms. Although arguably addressing an alternate demographic,[28] the Pachomian *Praecepta* mandate that each newly entering monk, if unformed, should be given 'twenty psalms or two of the Apostle's epistles, or some other part of the Scripture'.[29] Anyone who is illiterate (*litteras ignorabit*), is directed to go at the first, third and sixth hour:

> *hora prima et tertia et sexta uadet ad eum qui docere potest et qui ei fuerit delegatus, et stabit ante illum, et discet studiosissime cum omni gratiarum actione. Postea uero scribentur ei elementa syllabae, uerba ac nomina, et etiam nolens legere compelletur.*
> to someone who can teach and has been appointed for him. He shall stand before him and learn very studiously with all gratitude. Then the fundamentals of a syllable, the verbs, and nouns shall be written for him, and even if he does not want to, he shall be compelled to read.[30]

An accompanying Pachomian 'Precept' makes the aim of this instruction clear: 'There shall be no one . . . in the monastery who does not learn to read and does not memorize something of the Scriptures.'[31]

Material Evidence

The sequences described by Basil, Jerome and Pachomius find ready corroboration among monastic material remains.[32] Although this evidence has likewise often been subject to interpretive overlays that take monastic a-literacy as a starting point, even cursory perusal challenges conventionally caricatured dichotomies.[33]

Like broader school inventories,[34] artefacts that derive from monastic settings attest that students learned letters by name and by shape (Figure 1.1).[35]

Alphabets were orally recited, and copied out on boards, wax tablets and ostraca (Figure 1.2).[36]

Sequences were memorised in variously ordered configurations (Figure 1.3).[37]

Monastic syllabaries appear to preserve the same combinations encountered across a broader, non-monastic array of classroom artefacts.[38]

As students progressed to forming words, structural similarities are as patent. Extant wordlists include monosyllabic, disyllabic and trisyllabic combinations. Like their Graeco-Roman counterparts, monastic students arguably did not 'waste [their] labor in writing out [and reading] common words of everyday occurrence', but those that might prove useful at a later stage.[39] Following the

Figure 1.1 Letters of the Alphabet

Rogers Fund, 1914 (14.1.188). Image copyright: © The Metropolitan Museum of Art. Image source: Art Resource, NY

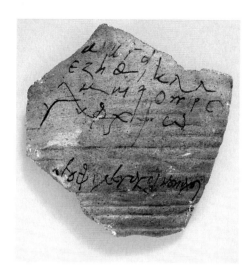

Figure 1.2 Alphabet followed by 'θεοφιλεστατοι μοναχοι'
Rogers Fund, 1912 (12.180.107). Image copyright: © The Metropolitan Museum of Art. Image source: Art Resource, NY

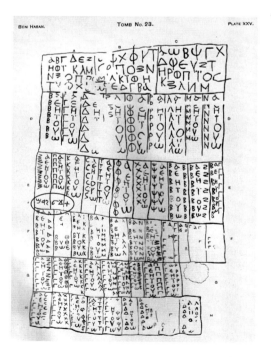

Figure 1.3 Alphabets and Syllabary
Source: Newberry 1893 (Plate XXV)

adjustments commended by Jerome, extant wordlists attest that 'the prophets or the apostles or the list of patriarchs from Adam downwards as . . . given by Matthew and Luke' served well in training both the 'tongue . . . [and] memory'.[40] Encouragement to work with 'strange, and/or difficult to pronounce words'[41] invited practice for which the Bible was particularly well suited.

Once students moved beyond forming letters, manipulating alphabets, reciting syllables and sounding out words, they progressed to copying gnomic maxims, sayings and longer passages. Here, practice that incorporates content encountered in conventional school settings is readily identifiable. For example, three ostraca provenanced to the Monastery of Epiphanius in Thebes preserve writing exercises comprised of lines from Homer (Figure 1.4).[42]

A larger ostracon, arguably a teacher's model, contains an alphabetical list of selected Sentences of Menander (Figure 1.5).[43]

Even seemingly obscure and highly specific formulations find attestation. For example, two of three extant examples of the χαλινός – a maxim formed by using every letter of the Greek alphabet[44] – are provenanced to Theban monastic establishments (Figure 1.6).[45]

Figure 1.4 Iliad 1.1–2

Rogers Fund, 1914 (14.1.139). Image copyright: © The Metropolitan Museum of Art. Image source: Art Resource, NY

Figure 1.5 Sentences of Menander

Rogers Fund, 1914 (14.1.210). Image copyright: © The Metropolitan Museum of Art. Image source: Art Resource, NY

Figure 1.6 Χαλινός

Rogers Fund, 1914 (14.1.219). Image copyright: © The Metropolitan Museum of Art. Image source: Art Resource, NY

The third is likewise linked to a monastic milieu.[46] Within this frame, the density of pedagogical artefacts that display lines drawn from scripture underscores the confluence that links classroom practice with the emergent rhythms of monastic life.[47] Such pieces have often been classified as 'biblical' rather than school related. However, beyond shifts in content, the routinised character of included practice suggests work with forms emblematic of those employed across the broader pedagogical landscape.[48] In turn – per Jerome, Basil and Pachomius – perhaps the density of artefacts that include material drawn from Psalms, Proverbs and the writings of Paul, the 'Apostle', should not surprise.[49]

Literary Evidence

If placing descriptive discussions in conversation with material remains raises questions about the adequacy of traditional reflections on the role accorded education in early monastic life, reading monastic sayings and stories in light of the literary genre to which they belong invites further re-assessment. The pedagogical purpose assigned to sayings and stories – material long used to argue against literate investment – is particularly well attested. In fact, Teresa Morgan has observed that 'more gnomic [sentences] survive [in schoolhands] than fragments of any other literature, or any other exercise'.[50]

Similar to learning pottery on a simple pot rather than a huge storage jar, work with gnomic sentences, sayings and stories served a central role in teaching skills foundational to more advanced composition and/or declamation. In a series of set exercises, students moved from rehearsing the basics of elementary grammar to practising modes of discourse that brought them to the 'threshold of rhetoric'. In turn, like the words in young Paula's lists, included gnomic content was understood to be doubly useful. Whether explicitly or by allusion, iteration was aimed not only at technical proficiency but also at promoting virtue and shaping character.[51]

As summarised by Raffaella Cribiore, 'a pupil's initial taste of a maxim, gained by copying a short text as an exercise in penmanship, was enriched when he [or she] attempted to read the same text with words and syllables separated'. In an iterative cycle, students 'chew[ed]' gnomic sentences and maxims 'over and over . . . making collections of them and expanding their content . . . until' they could (at an opportune moment or in a well-turned phrase) incorporate them into everyday speech and writing.[52] As outlined in handbooks that span half a millennium, the graded 'preliminary exercises' (προγυμνάσματα) that governed this work were so routinised they have been likened to the 'structural features of classical architecture'.[53]

Maxims (γνῶμαι)

At the most basic levels of composition, students were introduced to cryptic maxims like those attributed to the seven sages: γνῶθι σεαυτόν (know thyself), θεοὺς σέβου (fear the gods), γονεῖς αἰδοῦ (honour [your] parents). During subsequent

22 Lillian I. Larsen

stages, these small and infinitely malleable injunctions could be combined to create sentences similar to those encountered in the collected monostichs of Menander. For example: γονεῖς τιμῶν μάλιστα θεὸν φοβοῦ (Honor your parents, [but] fear God most of all).[54] As suggested by this sentence drawn from the Epiphanian ostracon discussed above, within a monastic frame, extant reformulations blur long instantiated boundaries between Christian and 'Graeco-Roman', elementary and advanced, 'lettered' and 'rustic', in provocative ways.[55]

Concise Reminiscences (χρεῖαι)

In the same progymnasmatic sequence, these elements might again be reformulated as a χρεία, 'a concise reminiscence', aptly attributed to a named or anonymous protagonist.[56] Standing between the simple 'maxim' and the longer 'reminiscence', χρεῖαι shared close and porous borders with each of these neighbouring forms.[57] Any 'aptly' attributed maxim might double as a χρεία. For example:

> [Γέρων εἶπεν·] γονεῖς τιμῶν μάλιστα θεὸν φοβοῦ.
> [An old man said:] 'Honour your parents, [but] fear God most of all.'

A lengthier reminiscence could be stripped of its narrative detail and readily reformulated.[58] Χρεῖαι could additionally be comprised of an attributed action (πρακτικαί).[59] For example:

> Ἔλεγον περὶ τοῦ ἀββᾶ Ἀγάθωνος, ὅτι τρία ἔτη ἐποίησεν ἔχων λίθον εἰς τὸ στόμα αὐτοῦ, ἕως οὗ κατώρθωσε τὸ σιωπᾶν.
> It was said of Abba Agathon that for three years he lived with a stone in his mouth, until he learnt to keep silence.[60]

They could alternatively be framed using a mixture of speech and action (μικταί).[61] For example:

> Ἀδελφός ποτε ἐσφάλη εἰς Σκῆτιν· καὶ γενομένου συνεδρίου, ἀπέστειλαν πρὸς τὸν ἀββᾶν Μωϋσῆν. Ὁ δὲ οὐκ ἤθελεν ἐλθεῖν. Ἀπέστειλεν οὖν πρὸς αὐτὸν ὁ πρεσβύτερος, λέγων· Ἐλθέ, ὅτι σε ὁ λαὸς περιμένει. Ὁ δὲ ἀναστὰς ἦλθε. Καὶ λαβὼν σπυρίδα τετρημμένην, καὶ γεμίσας ἄμμου, ἐβάστασεν. Οἱ δὲ ἐξελθόντες εἰς ἀπάντησιν αὐτοῦ, λέγουσιν αὐτῷ· Τί ἐστι τοῦτο, Πάτερ; Εἶπε δὲ αὐτοῖς ὁ γέρων· Αἱ ἁμαρτίαι μού εἰσιν ὀπίσω μου καταρρέουσαι, καὶ οὐ βλέπω αὐτάς· καὶ ἦλθον ἐγὼ σήμερον, ἁμαρτήματα ἀλλότρια κρῖναι. Οἱ δὲ ἀκούσαντες, οὐδὲν ἐλάλησαν τῷ ἀδελφῷ· ἀλλὰ συνεχώρησαν αὐτῷ.
> A brother at Scetis committed a fault. A council was called to which Abba Moses was invited, but he refused to go to it. Then the priest sent someone to say to him, 'Come, for everyone is waiting for you.' So he got up and went. He took a leaking jug, filled it with water and carried it with him. The others came out to meet him and said to him, 'What is this, Father?' The old man said to them, 'My sins run out behind me, and I do not see them,

and today I am coming to judge the errors of another.' When they heard that they said no more to the brother but forgave him.[62]

A μικτόν (or πρακτικόν) could as easily be reworked as a λογικόν. For example:

Εἶπεν ὁ ἀββᾶς Ἰωάννης· Τὸ ἐλαφρὸν φορτίον ἐάσαντες, τουτέστι τὸ ἑαυτοὺς μέμφεσθαι, τὸ βαρὺ ἐβαστάσαμεν, τουτέστι τὸ δικαιοῦν ἑαυτούς.
    Abba John said: We have put the light burden on one side, that is to say, self-accusation, and we have loaded ourselves with a heavy one, that is to say self-justification.[63]

As the latter examples suggest, whether expanded, condensed, collapsed and/or variously articulated, the same or similar χρεία could appear in a range of guises.[64] While χρεῖαι comprised of attributed action (πρακτικαί), or a mixture of words and action (μικταί), are well represented in extant source material, of the three classes of χρεῖαι, forms involving speech – that is, 'sayings' – are the most common. They are, likewise, the most differentiated.[65] A saying (λογικόν) could be articulated as a statement (ἀποφαντικόν) or as a response (ἀποκριτικόν). Each articulation could be further delineated by virtue of how a particular statement or response was structured.

Sayings Framed as Statements (ἀποφαντικαί)

At base, a saying framed as a statement (ἀποφαντικόν) was comprised of a 'word' (λόγος)[66] – generally, a maxim – aptly attributed to a well-known character (πρόσωπον), or something like a character.[67] This statement could be 'unprompted' (καθ' ἑκούσιον ἀπόφασιν).[68] For example:

Εἶπεν ὁ ἀββᾶς Ἀγάθων· Χρὴ τὸν μοναχὸν μὴ ἐάσαι τὴν συνείδησιν αὐτοῦ κατηγορῆσαι αὐτοῦ εἰς οἱονδήποτε πρᾶγμα.
    Abba Agathon said, 'Under no circumstances should the monk let his conscience accuse him of anything.'[69]

Alternatively, it could 'arise out of a specific circumstance' (κατὰ περίστασιν).[70] For example:

Ὁ ἀββᾶς Βενιαμὶν εἴρηκε τοῖς υἱοῖς αὐτοῦ ἀποθνήσκων· Ταῦτα ποιεῖτε, καὶ δύνασθε σωθῆναι· Πάντοτε χαίρετε, ἀδιαλείπτως προσεύχεσθε, ἐν παντὶ εὐχαριστεῖτε.
    As he was dying, Abba Benjamin said to his sons, 'If you observe the following, you can be saved. "Be joyful at all times, pray without ceasing and give thanks for all things".'[71]

As eminently straightforward stratagems were employed in transforming a λόγος/maxim into a saying, structural simplicity ensured implicit versatility.

24 Lillian I. Larsen

Sayings Framed as Responses (ἀποκριτικαί)

As delineated by Theon, a 'saying' (λογικόν) could as readily be formulated as a response (ἀποκριτικόν). This response could address a question (ἐρωτηματικόν), which required a 'yes' or 'no' answer.[72] For example:

Ἠρωτήθη ὁ αὐτὸς, εἰ ἀρκεῖ εἷς δίκαιος δυσωπῆσαι τὸν Θεὸν, καὶ ἔφη· Ναὶ, αὐτὸς γὰρ εἶπεν· Ἐρευνήσατε ἕνα ποιοῦντα κρῖμα καὶ δικαιοσύνην, καὶ ἵλεως ἔσομαι παντὶ τῷ λαῷ.

[On being] asked if one righteous man was enough to appease God, [Abba Epiphanius] replied, 'Yes, for he himself has written: "Find a man who lives according to righteousness, and I will pardon the whole people".

(Jer. 5.1)'[73]

It could alternatively be framed as a response 'to an inquiry' (τὸ κατὰ πύσμα) that required further elucidation (πυσματικόν).[74] For example:

Ἠρώτησεν ὁ πρεσβύτερος τῆς Νιτρείας, ὅπως ὀφείλουσιν οἱ ἀδελφοὶ διάγειν. Οἱ δὲ εἶπαν Ἐν μεγάλῃ ἀσκήσει, καὶ τηροῦντες τὴν συνείδησιν ἀπὸ τοῦ πλησίον.

The priest of Nitria asked [Abba Pambo] how the brethren ought to live. He replied, 'With much labour, guarding their consciences towards their neighbour'.[75]

It could be fashioned as a 'response . . . to a question calling for an explanation' (τὸ κατ' ἐρώτησιν αἰτιῶδες).[76] For example:

Ἠρώτησεν ὁ ἀββᾶς Μάρκος τὸν ἀββᾶν Ἀρσένιον λέγων· Καλὸν τὸν μὴ ἔχειν τινὰ ἐν τῷ κελλίῳ αὐτοῦ παράκλησιν; εἶδον γὰρ ἀδελφόν τινα ἔχοντα μικρὰ λάχανα, καὶ ἐκριζοῦντα αὐτά. Καὶ εἶπεν ὁ ἀββᾶς Ἀρσένιος· Καλὸν μέν ἐστιν, ἀλλὰ πρὸς τὴν ἕξιν τοῦ ἀνθρώπου· ἐὰν γὰρ μὴ ἔχῃ ἰσχὺν ἐν τῷ τοιούτῳ τρόπῳ, πάλιν φυτεύει ἄλλα.

Abba Mark asked Abba Arsenius, 'Is it good to have nothing extra in the cell? I saw a brother who had some vegetables and he has pulled them up.' Abba Arsenius replied, 'Undoubtedly that is good but it must be done according to a man's capacity. For if he does not have the strength for such practice he will soon plant others.'[77]

More generally, a responsive statement (λεγόμενον ἀποκριτικόν) could address neither a simple question nor an inquiry, but rather 'some remark to which [the] response [was] made' (λόγον δέ τινα ἔχουσαι πρὸς ὅν ἐστιν ἡ ἀπόκρισις).[78] For example:

Ἄλλοτε ἦλθον δύο γέροντες ἀναχωρηταὶ μεγάλοι ἀπὸ τῶν μερῶν τοῦ Πηλουσίου πρὸς αὐτὴν καὶ ἀπερχόμενοι ἔλεγον πρὸς ἀλλήλους· Ταπεινώσωμεν τὴν γραῖδα ταύτην. Καὶ λέγουσιν αὐτῇ· Βλέπε μὴ ἐπαρθῇ ὁ λογισμός σου, καὶ εἴπῃς, ὅτι Ἰδοὺ οἱ ἀναχωρηταὶ πρὸς μὲ ἔρχονται γυναῖκα οὖσαν. Λέγει αὐτοῖς ἡ ἀμμᾶς Σάρρα· Τῇ μὲν φύσει γυνή εἰμι, ἀλλ' οὐ τῷ λογισμῷ.

Two old men, great anchorites, came . . . to visit [Amma Sara]. When they arrived one said to the other, 'Let us humiliate this old woman [old hag].' So they said to her, 'Be careful not to become conceited thinking to yourself: "Look how anchorites are coming to see me, a mere woman".' But Amma Sara said to them, 'I am a woman by nature, but not in reasoning.'[79]

As demonstrated here, the general response readily lent itself to engagement with statements of praise, reproach or rebuke.[80]

Double Sayings (διπλοῦν)

The general response, in turn, retained fluid affinity with the 'double saying': a χρεία formed by using 'statements of two characters, either one of which creates a chreia of one character' (διπλῆ δέ ἐστι χρεία ἡ δύο προσώπων ἀποφάσεις ἔχουσα, ὧν καὶ ἡ ἑτέρα μεθ' ἑνὸς προσώπου χρείαν ποιεῖ).[81] For example:

Εἶπε ὁ ἀββᾶς Θεόδοτος Ἡ ἔνδεια τοῦ ἄρτου τήκει τὸ σῶμα τοῦ μοναχοῦ. Ἄλλος δὲ γέρων ἔλεγεν, ὅτι ἡ ἀγρυπνία πλέον τήκει τὸ σῶμα.

Abba Theodore said, 'Privation of food mortifies the body of the monk.' Another old man said, 'Vigils mortify it still more.'[82]

Suggesting that depictions of radically solitary monks are perhaps as caricatured as their 'a-' or 'exceptionally' literate counterparts, the double χρεία is particularly well represented in monastic sayings collections. In fact, judging by the inclusion of ancillary narrative detail,[83] the occasions for monastic engagement in clever repartee must have been myriad.[84]

Although elementary rhetorical instruction began with reading aloud, listening to others read and paraphrasing models, it was through iteratively re-framing, re-attributing and/or alternately re-working requisite forms that a student's emergent expertise was effectively displayed.[85] Having learned the rudimentary definition of a χρεία, its etymology, differentiation from related classes and sub-classes, students turned to exercises involving textual and narrative manipulation. To develop greater dexterity with the spoken and written word, they 'learned how to recite a *chreia*, to paraphrase it, to elaborate it, to confirm or refute its message, [and] to change its inflection through various cases and numbers'.[86] At a more advanced stage, respective elements of the same content could be seamlessly – or not so seamlessly – incorporated into longer narratives, lives, letters, travelogues and histories.

Conclusions

Placed in conversation with broader pedagogical norms, the emergent confluence that links early monastic descriptive, material and literary evidence is provocative. In fact, as elementary instruction comprised of learning letters, alphabets, syllables and words melds with copying maxims, devising χρείαι and manipulating requisite forms, a progressive picture of graded pedagogical investment begins to emerge. In turn, as one meets the same or derivative sayings and stories incorporated into the broader range of monastic source material, a strategic 'piece' in the enduring puzzle of monastic textual production falls into place. Countering anomalous attribution of burgeoning bodies of literature to communities of rustic, 'a-literate' monks,[87] this more plausible trajectory offers a provocative rubric for identifying monastic descriptive, material and literary evidence as inherently linked, rhetorically infused and pedagogically informed.

Correspondent with broader Graeco-Roman settings, the most extensive literary records that come to us from early 'monastic' communities are gnomic in form. This content shows evidence of having been shaped by the same rules, forms and models of discourse that governed more generally formulated sayings and stories. In addition, this preliminary survey suggests that the patterns identifiable in the familiar, and somewhat hybrid, collections of *apophthegmata* explored above are still more clearly defined in smaller χρεία compilations, of more focused character.[88] Although exploring the re-use of apophthegmatic content in complementary literary contexts underscores the degree to which requisite forms intersect, overlap and re-combine, whether the content that comprises various collections of *Apophthegmata Patrum* can be read as derivative of school settings remains an open question. It is, nonetheless, a question that bears serious consideration. Did gnomic sentences serve an educational purpose in monastic instruction similar to the traditional role accorded sayings in ancient pedagogical manuals? Were sayings, such as those attributed to the desert fathers and mothers, employed in teaching rudimentary (or advanced) grammatical skills, alongside moral discernment? Furthermore, is it possible that a portion of extant collections bespeaks the results of these investments? That is, might some subset of contemporary compilations record the literary prowess of young monks seeking (or being compelled) to progress in both grammatical-rhetorical and civic virtue?[89] Granting this frame makes it less surprising that a given saying appears in a variety of shapes and sizes, and/or that a measure of textual and narrative disparity separates respective articulations. Such fluidity – and repetition – is inherent to the genre.

If one accords serious weight to the parameters that define such practice, radical re-framing of the interpretive presuppositions with which discussion began is unavoidable. Re-examining the caricatured figures of Antony, Arsenius and Evagrius in this light imbues their legendary fame with an alternate register of resonance. Reading rhetorically (and generously), the same attributed sayings and stories that have long been used to argue against monastic involvement in literate pursuits in fact suggest the opposite. Situating these figures, and their reputed injunctions, within a diverse social landscape, comprised of a range of literacies, one is left to wonder whether efforts aimed at limiting, directing and/or controlling involvement in pedagogical pursuits, in fact, signal the inherent appeal of such investment.

Early Monasticism and the Rhetorical Tradition   27

Just as a 'no fishing' sign suggests good fishing,[90] in contexts where access to education was perhaps selectively available, the value of having a monastic founder, and two illustrious *literati*, affirms the importance of monastic/communal discipline, and shouldering one's share of the 'hard work' over 'softer' (and perhaps, more compelling) intellectual pursuits is clear. Imagining a more stratified framework, interactions between literate and less literate have been re-drawn in such a way that few might seek to cross them. Granting either scenario – or any number of hybrid, intermediate configurations – as descriptive, material and literary evidence coalesces, the caricatured figures of Antony, Arsenius and Evagrius are perhaps most accurately read as, at once, rhetorically performative and civically prescriptive. When understood as persuasive vehicles, the questions these articulations address may have had relatively little to do with debating the relative merits of literate education. Instead, it is arguable that they more readily register contests related to foundational pedagogical concerns. In fact, underlying tensions suggest that the most directive questions may result from asking not whether the monks invested in literate education, but rather to what degree and to what ends.

Notes

1 A portion of the research presented in this chapter was supported by funding from the Swedish Riksbankens Jubileumsfond, and undertaken in collaboration with the Monasticism and Classical Paideia Project at Lund University in Sweden. At an earlier, formative stage, the opportunity to explore ancient education under the tutelage of Raffaella Cribiore (NYU), and ancient sayings traditions in conversion with Kathy Eden (Columbia University), remains singularly foundational to this work.

2 Athanasius (*Life of Antony* 1 [PG 26, 841; Gregg 1980, 30]); the seminal consideration of Brakke 1995 offers a provocative re-assessment of Athanasius' political and ecclesial agendas. In turn, Rubenson 1995 presents a close counter-reading of Athanasius' caricature in light of Antony's letters. More recently, Gemeinhardt 2013 traces the contours of Antony's narrative trajectory as it moves to the West. The notable merits of each of these re-assessments have been widely affirmed. However, their critical effect has yet to dismantle the residual influence of well-rehearsed depictions of Antony as ἀγράμματος and, derivatively, the early desert ascetics as simple rustics. Despite compelling arguments to the contrary, the Egyptian monks remain fictively framed as 'uninterested in learning letters' and 'taught only by God'; cf. Wilken 2013, 99–108.

3 For the sake of argument, I have drawn excerpted portions of the *Life of Antony* and the *Sayings of the Fathers* from the most frequently cited translations. These include, respectively, the translation of Antony's *Life* in Gregg 1980 and Benedicta Ward's translations of collected sayings, the Greek Alphabetical (Ward 1975) and the Latin Systematic (Ward 2003). While, according to Chiara Faraggiana, these and other contemporary compendia are comprised of a 'stew' of sources, they remain the conduit through which many readers encounter the *Sayings of Fathers* (cf. Faraggiana 1997, 455–67).

4 *Sayings of the Fathers* (Latin Systematic Collection of Pelagius and John) X 5 [PL 73, 912–13; Ward 2003, 89]; cf. Πῶς ἡμεῖς ἀπὸ τοσαύτης παιδεύσεως καὶ σοφίας οὐδὲν ἔχομεν, οὗτοι δὲ οἱ ἀγροῖκοι καὶ Αἰγύπτιοι τοσαύτας ἀρετὰς κέκτηνται; Ἡμεῖς ἀπὸ τῆς τοῦ κόσμου παιδεύσεως οὐδὲν ἔχομεν· οὗτοι δὲ οἱ ἀγροῖκοι καὶ Αἰγύπτιοι ἀπὸ τῶν ἰδίων πόνων ἐκτήσαντο τὰς ἀρετάς (*Sayings of the Fathers* (Greek Alphabetical Collection), Arsenius 5 [PG 65: 88–9]). In the Greek version of this saying, Evagrius is replaced by an unnamed protagonist.

28   Lillian I. Larsen

5   *Sayings of the Fathers* (Greek Alphabetical Collection), Arsenius 6 (PG 65, 89; Ward 1975, 10).
6   Cf. Larsen 2013b, 5–12.
7   Burton-Christie 1993, 59; Guy 1974, 45; Harmless 2004, 71; cf. Larsen 2006, 1–25.
8   Marrou 1956, 333.
9   Marrou 1956, 330.
10 First published in France in 1948, Marrou's volume saw five further editions in French. Between 1950 and 1969, it was translated into Italian [1950], English [1956], German [1957], Greek [1961], Spanish [1965], Polish [1969] and Portuguese [1969] (cf. Too 2001). As a mid-twentieth century historian, Marrou's romanticised views of early monasticism echo those readily encountered across a broader swathe of the scholarly landscape. Repeatedly re-framed and re-assessed, however, the relative significance of Marrou's opus is illustrative (Cf. Larsen 2013, 60–62).
11 Too 2001, 2.
12 Rappe 2001, 423.
13 Cf. Cribiore 2001; Morgan 1998.
14 Cf. Larsen 2008, 30; Larsen 2013a, 75–7; Larsen 2013b.
15 Cf. Hadot 1995, 52.
16 *Asketikon* 15 [PG 31, 953; Clarke 1925, 176].
17 καὶ ἅμα οὐδὲ θόρυβον ἕξει ὁ οἶκος τῶν ἀσκητῶν ἐν τῇ μελέτῃ τῶν διδαγμάτων ἀναγκαίᾳ οὔσῃ τοῖς νέοις (*Asketikon* 15 [PG 31, 953; Clarke 1925, 176]).
18 ὥστε καὶ ὀνόμασιν αὐτοὺς τοῖς ἐκ τῶν Γραφῶν κεχρῆσθαι . . . καὶ γνώμαις παιδεύειν ταῖς ἐκ τῶν Παροιμιῶν, καὶ ἆθλα μνήμης ὀνομάτων τε καὶ πραγμάτων αὐτοῖς προτιθέναι (*Asketikon* 15 [PG 31, 953; Clarke 1925, 176–7]); cf. Gregory of Nyssa, *Life of Macrina* 962d.
19 καὶ ἀντὶ μύθων τὰς τῶν παραδόξων ἔργων ἱστορίας αὐτοῖς διηγεῖσθαι . . . εὔπλαστον οὖν ἔτι οὖσαν καὶ ἁπαλὴν τὴν ψυχὴν, καὶ ὡς κηρὸν εὔεικτον, ταῖς τῶν ἐπιβαλλομένων μορφαῖς ῥᾳδίως ἐκτυπουμένην, πρὸς πᾶσαν ἀγαθῶν ἄσκησιν εὐθὺς καὶ ἐξ ἀρχῆς ἐνάγεσθαι χρή (*Asketikon* 15 [PG 31, 953–6; Clarke 1925, 177]).
20 ὥστε τοῦ λόγου προσγενομένου, καὶ τῆς διακριτικῆς ἕξεως προσελθούσης δρόμον ὑπάρχειν . . . ἐκ τῶν ἐξ ἀρχῆς στοιχείων, καὶ τῶν παραδοθέντων τῆς εὐσεβείας τύπων, τοῦ μὲν λόγου τὸ χρήσιμον ὑποβάλλοντος, τοῦ δὲ ἔθους εὐμάρειαν πρὸς τὸ κατορθοῦν ἐμποιοῦντος (*Asketikon* 15 [PG 31, 956; Clarke 1925, 177]); cf. Quintilian, *Institutes of Oratory* 1.1.4.
21 Jerome, *Letter* 107 (Wright 1933, 338–71); cf. Quintilian, *Institutes of Oratory* 1.1.1–37.
22 *Fiant ei litterae vel buxeae vel eburneae et suis nominibus appellentur* (*Letter* 107 [Wright 1933, 344–7]).
23 . . . *et non solum ordinem teneat litterarum, ut memoria nominum in canticum transeat, sed ipse inter se crebro ordo turbetur et mediis ultima, primis media misceantur ut eas non sonu tantum, sed et visu noverit* (*Letter* 107 [Wright 1933, 346–7]); cf. Quintilian, *Institutes of Oratory* 1.1.27.
24 *Ipsa nomina, per quae consuescet verba contexere, non sint fortuita, sed certa et coacervata de industria, prophetarum videlicet atque apostolorum, et omnis ab Adam patriarcharum series de Matheo Lucaque descendat, ut, dum aliud agit, futurae memoriae praeparetur* (*Letter* 107 [Wright 1933, 346–7]); cf. Quintilian, *Institutes of Oratory* 1.1.30–35.
25 . . . *adhuc tenera lingua psalmis dulcibus inbuatur* (*Letter* 107 [Wright 1933, 344–5]).
26 *Discat primum Psalterium* . . . *et in Proverbiis Salomonis erudiatur ad vitam* (*Letter* 107 [Wright 1933, 364–5]). In direct reflection of young Paula's social stature, Jerome suggests that instead of 'jewels or silk' her treasures ought to be 'manuscripts of the holy scriptures'. In these, she should prefer 'correctness and accurate [punctuation]' rather than 'gilding, and Babylonian parchment, with elaborate decorations' *Pro gemmis aut serico divinos codices amet, in quibus auri et pellis Babyloniae vermiculata pictura, sed ad fidem placeat emendata et erudita distinctio* (*Letter* 107 [Wright 1933, 364–5]).
27 *magister probae aetatis et vitae atque eruditionis* . . . *initia ei traderet litterarum*. In fact Jerome offers to serve as 'both her tutor and her foster-father'. Carrying her on his shoulders, he will 'train her stammering lips . . . tak[ing] more pride in [his] task than . . . the worldly

philosopher; for . . . [rather than] teaching a Macedonian king, destined to die by poison in Babylon, [he will instruct] the handmaid and bride of Christ who one day [will] be presented to the heavenly throne' *Ipse, si Paulam miseris, balbutientia senex verba formabo multo gloriosior mundi philosopho, qui non regem Macedonum Babylonio periturum veneno, sed ancillam et sponsam Christi erudiam regnis caelestibus offerendam* (Letter 107 [Wright 1933, 368–71]).

28 Cf. Larsen 2012a; Larsen 2012b.

29 *dabunt ei uiginti psalmos uel duas epistulas apostoli, aut alterius scripturae partem* (Precept 139 [Boon 1932, 49–50; Veilleux 1980, 2.166]).

30 *Precept* 139 (Boon 1932, 49–50; Veilleux 1980, 2.166).

31 *et omnino nullus erit in monasterio qui non discat litteras et de scripturis aliquid teneat* (Precept 140 [Boon 1932, 50; Veilleux 1980, 2.166]).

32 John Chrysostom likewise proposes that Christian parents send their children to be educated in monasteries. Albeit providing little detail with regard to curricular content, like Basil and Jerome, Chrysostom emphasises the value of children being taught by spiritually approved masters who will encourage development of both intellectual and moral strength. He recommends that instruction begin once boys have reached the age of 10 and continue for at least 10 years. Marrou notes that, in later writing, Chrysostom appears to speak against such practice (Marrou 1956, 332). However, there is good evidence to suggest that these diverse positions, even within the writings of a single author, reflect wider debate (cf. Becker 2006, 169–70; Thomas of Marga, *Book of Governors* 1.74.3–10, 1.75.1–14).

33 See more detailed discussion in Larsen 2006, 67–70; Larsen 2013b, 16–19; Larsen, forthcoming.

34 Cribiore's catalogue (1996) offers a particularly rich register of Graeco-Roman artefacts. Monika Hasitzka's earlier compilation of Coptic remains attests comparable practice (Hasitzka 1990). In each, the character of included monastic evidence is notably unremarkable.

35 O.MMA 14.1.188 + O.BM. Inv 19082, 18816, 18798, 18972; cf. Winlock/Crum 1926, 2.298 n. 576; Hall 1905, 36, pl. 29 n. 2; et al.

36 O.MMA 12.180.107; cf. Winlock/Crum 1926, 2.136, 322 n. 620; et al.

37 As transcribed by Percy Newberry, this combination of alphabets and syllabary is preserved *in situ* on the wall of an abandoned pharaonic tomb, later used by Christian monks (Newberry 1893, 76–7 pl. 25; cf. Champollion 1889, 459–60). The patterned alphabetic sequences that introduce the inscription serve to elucidate practice commended by Jerome (*Letter* 107) and elsewhere, Quintilian (*Institutes of Oratory* 1.1.25). The first alphabet is written in conventional order, the second in reverse. The third preserves a 'mixed' sequence of letters, comprised of pairing the first with the last letter of the alphabet; the second with the second to last, and so on, thus: αω, βψ, γχ, δφ, ευ, ζτ, ης, θρ, ιπ, κο, λξ, μν; cf. Biedenkopf-Ziehner 2000, 2.137–44.

38 The syllabary portion of the Beni Hasan inscription likewise includes combinations characteristic of broader practice (Quintilian *Institutes of Oratory* 1.1.30–31; cf. Cribiore 1996, 191–6 nn. 78–97). The simplest sequences pair consonants and vowels in biliteral units, thus: βα, βε, βη, βι, βο, βυ, βω. . . . These are followed by triliteral combinations formed by adding an extra consonant after each vowel, thus: βαβ, βεβ, βηβ, βιβ, βοβ, βυβ, βωβ . . . (cf. Cribiore 2001, 23–4).

39 Quintilian, *Institutes of Oratory* 1.1.35 (Russell 2002, 80–81).

40 As transcribed by Newberry, wordlist inscriptions from Beni Hasan include: ⲛⲱⲣ[ⲉ], ⲁⲃⲣⲁⲅⲁⲙ, ⲓ[ⲥⲁ]ⲕ, ⲓⲁⲕⲱⲃ, ⲓⲱⲥⲏⲫ, ⲓⲉⲅⲉⲥ, ////////ⲥⲣⲥⲛⲏ, ⲓⲱⲣⲁⲛⲛⲏⲥ, ⲇⲁⲛⲓⲏⲗ, ⲁⲛⲁⲛⲓⲁⲥ, ⲙⲓⲥⲁ[ⲉⲗ], ⲁⲍ[ⲁ]ⲣⲓⲁⲥ. On the wall of an adjacent tomb, the term ⲁⲡⲁ is repeated 10 times (Newberry 1893, 2.67–8 nn. 69 and 75; cf. Champollion 1889, 459–60).

41 Quintilian, *Institutes of Oratory* 1.1.35 (Russell 2002, 80–81). Quintilian particularly recommends the inclusion of hard to pronounce words like λύγξ (lynx), στράγξ (drop), κλάγξ (howl) and κλώψ (thief).

30   *Lillian I. Larsen*

42   O.MMA 14.1.139; cf. Winlock/Crum 1926, 2.135, 320 n. 612.
43   O.MMA 14.1.210; cf. Winlock/Crum 1926, 2.135, 320–21 n. 615. It is striking that, in contrast to relatively mundane identification of non-monastic school texts, the pedagogical character of monastic material remains has elicited vociferous debate (cf. Bucking 2007; et al.). It is arguable that these discussions, too, remain tacitly informed by interpretive presuppositions grounded in highly caricatured visions of 'a-' and 'exceptional' monastic literacy.
44   Cf. Quintilian, *Institutes of Oratory* 1.1.37.
45   O.MMA 14.1.219. Cf. Winlock/Crum 1926, 2.136, 321 n. 616; Bellet 1982. A second fragmentary *exemplum* has been identified at Deir el Bahri.
46   Crum notes that a third, 'similarly enciphered', text is provenanced to the Monastery of Jeremias at Sakkara; cf. Thompson 1909, 58 n. 105.
47   Cf. Krueger 2004; Kotsifou 2007; Krawiec 2012.
48   Cf. Larsen, forthcoming.
49   Jerome, *Letter* 107; Basil, *Longer Rules* 15; Pachomius, *Precepts* 139–40; cf. Rönnegård 2010; McVey 1998.
50   Morgan 1998, 122.
51   Morgan traces the emergent protocol that governed work with gnomic maxims to Hellenistic and Roman preoccupation with inculcating a common civic ideal (1998, 120ff; cf. Morgan 2007). In his volume, Carr 2005 explores parallel use of gnomic content across a broader cultural spectrum; cf. Larsen 2008.
52   Cribiore 2001, 179.
53   Kennedy 2003, ix. Kennedy's compilation of the exercises attributed to Theon, Hermogenes, Aphthonius and Nicolaus offers an accessible introduction to this literature. Complementary treatments (Hock/O'Neil 1986 and 2002) flesh out applications that afford particular insight into the use of gnomic content in classroom settings.
54   O.MMA 14.1.210; cf. Winlock/Crum 1996, 2.135, 320–21 n. 615.
55   Larsen 2013a, 70.
56   As published by Hock/O'Neil 1986, 96–7, a papyrus scrap from Oxyrhynchus preserves a glimpse of the central role accorded χρεῖαι in the classroom. Comprised of a series of questions and answers, this 'schoolboy's rhetorical catechism' begins, appropriately enough, with: 'What is a chreia' (τί ἐστιν ἡ χρεία), for which the reply is recorded: '[the chreia is] a concise reminiscence associated with some character' (ἀπομνημόνευμα σύντομον ἐπὶ προσώπου τινὸς ἐπενεκτόν). Four subsequent questions, in turn, rehearse each of the form's salient features: 'Why is the chreia a "reminiscence"?' (διά τί ἀπομνημόνευμα ἡ χρεία); 'Because it is remembered so that it may be recited' (ὅτι ἀπομνημονεύεται ἵνα λεχθῇ). 'Why concise?' (διὰ τί σύντομον); 'Because often, once it has been expanded, it becomes a narrative or something else' (ὅτι πολλάκις ἐκταθὲν ἢ διήγησις γίνεται ἢ ἄλλο τι). 'Why with a character?' (διὰ τί ἐπὶ προσώπου); 'Because often, without a character, a concise reminiscence is a maxim or something else' (ὅτι πολλάκις ἄνευ προσώπου σύντομον ἀπομνημόνευμα ἢ γνώμη ἐστὶν ἢ ἄλλο τι). 'Why is it called "chreia"?' (διὰ τί εἴρηται χρεία); 'Because of its being useful, not because the other exercises do not have [this quality], but because of [its excellence], the name is a proper one instead of a common one' (διὰ τὸ χρειῶδες εἶναι, οὐχ ὡς οὐ καὶ τῶν ἄλλων τοῦτο ἐχόντων, ἀλλὰ κατ᾽ ἐξοχὴν ἴδιον ἐστὶ πρὸ κοινοῦ ὄνομα). Affirming the further rehearsal of forms suitable for classroom use, the fragmentary 'catechism' ends with a final, anticipatory line: 'What is the narrative' (τί ἐστιν ἡ διήγημα).
57   The chronological formation of monastic manuscript collections has long been a topic of wide debate. In contemporary scholarship, the work of Chiara Faraggiana is the most significant. Faraggiana has re-assessed the conventional dating assigned monastic apophthegmatic source material, as well as the trajectories assumed in defining its transmission. Informed by sustained and ongoing work with extant manuscript evidence, she has raised foundational questions about the adequacy of conclusions drawn from content included in the most frequently cited editions. Faraggiana suggests that on account of

Early Monasticism and the Rhetorical Tradition   31

the inherent fluidity that characterises apophthegmatic content, the blended manuscript evidence that undergirds the contemporary compilations has, per above, resulted in something of a 'stew' of sources – even as ready availability has made these editions the 'go-to' references for a broad range of scholarly analyses (cf. Faraggiana 1997). More recent work, undertaken in the context of the Monasticism and Classical Paideia Project at Lund University, builds directly on Faraggiana's foundational analyses. In this derivative context, the research results of Dahlman 2013 and Holmberg 2013 are particularly significant.

58   The name χρεία was ostensibly derivative of χρειώδες on account of the form's 'useful[ness]' in many ways for life' (πρὸς πολλὰ χρειώδες ἐστὶ τῷ βίῳ [Theon, *On the Chreia* 25–6 (Hock/O'Neil 1986, 83–4)]. However, such acknowledgement might as readily derive from deployment in classroom settings, where inherent malleability made the χρεία an essential component in grammatical and rhetorical (not to mention, philosophical) instruction.

59   In Theon's early delineation, πρακτικαί 'which reveal some thought without speech (πρακτικαὶ δέ εἰσιν αἱ χωρὶς λόγου ἐμφαίνουσαί τινα νοῦν) are further subdivided into effective/active (ἐνεργητικαί) and passive (παθητικαί) forms' (Theon, *On the Chreia* 96–104 [Hock/O'Neil 1986, 88–9]). However, these carefully delineated distinctions find scant corroboration in extant literary sources. Hock and O'Neil note that while distinguishing between active and passive forms may have been useful in classroom settings, these categories appear largely theoretical, surfacing almost solely as exempla in handbooks (1986, 67).

60   *Sayings of the Fathers* (Greek Alphabetical Collection), Agathon 15 (PG 65, 113; Ward 1975, 22). A still simpler version of this χρεία is preserved in Latin: *Quia per triennium lapidem in ore suo mittebat, donec taciturnitatem disceret* (For three years [Abba Agathon] kept a stone in his mouth in order to teach himself silence). *Sayings of the Fathers* (Latin Systematic Collection of Pelagius and John) 4.7 (PL 73; Ward 2003, 20).

61   Theon suggests that 'mixed chreiai are those which share characteristics of both the sayings-species and the action species but make their point with the action' [μικταὶ δέ εἰσιν ὅσαι τοῦ μὲν λογικοῦ καὶ τοῦ πρακτικοῦ κοινωνοῦσιν, ἐν δὲ τῷ πρακτικῷ τὸ κῦρος ἔχουσιν]; Theon, *On the Chreia* 105–7 [Hock/ O'Neil 1986, 88–9]). However, Aphthonius' later handbook simply affirms a juxtaposition of λόγος and πρᾶξις. For example: 'Pythagoras, on being asked how long human life can be, was visible for a short time and disappeared, making his visibility the measure of life' [Πυθαγόρας ἐρωτηθείς, ὅσος ἂν εἴη τῶν ἀνθρώπων ὁ βίος, βραχύ τι φανεὶς ἀπεκρύψατο, μέτρον τοῦ βίου τὴν θέαν ποιούμενος] (Aphthonius, *On the Chreia* 10–12 [Hock/O'Neil 1986, 224–5, 334–5 n. 54]).

62   *Sayings of the Fathers* (Greek Alphabetical Collection), Moses 2 (PG 65, 281–4; Ward 1975, 138–9).

63   *Sayings of the Fathers* (Greek Alphabetical Collection), John Colobos/John the Dwarf 21 (PG 65, 212; Ward 1975, 90).

64   Within a broader Graeco-Roman frame, parallel accounts appear in Hesiod, and again among the fables of Babrius; cf. Larsen 2013a, 71–5.

65   By virtue of chronological proximity, Aphthonius' fourth-century handbook is often relied upon when tracing rhetorical patterns in late ancient source material (cf. Rönnegård 2010, 172–82; et al.). However, of the progymnasmatic handbooks that remain extant, Theon's first-century exemplar is the most detailed. Likewise, Hock and O'Neil note that Theon's more particularised delineations warrant consideration because they so closely correspond 'to chreiai as they are encountered in ancient literature' (1986, 68). Bearing out Hock and O'Neil's assessment, the degree to which monastic forms align with Theon's more detailed delineations is provocative.

66   There is striking consonance between the technical terminology employed in handbook definitions and the quintessential desert query: 'Give me a word.'

67   Theon, *On the Chreia* 1–4 (Hock/O'Neil 1986, 82–3).

32 Lillian I. Larsen

68 For example: 'Diogenes the philosopher, on being asked by someone how he could become famous, responded: "By worrying as little as possible about fame"' [διογένης ὁ φιλόσοφος ἐρωτηθεὶς ὑπό τινος πῶς ἂν ἔνδοξος γένοιτο ἀπεκρίνατο· ὅτι ἥκιστα δόξης φροντίζων'] (Theon, On the Chreia 33–5 [Hock/O'Neil 1986, 84–5, 313 n. 22]).

69 Sayings of the Fathers (Greek Alphabetical Collection), Agathon 2 (PG 65, 109; Ward 1975, 20).

70 For example: 'Diogenes the Cynic philosopher, on seeing a rich man who was uneducated, said: "This man is silver-plated filth"' [Διογένης ὁ Κυνικὸς φιλόσοφος ἰδὼν μειράκιον πλούσιον ἀπαίδευτον εἶπεν· οὗτός ἐστι ῥύπος περιηργυρωμένος] (Theon, On the Chreia 41–4 [Hock/O'Neil 1986, 84–5, 313–14 n. 23]).

71 Sayings of the Fathers (Greek Alphabetical Collection), Benjamin 4 (PG 65, 145; Ward 1975, 44).

72 For example: 'Pittacus of Mytilene, on being asked if anyone escapes the notice of the gods in committing some sinful act, said: "No, not even in contemplating it"' [Πιττακὸς ὁ Μιτυληναῖος ἐρωτηθείς, εἰ λανθάνει τις τοὺς θεοὺς φαῦλόν τι ποιῶν, εἶπεν οὗ οὐδὲ διανοούμενος] (Theon, On the Chreia 56–8 [Hock/O'Neil 1986, 84–5, 331–2 n. 49]). Theon notes that a distinctive feature of this class is that after the affirmative (or negative) particle, any 'additional phrase is superfluous, since even with it removed the [particle] would be sufficient' [μετὰ γὰρ τὴν ἀπόφασιν τὸ προστιθέμενον περισσόν ἐστιν, ἐπεὶ καὶ ἀφαιρεθέντος αὐτοῦ ἐπήρκει ἡ ἀπόφασις] (Theon, On the Chreia 58–60 [Hock/O'Neil 1986, 84–5]).

73 Sayings of the Fathers (Greek Alphabetical Collection), Epiphanius 14 (PG 65, 165; Ward 1975, 58).

74 For example: 'Theano the Pythagorean philosopher, on being asked by someone how long after intercourse with a man does a woman go in purity to the Thesmorphorion, said: "With your own, immediately; with another's, never"' [θεανὼ ἡ Πυθαγορικὴ φιλόσοφος ἐρωτηθεῖσα ὑπό τινος ποσταία γυνὴ ἀπ᾽ ἀνδρὸς καθαρὰ εἰς τὸ Θεσμοφορεῖον κάτεισιν εἶπεν· Ἀπὸ μὲν τοῦ ἰδίου παραχρῆμα, ἀπὸ δὲ τοῦ ἀλλοτρίου οὐδέποτε] (Theon, On the Chreia 62–6 [Hock/O'Neil 1986, 86–7, 340–41 n. 64]).

75 Sayings of the Fathers (Greek Alphabetical Collection), Pambo 11 (PG 65, 372; Ward 1975, 197).

76 For example: 'Socrates, on being asked whether the Persian king seemed happy to him, said: "I can't say, for I can't know where he stands on education"' [Σωκράτης ἐρωτηθεὶς εἰ εὐδαίμων αὐτῷ δοκεῖ ὁ περσῶν βασιλεύς, εἶπε· οὐκ ἔχω λέγειν, μηδὲ γὰρ εἰδέναι πῶς ἔχει παιδείας] (Theon, On the Chreia 70–73 [Hock/O'Neil 1986, 86–7, 336–7 n. 57]).

77 Sayings of the Fathers (Greek Alphabetical Collection), Arsenius 22 (PG 65, 93; Ward 1975, 12).

78 For example: 'Once when Diogenes was having lunch in the market-place and invited [Plato] to lunch, Plato said: "Diogenes, how charming your unpretentiousness would be if it were not so pretentious"' [Πλάτων ποτὲ Διογένους ἀριστῶντος ἐν ἀγορᾷ καὶ καλοῦντος αὐτὸν ἐπὶ τὸ ἄριστον Ω Διόγενες, εἶπεν, ὡς χαρίεν ἄν ἦν σου τὸ ἄπλαστον εἰ μὴ πλαστὸν ἦν] (Theon, On the Chreia 80–84 [Hock/O'Neil 1986, 86–7, 332–3 n. 50]).

79 Sayings of the Fathers (Greek Alphabetical Collection), Sarah 4 (PG 65, 420; Ward 1975, 230). Even with the expansive detail that contextualises the monks' address, Sara's response offers a strikingly 'apt' reworking of a similar exchange, elsewhere attributed to the philosopher Anacharsis. As reported by Hock and O'Neil: 'Anacharsis, when reproached by someone because he was a Scythian, said: "I am by birth, but not manner of living"' [Ὁ αὐτὸς λοιδορούμενος ὑπό τινος, ὅτι Σκύθης εἴη, ἔφη· γένει, ἀλλ᾽ ὀχὶ τοῖς τρόποις] (Gnomologium Vaticanum 15 [Hock/O'Neil 1986, 30–31]).

80 Hock/O'Neil 1986, 30–31.

81 For example: 'Alexander the Macedonian king stood over Diogenes as he slept and said: "To sleep all night ill suits a counsellor" (Ilias 2.24), and Diogenes responded: "On whom the folk rely, whose cares are many" (Ilias 2.25)' [Ἀλέξανδρος ὁ τῶν Μακεδόνων βασιλεὺς

ἐπιστὰς Διογένει κοιμωμένῳ εἶπεν· οὐ χρὴ παννύχιον εὕδειν βουληφόρον ἄνδρα (*Il.* 2.24). καὶ ὁ Διογένης ἀπεκρίνατο· ὦ λαοί τ᾽ ἐπιτετράφαται καὶ τόσσα μέμηλεν (*Il.* 2.25)]. (Theon, *On the Chreia* 84–5 [Hock/O'Neil 1986, 86–9, 314–15 n. 24]).

82 *Sayings of the Fathers* (Greek Alphabetical Collection), Theodore of Eleutheropolis 2 (PG 65, 197; Ward 1975, 80).

83 The χρεία's structural malleability imbues questions of historicity with implicit uncertainty. In fact, Hock and O'Neil suggest that 'sayings', as a genre, can be used in reconstructing the life, message or circumstances of any given setting only if one exercises considerable caution and sophistication. Presenting a provocative rehearsal of the challenges inherent to distilling historical certainties from this genre of texts, they observe that 'each part of a *chreia* – the character, the prompting circumstance (if any), and the [statement] or action – can be manipulated in ways that do little to preserve historical certitude. Thus, attribution to a character, needing only to be apt, can vary, so that we cannot be sure *who* said or did something. The prompting question or circumstance can also vary according to the freedoms permitted in recitation and expansion or they can simply reflect a conventional setting, so that we cannot be sure of the exact *circumstance or question* that elicited the saying or action. And finally, the saying itself can be recited in different words, so that we cannot be sure of the exact *words* in the saying, only the general sentiment' (1986, 46). As importantly, however, Hock and O'Neil argue that if implicit malleability precludes assigning historical weight to the particular words or events used to structure a χρεία, the 'apt' narrative circumstances that frame a particular strain of articulation afford a rich rubric for re-imagining the general contours of the settings from which a body of articulations derive. Put simply, the criterion of 'apt' assignation that renders the form inherently fluid simultaneously imbues the rhetorical valence of a χρεία's descriptive details with real historical weight. Set within a rhetorical frame, the range of 'conventional circumstances' that make a given articulation plausible are essential to its persuasive function. As such, the recurrent detail that surfaces in a χρεία's narrative setting may well represent a normative spectrum of authentic praxis. So situated, both the density of extant monastic gnomic material and its diversity are provocative (Hock/O'Neil 1986, 41–7; cf. Larsen 2013b).

84 Plutarch explicitly connects classroom rehearsal of χρεῖαι with convivial exchange (*Convivial Questions* 1.1.2). Such juxtaposition, again, raises interesting questions about the contexts in which monastic sayings collections may have found their form (cf. Larsen 2012a; Larsen 2012b).

85 Cf. Larsen 2008.

86 O'Neil 1981, 20. In his volume *Threads and Images*, Per Rönnegård explores monastic incorporation of scripture into progressive manipulation of χρεῖαι, into patterned sequences of *ergasia*. However, by virtue of relying on Aphthonius' relatively late handbook, Rönnegård is less successful in identifying lines from scripture that have been reworked as attributed maxims to produce a more varied spectrum of χρεῖαι (Rönnegård 2010, 172–82).

87 Thanks to Kathy Eden, Professor of Classics and English Literature at Columbia University, for suggesting this apt metaphor in early discussion of reading the monastic *Sayings of the Fathers* in light of elementary rhetorical models (Autumn 2001); cf. Larsen 2006, 1–18.

88 Thanks to Chiara Faraggiana and Britt Dahlman for granting me access to their preliminary surveys of respective manuscript trajectories.

89 Cf. Larsen 2008; Larsen 2013a; Larsen 2013b.

90 Wire 1990, 3. Like a 'no fishing' sign, Wire premises that a given body of communication 'may indicate a situation opposite to what [it] say[s]' (5). Along commensurate lines, Vincent Wimbush (1997) argues that it is often the cracks and fissures, the inconsistencies in a body of texts that afford entry points for deciphering/discerning contested space and competing worldviews.

2 The Education of Shenoute and Other Cenobitic Leaders

Inside and Outside of the Monastery

Janet Timbie

'Who will inherit the kingdom of heaven and not be a ruler? Is there any (form of) rule except avoiding the coming wrath? Is there any kingdom except ruling over eternal life?'[1] Shenoute of Atripe (d. 465) punctuates his sermon with a series of rhetorical questions in the style of Paul's letters, but also in the manner of a philosophical or religious diatribe. Did Shenoute write in Coptic in this manner as the result of formal education? Or was he largely self-taught?

Monastic texts – including rules, sermons and letters – written in the fourth and fifth centuries by Pachomius and his successors, and by Shenoute and Besa, provide some information about the education of monks who joined their communities. But the sources offer only partial answers to the two separate questions that can be asked: What level of education did these leaders attain before entering cenobitic life? What kind of education was available inside the monastery? Many details in the texts indicate that monks in the Pachomian *Koinonia* and White Monastery Federation came from a range of socioeconomic levels, and their status might align with their pre-monastic level of education.[2] But the study of education in these monasteries is complicated by a language question, since the fourth and fifth centuries also saw the rise of written Coptic for both literary and non-literary material.[3] The works of Pachomius, Horsiesius, Theodore, Shenoute and Besa that survive were written in Coptic and in general show familiarity with the Bible in Coptic translation. However, it is not clear that exclusively Coptic education was available in Egyptian villages and towns during this period. If bilingual education was the rule in Coptic-speaking areas of Egypt, there should be evidence of Greek learning in the writings of those educated outside the monastery. And, on the other hand, was monolingual Coptic education the rule inside the monastery, since all surviving works from these communities were written in Coptic? These and other questions will be addressed below, though answers must be partial and preliminary due to the nature of the evidence that has survived in fragmented texts from late manuscripts and scattered archaeological investigations.

Monastic Rules and Practices

The starting point for any study of education in cenobitic monasteries is usually two Pachomian rules preserved by Jerome in Latin:[4]

139. Whoever enters the monastery uninstructed shall be taught first what he must observe; and when, so taught, he has consented to it all, they shall give him twenty psalms or two of the Apostle's epistles, or some other part of the Scripture.

And if he is illiterate, he shall go at the first, third, and sixth hours to someone who can teach and has been appointed for him. He shall stand before him and learn very studiously with all gratitude. Then the fundamentals of a syllable, the verbs, and the nouns shall be written for him, and even if he does not want to, he shall be compelled to read.

140. There shall be no one whatever in the monastery who does not learn to read and does not memorize something of the Scriptures. [One should learn by heart] at least the New Testament and the Psalter.

Jerome translated these rules from a Greek version kept at the Metanoia monastery near Alexandria, which operated on a Pachomian model though it was not formally part of the Pachomian *Koinonia*.[5] Comparison between the Latin text of Jerome and the surviving Coptic fragments of other rules suggests that his is a generally accurate text and translation. A monk who joined the Pachomian system learned basic rules for conduct ('what he must observe'), promised to obey and then memorised portions of scripture ('twenty psalms or two of the epistles'). If he did not know how to read, someone in the monastery would teach him. Memorisation of scripture and reading of scripture are separate tasks, but the new monk must work on both of them ('there shall be no one in the monastery'). Other rules show that books and reading were a normal part of the Pachomian environment: '100. No one shall leave his book unfastened when he goes to the *synaxis* or to the refectory.'[6]

Pachomian texts also indicate that written records were a regular part of monastery operations. The *Regulations of Horsiesius* (a successor of Pachomius) prescribe the conduct of certain monastic officers (*oikonomos*): 'It is fitting not to sell or buy or do anything, from great to small, without (the permission of) the superior of the community . . . (and for) everything to be written in the place of the steward (*oikonomos*), from small to large, openly and clearly.'[7] Monks who can read and write are carrying out these tasks. While it is clearly stated that monks are taught to read inside the monastery, it is not stated that some were also taught to write. However, as we will see from recent studies of education in Egypt, the statement in Rule 140 that 'the fundamentals of a syllable, the verbs, and nouns shall be written for him' when the monk receives reading instruction may indicate that reading was taught through writing, as it was in non-monastic elementary education.[8]

A similar pattern is found in the White Monastery rules that are quoted in the works of Shenoute, leader of the White Monastery Federation from approximately AD 385 until his death in the mid-fifth century.[9] First of all, it seems that some Pachomian rules were recorded and observed in the White Monastery in the time of Shenoute. Monks sarcastically quote a rule of Pachomius – 'No one shall speak to his neighbours in the dark' – and they are rebuked by Shenoute,

36   *Janet Timbie*

both for disrespect toward the great Pachomius and for not taking the rule seriously.[10] More than 500 rules are 'imbedded in Shenoute's nine-book work entitled *Canons*' and new monks would only gradually learn their contents and the punishments for disobedience.[11] Joining the White Monastery Federation is a gradual process that begins with a period at the gatehouse, where the newcomer is interviewed by the 'supreme Father', continues with a general description of the rules, and then includes an oral renunciation of property in favour of the monastery. This transfer of property is put in writing after two or three months.[12] Besa, the successor of Shenoute, states: 'He who enters to become a monk with us shall renounce first everything that belongs to him and (give them) in writing to the *koinonia* of God and the service of the poor.'[13] This is a literate environment in the sense that written records are kept and leaders and followers (monks and nuns) sometimes communicate in writing.[14]

The clear Pachomian rules about learning to read in the monastery if one was not already literate are not found in the works of Shenoute, but the latter are only preserved in partial manuscripts.[15] That reading is a normal activity in the White Monastery Federation is shown by rules dealing with acceptable books: 'If books or letters suitable to be read are brought to us, we shall not give them to anyone among us unless we have told him (the Male Eldest) about them. Nor shall any person among us read them whatsoever without first telling him.'[16] There is a library in the White Monastery and some monks are reading a variety of works, though Bible reading and recitation are the most important activity for all.[17] There are many references to meditation (using the Greek loanword *meleta*) in Shenoute, and this means the low-voiced recitation of prayers and scripture passages that accompanied all work in the monastery, as well as the time spent alone in one's cell.[18] So it is reasonable to conclude that new monks learned to read, if they were illiterate, in order to read the Bible and memorise portions for communal worship and private meditation.

The cenobitic monasteries of Upper Egypt therefore relied on a basic level of literacy to function. When the works of some leaders – in particular, Shenoute and Besa – demonstrate a higher level of literacy, the question is whether some kind of higher education went on inside the monastery. Or should we conclude that individuals who had achieved higher levels of education were joining communal monasteries and bringing their skills with them?

Socioeconomic Background of Cenobitic Monks

Was there a 'typical' cenobitic monk in the fourth and fifth centuries, at least in terms of previous occupation and residence? Did he or she come from a village or town in Upper Egypt? Ewa Wipszycka has reviewed the late antique sources that describe Egyptian monks, at least those who were Coptic-speaking, as illiterate peasants.[19] For example, Socrates Scholasticus, in narrating the events of the first Origenist controversy, states that most monks were 'pure, but intellectually simple and for the most part illiterate' and so were drawn to oppose Origenist ideas by a lack of understanding.[20] Wipszycka also notes that some modern scholars have argued that since a Greek-speaking elite dominated Byzantine Egypt, the Coptic-speaking majority in the monasteries must have come from a rural, and thus inferior and uneducated, environment. She counters this view by presenting evidence for a rural, Coptic-speaking elite and her evidence is consistent with passages in cenobitic literature.[21] In the *Bohairic Life of Pachomius*, Theodore (a successor to Pachomius) is described as 'born into a prominent family' and sent to school at age eight, and eventually joined Pachomius in the monastery at Pbow.[22] Petronius, from a wealthy Christian family near Diospolis Parva, founded the monastery of Thbew on his property, then 'asked to dwell in the shadow of the holy *Koinonia*', meaning that Thbew became one of the affiliated monasteries.[23] The Egyptian names of Petronius's family members (Pshenthbo, Pshenapalhi) place them in the Coptic elite category. Therefore, some leaders in the monasteries came from circumstances that probably provided them with an education beyond simple literacy. On the other hand, there is evidence from the White Monastery that some monks belonged to the rural poor category, because they were stealing food to give to relatives 'outside'.[24]

Less can be said about the family backgrounds of Pachomius and Shenoute, the most important figures in the cenobitic movement. The *Greek Life of Pachomius* states that he was conscripted into the army and, on his release, became a Christian and took up ascetic life.[25] The *Life of Shenoute* depicts a wonder-working Shenoute who also comes from a humble background.[26] But this work is probably a late compilation from *encomia* delivered on the feast day of Shenoute, and does not offer reliable information.[27] Pachomius and Shenoute have Egyptian names, wrote in Coptic and taught in a Coptic-speaking community. They grew up in the vicinity of towns (nome capitals) such as Panopolis and Diospolis/Thebes, where higher education was available. But in the case of these leaders, it may be necessary to infer from their writings how, where and to what level they were educated.

Schools and Education in Egypt: Content and Context

The general picture of educational practices in Egypt is becoming clearer. Archaeological research is increasingly alert to the possibility of finding school texts on ostraca and papyri, and actual schoolrooms may have been identified in towns and monasteries in Upper Egypt. There has been debate about certain ostraca, papyri, wall paintings and entire manuscripts: are they school texts and were they found in a classroom setting? But the debate about individual items does not change the overall picture.

Raffaella Cribiore published a compilation of educational texts coming from Greco-Roman Egypt, and she has continued to publish both primary sources and higher-level analysis.[28] The school texts suggest that learning to read and learning to write proceeded simultaneously. Students are copying the alphabet, syllables and words, but they are also copying short sayings and passages before they can read them.[29] This analysis relies, in part, on isolating handwriting types and sequencing them from the zero grade hand (the student just learning the

38   *Janet Timbie*

alphabet) up to the rapid hand (fluent).[30] Even zero grade hands are copying short selections from texts. Since the early cenobitic rules mandate learning to read and do not mandate learning to write (see above), it is possible that reading instruction in these monasteries proceeded in a different way – by alternating listening, memorisation and study of the written word. Perhaps the main goal was to read and memorise scripture passages and prayers in order to participate in meditative recitation (*meleta*).[31] On the other hand, the reference in Pachomian Rule 140 to the 'syllable' as well as verb and noun being written for the student monk suggests some overlap with non-monastic elementary education in which reading and writing went together.[32] For cenobitic monks who entered the monastery with previous education – as seems likely for Theodore, Shenoute and some others – the school text evidence is also important, since it shows what they would have done before entering the monastery and what they would have worked on after entry in order to become skilled preachers and writers.

School settings have been identified by archaeological work at some monastic sites, including the monastery of Epiphanius, the monastery of Phoibammon and the Naqlun monastery. Ostraca found in two monastic cells at the monastery of Epiphanius have received much attention, with Cell A seen as a site of scribal training and Cell B as the site of a monastic school. Scott Bucking has analysed the material evidence from the original excavations at the monastery of Epiphanius and argued for a 'multifunctional' interpretation that allows for the use of ostraca from Cell A not only in scribal training, but also for their use in private study or as recitation material for monks.[33] Finds in Cell B included word lists and short Homeric passages on ostraca, which led some to describe the site as a monastic school for children. Bucking has argued for other interpretations of these ostraca: education of adult monks, scribal training and simple pen trials.[34] Possible non-monastic school sites have also been identified. Trimithis, in the Dakhleh oasis, is the site of a large fourth-century house containing a room with painted texts on the walls (*dipinti*), whose content (Greek epigrams with classical vocabulary) indicates educational use.[35] The initial publication of this material argued that the painted verses use metrical form in the service of rhetorical education.[36] And this would indicate that some rhetorical training was available in a provincial, oasis town. More can be said about education in Panopolis, the town across the Nile from the White Monastery, because of the work that has survived from poets such as Nonnus and Pamprepius. Alan Cameron notes that such poets probably 'received at least their primary education in Panopolis'.[37] Primary education in this context may encompass both learning to read and write and also studying with a *grammatikos* to learn grammar and study literature.[38] But given the evidence for higher-level education in Trimithis, it seems likely that some rhetorical training was also available in Panopolis, a bigger and much more accessible town.

The organisation of the highest level of education is described in the writings of Libanius, a teacher of rhetoric in Antioch; and many handbooks of rhetorical exercises also lay out the steps for achieving eloquence after a long process of studying and memorising material from classical models.[39] Cribiore states that 'a student started by slavishly following a model, provided either by his own teacher or by a writer from the past; he began composing according to the pattern; and he learned to fly independently through a painful process of trial and error'.[40] This sequence may also be relevant for the compositions of Shenoute and other cenobitic leaders if scripture largely takes the place of all other 'writers of the past'.

The site of higher level education in Alexandria in the fifth and sixth centuries, Kom el-Dikka, has now been excavated, so there is material evidence to put alongside the descriptions that Libanius provides and also alongside the evidence from Trimithis for more modest educational premises. Edward Watts describes the layout of classrooms linked by a covered hallway, and adds that both Christian and pagan students attended the lectures and met and discussed the lessons in the hallway.[41] Higher-level education thus relied both on the efforts of the teacher and on discussion with fellow students. This suggests a pedagogical parallel with the cenobitic practice of formal community prayers and sermons followed by instruction and discussion in the smaller house unit.[42] The student or monk learned both from the teacher/monastic superior and from fellow monks.

Coptic and Greek in the Early Cenobitic Monasteries

The multilingualism of Egyptian society – and monasticism – at this period complicates study of the educational system.[43] The writings that survive from Shenoute, Pachomius and others are Coptic originals. Were the writers also literate in Greek, for both reading and writing? How was Coptic literacy achieved, and was it possible to be literate in Coptic only? These questions complicate the discussion of how much education the leaders had received and where they were educated. 'Literacy is not a single phenomenon but a highly variable package of skills' – according to Rafael Rodríguez – which could include reading, writing, access to certain types of texts only, and the ability to write one thing (name, personal letter) but not another.[44]

Jean-Luc Fournet describes the multilingual environment of Egypt in the fourth–seventh centuries using written evidence from the papyri; thus, the issue is one of 'multiliteracy' rather than multilingualism.[45] The relationship between Coptic and Greek is one of 'diglossia with real bilingualism'.[46] Coptic and Greek had different functions (diglossia) and some people were also fully bilingual, whether in speech, reading or writing. Coptic as a medium for writing the Egyptian vernacular in an alphabetic system, mainly borrowed from Greek, developed rapidly beginning in the third century, among Egyptian Christians who also spoke Greek. Fournet summarises the changes:

> In the following century, Coptic expanded dramatically not only as a literary medium but also for ordinary use, still in Christian circles. The Egyptian population, which had become mainly Christian in this period, had from this point on its own means of writing, which allowed it to communicate in its own languages.[47]

40   *Janet Timbie*

And this is exactly the period of the founding and rapid growth of the cenobitic communities in Upper Egypt. The rapid expansion of Coptic must have included rapid development of educational settings for achieving Coptic literacy, since leaders such as Pachomius (d. 346) and Shenoute, who is writing fluently in Coptic before 385 when he becomes abbot, are using Coptic as their means of written communication. The dominance of Coptic in these communities is also shown by the *Letter of Ammon*, in which the Greek-speaking Ammon describes his experience in the monastery at Pbow when Theodore was the leader. Theodore the Alexandrian translates the oral teaching of Theodore the abbot for Ammon, and guides him to the house where 20 Greek-speaking monks discuss the teaching. Ammon is also directed to 'learn the divine scriptures' with this group, presumably in Greek, because there is no indication that Ammon learns Coptic.[48] Near the end of his three-year stay at Pbow, Ammon is still listening to interpreters.[49]

Greek and Coptic educational texts (ostraca, papyri, wooden boards) follow the same pattern. Alphabets, syllabaries, word lists and short texts have been found in both languages.[50] The texts in Coptic are religious (Bible, prayers, stories), but Cribiore points out that the school setting for such material is not proven: 'When one can rely only on the quality of the hand, in the absence of other characteristics of school exercises, it is easy to mistake texts that were written by barely literate monks for exercises.'[51] However, if some monks in cenobitic monasteries were taught writing as well as reading, there would be another explanation for the 'practice' religious texts. They would be monastic school exercises.

Greek school texts also start to use religious material in place of classical texts during the Byzantine period. Cribiore points to two differences between Greek and Coptic school exercises: first, students of Coptic copied epistolary formulas to practise their writing; and second, grammatical exercises (declensions, conjugations) are largely absent from the Coptic school material.[52] There is no clear evidence for higher-level education – the teaching of grammar and rhetoric – in Coptic, yet there is evidence of composition in Coptic that follows rhetorical patterns found in Greek patristic literature. Mark Sheridan analysed four Coptic sermons from the fifth–sixth centuries and classified two as text-based homilies, one as an encomium and the last as showing 'extensive affinity with the forensic rhetorical tradition'.[53] The sermon by Shenoute that was quoted at the beginning of this chapter uses rhetorical questions that assume some response from the audience, as in a philosophical or religious diatribe.[54] The question for Shenoute, and other early cenobitic leaders, is how and where did they study the literary models before composing original material in Coptic?

Conclusion: Continuing Education in the Monastery

'While it is true that Christians adopted Classical education and progressively retooled it to meet their needs, in some circles, such as monasteries, education was limited to the reading of the Scriptures.'[55] This statement by Sofia Torallas

Tovar, a Coptic papyrologist, in a discussion of word lists on ostraca and papyri that enabled readers of the Bible in Coptic to learn some obscure Greek loanwords, suggests that the Pachomian rule still dominates some of the published research. But the picture is more complicated, since everyday writing and original composition are also going on in the cenobitic monasteries.

If the stages of education in antiquity are fairly clear and the documentary evidence in support is accessible, thanks to the work of Cribiore, then the problem is how to fit the cenobitic leaders on the grid.[56] Alberto Nodar has summarised the stages clearly in recent work. The student began with the *didaskalos*, either in a schoolroom or at home, learning reading, writing and basic maths. Some students continued with the *grammatikos* to study grammar in the context of intensive reading of literature, and maths studies continued. A few students then studied with a *rhetor* in order to learn persuasive speech by means of formal exercises (*progymnasmata*) in standard forms such as declamations or encomia.[57] For each of the early cenobitic leaders from whom we have written work, it is possible to ask whether their work fits any of the standard forms and therefore indicates higher-level education.[58]

Each cenobitic leader presents a different picture. Pachomius cannot be identified with confidence as the author of the *Instructions* that circulated under his name.[59] His letters have better support; Shenoute even quotes one letter.[60] But his letters are not very helpful if the goal is to examine the education of Pachomius, since they feature a 'cryptic use of the letters of the alphabet' that is 'unintelligible to all but the recipients'.[61] Joel Kalvesmaki has recently reviewed all research on the letters and usefully compared them to works such as *On the Mystery of the Letters* and the *Apocalypse of Charour.* Just as ordinary schooling started with letters, syllables and then words, the secret communication started with an alphabetic code that elevated the standing of Pachomius as a holy man.[62] But it is not clear that such coded communications were associated with higher levels of formal education, for cryptography is common in late antique Egypt.[63] So there is no reason to conclude that Pachomius had more than primary education before founding a monastery, where he read the Bible intensively in Coptic and began to use a secret language for some aspects of monastic guidance.

The successors of Pachomius left written work that is more useful for answering questions about education. Both Theodore and Horsiesius wrote *Instructions* and *Letters* that resemble contemporary sermons and biblical letters such as Ephesians.[64] The *Testament of Horsiesius* connects many biblical quotations and allusions, with a minimum amount of original text, in response to some kind of crisis in the *Koinonia*.[65] The *Life of Pachomius*, whether in Coptic or Greek versions, does not say anything about the background of Horsiesius, simply noting that he had been with Pachomius for many years before being appointed head of Chenoboskion.[66] According to the *Greek Life of Pachomius*, Theodore joined the Pachomian movement at 14 (around AD 328) and thus could have completed the second stage of education (*grammatikos*), since he was 'from a great home thriving according to the world'.[67] Theodore may have become literate – reading and writing – in both Greek and Coptic before entering the monastery, and studied

42   *Janet Timbie*

Greek at the *grammatikos* level; but, as noted above, there is no evidence in the school texts for study of Coptic grammar. A minimal conclusion would be that Theodore and Horsiesius composed their works following years of Bible reading, as well as study of the festal letters sent annually by the archbishop of Alexandria. Armand Veilleux has noted similarities between the festal letters announcing the dates of Lent and Easter and the letters sent by Pachomian leaders calling everyone to Pbow for the annual meeting at Easter.[68]

Shenoute, third in line after Pcol and Ebonh as head of the White Monastery Federation, is also the author of the largest body of original Coptic writing that survives. His chronology can only be reconstructed from statements in his own writings and in the small corpus of works by his successor, Besa, because he is not mentioned in non-Egyptian patristic sources. Statements such as 'after we went to Ephesus', meaning the Council of Ephesus in AD 431, and 'more than a hundred years I have been in the desert' imply a very long life and an early entry into the monastery.[69] One chronology has him entering the monastery at age nine, which agrees with Coptic tradition, becoming leader around 385 and dying in 465/66 at the age of 102.[70] If he was older at entry, then he was older at death. Coptic tradition says he lived to 118, so he was born 346/47 and died 464/65. This chronology has been criticised; but the relevant point here is how much basic education Shenoute might have received before he joined the monastery.[71] A student who began to study rhetoric at 14 or 15, following the usual pattern, must have already completed the two earlier stages (*didaskalos* and *grammatikos*), but 'length of schooling . . . depended a great deal on environment, students' social status, and . . . accessible teachers', as Cribiore states.[72] If Shenoute entered the monastery at nine (the traditional view), he might have received some instruction in Greek and Coptic reading and writing, and in arithmetic, in the general vicinity of Panopolis. But there would be little time for instruction at the next level, when Greek grammar was taught. Shenoute's own statement in 431–32 – 'I have been reading the holy gospels for more than sixty years' – only implies that he was a monk by 371–72, and so might have been in his mid-20s at entry.[73] In that case, there would be time to complete the first two stages of education and have some contact with rhetorical training, perhaps in Panopolis.[74] But the chronology of Shenoute is uncertain apart from a few points, so it does not offer a firm basis for reconstructing his formal education.

There is another potential starting point for a discussion of the education of Shenoute: the content of his written work.[75] His letters and sermons for monastic and non-monastic audiences have features that may make it possible to answer questions such as whether he was literate in Greek, knew any standard classical or patristic works, and was trained to compose according to models such as the diatribe or encomium. The answers would then direct attention to education as it was organised in the late fourth and fifth centuries in Egypt. Either Shenoute learned these things in childhood or youth in a school setting or he learned them inside the monastery mainly through independent study. On the question of Greek literacy, most would agree with Stephen Emmel that 'there is no good reason to doubt that Shenoute was capable of both reading and speaking Greek, and

The Education of Shenoute and Other Cenobitic Leaders   43

therefore also of writing it with at least some facility'.[76] Some of his works refer to visits from high-ranking officials or 'philosophers', who came with questions or simply to hear him preach, and conversation in Greek is likely.[77] Other works contain material that Shenoute translated from Greek into Coptic: *I Am Amazed* (*Discourses*, Book 7) contains a long excerpt from Theophilus's *Festal Letter* of 401 translated into Coptic by Shenoute; and *Canons*, Book 1 has a passage in which Shenoute blends his own words with his Coptic translation of Isaiah 1:9.[78] Only a small part of Shenoute's work is available in modern critical editions, which makes it difficult to identify classical and patristic works that he has read or cited. Anne Boud'hors notes a possible allusion to the *Physiologos* in *My Heart Is Crushed*, as well as similarity to the phraseology of a letter of Basil of Caesarea.[79] *I Have Been Reading the Holy Gospels* quotes an unidentified work by Athanasius,[80] while *I Am Amazed* quotes Athanasius's *Festal Letter* of 367 on the canon of scripture.[81] Other parts of *I Am Amazed* quote statements by Nestorius that are accurately translated into Coptic, based on comparison with the Greek of various sources.[82] More examples of reading, translating, and quotation of Greek material will probably be identified in future critical editions of the works of Shenoute.

Finally, there is the question of whether his work follows known rhetorical models. Very little has been published that tackles the problem, though some studies can be expected fairly soon. Given the evidence for Shenoute's knowledge of Greek language, familiarity with some Greek authors, and apparent use of rhetorical models (whether imitating Paul or following classical models), Emmel's conclusion that Shenoute had 'rhetorical and notarial training in Greek (and in Coptic, such as it may have been in the middle of the fourth century)' seems reasonable.[83] This training was fused with intensive reading of the Bible in Coptic from the time he entered the monastery – and with his own genius – and the result was highly original work in Coptic.

Therefore, Shenoute probably passed through the first two stages of education before entering the monastery. He may also have studied at the next level for a time to learn some of the rhetorical models. But, for the most part, his literary achievement illustrates the way education in Late Antiquity was meant to work: first, acquire basic skills in reading and writing; second, read deeply with attention to grammatical features; and, finally, produce written or oral compositions following standard patterns.[84] In Shenoute, the second stage is, in effect, repeated in the monastery through years of intensive reading of the Bible in Coptic, and also in Greek. Emmel describes the self-education of Shenoute that took place after he entered the monastery and before he became leader around AD 385: 'He spent most of his time reading, memorizing, and meditating upon the Holy Scriptures, by which I mean, of course, the Coptic Bible . . . [and] he learned to compose in Coptic in wonderful imitation of its cadences.'[85] Even an early work such as the open letter of *Canons*, Book 1 weaves allusions to the 'Destroyer' with prophetic-sounding language and wraps up with a quotation from Isaiah:

A voice came three times around our community saying 'The Destroyer (cf. 1 Cor 10:10, Num 16:1–35) entered you, the Destroyer ruled over a portion

44   *Janet Timbie*

of you and took it captive to a distant land . . . and destroyed the choice bunches of grapes . . . (and) he destroyed the older rams among the sheep'. Except that the Lord has left a remnant among us, 'we would have become like Sodom and we would resemble Gomorrah' (Isa 1:9).[86]

Future critical editions of the works of Shenoute may focus attention on Greek influences, perhaps going back to his pre-monastic education, and also on his radical choice of Coptic as a vehicle for oral and written rhetoric when there were hardly any models to follow.

Notes

1 Shenoute, *Discourses*, Book 8, Leipoldt 1913: CSCO 73, 5. This sermon from Book 8 is partially preserved and so may be identified as either *The Idolatrous Pagans* or *And We Will Also Reveal Something Else*. See Emmel 2004a, 656–7.
2 Wipszycka 1996a, 329–36.
3 Fournet 2009, 430–37.
4 *Precepts* 139–40; see Boon 1932, 49–59 (Latin) and Veilleux 1981, 166 (English).
5 Veilleux 1981, 7.
6 Lefort 1956, CSCO 159, 31 (Coptic); Veilleux 1981, 162 (English). Rule 101 also deals with the care of books. The *synaxis* is the communal prayer session that took place daily.
7 Lefort 1956: CSCO 159, 90; Wipszycka 1996a, 133 cites this passage in her critique of scholarship that assumed rural illiteracy.
8 Boon 1932, 50 (Latin); Veilleux 1981, 166 (English). Cribiore 2001, 176–8 describes the tight connection between reading and writing in primary education, and contrasts this with practice in medieval monasteries in Europe that reserved writing for a small minority.
9 In contrast to the Pachomian rules, there are no surviving manuscripts that contain only White Monastery rules. They must have existed because Shenoute several times mentions the records of the monastery that preserve the rules; see for example *Canons*, Book 3, work A22 in Leipoldt 1913: CSCO 73, 126–7. See also Schroeder 2014, including a comparison of Pachomian and White Monastery rule manuscripts.
10 In Shenoute; see *So Listen*, Boud'hors 2013, 87. The Pachomian rule is found in Lefort 1956: CSCO 159, 31.
11 Layton 2007, 67.
12 Layton 2007, 60. Also discussed in Wipszycka 1996a, 133.
13 *Letters and Sermons of Besa*, Kuhn 1956: CSCO 157, 105.
14 See Krawiec 2002, 31–50 on the disagreements between Shenoute and the women's monastery, with references to written communication to and from all parties.
15 Layton 2014 offers a complete text and translation of the more than 500 White Monastery rules that survive.
16 Layton 2007, 49 n. 19, quoting *Canons*, Book 5. See also Albarrán Martínez 2012, 210.
17 Orlandi 2002.
18 See Layton 2007, 71 for some specific references and a description of the monastery as filled with 'a constant buzzing sound like a flight of bees, as everyone continually mumbles prayers and passages of Scripture in a low voice'.
19 Wipszycka 1996a, 330–31.
20 Socrates Scholasticus, *Ecclesiastical History* 6.7, Maraval 2004–07, 3.292.
21 Wipszycka 1996a, 331.

The Education of Shenoute and Other Cenobitic Leaders 45

22 *Bohairic Life of Pachomius* 31, Veilleux 1980, 55–7. There is some disagreement between the versions of the *Life of Pachomius* on the age of Theodore when he joined Pachomius; see Veilleux 1980, 272–3.

23 *Bohairic Life of Pachomius* 56, Veilleux 1980, 77. See Rousseau 1999a, 153.

24 Layton 2002, 49 n. 103.

25 *Greek Life of Pachomius* 4–6, Veilleux 1980, 300–301.

26 *Life of Shenoute* 3–4, Bell 1983, 42–3, where the child Shenoute is a shepherd and has miraculous experiences.

27 Lubomierski 2007, 201–11.

28 See Cribiore 1996, 2001, 2007a, 2009; Cribiore et al. 2008.

29 Cribiore 2009, 327.

30 Cribiore 1996, 112; Bucking 1999, 199.

31 Timbie, forthcoming b.

32 Boon 1932, 50 (Latin); Veilleux 1981, 166 (English).

33 Bucking 2007, 36; Larsen 2013b, 16–19 analyses the Epiphanius evidence as part of an effort to correct the stereotypical picture of the 'a-literate' monk.

34 Bucking 2007, 36–41.

35 Cribiore et al. 2008.

36 Cribiore et al. 2008, 190.

37 Cameron 2007, 34.

38 Cribiore 2001, 50–53. See also Egberts et al. 2002 for essays on topics related to Panopolis, including the library of the White Monastery.

39 Cribiore 2007b.

40 Cribiore 2001, 221.

41 Watts 2010, 5–9.

42 Rousseau 1999a, 85.

43 Bagnall 1993, 231 discusses Latin as the 'third' language in Egypt, used in a narrow range of administrative and military matters. Fournet 2009, 421–30 surveys the use of Latin in late antique Egypt based on the evidence of the papyri, and concludes that the situation is 'diglossia with limited or imperfect bilingualism' (421).

44 Rodríguez 2009, 158, with many useful references and good discussion of the interface between orality and literacy.

45 Fournet 2009, 419.

46 Fournet 2009, 430.

47 Fournet 2009, 431.

48 *Letter of Ammon* 7; Goehring 1986a, 129.

49 *Letter of Ammon* 29; Goehring 1986a, 151–2.

50 See Cribiore 1999 for a clear summary and analysis of the evidence. Torallas Tovar 2013 uses school texts as a means to explore the complicated role of Greek loanwords in Coptic.

51 Cribiore 1999, 279.

52 Cribiore 1999, 280–81.

53 Sheridan 2007, 47; see also Emmel 2007, 91.

54 Timbie, forthcoming a; Schenkeveld 1997, 232; and Siegert 1997, 421–33. On the structure of the works of Shenoute (*Canons* and *Discourses*) see Emmel 2004a, 3–5.

55 Torallas Tovar 2013, 112.

56 Cribiore 1996, 2001, 2007a.

57 Nodar 2012, 185.

58 See above for evidence of writing practice in monastic settings, and Cribiore 2001, Bucking 2007.

59 Veilleux 1982, 1–3.

60 Kalvesmaki 2013, 24.

61 Kalvesmaki 2013, 11.

62 Kalvesmaki 2013, 24.

46   Janet Timbie

63   Dieleman 2005, 84–7.
64   See the many quotations and allusions to Ephesians and other Paulines in Theodore, *Instruction* 3, Veilleux 1982, 93–119. Rousseau 2007, 140–57 examines all the instructional works of the successors of Pachomius and identifies shared ideas.
65   *Testament of Horsiesius*, Veilleux 1982, 171–215.
66   *First Greek Life of Pachomius* 119, Veilleux 1980, 381.
67   *First Greek Life of Pachomius* 33, Veilleux 1980, 320.
68   Veilleux 1982, 6–7. Rousseau 1999a, 75 describes the two annual meetings, one at Easter and one in August, that brought together monks from all the monasteries in the *Koinonia*.
69   Emmel 2004a, 9, 11 cites the works (*I Have Been Reading the Holy Gospels* and acephalous work A22) that contain these statements.
70   Emmel 2004a, 11.
71   Emmel 2004b, 157 makes another case for the 346–465 chronology; Luisier 2009 criticises it and maintains that Shenoute died around 450, before the Council of Chalcedon (AD 451).
72   Cribiore 2001, 56 (14 or 15 as the age for studying rhetoric), 162.
73   Emmel 2004a, 9; Emmel 2004b, 157.
74   Van Minnen 2002, 178–9. Van Minnen points out that the Bodmer collection of codices may have come from Panopolis and so provide evidence for advanced education there. Documentary material also points to the presence of a philosophical school.
75   Emmel 2004a, 3–5 summarises the structure of Shenoute's literary corpus.
76   Emmel 2007, 90.
77   Shenoute, in *As I Sat on a Mountain* (*Discourses*, Book 3; Leipoldt 1908: CSCO 42, 44) begins by stating that the audience included a pagan philosopher, officials and rich people.
78   Emmel 1995 identified the festal letter in Shenoute; Emmel 2004a, 166 comments on Shenoute's use of *Isaiah* 1:9. A critical edition of *I Am Amazed* is available in Cristea 2011.
79   Boud'hors 2013, 71.
80   Moussa 2010, 142.
81   Cristea 2011, 66–80.
82   Cristea 2011, 88–9.
83   Emmel 2007, 91.
84   Cribiore 2001: chapters 6, 7 and 8 discussing the curricula in all three stages.
85   Emmel 2004a, 160.
86   *Canons*, Book 1, Leipoldt 1908: CSCO 42, 195–6. See Emmel 2004b, 166 for the full manuscript citation and further discussion.

3 Teaching the New Classics

Bible and Biography in a Pachomian Monastery

Edward Watts

> When [Theodore] sat to instruct the brothers, they would ask him about many things
> he had said to them since they did not understand the full depth of their significance.
> On the other hand, if he was standing, no one except the interpreter questioned
> him, according to the rule laid down from the beginning. But they would stand
> completely attentive, taking in everything he said.
>
> (*The Life of Saint Pachomius* 188, trans. Veilleux)[1]

This passage from the *Bohairic Life of Pachomius* offers a rare chance to confront
one of the greatest challenges scholars face when trying to reconstruct the social
dynamics of the late antique educational environment. Education in all periods
and all contexts depends upon a profound and personal exchange of information
between a master who possesses knowledge and a disciple who wants to gain
that knowledge. The knowledge a teacher possesses gives him or her a sort of
authority that the student willingly accepts in exchange for instruction. Even
students like Apollonius of Tyana, Proclus and Antony whose natural abilities
far outstripped those of some of their teachers accepted a subordinate status as
long as their mentors could still teach them something useful.[2]

The power dynamic animating a teacher–student relationship is so basic that
we often do not think it worth examining, but it has profound implications
for the study of late antique education. Teaching was an activity whose success
depended upon a master's ability to continue to assert direct, personal authority over disciples. But this authority was not remote. It was instead something
exercised through personal interactions and oral communication. The words
of a teacher, spoken directly to a student or group of students, simultaneously
conveyed information and either reinforced or undermined the teacher's dominant position.

The *Bohairic Life of Pachomius* describes teaching in a large monastic community, not a conventional school; but it shows that Pachomian leaders understood
both the authority that followers yielded to masters and the importance of
limiting the moments when this formal power was fully exercised. Theodore,
the head of the Pachomian federation (the Koinonia) from 350 to 368, taught

48   *Edward Watts*

in two ways. At certain times, he would sit and discuss things conversationally with his subordinates. In these moments, he fielded their questions; explained things that they found unclear; and took pains to ensure that they understood his ideas. His authority was never challenged, but its full power was also deliberately suppressed. At other times, however, Theodore asserted the full power of the ascetic master. He stood before the brothers and taught without interruption. They were expected to listen and absorb his ideas without question. He was the master, they were the subordinates, and everything about the setting communicated this fundamental inequality.

A successful teacher needed to master both dynamics. A teacher or ascetic master who never exercised his full authority ultimately relinquished the parts of that authority he failed to use.[3] At the same time, the head of a scholastic or monastic circle who insisted on dominating his students often encountered pushback from followers who felt no personal connection with him.[4] As Theodore's interactions with his fellow monks show, Pachomian communities did a particularly good job of documenting the ways in which their leadership balanced the exercise of the authority of a teacher with the informal, personal interactions that gave meaning to a monk's membership in the monastery's community.

The rest of this chapter examines how this was done. The Koinonia worked simultaneously as a cooperative enterprise that collectively guided monks towards ideal monastic practices and as a steeply hierarchical environment in which authority was strictly defined. Pachomian leaders explained the nature of this community to the members of the Koinonia by deftly mixing the oral exegesis of biblical passages with orally transmitted anecdotes about the community's founders that illustrated how these passages applied to Pachomian monastic life. Beneath this system of education, however, lay a support structure that managed the relationships between masters and their followers that made teaching personally meaningful. The chapter then concludes by showing how the Koinonia adapted these personal relationships so that they also reinforced a steep, inflexible and occasionally remote ascetic hierarchy.

The Koinonia

The Pachomian community began in the early decades of the fourth century as a communal enterprise dedicated to mutual ascetic improvement. Pachomius, the master who established the Koinonia, organised it around the notion that each monk became 'a subject of edification to his neighbor and a way [for him] to enter into the joy of the kingdom of heaven'.[5] A Pachomian ascetic watched the behaviours and practices of other members of the community because this 'incited him to imitate their actions and the excellent practices they perform in order to do the same himself'.[6] If, however, other monks were doing things detrimental to their ascetic practice, a fellow monk was supposed to correct them before they wandered from the true path.[7]

The Pachomian way of life initially centred on a small cluster of ascetics who lived together and offered one another support. By the middle of the fourth century, the enterprise had grown into a network of at least seven different monasteries and thousands of monks scattered across the Nile Valley.[8] Pachomius established Pbow as the administrative centre of the Pachomian system, but a range of monastic foundations also eventually joined it.[9] This included a monastery called Thbew founded by a wealthy landholder named Petronius and located on his family lands; and another, Thmoušons, that had substantial independent commercial interests.[10] By 350, it had become clear that these monastic franchises could not be governed effectively without a strong, well-defined central authority that managed affairs.[11] To ensure the integrity of the community, Pachomian leaders needed to be forceful, their orders needed to be communicated clearly, and they needed to be obeyed. All of these things, however, involved the assertion of an authority that seemed to run against the ideal that members of the community worked collectively to monitor and (if necessary) correct each monk's ascetic practices. The rigid hierarchy that the Pachomian monastic structure required and the egalitarian ideal of mutual correction that it espoused fit together rather awkwardly.

As the system developed, Pachomian leaders created a sophisticated way of explaining how these two seemingly contradictory elements of the Koinonia reinforced one another. This explanation centred primarily on the oral and literary fashioning of the figure of Pachomius himself. Pachomius was said by his successors to have based his model for the Koinonia on instructions that he received from a series of divine visions.[12] These instructions led to a set of regulations that steered the monks towards behaviours designed to strengthen their ascetic practice. Pachomius was said to have described the project as one in which 'the Lord knows that if you do not observe the laws which I have laid down for you and, if you do not put them into practice and carry them out, you will not see any place of rest for your souls'.[13]

However divinely inspired these rules may have been, they were extremely intrusive. The Pachomian hierarchy regulated the daily schedule monks followed, the tasks they performed and even such mundane things as whether a monk could change clothes or pull a thorn out of his finger.[14] The Pachomian leadership understood that this degree of regulation was, at best, annoying and, at worst, an excessive and arbitrary exercise of power. They then made it clear that Pachomius had understood and responded to these types of complaints. In what the community would come to believe was Pachomius' final words to his followers, he was said to have claimed that 'I never corrected any one of you as one having authority except for the sake of his soul's salvation.'[15] In addition, Pachomius explained that all of the micromanaging he did came about because of God's wishes. Never, he asserted, 'did I move any of you from one place to another or from one occupation to another unless I knew that it was to his advantage according to God that I did it'.[16] He also claimed never to have chastised anyone, got angry with anyone or reacted angrily in a way that differed from what God had ordained.[17] The community was then created, structured

50   Edward Watts

and continually managed according to a divine plan uniquely understood by Pachomius and continued by those who followed him at the top of the monastic hierarchy.

Pachomian Teaching

When Pachomius' successors spoke to their followers in a formal setting, they regularly reinforced how Pachomius' project fulfilled the mission of the Apostles. They liberally referenced the biblical passages that underpinned the Pachomian lifestyle and the ways in which Pachomius implemented biblical instructions. They also emphasised how, practically speaking, these ideas and the founder's example could guide them in the present.

In the text now preserved as his *Third Instruction*, Theodore explains what the Koinonia delivered to its members by artfully blending the words of Jesus, the legacy of the Apostles and the model of Pachomius. The fifth chapter of the text gives an example of his method. He began by quoting 2 Corinthians 1.3–4: 'We give thanks to God', he said, 'for enabling us to forget our sorrows and our distress in the fragrance of obedience and with the firmness of a firm faith in the law of the holy and true Koinonia.' The Koinonia then represented the fulfilment of the promise of release from suffering that 2 Corinthians laid out. But Theodore was not done. He next tied the Koinonia and Pachomius to the Apostolic tradition. The Koinonia, Theodore continued, 'has as its author, after the Apostles, Apa Pachomius, the man whose God-given promises we are ready to inherit if we only observe his commandments'. Theodore then concludes the thought with another quotation, this time from 2 Corinthians 7, speaking about the washing away of 'every defilement of flesh or spirit, and perfectly practicing purity in the fear of God'.[18]

The rest of the *Instruction* proceeds similarly. Biblical quotations comprise nearly half of the surviving the text, but Theodore rarely quotes Scripture at length. Instead, what one finds is an elaborate textual tapestry woven from Scriptural quotation, Apostolic example and the history of the Pachomian community. This was by design. Theodore says, for example, that because monks were 'acquainted with the wholesome knowledge of Holy Scripture and the works by which God trained the saints and the fathers of the Koinonia' they are able to avoid despairing about the challenges of ascetic life.[19] The success that the Pachomian system promised ascetics grew out of the effective blending of these three elements from which Pachomian identity derived.

This message was indeed powerful, but only if the code in which it was expressed could be deciphered. It is easy to see in a modern, annotated edition of Theodore's *Third Instruction* or another similar Pachomian text the degree to which rapid-fire biblical quotation, mentions of the Apostles and references to the history of the Pachomian community combine to give authority to the ideas for which the speaker argues. An ancient audience listening to the text would have had a much different experience. The power of the ideas Theodore expressed, the passages he quoted and the stories to which he connected them would all have been lost on the audience unless they had an intimate knowledge of both Scripture and Pachomian communal history.

It is clear, however, that Pachomian monks lived in a world designed to give them the background to appreciate the tapestry of textual and historical references that leaders like Theodore expertly wove. This process began as soon as a monk joined the monastery. According to Pachomian sources, a potential community member would wait in the gatehouse of the monastery he hoped to join until he could be interviewed by its head.[20] While he waited, the monks in charge of the gatehouse taught the prospective member the Lord's Prayer and a few Psalms.[21] If the head of the monastery determined that the new arrival truly understood what it meant to commit to the monastic life and was willing to do what it required, he would then be welcomed to the community.[22] An intense period of study followed this in which the novice was taught about the rules and traditions of the Pachomian monastery.[23] In this period he was also required to learn a number of Psalms and other passages of Scripture by heart. If he could not read, he was taught to do this so that he could better engage in the study of biblical texts.[24]

Monks continued to receive regular instruction in Scripture and the divinely inspired principles on which Pachomius had organised the life of his community for as long as they remained a part of the Koinonia.[25] Each day began with a horn or gong that called the monks to assemble for the *synaxis*, communal morning prayers.[26] From the time that he left his cell until he entered the *synaxis*, each monk was to 'recite something from the Scripture'.[27] The assembly itself included a great deal of reading from the Scriptures as well as collective prayers and time for silent reflection among the monks.

The monks continued reciting texts, praying and contemplating God's word while they worked during the day.[28] The workday was interrupted by a mid-day meal and it concluded with a smaller supper.[29] The hours following the evening meal were for instruction, communal prayer and discussion within the individual houses. On certain days of the week the superiors of each monastery presented a short lesson to all of the monks before leading them in common prayer.[30] On other days, this lesson seems to have been presented in the houses by the various headmasters.[31] As they withdrew, the monks again did so while repeating passages from Scripture and, potentially, pondering the connection these passages had to the lifestyle that they had collectively adopted. The evening concluded with discussion of the night's catechesis in the houses.

The Pachomian daily routine depended upon a set of patterns determined by Pachomius and his successors, and inspired by the example of the Apostles. The monks spent most of their time hearing, reciting and thinking about Scripture. But it is also clear that there was a selective engagement with Scripture in these communities that was mediated by the Pachomian hierarchy. The leaders of the community determined what Scripture was recited, discussed and thought about in the community as well as the way in which it was presented. The teaching was also done in a way that reinforced this hierarchy and a monk's place in it. The monks were hearing Christian Scripture, but they were receiving a Pachomian

52   Edward Watts

version of it that related specifically to the life they lived and the social context in which they lived it.

Social Dynamics

As we saw at the outset of this chapter, Pachomian leaders understood that effective teaching involved not just the exercise of formal authority but also the cultivation of personal relationships that made people willing to cede authority to a mentor. When a novice joined the community, he was compelled to renounce his attachments to family and property and embrace a new ascetic family.[32] This concept of family replacement echoes an old model of framing the relationship between a master, his disciple and the circle to which they each belonged that reached back at least as far as the Old Academy of the fourth century BC.[33] In philosophical circles, however, the community tended to be small, and organised in such a way that students knew all of their teachers and peers.[34] The philosopher who headed them could easily serve as an authoritative figure who commanded the full attention and devotion of students in class as well as a mentor who built personal relationships with his students outside of class.[35]

The size of the Pachomian Koinonia had, by the mid-fourth century, made it impossible for the community's leadership to do these things. The Pachomian leaders then wisely decided to add additional layers to this spiritual family. Each monk belonged to a massive association with thousands of spiritual brothers, a group so large that the notion of all monks belonging to one family could seem more theoretical than real. The Koinonia, however, ensured that the monks had a multi-layered understanding of their ascetic clan. All Pachomians belonged to the Koinonia, but they were also living in a specific monastery within the Koinonia. The monasteries themselves were also subdivided into monastic houses of approximately 20 monks.[36] In addition, a newcomer was immediately placed in a sort of spiritual sonship to an ascetic mentor who was described as 'your father after God'.[37] The novice was to model his practices on those exhibited by his ascetic father and learn the ways of the community by following his father's example. If the relationship worked, the ascetic father provided the novice with personalised guidance and support.

The heads of monastic households exercised a different sort of authority over their monks. Every part of the daily routine in which a novice participated reinforced the fact that he ranked below the head of his household and was subject to his control. When the entire monastery assembled for the *synaxis*, for example, the rules of the Koinonia stated explicitly that 'no one may walk ahead of his housemaster and his leader'.[38] During an assembly, 'no one was allowed to sing Psalms apart from the housemasters and the elders of the monastery'.[39] Within the individual houses, the housemasters taught three times a week and would lead the discussions in which the brothers sought to understand the occasional lectures that the head of the monastery sometimes gave.[40] They ensured that individual monks understood the practical application of this teaching and punished those monks who failed to follow the monastery's rules.[41]

Teaching the New Classics   53

Their authority was, however, wielded in intimate quarters. The 20 monks in a Pachomian house would have known each other very well and the head of the house would have been a very familiar figure to them. While the daily assemblies would have served to introduce monks to the passages of Scripture that Pachomian leaders thought were important, it is likely that the Pachomian communal history that gave these Scriptural passages their specific resonance in the community was mainly transmitted through the more intimate personal conversations in the houses.

No existing Pachomian source records what was said in those house meetings, but a good sense of what was discussed orally in these small groups can be gained from looking at the oral transmission of anecdotes at the next level up in the Pachomian hierarchy. A range of Pachomian literary sources claim that Pachomius regularly would tell stories to 'the fathers of old who lived a long time ago with him . . . after explaining the words of the Holy Scriptures'.[42] Once Pachomius died, the monks who had known him continued to retell the stories that they had heard from the master. When Theodore took over the community in 350, he encouraged others to recall stories that they had heard from Pachomius. Theodore himself spoke at length about Pachomius' life, the process through which he established the Koinonia and his own interactions with the community founder. This process, the Greek *Vita Prima* of Pachomius says, was like that of 'children eagerly desiring to recall the memory of the fathers who brought us up'.[43]

While these materials eventually formed the basis of the substantial biographies that the community wrote of Pachomius, Theodore and the generation of founders who helped the community take shape, they did not begin as written texts. During the life of Theodore, they were instead discrete oral traditions passed down personally from the head of the monastery to his followers. They travelled down the monastic hierarchy from Theodore either to the heads of each Pachomian monastic franchise or to the heads of the individual houses in his monastery. From there, they would ultimately wind their way down to individual monks. Unlike the Scripture reading, however, these traditions were referenced but seldom transmitted in the large, impersonal settings of a formal oral instruction. This was not the sort of material to which monks were expected to simply listen without comment. These oral traditions instead moved in informal settings where conversation, questions and discussion were encouraged. They then served as an important bridge between the top of the Pachomian hierarchy and the individual monks who rested at its bottom. A figure like Theodore could seem remote and quite distant to novices who processed in ranked order into an assembly at which he spoke. But these oral traditions passed down personally from the head of the Koinonia to his deputies and from those deputies down to individual houses emphasised that all members of the Koinonia belonged to the same monastic family as Theodore. These traditions showed that they were all ascetic descendants of Pachomius.

An additional feature of Pachomian life further intensified the power of these oral exchanges. Conversation between monks was highly regulated in all

54   *Edward Watts*

Pachomian monasteries. The set of rules attributed to Pachomius by Jerome in 404 contains a large number of restrictions on when monks could speak.[44] They were not allowed to talk when walking to meetings of the monastery, and were publicly punished if they spoke during prayers or meetings.[45] They were expected to eat silently; they were not permitted to ask for anything at mealtimes; and they were required to come and go from the dining area without speaking.[46] They were 'to talk about no worldly matter' when working, a rule that was so strictly enforced that Theodore was demoted from supervising the bakery when he failed to get the monks there to obey it.[47] They were also not allowed to speak to other monks when they sat in their houses; nor was a monk allowed to say anything 'in the place where he sleeps'.[48]

While this collection of rules contains many injunctions against speaking, it also contains a few instances in which speaking is mandated. After the morning prayers are concluded, monks 'shall not return right away to their cells but they shall discuss among themselves the instruction they heard from their housemasters'.[49] In addition, 'everything that is taught in the assembly of the brothers they must absolutely talk over among themselves, especially on the days of fast when they receive instruction from their masters'.[50] These settings in which monks were required to speak are the very places in which the transmission of anecdotes and other Pachomian communal history was most likely to occur.

Bentley Layton noted recently that monastic communities worked hard to fashion a 'totalizing discourse' that replaced the values, ideals and behaviours of the world with those that would enable them to succeed in a monastery.[51] That process, which is most familiar to us from the White Monastery of Shenoute, is certainly at work in the Koinonia too. The Pachomians, however, show a particularly shrewd appreciation of the way that social dynamics could be manipulated to create this totalising discourse. By regulating speech so tightly, the Pachomian leadership attempted to ensure that the only personal conversations that ordinarily were permitted involved either analysis of Scripture or the exchange of Pachomian communal history. The social relationships that these conversations created were then based entirely around the shared experience of belonging to the ascetic family of Pachomius and the process of trying to figure out what membership in this family actually involved. These conversations all served as opportunities for the further education of the monks and their deeper integration into the monastic community. They also, not coincidentally, created highly controlled moments in which individual monks were given the opportunity to learn without feeling the full weight of the authority they had given to a monastic master.

Conclusion

Oral testimony and informal interactions between teachers and students had long served to moderate any discomfort that students felt about granting power and control to their teachers. This process had been going on in Greek scholastic settings since at least the fourth century BC. In Greek philosophical schools, one sees teachers and students interacting outside of class in ways designed to blur the strict hierarchy that existed inside the classroom. Like the Pachomians, they shared anecdotes about the founders of their communities, and discussed the ways in which the actions of these scholastic ancestors reinforced and illustrated the ideas presented in the written texts students studied.[52] Unlike the Pachomians, however, these conversations among philosophers often took place over dinner in the homes of the teachers or on leisurely walks through cities.[53] They were social occasions with an informal dynamic that appears to have mixed the business of sharing communal historical traditions with pleasurable activities.

The Pachomians differed from these non-monastic circles in another important way. Most ancient schools were small and organised in such a way that students knew their teachers and peers quite well. By the time that most of our Pachomian sources were written down, however, the Koinonia was a multi-site ascetic franchise spread across a number of different locations and involving thousands of people. No monk could know every member of the community, and few regular monks would have had the opportunity to interact with a leader like Pachomius or Theodore very often. Despite the challenges presented by the size and diffuse nature of the Koinonia, the Pachomians succeeded in replicating much of the informal dynamic that worked so well in conventional schools. They did this not by expanding the amount of time in which monastic leaders made themselves available to their 'sons'. Instead, they simultaneously restricted the amount of informal interaction those sons had with other people and directed the sorts of things discussed during these conversations. This allowed the informal instruction that a figure like Theodore gave personally to his associates to echo down the hierarchy to ordinary monks.

This brings us back to the point with which this chapter began. Like most successful teachers in antiquity, Theodore very clearly understood the need to balance the strong exercise of a teacher's intellectual and spiritual authority with informal personal interactions in which that authority was deliberately downplayed. The Pachomians, however, appear to have been the first teachers to simultaneously exercise the authority of a teacher and develop the intimate bond between a mentor and disciple that underpinned it across a large, vertically integrated organisation made up of many thousands of followers. Some of the methods that Pachomians employed to create this bond would have horrified teachers who headed more conventional circles, but these teachers would certainly have understood the essential nature of the relationships Pachomian leaders worked to create. The extreme efforts made by Pachomians to adapt the social dynamics of ancient schools to serve the needs of a much larger organisation help us to appreciate the importance of personal relationships and oral teaching in sustaining large monastic communities. It also points to the essential role that similar exchanges played in the success of other, smaller schools.

Notes

1 *Bohairic Life of Pachomius* 188. All translations of Pachomian texts follow those of Veilleux 1980–82.

2 Apollonius, for example, stayed alongside his flawed Pythagorean teacher Euxenus for a time 'like young eagles who, as long as they are not fully fledged, fly alongside of their parents and are trained by them in flight, but who, as soon as they are able to rise in the air outsoar the parent birds' (Philostratus, *Life of Apollonius* 1.7). Proclus had a similar experience when studying under the Aristotelian teacher Olympiodorus (*Life of Proclus* 9). For Antony and his studies under local holy men living outside Egyptian villages see *Life of Antony* 3 and the discussion of Gemeinhardt 2013a, 38–40.

3 According to Pachomian biographical traditions preserved in Sahidic – e.g. *First Sahidic Life of Pachomius* III (10) – the first circle of followers that Pachomius established failed to respect him or listen to his guidance because he proved too eager to please them. For discussion see Rousseau 1999a, 60.

4 The rebellion that toppled the Pachomian leader Horsiesius seems to have resulted from the inflexible and slightly imperious way that he asserted his authority during a dispute about whether monasteries could expand their economic activities beyond basket making. For discussion of this see *Bohairic Life of Pachomius* 139; *First Greek Life of Pachomius* 127; Watts 2010, 95–9.

5 Theodore, *Instruction* 3.4. The text of Theodore's Third Instruction is found in Lefort 1956, 40–60. For an English translation see Veilleux 1982, 92–119. Anyone studying the Pachomian monasteries of the fourth century immediately confronts a significant source problem. Nearly all of the written materials that we possess for the history and functioning of Pachomian communities date well after the death of Pachomius and first appear in the aftermath of a split in the 340s that nearly destroyed the community. They then reflect and justify the structures put in place to prevent further splits within the community. See here the helpful discussion of Rousseau 1999a, 39–54.

6 *Bohairic Life of Pachomius* 105.

7 *Bohairic Life of Pachomius* 105.

8 It is uncertain how many Pachomian franchises existed in 350, but there were at least seven. For discussion of this question see Rousseau 1999a, 56 and Rousseau 1999b. For the number of monks see the estimates in Palladius, *Lausiac History* 7.6, 18.13, 32.8 and 32.9. If Palladius is to be trusted (and there is no strong ancient evidence either supporting or refuting his information), the Koinonia probably involved nearly 7,000 monks at the end of the fourth century.

9 Pbow was near Tabennisi, the location of Pachomius' first community. On Pachomius' initial efforts to grow the community, see Rousseau 1999a, 70–76.

10 *First Greek Life of Pachomius* 89, *The Life of Saint Pachomius* 56. For the economic diversity and sophistication within the Koinonia see Wipszycka 1996b.

11 This followed the end of the rebellion of the monastery at Thmoušons (discussed above) that caused the Koinonia's leader Horsiesius to step down.

12 Cf., e.g., *First Greek Life of Pachomius* 12; *Bohairic Life of Pachomius* 17, 88.

13 *Bohairic Life of Pachomius* 118.

14 *Precept* 96; cf. *Precept* 82; 97–8. It is worth noting that these rules were almost certainly not applied all of the time. The distance between an ascetic ideal and the messy practicalities of running a large and complex organisation on a daily basis would have been considerable.

15 *Bohairic Life of Pachomius* 118.

16 *Bohairic Life of Pachomius* 118.

17 *Bohairic Life of Pachomius* 118.

18 *Instruction* 3.5, quoting 2 Corinthians 7.1.

19 *Instruction* 3.6.

20 The initial process of initiation is somewhat obscure within the Pachomian sources themselves, though its nature is suggested by the accounts of Pachomius' initiation of his early

Teaching the New Classics   57

followers. See, for example, *First Greek Life of Pachomius* 24 and *Bohairic Life of Pachomius* 23 (on Pachomius' early disciples); *First Greek Life of Pachomius* 36 and *Bohairic Life of Pachomius* 30 (on Theodore's initial moments in the community). For discussion, note Rousseau 1999a, 70. On the process in the later fourth century see the detailed description in *Precept* 49.

21   On this instruction, see *Precept* 49 and Rousseau 1999a, 70. For the porters and their teaching responsibilities note *Bohairic Life of Pachomius* 26. The learning of the Psalms is also perhaps suggested by *Bohairic Life of Pachomius* 15 and 23.

22   This entire process is described by Rousseau 1999a, 70–71. For the clothing in monastic habit see *Bohairic Life of Pachomius* 26. For the questioning of a new arrival note *Bohairic Life of Pachomius* 23 and *First Greek Life of Pachomius* 24.

23   The learning of these traditions is suggested by *Bohairic Life of Pachomius* 23 and *Precept* 49. Although this purports to describe Pachomius' training of his first disciples, the pattern of initiation described here likely resembles that of the broader Pachomian community at the time that this description was written.

24   *Precepts* 49, 139. Note as well, Rousseau 1999a, 70.

25   The following description of the daily routine in the Koinonia draws heavily upon the reconstruction of Rousseau 1999a, 77–85. Rousseau draws upon sources written under Theodore, Horsiesius and later heads of the Koinonia to reconstruct the period when Pachomius himself governed the monastic community. While one can question how well this represents life under Pachomius (e.g. Goehring 1986b, esp. 239–40), one can confidently use these sources to illustrate patterns of life under the supervision of Theodore and Horsiesius.

26   Note *Rule* 2 as well as *Precepts* 3, 9.

27   *Precept* 3.

28   *Precept* 28. Note here the comments of Rousseau 1999a, 82 n. 28.

29   For mealtimes see the description of Palladius, *Lausiac History* 32.6.

30   There seem to have been three scheduled each week, with the superiors leading the collective instruction on Saturdays and Sundays (*Bohairic Life of Pachomius* 26; cf. *First Greek Life of Pachomius* 58 and Rousseau 1999a, 85).

31   *First Greek Life of Pachomius* 28; *Bohairic Life of Pachomius* 26. See as well the discussion of Rousseau 1999a, 85.

32   *Bohairic Life of Pachomius* 23.

33   For discussion of these concepts and the identification with a specific intellectual circle they were supposed to engender in students see Watts 2005 and 2007. The relationship is explicitly theorised in the pseudo-Platonic *Theages*, a dialogue likely composed in the Old Academy (e.g. *Theages* 127–8).

34   The largest number of students said by an ancient source to belong to one teacher's circle is the 100 paying pupils attributed to Chrestus of Byzantium by Philostratus (*Lives of the Sophists* 591). Most other circles were presumably much smaller. The school of Libanius seems to have topped out at around 50 students at one time, and only 196 different students are mentioned in the 15 years covered by his collected letters. For discussion see Cribiore 2007b, 96–7.

35   On these informal relationships between teachers and students see Watts 2010, 33–45, 60–62.

36   For these monastic houses see the important discussion of the economic role they played in Wipszycka 1996b, 167–79.

37   *Fifth Sahidic Life of Pachomius* 93 and the discussion of Rousseau 1999a, 68.

38   *Precept* 130.

39   *Precept* 16.

40   See above, note 30.

41   *Precept* 133.

42   *First Greek Life of Pachomius* 10. This is probably not unlike the oral traditions that came to form the various versions of the *Apophthegmata Patrum* discussed in Chapter 1 of this volume by Lillian Larsen, though one suspects that the internal Pachomian traditions

58 *Edward Watts*

proved less fluid because of the more controlled institutional context in which they were transmitted.

43 *First Greek Life of Pachomius* 99.
44 On the dating of the text see Rousseau 1999a, 48–9 and the edition of Boon 1932, 13–74.
45 *Rule* 59 (on silence when walking to processions); *Rule* 8 (no talking during meetings and prayers).
46 *Rules* 31, 33, 34.
47 *Rule* 60. On silence in the bakery in particular, see *Rule* 116. On Theodore's demotion see *Bohairic Life of Pachomius* 74.
48 *Rule* 122 (in houses); *Rule* 88 (place where he sleeps).
49 *Rule* 19.
50 *Rule* 138.
51 Note on this the important discussion of Layton 2007, esp. 58–69.
52 For this process in philosophical communities see Watts 2011.
53 Watts 2010, 60–62.

Part II

Gnomic Knowledge

4 An Education through Gnomic Wisdom

The *Pandect* of Antiochus as *Bibliotheksersatz*

Yannis Papadogiannakis*

Almost everything we know about Antiochus, characterised as 'a ghostly character whom Migne's PG has patched together from various texts',[1] is based on the information that he provides us with, as well as/on top of a short biographical note that prefaces many manuscripts preserving the text of the *Pandect*.[2] To Gibbon's readers (and subsequent generations) Antiochus may be remembered, if at all, by Gibbon's famous sneer.[3] The truth of the matter, however, is that the *Pandect* became a classic of Eastern Christian spirituality, which is still read to this day. In the preface to his *Pandect*, we are told that Antiochus was abbot of the Great Laura of St Sabas in Palestine. Around 620, at the request of his compatriot Eustathius, an abbot of a monastery in Ancyra, he composed the famous *Pandect of the Holy Scriptures*, consisting of 130 homilies which form a compendium on the monastic life. Antiochus prefaces this work with an account of the martyrdom of 40 monks of the Great Laura, tortured and put to death by the Saracens at Kedron just before the fall of Jerusalem to the Persians.[4]

The title *Pandect* recalls another ambitious effort by Justinian and his legal experts to distil several thousand textbooks of Roman law into the legal Pandects, which became the most authoritative legal collection for centuries.[5] In the beginning of his letter to Eustathius, Antiochus refers to the fact that, due to the Persian invasions, Eustathius and his monks, in his words, had to move from one place to another. As they could not be weighed down by books, and as it was not always easy to find the necessary books in any of the areas to which they moved, the monks asked Antiochus to summarise ('condense' is more appropriate) the Old and the New Testament. Thus they would not be burdened too much, but also they would not lack access to their salvific teachings. In response to this request Antiochus notes that he put together all the materials from the Scriptures that he was asked to, and divided them into 130 *kephalaia*/capita, joined together but separate from each other in order not to confuse the reader.[6] In return, Antiochus, following a common formula, asks Eustathius to pray for his labours and to show understanding in regard to any deficiencies he may come across in his work. There follows an account of the martyrdom of 40 monks, and Antiochus concludes his letter with a metaphor illustrating his enterprise. He has woven together several different threads from the Bible to produce a cloak that will keep the monks warm just as the predictions of the Scriptures make up the cloak of flesh that Christ put on in his incarnation.[7]

62 Yannis Papadogiannakis

In terms of the contents of the *Pandect*, the list of the titles of the *kephalaia/homilies* in the appendix provides an overview of their subject matter. Given the status of the *Pandect* in Eastern Orthodox spirituality, modern scholarly interest has remained sparse and uneven. What little work has been done on the *Pandect*, other than the brief descriptions in reference works,[8] is philological and codicological[9], primarily related to finding fragments of lost works that Antiochus cited[10] or to mining the text for historical information.[11] We are clearly dealing with a text made of texts, where pride of place is taken, of course, by the Bible, which has been distilled in gnomic sayings: 'The point [or aim] is a maximum of meaning in a minimum of words.'[12] On the basis of what little work has been done we also know that Antiochus is quoting Irenaeus, Ignatius, Clement of Alexandria (*Quis dives salvetur*), the letter of Polycarp to the Philippians, Evagrius (including the works *de Oratione* and *de octo spiritibus malitiae* traditionally ascribed to Saint Nilus)[13] and, above all, his favourite ps. Clement's *Letter to the Virgins*. There are also several allusions to the works of Dionysius the Areopagite. One of the very few scholars who studied the *Pandect*, mostly in search of quotations of ps. Clement's *Letter to the Virgins*, has remarked on Antiochus' working methods thus: 'Antiochus so seldom names the author from whom he borrows, that the reader of the *Homilies* has to rely entirely upon his perception of a change in Antiochus' style, and in the savour of his language for the detection of a quotation.'[14] This calls for more philological research in order to fully document Antiochus' sources. Despite the efforts of the editors of the PG and of other scholars there remains a lot to be done in regard to the sheer bulk of unattributed sources that need to be traced.

It is not my aim to dwell on *Quellenkritik*, however, important and much needed as it may be in the case of Antiochus' *Pandect*. Bardy has remarked that the work lacks originality, pointing out at the same time that Antiochus sought to create a code of monastic practice but that he doubts that Antiochus fully succeeded in doing so.[15] This attitude is typical not only of scholars of past generations but also of many modern scholars, and has been summed up well by Konstan who, apropos of Stobaeus' *Anthologion*, writes:

> Excerptors, generally speaking, have a bad name. As mere compilers, their own thoughts, if they had any, are concealed behind the wisdom of others. They are essentially derivative, secondary; at best, they may be classed with authors of synopses and abridgments, or with scholiasts, or even, at a stretch, with commentators, writers who take it upon themselves to make important works composed by others (or sometimes composed by themselves) more accessible to the general reader [. . .] Of these, excerptors seem the most anonymous and impersonal, even mechanical: they cut and paste, and so lack any voice of their own. We are grateful, of course, when they preserve fragments that would otherwise have been lost, and in this respect we particularly value their dutifulness as copiers: we do not want them to tamper with the extracts they reproduce, but leave them exactly in the form in which they found them (and can only hope that they chanced upon reasonably good manuscripts). The less creativity they exhibit, the better.

An Education through Gnomic Wisdom   63

What is more, excerptors represent, according to the common view, a decadent phase of civilization. They copy out bits and pieces of works that are no longer available, or that no one is willing or able to read, any longer, in complete versions. Culture is in decline, and literature must be pre-digested, simplified, abbreviated. In a sense, the excerptors have assumed the noble task of preserving something of the great tradition that has now diminished to a trickle, but their very activity is a sign of loss and diminishment.[16]

Whether this preconception is justified will partly inform the following analysis.

Kephalaia

The literary format that Antiochus employs is the *kephalaia*/capita. As a format it proved very popular, not least among monastic authors.[17] *Kephalaia* is a versatile, capacious but ill-defined literary format of great didactic potential that has been put to different uses.[18] In literary practice, however, the term *kephalaia* is used both as a heading for the organisation of clusters of *gnomai* and arguments in the form of *topoi*,[19] as well as of questions and answers (*erotapokriseis*). In a study with important implications for the understanding of works such as those of Antiochus, Pierre Hadot has drawn attention to the literary practice (and its implications) of presenting philosophical traditions in the form of short sentences, maxims, *sententiae* and *gnomai*, which made easier their memorisation and their meditation.[20] Both *apophthegmata* and *kephalaia* were already in existence in the philosophical tradition and Hadot has pointed to numerous examples of them in the works of Diogenes Laertius, Marcus Aurelius' *Meditations* and Porphyry's *Sentences*. Both of these literary genres are responses to the requirements of meditation.

In the case of Antiochus' *Pandect*, *kephalaia* designates a unit of text that includes a dense clustering of related biblical proofs with the chosen heading embedded in a short homiletic piece of varying length that renders explicit what links the different *gnomai* together. Some scholars have criticised the use of the term 'homily' for Antiochus' *kephalaia*, possibly on account of the sheer bulk of *gnomai* that, more often than not, are strung together in succession. However, there is a strong homiletic flavour in most of these textual units that lends itself to this characterisation. This is a conscious attempt on Antiochus' part to provide his readers not only with the raw materials for the subject matter of each *kephalaion* but also with a way in which they can be understood as sitting together.

Halfway into his work Antiochus offers a clue as to his working method and to the literary nature of his work, writing 'yesterday we discoursed . . . today not only'.[21] Two things stand out here: the indications of time here may point to a set of lectures that may have been reworked in the form of the short homilies/*kephalaia* of the *Pandect*. That this may be the case is reinforced by the term διελέχθημεν, which alludes to the literary format of *dialexis*, which can designate a philosophical discourse or a more informal element in the repertoire

64   *Yannis Papadogiannakis*

not of the philosopher, but of the epideictic orator. Maximus of Tyre (second century AD)[22] and, as has been shown recently, Theodoret of Cyrrhus, in his *Graecarum Affectionum Curatio*, used the format of *dialexis* to great effect.[23] In monastic literature Dorotheus of Gaza and Diadochus of Photike are two other examples.

Citations/*gnomai* play a crucial role in developing Antiochus' themes. They are an integral part of each *kephalaion*/homily and they are clustered either in the beginning, the middle or the end of each homily. They are juxtaposed often with only a couple of words connecting them, such as 'and again', 'and thus', etc. (καὶ αὖθις, καὶ ἐπάγει, καὶ πάλιν καὶ ὁ Ἡσαίας λέγει, καὶ ὡς ὁ Κύριος φησί, καὶ ἄλλος φησίν, λέγει ἡ Γραφή etc). Like other gnomic anthologists, Antiochus is unafraid of repetition, sometimes reusing the same saying in different contexts and combinations. *Gnomai* are found sometimes in isolation, sometimes bundled in various combinations so as to create rhetorically coherent exhortatory clusters. Each homily ends with a doxological formula: 'For His is the glory unto the age and ages, Amen.' A number of these homilies/*kephalaia* reflect recognised ascetic themes: 'on virginity', 'on vainglory', 'on sloth', 'on obedience', 'on chanting' and so on.

In his treatment of vices and praise of virtues Antiochus follows a well-established monastic literary tradition which was indebted to Graeco-Roman education. We know, for example from Aristotle and Quintilian among others, that ancient orators were trained by undertaking written exercises on moral themes, such as denouncing typical instances of particular vices, and that they customarily made collections of such themes for all-purpose use.

Antiochus' methods of compiling *gnomai* are also based on ancient literary practices. He strings together excerpts from the Greek Bible at a rather breathless pace, using scriptural excerpts drawn from many separate biblical books, arranging them around an organising idea or theme, and splicing together various passages dealing with the same topic to give a coherent whole. Thus the Bible is interrogated to see what biblical warrants it can yield on the themes Antiochus is pursuing.

Since at least Aristotle, aphorisms, maxims, excerpts, etc. had been bound up with the construction of cogent argument and the gathering of material to develop a composition. According to him, they comprised the most effective ways of arguing from the basis of generally accepted opinions and provided models for making deductions. David Konstan has recently highlighted the rhetorical underpinnings of the art of excerpting by showing how Aristotle, in *Categoriae* (1.14, 105a34–b14), advises on the manner in which one ought to select (ἐκλεκτέον) propositions or opinions (δόξας) as a basis for argument, for example those of the majority or of the wise, or of those that are best known. Aristotle continues by urging his readers:

> it is good to select also from written arguments, and make outlines for oneself for each type, setting them down separately, for example 'concerning the good' or 'concerning animals'.

ἐκλέγειν δὲ χρὴ καὶ ἐκ τῶν γεγραμμένων λόγων, τὰς δὲ διαγραφὰς ποιεῖσθαι περὶ *ἑκάστου* γένους ὑποτιθέντας χωρίς, οἷον περὶ ἀγαθοῦ ἢ περὶ ζῴου.[24]

Aristotle's testimony highlights how reading and writing were closely linked operations. The resulting compilations were the result of an intellectual process of selection, extraction and archiving of useful material: exempla, proverbs, *gnomai*. The processing of the selected excerpts involved successive steps of rewriting and reorganising these textual units in various formats.

Like many authors before and after him (all the way to Renaissance scholars) Antiochus aided his process of reading texts by producing excerpts; and with his *Pandect* he produced a repository of biblical extracts for the edification of monks, drawn from his reading notes. In putting together the *Pandect* as a *Bibliotheksersatz* Antiochus was putting together a library that was at the same time a collection of books as well as a book that encompassed the reading notes excerpted from one or many other books. This portable library created a new textual frame within which the Bible was inscribed and where the content of other books was merged according to a thematic filter reflected in the head or subject matter, which functions as a structuring principle.[25] This is consistent with the process with which commonplace books were put together.[26]

Commonplaces, in the form of apophthegms, maxims, etc., were intrinsic to the construction of cogent arguments and to the process of composition and of rhetorical amplification.[27] Collecting excerpts on subjects of interest, organising them and setting them in a frame tailored to the question at hand was what students expected of their teachers. By producing and using anthologies Christian teachers like Antiochus were working within established patterns of school practice.[28] The importance of these collections of commonplaces for ancient, medieval and Renaissance education cannot be overestimated. This is reflected in their continued usage well into the early modern period, when *topoi* began to develop 'modern connotations of banality, identical to "trite truism", a degenerative slide . . . to empty verbiage'.[29]

The textual frame of the *Pandect* and the practice of marshalling biblical quotations on that scale addressed broader practical concerns too, in terms of the availability of reading materials. For, even if the concept of a fixed scriptural canon existed, biblical texts were much more likely to survive and circulate in collections such as that of Antiochus.

But there is an additional aspect of the *Pandect* that connects it with education and which deserves our attention. *Kephalaia* made of extracts were intended to be morally and religiously formative. Antiochus' objective is not simply to provide biblical readings to a dislocated monastic community, but also to show how it is possible to help this community establish habits of thought that will shape and cultivate their capacities for moral reasoning and perfection. Many of the themes, the advice offered in short, striking sayings or extracts, lend themselves to easy recitation and memorisation and are meant to

66   *Yannis Papadogiannakis*

foster such habits of thought, both by reshaping the readers' patterns of thought and by facilitating the translation of thought into action. In doing so, they inscribe the *Pandect* in the tradition of spiritual exercises that had been integral to the pursuit of the philosophical life.[30] For example, in *kephalaion* 61, 'On attention to oneself', Antiochus employs Deut. 4:9 ('But take care and watch yourselves closely, so as neither to forget things that your eyes have seen nor to let them slip from your mind all the days of your life'); Deut. 15:9 ('Be careful that you do not entertain a mean thought'); and Prov. 4:23 ('Keep your heart with all vigilance, for from it flow the springs of life'). In *kephalaion* 87 περὶ, σπουδῆς', Antiochus plays with the various meanings of σπουδή and urges vigilance regarding one's thought and intentions, pressing into service Eccles./ Sirach 6:37 ('Reflect on the statutes of the Lord and meditate at all times on his commandments') spliced with Sirach 9:15–16 ('Let your conversation be with intelligent people, and let all your discussion be about the Law of the most High. Let the righteous be your dinner companions'). At issue here is not just a mere exercise of the moral conscience: it is an exercise relating to the monks' relationship to God; a perpetual reference to God at each instant of life. Ἀμέλεια (lack of watchfulness), even for an hour, can make God's grace grow cold.[31] Thus 're-framed', the Bible may well have been the script for many a performance of scripture.

Pierre Hadot, in his book *Exercices spirituels et philosophie antique*,[32] has convincingly argued and demonstrated how in ancient philosophy techniques such as that of attention to oneself (προσοχή) required meditating on and memorising rules of life (κανόνες), those principles which were to be applied in each particular circumstance, at each moment in life. It was essential to have the principles of life, the fundamental 'dogmas', constantly 'at hand'. Hadot demonstrated how this same theme is operative once again in the monastic tradition – except that in the monastic tradition philosophical dogmas are replaced by an evangelical rule of life inspired not only by the words of Christ but also by biblical exempla and proverbs, the words and deeds of the 'ancients'; in other words, of the first monks.[33] 'Both the evangelical commandments and the words of the ancients were presented in the form of short sentences, which – just as in the philosophical tradition – could be easily memorized and meditated upon.'[34] Galen, among other ancient authors, famously referred to this practice thus: 'You may be sure that I have grown accustomed to ponder twice a day the exhortations attributed to Pythagoras. First I read them over and then I recite them aloud.'[35] The numerous collections of *apophthegmata* and of *kephalaia* we find in monastic literature are a response to this need for memorisation and meditation.[36] It is for this reason, among others, that Hadot was led to conclude: 'Like philosophical meditation, Christian meditation flourished by using all available means of rhetoric and oratorical amplification, and by mobilizing all possible resources of the imagination.'[37]

Seen in this light, Antiochus' *Pandect* is far from the relaying of a formalised distillation of the Bible and of other works, even as Antiochus' effort presupposes and builds on extensive experience with reading techniques and with systems of text retrieval and reference that stretched all the way back to the classical world.

As it turns out, the *Pandect* owes a lot to the learned mechanisms of persuasive argument known not only to ancient, but later to medieval and Renaissance readers. It replicates the way didactic discourse might be organised, engaging the recipients' attention and their eventual adherence by taking them through associations triggered by likenesses, affinities and contrasts. Being a resource which was meant to be shared by the members of the monastic community, it was also a cohesive factor, bonding the community whose collective memory was stocked from biblical texts amassed and arranged in labelled *kephalaia*.[38]

Conclusion

As well as making these texts available to Eustathius' monastic community, the collections in the *Pandect* adapted the biblical text and other texts to the (perceived) demands of a particular time and place in relation to reading, interpretation and understanding. For the monastic community (but also for the subsequent lay readers), Antiochus' *Pandect* mapped their religious and moral universe and imprinted on their minds Antiochus' vision of that universe.

We must not lose sight of the dire circumstances under which this work was put together – if only because it was these circumstances that spawned this work – and their implications for our understanding of the *Pandect*. 'We must bitterly grieve', Antiochus laments quite appropriately in *kephalaion* 107, *on Compunction*, 'over the burning of the Holy City, Jerusalem, over the removal of the Holy Cross of Christ, our God, in Persia, over the so many who were killed in the wars, for they were ones of us/part of us and shared our faith (ὅτι σύσσωμοι ἡμῶν εἰσιν καὶ ὁμόπιστοι)'.[39] The grief over the fall of the Holy City makes its mark elsewhere, sporadically not only in the *Pandect* but also in a moving prayer ascribed to Antiochus, which is saturated with the language of the Psalms appended at the end of the *Pandect*, in which Antiochus could well have been taken to express the prevailing, collective feeling of the Christians after the fall of Jerusalem. All this brings to mind Grenzmann's remark that the situation of the aphorist is usually that of intellectually uncertain times.[40] Such, I hope, are the incentives for and merits of pursuing a more thorough study of Antiochus' *Pandect*, which still awaits the critical edition that it so richly deserves.

Appendix

1. Περὶ πίστεως (On Faith)
2. Περὶ ἐλπίδος (On Hope)
3. Περὶ ἑστιάσεως (On Feasting/Banqueting)
4. Περὶ γαστριμαργίας (On Gluttony)
5. Περὶ μέθης (On Drunkenness/Inebriation)
6. Περὶ ἐγκρατείας (On Continence/Temperance/Self-Control)
7. Περὶ νηστείας (On Fasting)
8. Περὶ φιλαργυρίας (On Love of Money)
9. Περὶ δωροληψίας (On Bribery)
10. Περὶ σκνιφότητος (On Parsimony/Stinginess)
11. Περὶ δανειζόντων (On Moneylenders)
12. Περὶ τόκων (On [Exacting] Interest)
13. Περὶ πλεονεξίας (On Greed)
14. Περὶ περισπασμοῦ (On Distraction)
15. Περὶ τοῦ μὴ ἀγαπᾶν τὸν κόσμον (On Not Loving the World)
16. Περὶ *παρρησίας* (On Boldness/Liberty/Frankness of Speech)
17. Περὶ τοῦ ἀπέχεσθαι γυναικῶν (On Abstinence from Women)
18. Περὶ τοῦ μὴ ἐνδελεχίζειν ψαλλούσαις γυναιξίν (On Not Being Often Around/ Together with Women Chanters/Chantresses?)
19. Περὶ πορνείας (On Fornication)
20. Περὶ σωφροσύνης (On Prudence)
21. Περὶ παρθενίας (On Virginity/Chastity)
22. Περὶ προπετείας (On Petulance)
23. Περὶ ὀργῆς (On Rage/Wrath)
24. Περὶ θυμοῦ (On Anger)
25. Περὶ λύπης (On Sorrow/Grief)
26. Περὶ ἀκηδίας (On Listlessness/Despondency)
27. Περὶ ἀπογνώσεως (On Despair)
28. Περὶ γογγυσμοῦ (On Grumbling)
29. Περὶ καταλαλιᾶς (On Detraction/Backbiting)
30. Περὶ ψιθυρισμοῦ (On Gossipy Slandering)
31. Περὶ τοῦ μὴ μέμφεσθαι (On Not Reprehending/Reproaching Others)
32. Περὶ ἀντιλογίας (On Not Gainsaying/Speaking Against)

An Education through Gnomic Wisdom   69

33. Περὶ ἀργολογίας (On Idle Chatter/Talk)
34. Περὶ περιεργίας (On Idle Curiosity)
35. Περὶ καταφρονήσεως (On Not Looking Down Upon/Despising/Disdaining [Others])
36. Περὶ ὀκνηρίας (On Sloth)
37. Περὶ τοῦ μὴ ἐρίζειν μετὰ δυνάστου (On Not Contending/Arguing with Potentates/Rulers)
38. Περὶ παρακοῆς (On Disobedience)
39. Περὶ ὑπακοῆς (On Obedience)
40. Περὶ συκοφαντίας (On Calumny/Slander)
41. Περὶ κλοπῆς (On Theft)
42. Περὶ ψεύδους (On Falsehood)
43. Περὶ κενοδοξίας (On Vainglory)
44. Περὶ ὑπερηφανίας (On Pride/Arrogance)
45. Περὶ ὑψηλοφροσύνης (On Haughtiness)
46. Περὶ τοῦ μὴ μεγαλοφρονεῖν *παρ' ἑαυτῷ* (On Not Being Arrogant)
47. Περὶ τοῦ μὴ ἐξουθενεῖν τινα (On Not Despising One/Being Contemptuous)
48. Περὶ τοῦ μὴ καταγελᾶν (On Not Deriding One)
49. Περὶ τοῦ μὴ κατακρίνειν (On Not Censuring One)
50. Περὶ τοῦ μὴ σκανδαλίζειν (On Not Causing Scandal/Giving Offence)
51. Περὶ τοῦ μὴ ὀνειδίζειν *ἀλλὰ* μᾶλλον ὀνειδίζεσθαι (On Not Ridiculing But Rather Being Ridiculed)
52. Περὶ τοῦ μὴ ἀνταποδοῦναι κακόν (On Not Retaliating/Against Retribution)
53. Περὶ τοῦ μὴ μνησικακεῖν (On Not Being Rancorous)
54. Περὶ τοῦ μὴ ἐχθραίνειν (On Not Hating)
55. Περὶ τοῦ μὴ φθονεῖν (On Not Envying)
56. Περὶ τοῦ μὴ ἐρίζειν (On Not Wrangling/Quarrelling)
57. Περὶ τοῦ μὴ μισεῖν (On Not Hating)
58. Περὶ τοῦ μὴ ἐπιχαίρειν (On not Rejoicing over/Being Malignantly Pleased in One's Ills/Misfortune)
59. Περὶ τοῦ συγχαίρειν (On Sharing in One's Joy)
60. Περὶ τοῦ μὴ λυπεῖν τινα (On Not Causing Grief to Someone)
61. Περὶ τοῦ προσέχειν ἑαυτῷ (On Watching Oneself)
62. Περὶ χρηστολογίας (On Speaking Kindly)
63. Περὶ τοῦ μὴ ὀμνύειν (On Not Swearing Oaths)
64. Περὶ τοῦ φυλάσσειν μυστήριον (On Safeguarding the Mystery)
65. Περὶ τοῦ μὴ ἀκαίρως θαρρεῖν (On Not Hoping Untimely/Unsuitably)
66. Περὶ ἀληθείας (On Truth)
67. Περὶ τοῦ ἐλέγχειν (On Reproving)
68. Περὶ τοῦ ἐλέγχεσθαι (On Being Reproved)
69. Περὶ τοῦ αἰσχύνεσθαι (On Feeling Shame)
70. Περὶ ταπεινοφροσύνης (On Humility)
71. Περὶ τοῦ συγχωρεῖν τῷ πλησίῳ (On Forgiving Your Neighbour)
72. Περὶ τοῦ εὔχεσθαι ὑπὲρ ἀλλήλων καὶ τῶν ἐχθρῶν (On Praying for Each Other and for One's Enemies)

70   *Yannis Papadogiannakis*

73. Περὶ τοῦ μὴ ζητεῖν τὰ ἑαυτοῦ (On Not Seeking One's Own Advantage)
74. Περὶ τοῦ μὴ ἐπιθυμεῖν (On Not Longing/Desiring For)
75. Περὶ δικαιοκρισίας (On Righteous Judging)
76. Περὶ δικαιομετρίας (On Measuring Justly)
77. Περὶ μετανοίας (On Repentance)
78. Περὶ ὑπομονῆς (On Patience/Patient Endurance)
79. Περὶ ἀγῶνος (On Struggle)
80. Περὶ *ὁμονοίας* (On Unanimity/Concord)
81. Περὶ λογισμῶν (On Thoughts)
82. Περὶ παιδείας (On Discipline/Corrective Training)
83. Περὶ συμβουλίας (On Counsel)
84. Περὶ ἐνυπνίων (On Dreams)
85. Περὶ ὀλιγοψυχίας καὶ διψυχίας (On Faint-Heartedness and Duplicity)
86. Περὶ κόπου (On Toil)
87. Περὶ σπουδῆς (On Zeal/Pains/Seriousness)
88. Περὶ διακονίας (On Ministry)
89. Περὶ ἀκτημοσύνης (On Lacking Possessions/Poverty)
90. Περὶ πένθους (On Mourning)
91. Περὶ τοῦ, Καιρὸς τοῦ παντός (On the [Biblical] Phrase 'There is a Right Time for Everything' Eccl. 3,1)
92. Περὶ τοῦ συμπάσχειν (On the Act of Compassion)
93. Περὶ τοῦ μὴ προσωπoληπτεῖν (On Not Being Partial)
94. Περὶ τοῦ οἰκεῖν μετὰ ὀλίγων καλῶν (On Living Together with Few but Good [People])
95. Περὶ τοῦ μὴ γελᾶν (On Not Laughing Immoderately)
96. Περὶ τοῦ ἀγαπᾶν τὸν πλησίον (On Loving Your Neighbour)
97. Περὶ φιλοξενίας (On Hospitality)
98. Περὶ φιλοπτωχίας (On the Love of the Poor)
99. Περὶ τοῦ ἐπισκέπτεσθαι (On Visiting [Others])
100. Περὶ τοῦ μὴ ἐλπίζειν ἐπ' ἄνθρωπον (On Not Putting Too Much Hope on/Hoping on Humans)
101. Περὶ τοῦ μὴ πεποιθέναι ἐπὶ τῇ ἰδίᾳ ἰσχύϊ (On Not Putting too Much Trust/Faith in One's Own Strength)
102. Περὶ τοῦ παραιτεῖσθαι τὰς ἀκαίρους συντυχίας (On Forgoing Untimely Meetings)
103. Περὶ ἡσυχίας (On Tranquillity/Silence)
104. Περὶ ἀγρυπνίας (On Vigil)
105. Περὶ ψαλμῳδίας (On Chanting)
106. Περὶ προσευχῆς (On Prayer)
107. Περὶ κατανύξεως (On Compunction)
108. Περὶ τιμῆς γονέων (On Honouring One's Parents)
109. Περὶ τοῦ εὐλαβεῖσθαι πρεσβυτέρους (On Reverencing the Elderly)
110. Περὶ μακροθυμίας καὶ ὀξυχολίας (On Forbearance and On Being Quick-Tempered)
111. Περὶ ἡγουμένων (On Abbots)

An Education through Gnomic Wisdom 71

112. Περὶ ἀποταγῆς (On Renunciation)
113. Περὶ ὑποταγῆς (On Submission)
114. Περὶ τοῦ φυλάσσειν ἐντολὰς (On Keeping the Commandments)
115. Περὶ πραότητος (On Meekness)
116. Περὶ τοῦ ἀδικεῖσθαι καὶ μὴ ἀδικεῖν (On Being Wronged and Not Doing Wrong to Others)
117. Περὶ εὐχαριστίας (On Thanksgiving)
118. Περὶ τῆς ἐν Θεῷ εὐφροσύνης (On Joy/Gladness in God)
119. Περὶ τοῦ μὴ μεριμνᾶν (On Not Caring too Anxiously about Daily Cares)
120. Περὶ ἀπαρχῶν (On First Fruits)
121. Περὶ ἐξιλασμοῦ (On Atonement/Propitiation)
122. Περὶ ἀρχιερωσύνης (On Highpriesthood)
123. Περὶ διαταγῆς κλήρου (On Setting in Order the Clergy)
124. Περὶ τοῦ αἰδεῖσθαι ἱερεῖς (On Showing Deference to Priests)
125. Περὶ προσδοκίας τῶν μελλόντων (On the Expectation of Last Things)
126. Περὶ κλήσεως Θεοῦ (On God's Vocation)
127. Περὶ φόβου τοῦ Θεοῦ (On Fear of God)
128. Περὶ τῆς εἰς Θεὸν ἀγάπης (On the Love Towards God)
129. Περὶ υἱοθεσίας (On Adoption)
130. Περὶ βασιλείας οὐρανῶν (On the Kingdom of Heaven)

Notes

* The author gratefully acknowledges the generous support of the European Research Council for funding the research project 'Defining Belief and Identities in the Eastern Mediterranean' out of which this contribution has been developed.
1 Bowersock 2012, 36.
2 On the biographical note see Nau 1906 and Odorico 1988.
3 'the lamentations of the monk Antiochus whose one hundred and twenty-nine homilies are still extant, if what no one reads may be said to be extant'. Gibbon 1807, 221, n. 61.
4 On Antiochus' historical context see Schick 1995, 1–84; Booth 2014, 94–100.
5 Harries 2013.
6 'διὰ τὸ μήτε δύνασθαι ὑμᾶς βάρος βιβλίων ἐπιφέρεσθαι, μήτε ἐν τοῖς τόποις ἐν οἷς ἐπιδημεῖτε εὑρίσκειν εὐχερῶς τα ἐπιζητούμενα, ἐκελεύσατε τῇ ἐμῇ βραχύτητι ἐν συντόμῳ πᾶσαν συστεῖλαι τὴν θείαν Γραφήν, Παλαιάν τε καὶ Καινήν, ὥστε μήτε ἄχθος ἡμῖν γενέσθαι βαστάγματος, μήτε πάλιν ἐλλειφθῆναί τι τῶν τεινόντων ἐπ'ὠφέλειαν καὶ σωτηρίαν ψυχῆς, εἶξα προθύμως τῇ ὑμετέρᾳ κελεύσει, εὐθέως περιστήσας πάντα τὰ παρ' ἡμῶν ἐκ τῆς θείας Γραφῆς ἐπιζητούμενα, εἰς ἑκατόν τριάκοντα κεφάλαια ἡνωμένα τε καὶ διακεκριμένα ἀπ'ἀλλήλων, ὡς μὴ σύγχυσιν καὶ φυρμόν ὑπομεῖναι τὸν ἀναγινώσκοντα.' PG 89, 1421 B–C.
7 'Ἐκ τοῦ ἱστοῦ οὖν τῶν εξήκοντα βασιλίδων τούτων ὀλίγους στήμονας ἀνείλαμεν, καὶ ἐποίησα περίζωμα εἰς θέρμην τοῖς μετὰ πίστεως ἐντυγχάνουσιν. Ὥσπερ οὖν ὁ ἱστὸς πολυμερὴς ὢν εἰς μονομερῆ χιτῶνα ἀποτελεῖται; οὕτως καὶ πᾶσαι αἱ προρρήσεις τῶν θεοπνεύστων Γραφῶν εἰς τὸν τῆς οἰκονομίας Δεσποτικὸν χιτῶνα κατέληξαν, ὅν ἀνείληφεν ἐκ τῆς ἁγίας ἐνδόξου καὶ ἀειπαρθένου Μαρίας.' PG 89, 1429 A–B.
8 Bardy 1936, 701–2.
9 Rapp 2005a; Binggeli 2008.
10 Cotterill 1884; Haidacher 1905.

72   *Yannis Papadogiannakis*

11   Mayerson 1984; Olster 1994, 79–84; Booth 2014, 94–5.
12   Williams 1980, 39.
13   Haidacher 1905.
14   Cotterill 1884, 38.
15   Bardy 1936, 701.
16   Konstan 2011, 9–10.
17   Von Ivánka 1954.
18   See Géhin 2013 and Van Deun 2013.
19   Pernot 1986, 265–6.
20   Hadot 1981.
21   PG 89, 1644 A.
22   For an exquisite literary analysis of Maximus' *dialexeis* see Trapp 1997.
23   Papadogiannakis 2012, 119–40.
24   Konstan 2011, 14. Konstan also cites Isocrates' *Ad Demonicum* 51–2, 'in which [. . .] the orator advises the young prince to read widely, seeking examples of virtue and learning not only from Isocrates himself but the best of what the poets and wise men have written'. On the Graeco-Roman background of collecting and arranging excerpts, *gnomai* and maxims, see also Kirk 1998, 87–151. For these literary practices in late antiquity and Byzantium see Odorico 1990, Odorico 2004 and the contributions in Piccione/Perkams 2003.
25   On the origins and significance of this literary practice see Jacob 1997 and Jacob 2002.
26   Moss 2011, 7; Blair 2010.
27   Pernot 1986; Moss 2001; Moss 2011, 1–17.
28   On these school practices see Snyder 2000.
29   Moss 2001, 119.
30   Hadot 1995, 107, arguing that ancient philosophy in its most fundamental nature is not a systematic theoretical construct, but consists in a series of practical exercises destined to transform our perception and our being.
31   PG 89, 1701 B–C.
32   Hadot 1981. On the reception of Hadot's ideas see the contributions in Chase et al. 2013.
33   Hadot 1995, 133.
34   Hadot 1995, 133.
35   *De propriorum animi cuiuslibet affectuum dignotione et curatione*, 6 cited in Wilson 2012, 34.
36   Hadot 1995, 133.
37   Hadot 1995, 133.
38   Moss 2011, 6 notes the similar effect that commonplace books had in Western Europe: '[They] [. . .] bonded the Latin-literate elite in a community of shared points of reference, core texts, and common practice, that resisted dissolution when Europe fractured along confessional lines.'
39   PG 87, 1764 B–C.
40   'Systemfeindlichkeit, die Zusammenhanglosigkeit der Sätze, das Selbstbedenken als Grund-lage der geistigen Zeugung weisen auf einen Denktypus hin, der in geistig ungesicherten Zeiten beheimatet ist. Die "aphoristische Situation" findet sich in Perioden geschichtlicher Krisen, in denen festgefügte Anschauungen zerbrechen und neue Wirklichkeiten entdeckt werden. Der echte Aphoristiker ist der staunende Mensch.' Grenzmann 1976, 207.

5 Syriac Translations of Plutarch, Lucian and Themistius
A Gnomic Format for an Instructional Purpose?

Alberto Rigolio

A selection of texts by Plutarch, Lucian and Themistius were translated into Syriac during Late Antiquity. Plutarch's *De cohibenda ira*[1] and *De capienda ex inimicis utilitate*,[2] Ps.-Plutarch's *De exercitatione*,[3] Lucian's *De calumnia*[4] and Themistius' *De amicitia*[5] and *De virtute*[6] are literary works by pagan authors that were translated between the fifth and the sixth centuries. They survive today in Syriac manuscripts that were written between the seventh and the ninth centuries.[7] Given the absence of prefaces, colophons or any information external to the texts, there is no explicit indication about the identity of the translators or about the origin of the translations. The only viable path to understand why Syrian scholars were interested in Plutarch, Lucian and Themistius is a close analysis of what the texts themselves (and their manuscripts) say.

Luckily, translations are a special kind of literature. The editing and abridgement strategy that the translators adopted allows us to catch a glimpse of their aims as well as of the audiences that they foresaw. I have argued elsewhere that the omission of most references to pagan religion and mythology as well as the practice of anonymising and glossing proper names of figures of the historical past reveals that the translators intended to make use of Plutarch, Lucian and Themistius as instructional texts suitable for Christians.[8] The present chapter focuses on the translators' aims by analysing the form in which the texts were reshaped and presented to the target audience. It will be shown that the translators paid special attention to the form of the text, and it will be argued that the gnomic sequences that they introduced display important similarities with wisdom literature. A close textual analysis of the Syriac translations of Plutarch, Lucian and Themistius can thus help remove them from the scholarly isolation to which they have been so far relegated, and can open new paths to a more organic understanding of the translations within established literary traditions and, beyond that, within the cultural life of Late Antiquity.

Editing the Texts

The process of editing that the Syriac Plutarch, Lucian and Themistius underwent reveals that the translations were meant to be used as instructional texts suitable for a Christian readership. The first concern for the translators was the

74   *Alberto Rigolio*

references to pagan religion that they found in the Greek originals. The translators systematically omitted mentions of pagan deities; or, whenever possible, they rendered them with the word 'God'. Secondly, the translators went about carefully in their rendering of the anecdotes based on mythological figures, such as Achilles, Agamemnon and Athena, which were for the most part omitted in translation. While the *exempla* based on historical personalities were mostly translated, the *exempla* based on mythological figures were mostly omitted.[9] A third noticeable change that the translators applied to the texts relates to the rendering of proper names. On many occasions the proper names of characters appearing in anecdotes are omitted and replaced with generic and anonymous designations, such as 'a king', 'a wise man' and 'a philosopher'. To give a few examples, 'Xerxes' became, in Syriac, 'a Persian king', 'Pindar' became 'a wise man' and the Pontifex Maximus 'Spurius Minucius' became 'the judge'. It is difficult to imagine that somebody able to read Plutarch in Greek would not be aware of the identity of Xerxes or Pindar, and such changes should instead be understood as indicative of the translators' instructional aims. It is especially remarkable that some of such descriptions correctly identify even lesser-known figures when such information was not immediately available in the text: such as 'Porus', who was described as 'the king of the Indians'; 'Arcesilaus', who was termed 'a philosopher'; and 'Pylades', who was called 'Orestes' friend'.[10]

The present analysis focuses on another notable feature that likewise betrays the aims that guided the Syriac translators of Plutarch, Lucian and Themistius. Among the changes that they applied to the Syriac texts, a number of textual additions and re-phrasings reveal the translators' familiarity with gnomic compositions that are commonly used in wisdom literature. Often the translators rewrote the original text following patterns such as programmatic admonitions, aphorisms and *inclusiones* that reveal a concern to break down the text into independent and reproducible units with edifying content. The practice of expanding on the original texts was not uncommon in early Syriac translations, yet the expansions of the Syriac Plutarch, Lucian and Themistius display the introduction of gnomic formats.[11]

In the following passage, the translator paraphrased a quotation from Hippocrates, and he broke down Plutarch's argumentation so as to obtain an independent gnomic unit. Also, the explicit reference to Hippocrates was omitted in Syriac, and one finds, instead, two additions (in *italics*):[12]

Καὶ πρῶτον μέν, ᾗ φησιν Ἱπποκράτης χαλεπωτάτην εἶναι νόσον ἐν ᾗ τοῦ νοσοῦντος ἀνομοιότατον αὐτῷ γίνεται τὸ πρόσωπον, οὕτως ὁρῶν ὑπ' ὀργῆς ἐξισταμένους μάλιστα καὶ μεταβάλλοντας ὄψιν, χρόαν, βάδισμα, φωνήν [. . .]

First of all, as Hippocrates says that the most dangerous disease is that in which the countenance of the patient becomes most unlike how it was, so firstly I saw that those who are moved by anger are also changed in (their) countenance, skin, gait and voice [. . .]

First of all, we notice that as in the sick to see their faces different from usual is a sign of death, *so also in the irascible the ugliness of their appearance is a sign of their defeat*. Indeed, not only the colour of their faces is changed, but also their voice (189.5), their movements and their sight, *and their outside is the image of what is in the inside.*

The first addition is explicative, and it relates the *general* example about the sick with the *specific* example about the irascible man. The second addition repeats the concept expressed above by playing on the correlation between the inner condition of the angry person and his appearance. As a result, the translator used the Greek text to produce a self-standing gnomic sequence that could be easily extrapolated from the original Plutarchan text.

Similarly, the Syriac additions to another passage break down the course of the argumentation in order to create an independent textual unit:[13]

Καὶ τῶν πραγμάτων ἄφιλα πολλὰ καὶ ἀπεχθῆ καὶ ἀντίπαλα τοῖς ἐντυγχάνουσιν, ἀλλ' ὁρᾷς ὅτι καὶ νόσοις ἔνιοι σώματος εἰς ἀπραγμοσύνην ἐχρήσαντο [. . .]

ܘܣܓܐܐ ܡܢ ܣܘܥܪ̈ܢܐ ܣܩܘܒܠܐ ܐܢܘܢ ܠܗܠܝܢ ܕܒܗܘܢ. ܐܠܐ ܡܨܝܐ ܕܢܚܙܐ ܗܟܢܐ ܣܓܝܐܝܢ. ܠܒ̈ܢܝ ܐܢܫܐ. [3.10]

Many situations are unkind, hostile and adversary to those who meet them; but you see that some have used the sickness of the body to live a quiet life [. . .]

It is possible to see that many things, although adverse and harmful to *us, in other respects benefit us.* How many have fallen sick in the body, and this (3.10) sickness of theirs *refrained and hindered them from evil.*

The first addition results in the creation of an aphorism, while the second addition interrupts the original text and it closes the gnomic composition by repeating the message already provided in the opening aphorism.

On other occasions, the Syriac translators elaborated on the gnomic structures already contained in the original text. In the following passage, while the expansions simply add to the already binary structure of the Greek text, the introduction and repetition of the words ܓܒܐ [*gabō*] 'side' and ܙܟܘܬܐ [*zōkūtō*] 'victory' betray an interest for the gnomic format of the text:[14]

Φιλονεικίαν γε μὴν καὶ τὸ δύσερι καὶ πᾶσαν <***> ἐκποδὼν μεταστατέον, οἷον σπέρματα ἔχθρας εὐλαβουμένους. Οὐ γὰρ ἐν ἀνταγωνισταῖς, ἀλλ'ἐν συναγωνισταῖς ἡ φιλία.

ܚܪܝܢܐ ܕܝܢ ܘܦܠܓܘܬܐ ܢܬܚܠܘܢ ܡܢ ܡܢܢ ܚܠܦ.
ܕܡܢܗܘܢ ܫܘܚܐ [60.10] ܕܒܥܠܕܒܒܘܬܐ. ܠܐ ܗܘܐ
ܓܝܪ ܐܝܟ ܕܥܡ ܒܥܠܕܒܒܢ ܡܢ ܟܬܫܐ ܗܕܐ ܢܫܩܘܠ.
ܙܟܘܬܐ ܕܗܘܝܐ ܡܢ ܓܒܐ ܠܓܒܐ ܢܣܒ. ܐܠܐ
ܥܡܗܘܢ ܕܡܢ ܓܒܢ ܡܬܟܬܫܝܢܢ ܕܡܢܘ ܒܢ ܢܗܘܐ ܗܘ
ܩܕܡܝܐ ܘܢܣܒܝܗ ܠܙܟܘܬܐ.

Competitiveness, contention and all <rivalry> should be put aside, (and we should) beware of them as seeds of enmity. For there is no friendship among enemies, but (there is) among fellow-combatants.

Contention and division must be taken away, for (60.10) enmity sprouts from them. Indeed, it is not as if we fight our *enemy so that we may take the victory from one side to the other side,* but we compete with those who are *from our side about who shall be the first and take the victory.*

The same observation can be made regarding another passage in which the Syriac translator elaborated a gnomic sequence already attested in the Greek original. The passage is composed of an admonition (the opening sentence) followed by a course of argumentation. The Syriac expansions (in *italics*) do not add anything to the contents, but they elaborate the text by expanding on the structure of the Greek sentence. The opening admonition is expressed in greater length by the Syriac, and the Syriac text then provides the same course of argumentation as the Greek:[15]

Οὐκ ἄρα οὐδὲ ἐν φιλίᾳ τὸ σφόδρα. Ἑκατέρα γὰρ ταῖν <ὁδοῖν> ἄλλοσέ ποι ἐκφέρει ἢ ὅποι δεῖ καταλῦσαι. Ἡ μὲν γὰρ ἐπὶ κολακείαν ἄγει, τῆς δὲ ἐπ'ἔχθραν ἡ τελευτή.

ܡܕܝܢ ܐܦ ܠܐ ܠܪܚܡܐ ܗܘ [63.1] ܡܫܒܚ ܐܢܐ.
ܕܒܣܝܡ ܛܒ ܐܘ ܕܩܫܐ ܛܒ. ܬܪܬܝܗܘܢ ܓܝܪ
ܐܝܟ ܫܒܝܠܐ ܦܪܝܫܝܢ. ܠܗܪܟܐ ܘܠܬܡܢ. ܡܢ ܗܝ ܐܘܪܚܐ
ܕܡܩܪܒܐ. ܠܐܘܢܐ ܘܗܘ ܕܨܒܝܢ ܠܢ ܠܡܐܙܠ.
ܒܒܣܝܡܘܬܐ ܓܝܪ ܝܬܝܪܬܐ. ܠܘܬ ܫܘܥܒܕܘܬܐ
ܢܦܩܐ. ܘܩܫܝܘܬܐ ܬܘܒ ܝܬܝܪܬܐ. ܠܘܬ
ܒܥܠܕܒܒܘܬܐ ܡܩܪܒܐ.

Then, (there should be) no excess in friendship. Either <way> leads to a different place than to where one should end up: the one leads to adulation, while the end of the other to enmity.

Neither do I praise the friend who is too benevolent nor (the one) who is too harsh. For both things are separate as a road (leading) *hither and thither,* rather than the path that brings us to the lodging *where we intended to go.* Indeed, *excessive benevolence* ends up in adulation, and *excessive harshness* too fosters enmity.

At the same time, however, the Syriac adaptor added and repeated the words with the same roots 'benevolent-benevolence' and 'harsh-harshness' both at the beginning and at the end of the passage. The repetition of the same words or

Syriac Translations of Plutarch, Lucian and Themistius   77

formulas both at the beginning and at the end of a gnomic unit constitutes a textual device known as *inclusio*.[16]

Another instance of *inclusio* may be detected in the following passage from *De cohibenda ira*. Although the passage is problematic since the translator misunderstood what the Greek text expresses about the role of time in quenching anger, it is nonetheless clear that the translator repeated the specific example about anger in the close of the passage, despite the fact that it had been already expressed in the opening:[17]

Αὕτη μὲν οὖν ἴσως οὐκ ὀργῆς ἰατρεία φανεῖται, διάκρουσις δὲ καὶ φυλακὴ τῶν ἐν ὀργῇ τινος ἁμαρτημάτων. Καίτοι καὶ σπληνὸς οἴδημα σύμπτωμα μέν ἐστι πυρετοῦ, πραυνόμενον δὲ κουφίζει τὸν πυρετόν, ὡς φησιν Ἱερώνυμος.

Perhaps this [i.e. gaining a delay] will not seem a cure for anger, but rather a respite and a guard for the mistakes of the irascible. Certainly the swelling of the spleen is a symptom of the fever, and once it has been calmed it assuages the fever, as Hieronymus says.

Hastiness is not therapeutic for anger, but it assuages it for a moment, as if it were a guard to it. Behold, the swelling of the spleen is due to fever, and the care of it brings the trouble to an end; *and the hastiness that comes from anger, it is the care of it that puts anger to an end.*

In the close, the translator substituted the reference to Hieronymus of Rhodes with the specific example about anger, where he repeated the word 'hastiness' ܪܗܝܒܘܬܐ [*rhībūtō*] used above, possibly aiming at the composition of an *inclusio*.

The use of *inclusiones*, repetitions of the same words or same moral recommendations both at the beginning and at the close of a gnomic sequence, is a strategy that the translators used on a number of occasions. As a result, the Syriac text appears broken down into smaller and independent units that could be easily reproduced out of their contexts. Two other instances of *inclusiones* affected passages of the Greek text that are too long to be reported in full here. In the *De capienda ex inimicis utilitate*, Plutarch reported an anecdote about the cytharedes, who play better when they are in competition than when they train by themselves in solitude. Accordingly, Plutarch explained that we should take our enemies as competitors for fame, and that we should regulate our deeds and customs as if we were always in competition with our enemies. At the close of the anecdote, the Syriac adaptor added a reference to the specific example of the cytharedes mentioned only a few lines above.[18] Another instance of *inclusio* is attested in the *De amicitia*, where, following a comparison between the practice of reproaching friends and that of healing the sick, the Syriac adaptor added a closing sentence that reiterates the similarity between the deeds of a friend and those of a physician.[19]

Adding Advice

Another set of additions to the texts brings the translations closer to wisdom literature. Such additions contain instructional remarks of an edifying nature, and they can likewise be taken as indicative of the didactic aim that guided the translators. In the following passage, the translator broke down the argumentative sequence of the text by inserting an instructional addition (in *italics*):[20]

Ἐφεδρεύει σου τοῖς πράγμασιν ἐγρηγορὼς ὁ ἐχθρὸς ἀεὶ καὶ λαβὴν ζητῶν πανταχόθεν περιοδεύει τὸν βίον [. . .]

The enemy, always awake, lies in wait of your deeds and patrols (your) life on every side seeking a grip [. . .]

(The enemy) tracks your customs, he does not rest from inquiring into your ways, and he strives to find a cause against you, while he roams hither and thither. *Well then, his watchfulness does not harm you, but it recalls you to beneficial customs.*

Not unlike the passages reported above, the addition creates an independent gnomic unit; but, in this case, its content consists of moral advice that is in accordance with the edifying message of the *De capienda ex inimicis utilitate*.

Other additions with moral contents do not radically alter the format of the Greek text. The following passage from Themistius' *De amicitia* describes the attitude that a person should adopt in his relations with friends. In addition to the Greek, the Syriac recommended that:[21]

ἀπὸ τῶν σμικρῶν καὶ φαυλοτάτων ὡς ἂν δόξειεν ἀρχομένους, οἷον τοῦ προσορᾶν εὐμενῶς καὶ διαλέγεσθαι ἐπιδεξίως καὶ συμπαρακαθέζεσθαι καὶ συμβαδίζειν, καὶ δῆλον γενέσθαι ὅτι ἥδοιτο ὁρωμένῳ.

We should begin with what might seem to be small and very insignificant steps, such as casting kind glances (at our friend), conversing with him tactfully, sitting and walking with him, and making it clear that we are happy to see him.

Let us begin from the very small things. First of all, let us look at them with (56.10) benevolence, and let us sit next to them with a pleasant talk; let us stick to their steps and let us show that we rejoice at their sight; *and let us implant in ourselves the customs that they have.*

A few chapters below, the Syriac translator invited to give advice to friends 'without being detached from the (friend's) issues, but rather bearing with the friend part of their burden, even if the issues are impure':[22]

[. . .] πρὸς ἑκάστην χρείαν τοῦ φίλου τὸ πρόσωπον οἰκεῖον μεταλαμβάνειν, ἐν ἀρρωστίᾳ μὲν ἰατροῦ, ἐν δίκαις δὲ συνηγόρου, συμβούλου δὲ ἁπανταχοῦ καὶ συνεργοῦ ἐπὶ τῇ γνώμῃ.

[59.10] ܐܠܐ ܕܐܢܬ ܡܢ ܢܦܫܟ ܡܠܒܟܐܝܬ ܡܫܬܘܬܦ ܐܢܬ ܠܟܘܪܗܢܗ. ܟܕ ܗܘܐ ܐܢܬ ܠܗ ܐܝܟ ܒܟܘܪܗܢܐ ܕܒܣܘܡܬ ܐܣܝܐ. ܘܗܟܢܐ ܥܕܪܐ ܒܨܒܘܬܐ ܕܬܚܠܬܐ ܕܡܢܐ. ܘܡܗܒ ܐܢܬ ܠܗ ܡܠܟܐ. ܠܐ ܟܕ ܦܪܝܫ ܐܢܬ ܡܢ ܨܒܘܬܐ. ܐܠܐ ܟܕ ܫܩܠ ܐܢܬ ܥܡܗ ܡܢ ܝܘܩܪܗܝܢ. ܘܐܦܠ ܐܢ ܕܛܢܦܢ ܨܒܘܬܐ.

[. . .] you shall keep changing the role you play according to the need (of the friend). When he is sick, (play the role) of a physician; when he is in trials, (play the role) of a lawyer; play (the role) of an adviser on every occasion, and of a helper when he is taking a decision.

But you yourself shall promptly (59.10) participate in his grief, being like a doctor when he is sick, like a defender in the issues that are disputed; and you shall give him advice *without being detached from the issues, but rather bearing with him part of their burden, even if the issues are impure.*

Another moralising addition seems to directly reveal the instructional aims of the translators. After a negative *exemplum*, the addition 'we shall instead emulate excellent men' opens a section of the text in which Plutarch reported *exempla* of philosophers who were imperturbable in conditions that would have easily made ordinary men angry:[23]

Καὶ δεινὸν οὐδὲν ἀρξαμένους ἀπὸ τῆς τροφῆς σιωπῇ χρήσασθαι τοῖς παρατυγχάνουσι, καὶ μὴ πολλὰ χολουμένους καὶ δυσκολαίνοντας ἀπερπέστατον ὄψον ἐμβαλεῖν ἑαυτοῖς καὶ φίλοις τὴν ὀργήν.

ܟܕ ܠܐ ܡܬܚܡܬܝܢ ܥܕܢ ܫܪܘܬܐ. ܘܚܠܦ ܡܐܟܠܬܐ ܕܒܣܝܡܢ. ܡܪܝܪܘܬܐ ܕܚܡܬܐ ܩܕܡܝܢ ܘܩܕܡ ܪ̈ܚܡܝܢ ܣܝܡܝܢ. ܐܠܐ ܢܛܢܐ ܠܓܒܪ̈ܐ ܡܝܬܪ̈ܐ.

To start with food, it is nothing unpleasant to stay quiet with guests, and not, by being angry and peevish about many things, to throw to ourselves and to (our) friends the most unpleasing food, anger.

By not being angry during the time of the meal – and (otherwise) instead of delicious dishes we (would) put in front of us and in front of (our) friends the bitterness of anger – *we shall instead emulate excellent men.*

These passages show, then, that the translators' interest lay in the morally edifying anecdotes that make up most of the texts by Plutarch, Lucian and Themistius.[24] Thanks to the process of editing, the translations appear structured as

80   *Alberto Rigolio*

collections of anecdotes and pieces of moral advice that could be extrapolated and reused outside the original context. The phenomenon is especially evident in Plutarch's *De cohibenda ira*, whose Greek text opens as a dialogue between two characters, but whose translation omits the dialogic sections and adopts the format of a treatise that is mostly made up by maxims and moralising anecdotes.

The translators have thus rendered the Syriac Plutarch, Lucian, and Themistius closer to wisdom literature. The editing process ultimately betrays a didactic strategy based on the use of moralising texts arranged in gnomic formats such as *exempla*, aphorisms and *inclusiones* that could be potentially reproduced in different instructional settings. Instances of wisdom literature, especially in the form of *gnomologiai* or collections of sentences and anecdotes, are fairly common in early Syriac manuscripts; and, in particular, Greek traditions had a major impact on the composition of wisdom literature in Syriac. The *Advice of Theano*, *Sayings of Menander*, *Sayings of Pythagoras*, *Sayings of the philosophers on the soul*, *Definitions of Plato*, *Advice of Plato to his disciple* and the *Instructions of Anton, Plato's physician* are just some of the Syriac collections of wisdom literature that reveal the impact of Greek literary traditions.[25]

Contexts and Use

The composition of Syriac wisdom and instructional literature provides a possible cultural environment within which to understand the Syriac translations of Plutarch, Lucian and Themistius. Although still in need of systematic scholarly attention both at a microscopic (editions, translations, textual criticism) and at a macroscopic level (what they can say about the cultural life of the time), Syriac wisdom literature displays a thrust towards literate instruction that finds major parallels in early Christian literature in different languages. A remarkable example is represented by the *Apophthegmata Patrum*, the edifying anecdotes which could be used independently and reproduced in a variety of instructional settings.[26] The Evagrian ascetic *corpus*, which is mostly structured as a series of sentences and anecdotes, is another Christian collection of instructional literature. The transmission of gnomic literature to ascetic settings via translation is represented by Rufinus' Latin translations of the *Sentences of Sextus* and of the Evagrian ascetic *corpus*.[27]

It is especially remarkable that a Syriac author whose life was roughly contemporary with the Syriac translations of Plutarch, Lucian and Themistius confronts the modern reader with a very similar didactic strategy based on the use of anonymised anecdotes and maxims as instructional texts: John of Apamea, a prolific Syriac writer of the fifth century and who is also known as John the 'Solitary', ܝܚܝܕܝܐ [*iḥīdōyō*].[28] Within the works transmitted under his name, two dialogues are especially relevant to the present analysis because they depict a Syriac setting in which anecdotes and maxims were used as instructional texts. The two dialogues, which betray some familiarity with the dialogic genre of the Greek literary tradition, feature John the Solitary conversing with less experienced ascetics, all of whom bear Greek names; and their conversations are set in a monastic setting, namely John's own ܟܘܪܚܐ [*kūrḥō*], 'cell' or 'hut', for the *Four dialogues*.[29] The references to the daily prayers at the beginning of most dialogues are reminders of the communal life pattern of the speakers of the dialogues. The *Six dialogues with Thomas* deal with philosophical and theological issues concerning the soul and its relation to virtues and passions, and with the spiritual and ascetic life.[30] The *Four dialogues with Eusebius and Eutropius on the soul* deal with the nature of the soul and the incorporeal, with the body, with the creation and with divine economy.[31]

The literary nature of the fictitious setting of the dialogues is a feature to bear in mind, and one should avoid accepting John the Solitary's picture as a faithful description of early Syrian monasticism or as indicative of a standardised sort of monastic education. At the same time, however, John's dialogues betray an instructional strategy that has much in common with the efforts of the Syriac translators of Plutarch, Lucian and Themistius. If anything, the unfolding of the dialogues has a prominently didactic character, and the most suitable way to qualify the exchanges between John the Solitary and the other speakers is that of a teacher–pupil relationship. The speakers' attitude towards John is well represented by their profound admiration for the solitary, which itself led the young monks to John's hut, and thus provided the occasion for the encounter.[32]

The occasions of the encounters of John the Solitary with his interlocutors in the two dialogues are similar. Thomas on the one hand, and Eusebius and Eutropius on the other, have all spent some time as hermits – Thomas after gaining the 'excellent education of the Greeks' (ܝܘܠܦܢܐ ܡܝܬܪܐ ܕܝܘ̈ܢܝܐ)[33] – when they got to know John through literary pieces that John himself had written. Thomas came across a book of hymns composed by John, while Eusebius and Eutropius received a letter from John, presumably dealing with Christian ascetic life. Positively impressed by the reading, the young ascetics decided to meet John in person, and approached him with a number of questions on the soul, on the body and on divine economy. Also, Thomas confessed that his doubts derived from the variance that he found among the opinions of pagan poets.[34]

The instructional relationship among the speakers of John's dialogues is striking in the *Four dialogues*. Here John routinely draws anecdotes from a straightforward imagery, such as the coxswain, animals and musical instruments.[35] But something unexpected happens towards the end of the second of the four dialogues, when John decides to leave aside the dialogic format that he had employed so far, and instead recounts to his audience a series of fourteen morally edifying anecdotes about generic wise men and solitaries. John declares that he intends to narrate such stories 'so that the narration of them may be profitable for you' (ܡܛܠ ܕܬܫܥܝܬܐ ܕܝܠܗܘܢ ܬܗܘܐ ܠܟܘܢ ܠܥܘܕܪܢܐ).[36]

The anecdotes are very similar to those that one can find in the Syriac translations of Plutarch, Lucian and Themistius, not least because they are anonymised

82 *Alberto Rigolio*

and they often close with moral remarks. To give an example, the first anecdote is about:

> a *certain wise man*. In order not to be hindered from study, he ceased to live in the city, and he built for himself a hut outside the wall. He had next to his dwelling place a piece of land that was cultivated with wheat, and he was always passing by its side. When somebody from his town asked him if its seed had sprouted, he replied: 'I do not even know if it has been seeded!' Look how useful to the soul the love of study is! For, once the soul is accustomed to studying, it is not possible for the mind to wander outside it.[37]

It is regrettable that neither the editor nor the modern translator of the dialogue systematically traced back the origin of the anecdotes that John recounted. One of the anecdotes, which deals with anger, does not have a Christian origin and is found in Epictetus' *Encheiridion*,[38] but it is referred to a monk in John's version. Another anecdote, instead, is found in the *Apophthegmata Patrum*.[39]

In the structure of the *Four dialogues*, the switch from the dialogic format to the narration of *exempla* to describe the ascetic lifestyle is a considerable discontinuity. In spite of wishing to convince by the use of arguments, the *exempla* reiterate models of worthy conduct and they are underpinned by a different strategy of persuasion, as John explains. Indeed, after pronouncing the fourteenth and last *exemplum*, John gives the reason why he narrated such stories:

> because of the simplicity of those brothers who were present (at the discussion) but have not completely understood what has been previously said, lest they withhold their good will, *I wanted to help their minds through the narration of stories.*[40]

In the setting of the *Four dialogues*, it is the expected background of the audience that prompted John to report such anecdotes. It is John's assumption that a part of the audience would be happy to hear *exempla* of worthy conduct by generic wise men, philosophers and hermits. At the same time, however, the audience included also individuals like John himself, Eusebius and Eutropius, who must have experienced some sort of philosophical training as shown in the arguments that they used. In the case of Thomas, it may be that he was educated in Greek, perhaps even in the city of Alexandria.[41]

While about half of the *Four dialogues* adopts a dialogic format, the same work also contains gnomic material that reveals a different sort of didactic strategy. This strategy appears again and even more strikingly in the fourth and last book of the *Four dialogues*. Here, Eusebius puts forward a surprisingly elementary request. He asks John for the definitions of a series of more than sixty words with meanings related to virtue, such as 'sufferance', 'poverty', 'mercy', 'charity' and so forth:

in order that we may discern clearly the words that are said about virtue, we would like to learn the meaning of each of them, both physically and spiritually, for, with the understanding of their difference, our mind will be even more enlightened about the many varieties of virtue.[42]

John agrees to provide the definitions of such terminology, and, as a result, the fourth dialogue consists entirely of a collection of moral sentences. Again, as opposed to the dialectic arguments previously adduced in the *Four dialogues* – which, incidentally, required familiarity with philosophical concepts such as 'element' (στοιχεῖον 1.14) and 'substance' (οὐσία 2.1) – the definitions offered in the fourth dialogue reveal a different strategy of persuasion: they respond to a concern for straightforwardness, and they could be easily understood and memorised without previous experience in philosophy.

Conclusion

John the Solitary's choice to reproduce anonymous *exempla* and gnomic sentences, then, betrays the same didactic strategy implemented by the Syriac translators of Plutarch, Lucian and Themistius; and the anonymised anecdotes of the *Four dialogues* share the textual format of several passages in the *corpus* of Syriac translations that have been considered here. The analysis of the translators' editing and abridgement strategy suggests a path that can help put the Syriac Plutarch, Lucian and Themistius into context, and relate them to more familiar strands in Syriac literature. Wisdom literature in particular is abundantly attested in early Syriac manuscripts, and its overall significance for the study of Early Christianity awaits full appreciation.[43]

Through a close analysis of the texts, it has been argued in this chapter that textual formats employed by the Syriac translators of Plutarch, Lucian and Themistius can shed light on the enterprise of transmission of Greek secular literature into Syriac. The introduction of gnomic formats such as aphorisms, *exempla* and *inclusiones*, and the addition of moral expansions, reveal the same didactic strategy used in the dialogues by John the Solitary. Also, these textual formats ultimately suggest a link to wisdom and instructional literature, and they show a didactic thrust within which to understand the transmission into Syriac of Plutarch, Lucian and Themistius.

Notes

1 MS *Sin. Syr.* 16 (seventh century) and MS *BL Add.* 17209 (ninth century); De Lagarde 1858, 186–95, only from MS *BL Add.* 17209.
2 MS *Sin. Syr.* 16; edition and English translation in Nestle 1894.
3 MS *BL Add.* 17209 and *Sin. Syr.* 16; edition De Lagarde 1858, 177–86, only from MS *BL Add.* 17209 (the beginning is missing), and Rohlfs 1968, only from MS *Sin. Syr.* 16 (only the beginning); English translation in Rigolio, forthcoming.

4 MS *Sin Syr.* 16 and MS *BL Add.* 17209; edition Sachau 1870, 48–65, only from MS *BL Add.* 17209.

5 MS *BL Add.* 17209; Sachau 1870, 48–65.

6 MS *BL Add.* 17209 and MS *Sin. Syr.* 14 (excerpts; tenth century); Sachau 1870, 17–47, only from *BL Add.* 17209; German translation from Sachau 1870 in Gildemeister/Bücheler 1872b; Latin translation from Sachau 1870 in Downey/Norman 1971, III 8–71; Italian translation in Conterno 2014.

7 The editions of the Greek texts used here are Pohlenz et al. 1929, Bompaire 1998 and Downey/Norman 1971 respectively; the translations from Greek and from Syriac are my own.

8 Rigolio 2013.

9 Rigolio 2013.

10 The same strategy of reproducing moralising anecdotes from Plutarch's *Moralia* in an anonymous way is attested in Greek Christian writers such as Clement of Alexandria, in the *Paedagogus*, and Basil of Caesarea, in the *Ad adulescentes*.

11 Brock 1980.

12 Plutarch, *De cohibenda ira* 455E: Syr 189.1–5.

13 Plutarch, *De capienda ex inimicis utilitate* 87A: Syr 3.6–10.

14 Themistius, *De amicitia* 275CD: Syr 60.8–13.

15 Themistius, *De amicitia* 277C: Syr 62.23–63.5. Lucian, *De calumnia* 30 : Syr 15.21–3 is another passage that reveals an elaboration on the Greek text possibly aimed at obtaining a parallel structure: 'for it would be ridiculous to set doorkeepers for our house but to leave our ears and mind open' (καὶ γὰρ ἂν εἴη γελοῖον τῆς μὲν οἰκίας θυρωροὺς καθιστάναι, τὰ ὦτα δὲ καὶ τὴν διάνοιαν ἀνεῳγμένα ἐᾶν) was translated as 'for it is very foolish that we put *doors* and guardians to our houses, but we leave our ears and our thoughts open' (ܐܦ ܓܝܪ ܣܟܠܘ ܛܒ ܗܝ ܕܠܒ̈ܬܝܢ ܢܣܝܡ ܬܪ̈ܥܐ ܘܢܛ̈ܪܐ، ܘܐܕܢ̈ܝܢ ܕܝܢ ܘܡܚܫ̈ܒܬܢ ܢܫܒܘܩ ܟܕ ܦܬܝ̈ܚܢ), in which the addition of 'doors' provides a counterpart to 'ears'.

16 Kirk 1998, 149–51.

17 Plutarch, *De cohibenda ira* 460C: Syr 193.14–18.

18 Plutarch, *De capienda ex inimicis utilitate* 87F–88A: Syr 5.24–6.9.

19 Themistius, *De amicitia* 277BC: Syr 62.6–20.

20 Plutarch, *De capienda ex inimicis utilitate* 87BC: Syr 4.6–9.

21 Themistius, *De amicitia* 272AB: Syr 56.9–12.

22 Themistius, *De amicitia* 274D: Syr 59.9–14.

23 Plutarch, *De cohibenda ira* 461C: Syr 194.16–18.

24 There is the possibility that the change in the title of Lucian, *De calumnia*, likewise emphasises the instructional message of the text: 'On not believing lightly in slander' (περὶ τοῦ μὴ ῥᾳδίως πιστεύειν διαβολῇ) was translated as 'On that one should not believe in slander against friends' (ܥܠ ܗܝ، ܕܠܐ ܙܕܩ ܕܢܗܝܡܢ ܠܡܐܟܠܩܪ̈ܨܐ ܥܠ ܪ̈ܚܡܝܢ).

25 Zeegers-Vander Vorst 1978; Possekel 1998; Brock 2005; Brock 2012; Arzhanov 2013. The afterlife of Syriac wisdom literature and its use in the composition of Arabic wisdom literature are promising lines of research in need of systematic scholarly attention. Recent work on the Greco-Arabic tradition is accessible at www.ancientwisdoms.ac.uk.

26 See the chapters by Lillian Larsen and Yannis Papadogiannakis in the present volume.

27 Pevarello 2013. A systematic treatment of the benefits of the use of the example and the enthymeme (maxims being included in the latter) in rhetoric is provided by Aristotle, *Rhetoric* 2.20–21; and classical authors who made large use of *gnomai* in their work include Isocrates, *Ad Nicoclem*, Xenophon, *Oeconomicus* and *Cynegeticus*, and Plutarch, *Apophthegmata*.

28 De Halleux 1983; Brock 1982, 31–2; Lavenant 1984, 15–19; Hausherr 1939, 91–2.

29 John the Solitary, *Four dialogues* 1.6.

30 Edition and German translation in Strothmann 1972; French translation in Lavenant 1984, 47–119.

Syriac Translations of Plutarch, Lucian and Themistius   85

31 Edition in Dedering 1936; French translation in Hausherr 1939.

32 For instance, John the Solitary, *Four dialogues* 80.3–6: ܣܝܡܬܐ ܠܟܘܢ ܡܢܟܘܢ ܐܘܡܪܟܝ ܚܒܝܠܬܐ ‏.ܟܒܡܘܒ ܗܠ ܗܝܡ ܠܟ ܡܘܢ ܐܟܣܝܘܒ ܙܟ ‏.ܗܝܬܘܒ ܠ ܡ ܢܕܗ܇ 'you have laid a pile of good things in our soul through the acquaintance that we have (gained) with your virtue. We glorify and praise Him who gave you such a gift!'

33 John the Solitary, *Six dialogues* 1.5.

34 John the Solitary, *Six dialogues* 1–7; Thomas uses the word ܦܘܝܛܐ [*pūyiṭē*] 'poets' (1.21); see Lavenant 1984, 48 n. 1.

35 John the Solitary, *Four dialogues* 10, 26 and 49 respectively.

36 John the Solitary, *Four dialogues* 50.15.

37 John the Solitary, *Four dialogues* 50.16–23: ܕܚܫܒܬܐ ܙܘ ܐܝܬ ܗܘܐ܇ ܘܡܢ ܕܠܗ ܢܦܘܩ ܕܝ ܒܝ ܗܠܘܒܝ ܘܡ ‏.ܩܠܘܒܐ ‏.ܡܘܡܪ ܕܝ ܒܘܒܕܐ ܕܝ ܕܒܗ ܐܝ ܡܢ ܒ ܩܘܒ ܐ ‏.ܩܠܐܘܠܐ ܒ ܐܝܥܪ ܒܝ ܕܝ ܐܬܪܐ ܘ ܕܝܒܝ ‏.ܢܝ ܡܠܟܐ ܕܗܒܝ ܢ ܨܕ ܒ ܒܝ ܗܠ ܒ ܝ ܗܘܐ ‏.ܡܠܗ ܒܝܘܒܘܡ ‏.ܥܝ ܐܘܒ ܒܘܒ ܘ ܒܝ ‏.ܒܬܝ ܐܪ ܐܕ ܕܪ ܐܝܢܝ ‏.ܐ ܐܝܕ ‏.ܐܕ ܒ ܘܒ ‏.ܘܢ ‏.ܩܘܒܠܐܘܒܐ ‏ܕܘܒܬܐ ܡܘܒܝܗܝ ܐܝܬܗܒ ‏.

38 John the Solitary, *Four dialogues* 52.13–17: ‏.ܘܡ ܗܘܐ ܚܙܝ ܡܘܡܒ ܡܬܒܠܗ ܐܒ ܙܘ ܐܝܢܝܒ ‏.ܐܕܝܕܘܒ ‏ ‏.ܡܘܒܠܗܠ ܒܘܪ ܐܒ ‏.ܢܝܐܘ ܐܕܟ ܠܝ ܗܘܐ ܗܝܒ ‏.ܒܝܠܒ ‏.ܡܠ ܒܘܒܗܘܒ ܘܒ ‏ܩܘܡ ܐܝܢ ܟܝܘ ܒܘܒܝܐ ‏.ܕܒܠ ‏.ܒܝܒܬܐ ܒܬܗܒ ܐܬܘ ܒܝܒܘܒ ܒܢ ܗܠ ‏: 'a solitary, when his disciple broke the vessel with which he used to drink and he believed that (the solitary) would be angry at him, for he did not own another vessel, he answered and told the disciple: "Do not be distressed for this, for nothing unbreakable has been broken!" He observed this on every occasion.' Epictetus, *Encheiridion* 26 (trans. Boter 1999, 304): 'For instance, when someone else's slave breaks a cup, our immediate reaction is: "It is just one of those things that happen." Realise, then, that when your own cup is broken, you must react in the same way as when someone else's cup was broken.' Contrast Plutarch, *De cohibenda ira* 461EF.

39 John the Solitary, *Four dialogues* 77.7–13; Hausherr 1939, 92; *PG* 65.376; Wallis Budge 1904, 572–3; Ward 1975, 200.

40 John the Solitary, *Four dialogues* 53.23–54.1: ‏.ܡܒܬܚ ܕܝ ܒܘ ܡܠܘ ‏.ܚܒܝ ܒܝܘܒܝܠܒ ܡܘܒ ܐܬܘܗܠܐܕ ܚܒܠ ‏.ܒܐܬܘܒܘܒܠܐ ‏.ܚܠܒ ܝܒܘܒܝܬ ܐܝܥܘܒܐ ܘܡܘ ܡܘܒ ܒܘܒܘ ‏.ܢܒ ܒܝܐ ܐܟܕ ‏ ‏.ܒܘܒܐ ܚܝ ‏ܝܒ ܝ ܥܘܡܘܒ ‏ܝ ‏.

41 Thomas mentions the library of Alexandria (55.538), but the passage does not necessarily imply familiarity with the place (Lavenant 1984, 96 n. 3).

42 John the Solitary, *Four dialogues* 80.7–11: ‏ܕܠܗ ܗܘܡ ܣܝܡ ܚܒܠܒ ܐܝܬܘܒ ܒܚܒܗ ܐܚܒܘܒ܇ ‏ܒܝܘܒܝܗܒ ‏ܟܒܗܘܒ ܓ ܒܝ ‏ܒܘܒܠ ‏.ܐܟܠܒܕ ‏ܐܘܒ ‏ܒܝ ܓ ‏ܒܝ ‏.ܣܠ ‏.ܡܘܒܐܝܪ ‏ܕܐܝܒ ‏ ‏ܘܒܝ ‏.ܘܡ ‏ܘ ‏ܒܘܒܝ ‏ ‏.ܒܝܘܒܝܗܒ ‏ܐܕܐ ‏ܐܪ ‏ܩ ܒܘ ‏ܩ ‏ܒܘܒ ‏ ‏ܕܒ ‏ܒܝ ‏.

43 A systematic analysis of the advantages of the uses of wisdom literature (the example and the maxim in particular) in a rhetorical setting is provided by Aristotle, *Rhetoric* 2.20–21; but see also Gregory of Nazianzus, *Letter* 51.5 about the use of γνῶμαι, παροιμίαι and ἀποφθέγματα in the composition of letters.

6   Athens and/or Jerusalem?

Basil's and Chrysostom's Views on
the Didactic Use of Literature
and Stories

Jan R. Stenger

Late Antique Christianity and the Challenges of Socialisation

As Christianity after Constantine started spreading across the Empire and moving up the ladder of society, two emerging lifestyles marked the extremes of experiences that were available to the faithful believer. On one end of the scale, charismatic ascetic figures appealed to an ever-growing number of Christians, despite their anti-social mode of living in the desert and lack of cultivation.[1] On the other end, the fourth century saw the rise of the well-educated elite bishop who, deeply rooted in Greek polis culture, acted as a benefactor and political leader of his city.[2] Both ways of life responded to the new challenges that Christianity faced as its appeal stretched out to all segments of society and its adherents became increasingly entangled in this world here. Christian religion came to embrace a broad spectrum of classes, professions, occupations and habits that did not always differ from those of contemporary pagans. Consequently, it was no longer advisable to address only illiterate fishermen and tentmakers (if early Christianity had ever done so), but it was key to success to reach out to the urban upper class as well. This is why educational matters and the issue of socialisation came to the fore among Christian intellectuals of this period.[3] More generally, the ongoing changes meant that Christian thinkers still had to come to grips with the issue of the relation between faith and classical culture. Now this discussion was continued in more comprehensive fashion and with greater attention to the institutional setting of education than before.

The question that will be addressed in this chapter is whether Christians found an answer to this challenge; and, more precisely, whether they designed a genuinely religious education that would win over the upper echelon of society without alienating them from their cultural roots. First, some remarks are in order on what is meant by 'religious education'.[4] To give a working definition, I view as religious an education that pursues an outspokenly religious goal; is based on sacred values and dogmas; makes use of media and methods informed by a set of beliefs; and is located in an institution under the control of religious agents. Among numerous texts from this period that tackled pedagogical issues in various ways,[5] I shall deal with two famous responses which stem from an identical cultural background and roughly pursue the same end, namely to implant an ideal of Christian conduct in the souls of children.

The one is the treatise *On Vainglory or the Education of Children*, written by the preacher John Chrysostom (c. 349–407) in Antioch sometime in the 390s. This is the first surviving Christian text to be devoted exclusively to educational matters. The other is the *Address to the Young* by Basil the Great (c. 330–79), a work purporting to be written for his two nephews, but unmistakably directed to a larger audience (c. 370/75). Both documents not only share the aim of forming virtuous and faithful men but also display a common interest in the role of texts and narratives in teaching boys. This can provide a springboard for our discussion as it reveals how the two authors, erudite figures themselves, understand the relationship between religion and secular schooling. It will be argued that, despite offering two complementary avenues to education, neither Basil nor Chrysostom reaches a conclusive and satisfactory result.

The Household: a School or the Clash of Civilisations

First, departing from the chronological order, Chrysostom's treatise will be discussed, as it has the broader scope and seems at first glance more decided in its views.[6] This work was devised when the preacher was still under the spell of his ascetic experience in the mountains surrounding Antioch, and sought to translate components of the monastic life into urban everyday doings.[7] As the first sentence indicates, Chrysostom in his treatise wanted to follow up what he had taught to his congregation on a previous occasion.[8] However, its transmitted title, *On Vainglory*, suggests that it was targeted primarily at the upper stratum of the city's population, which in Chrysostom's view stubbornly stuck to the competitive values of Greek culture as they shone through multifarious modes of conspicuous consumption.[9] Possibly, John regarded the wealthy members of the congregation as instrumental in shaping the habits of the entire community. Although he conceded that it was not feasible to convert the entire city into a monastery or a church,[10] he did not relinquish the hope of eradicating the vice of vainglory and introducing Christian humility in its place. The most promising vehicle for this aim seemed to him the fortification of the child's soul against all harmful desires, nicely encapsulated in the image of the newly built city, which runs through the treatise as a red thread.[11]

What immediately catches the eye in a discussion centring on upper-class education is that John's text is almost completely silent on secular schooling. Although the urban elite laid great emphasis on the rhetorical training of their sons, Chrysostom has virtually nothing to say on this issue, except some brief remarks which show that he accepts traditional education as non-negotiable in this milieu.[12] This is even more surprising when we consider that the well-to-do in Greek cities took considerable pride in their *paideia*, and that Chrysostom himself had undergone this very kind of schooling, possibly with the famous sophist Libanius and obviously with some success.[13] Yet, his silence seems to be indicative of his dismissal of secular schooling as unsuitable

88   *Jan R. Stenger*

for engendering morality in the soul of boys. When we look beyond this treatise we encounter in his gigantic oeuvre frequent passages in which Chrysostom even explicitly posits a contradiction between formal education along the lines of the traditional curriculum and blameless conduct.[14] We also might draw in here the opening paragraphs of *On Vainglory* where he vividly portrays the detrimental consequences of the elite habitus, thereby intimating that the established *paideia* falls far short of precluding vanity and misled ambition.[15] From these observations we can surmise that Chrysostom presupposes the continuance of the given education in this social environment and deliberately relegates it to the established schools.

What attracts his genuine interest is instead religious teaching, with a decisively moral stance on the issue. The preacher's original contribution to the debate on education is that he places the Christian household at the heart of the matter, to the extent that the family would replace the school as the key institution. Chrysostom assigns the task of the child's formation to the father and, to a lesser degree, to the mother. Theirs is the obligation to nourish in the boy's soul the virtues that will manifest themselves in wholesome conduct.[16] Religious education is thus implemented in a top-down process: Chrysostom envisions a chain of instruction where laymen, after having been morally improved by the preacher, become instructors of others and collaborate with Chrysostom in the formation of Christian citizen-athletes.[17] In this network of teachers and followers, parents play a vital part because of their familial authority. Since the entire pedagogical process is oriented towards *philosophia*, that is, Christian ethics,[18] instead of formal knowledge, it is crucial to make the child familiar with suitable role models so as to stimulate the emulation of these exemplars.[19] For one thing, this aim is achieved by guiding the boy to monks and other saintly men so that he can form an idea of what is required in a blameless life.[20] Of equal if not greater importance, though, is the instruction through edifying stories. The relevance of this method can be judged from the fact that the detailed discussion of how to present suitable narratives occupies the centre of the entire treatise (37–53).

Over several pages in the modern translation, Chrysostom gives substantial advice on the ways in which a father should recount biblical tales to his child, modify them to his needs, draw ethical lessons from them and ensure that the intended message takes root in the boy's mind:

> Speak to him and tell him this story: 'Once upon a time there were two sons of one father, even two brothers'. Then after a pause continue: 'And they were the children of the same mother, one being the elder, the other the younger son. The one, the elder, was a farmer, the other, the younger, a shepherd; and he led out his flocks to woodland and lake'. Make thy stories agreeable that they may give the child pleasure and his soul may not grow weary. 'The other son sowed and planted. Both decided to do honour to God. And the shepherd took the firstlings of his flocks and offered them to God'. Is it not a far better thing to relate this than sheep with golden

Athens and/or Jerusalem? 89

fleeces and such fairy tales? Then arouse him – for not a little depends on the telling of the story – introducing nothing that is untrue but only what is related in the Scriptures.[21]

Then Chrysostom goes on to expound at length how the father should break up the story of Cain and Abel into chunks, relate the stages of the narrative and lay stress on the implied moral meaning. Finally, after the child has listened to the story several times, he should be asked to retell it from memory so as to show that he has fully internalised the lesson. Alongside churchgoing, storytelling occupies centre stage as the most valuable resource in implanting Christian values and habits. As indicated in the quoted passage, Chrysostom recommends, or rather prescribes, that stories taken from the Scriptures supersede the pagan myths that families as well as school teachers were used to accustom children to. Instead of admiring Greek heroes such as Jason, the Christian boy will learn of the deeds of Cain and Abel or Jacob and Esau so that he develops a sense of what is right and what is wrong.[22] It is interesting to note that Chrysostom, otherwise a despiser of entertainment and joy, acknowledges the need to dress up the biblical tales by adapting their wording and creating suspense.[23] Thus, the narrative style is carefully crafted so as to enhance the effectiveness of teaching by a blend of entertainment and instruction.[24] As to the moral lesson, the form cannot be easily abstracted from the content of the stories.

Yet, it is not only for the sake of pleasure that Chrysostom suggests altering the stylistic presentation of the stories. A more important reason is the level of the child's understanding. As a young boy is not yet capable of fully grasping the moral import of the tales, it is of utmost importance to adjust the narratives to his abilities to drive the point home. The father is advised to use vivid and powerful language and make sure that the meaning of the events is made explicit and sufficiently clear. One technique for securing the success of the story is, for instance, to draw parallels between biblical events and the everyday experience of the boy so that he is able to translate the moral lesson into his own life.[25] Further, it is paramount not only to appeal to the intellect and moral conscience but equally to arouse strong feelings. After pointing out the devastating effect of greed and envy as embodied by Cain, the father will recognise how deeply his storytelling impresses itself on his son's state of mind: 'If only you sow this teaching in the child, he will not need his tutor, since this fear that comes from God, more than any fear has possessed the boy instead and shakes his soul.'[26]

The emotional response to the tales is the core vehicle for moulding a child's soul in Chrysostom's pedagogical programme.[27] As he also claims elsewhere, in reading or listening to texts and viewing theatre performances, a psychological mechanism operates on the audience's soul, to the effect that they involuntarily tend to emulate what they have viewed or heard.[28] As the spectators in the theatre are drawn into imitating the shameless behaviour of the actors on the stage, so the child will be frightened by the prospect of God's punishment if this is told in powerful language. This important mechanism of fear then inevitably engenders in the child the desire to emulate worthy characters like Abel and

90   Jan R. Stenger

Jacob and detest base ones such as Cain. What is especially significant about this pedagogy is that it aims at the imitation of models of Christian origin. While the individual in everyday life is engulfed by the inherited values of the pagan upper class or the ethics epitomised by mythological heroes, the biblical tales read out in church or in the household provide genuinely Christian exemplars. So specifically Christian virtues or what Chrysostom calls 'philosophy' will gradually be assimilated into profane life and annihilate the vainglory of the traditional elite. This is put forward with utmost clarity in the context of the story of Jacob and Esau:

> Narrate further the story of his bride and his return home, and the boy will profit much therefrom. Consider how many things he will learn. He will be trained to trust in God, to despise no one even though he is the son of one who is well born, to feel no shame at thrift, to bear misfortune nobly, and all the rest.[29]

The Church Father's guidelines on education include, to be sure, many lessons that resemble the teaching of the established philosophical schools, for instance the rejection of bodily pleasures; after all, his ethics did not differ substantially from the mainstream of popular Stoicism.[30] However, it is Christian virtue that is the lifeblood of Chrysostom's education, as the entire formation process is designed to inculcate fear of God, brotherly love and humility.

At first glance, it seems as though Chrysostom found a sensible solution to the problem of the elite values which form the backbone of Greek polis culture. He sees the need to furnish the children of Christian families with specifically religious role models in order to instil the desirable attitudes and habits. Since traditional education at the top of the social ladder relied heavily on the use of literary texts as a vehicle of ethical teaching, the Church Father adopts this successful strategy, but promotes a different canon of authoritative texts, the Scriptures. Furthermore, he recognises that Christian moral instruction requires a new institution and setting: the burden of the moral upbringing is placed on the Christian household as the kernel of a Christian society.[31]

Yet, consistent though it may appear, this educational concept is fraught with some pitfalls which seem to have escaped its designer's notice. Paradoxically, the major strength of the concept, its unequivocally religious fingerprint, simultaneously proves its major weakness. As mentioned earlier, Chrysostom chooses to exclude secular schooling from further consideration because it was deemed indispensable by the elite anyway. The Church Father is ready to concede that, after the moral upbringing within the household, the young Christian will embark on a public career, either in the administration or in the army (81). In other words, Chrysostom shies away from a radical change of entrenched life planning. The envisaged careers, however, cannot be pursued without formal education, which remains the domain of the traditional schools. A sceptic may wonder how the two branches of education, the secular one and the Christian, can be brought together. Given that secular teachers without exception claimed to convey, alongside skills, ethical values, is it not inevitable that their goals collide with those of Chrysostom's Christian education? As he strenuously seeks to detach the moulding of the soul from the intellectual training, Chrysostom circumvents this hurdle and allows only for weak connections between the two spheres. At one point at least, he suggests that Christian virtues are likely to spill over into the secular sphere of the profession:

> Let us encourage him to handle political affairs, such as are within his capacity and free from sin. If he serves as a soldier, let him learn to shun base gain; and so too, if he defends the cause of those who have suffered wrong, or in any other circumstance.[32]

However, Chrysostom does not elaborate upon this point; nor does he advise how to deal with potential clashes of public and religious demands. Occasionally, he even hints that the conventional values of the upper class likewise feed into the formation of the soul. For instance, the sense of reputation, which pervades the thinking of the educated elite, brings about the self-restraint of the individual.[33]

The reason why the preacher perseveres in ignoring secular schooling and its concomitants is that he splits the individual into two parts, an outer aspect and an inner one. While in the public sphere each individual plays a role in his profession according to the expectations of society, with regard to ethics and religion he should seek to live up to Christian ideals lest he jeopardise the reward in heaven. For the former, he relies on reasoning and knowledge; for the latter, the key to success is not the intellect but wisdom, as Chrysostom stresses unambiguously.[34] Wisdom, he tells us, is the master principle and is roughly identical with fear of God (85–7). This clear separation of intellect and morals is intended to cast away the classical *paideia* and its repercussions. What Chrysostom fails to address, though, is the question of whether it is feasible in the first place to skip over the content of classical culture and the impact of the schools on ethical norms. His admonitions are spoken in a vacuum as if it were possible to buy the practical skills transmitted by the schools without their ethical implications. A religious education in Chrysostom's eyes is instrumental in overcoming established social norms such as vainglory, but he assumes that the Christian household as a kind of monastery will implement the overall change almost automatically and smoothly. That cannot count as an integrated approach to religious education.

Blending Cultures or Basil's Consensual Approach

Whether any father among the congregation in Antioch was prepared to follow Chrysostom's pedagogical principles to the letter need not concern us here. An alternative path was opened by his older contemporary Basil the Great, who hailed from a similar background.[35] In a sense, there is even a connection between him and Chrysostom, as the ancient tradition also made Basil a student of Libanius, and even a correspondence between the Church Father and the

92 *Jan R. Stenger*

sophist, though of doubtful authenticity, has come down to us.[36] Further, he was immersed in classical culture to no lesser extent but decided to devote himself to an ascetic life.[37] In contrast to Chrysostom, Basil in his *Address to the Young* reveals an intense personal interest: not only is his educational programme cast in the mould of a private letter, as an advice to his nephews, but right from the beginning he fashions himself as the teacher and model for his young disciples.[38] However, it is beyond doubt that the author had a general audience in mind when he expounded his views on education. His guidelines would have been relevant to all Christian boys around the age of 15, who were following the curriculum in the traditional schools. In a similar way as Chrysostom, Basil seems to have regarded as his target audience Christian families among the affluent elite, who continued to value a thorough training in literature as the ticket to a successful and honourable life. It is important to note that Basil's letter was more limited in scope than Chrysostom's instructions; neither did he undertake to outline a general theory of education, nor did he claim to assess the value of pagan literature as such. His was the aim to discuss how far Christian students can benefit from reading pagan texts.[39] The work roughly falls into two parts: first, Basil discusses the value of pagan literature for a Christian upbringing (2–6), and then he focuses on the individual's morals in general (7–10).[40] His ideal, on which his precepts rest, is the consonance of profession and life, accompanied by the purification of the soul and the dismissal of earthly goods. Basically, we see here the same vision as in Chrysostom's guidelines, the promotion of Christian virtue intended as the preparation for afterlife.[41]

The identity of their aims notwithstanding, Basil's mode of conveying his insights is completely different from Chrysostom's. The Antiochene preacher carefully avoided explicit allusions to pagan literature and culture, although his teachings betrayed the marks of them throughout. The Cappadocian Church Father, by contrast, seasons his didactic epistle with an exceptional cornucopia of quotations, allusions and similes taken from the classics; of this practice he does not even make a secret, as he often refers to the classical authors by name. His letter virtually amounts to a contextualised anthology because it is interspersed with the most famous and memorable sayings of Greek authorities, such as Hesiod, Theognis and Solon.[42] The inclusion of their verses and ideas should not be considered ornamental; rather, it is crucial for Basil's didactic purposes: by his very discourse, Basil displays the usefulness of the poets and, to a lesser degree, of prose writers for the edification of the young. The abundance of quotations, references and big names is testament to the central place that Basil is willing to allocate to classical literature in the education of Christians. It goes without saying that this approach, like Chrysostom's, is recommended exclusively to the upper echelon of society who could afford to spend their time in reading literary works. Further, it is important to note that this mode of presentation is itself part of the message, as the author's polished style, quotations and arguments all enunciate the usefulness of classical erudition in a Christian leader.

How does Basil envisage the contribution of literature to ethical instruction? He distinguishes between poetry and prose, with the latter comprising narratives, rhetoric and philosophy.[43] As the Greeks since the classical era were convinced, it is especially the poets who play a vital role in imparting ethical insights on the students.[44] In his choice of profitable set texts Basil does not differ from earlier or contemporary evaluations, since pride of place is given to the ancient paragon of poetical wisdom, the epic poet Homer.[45] Second ranks the didactic poet Hesiod, represented by numerous quotations, and then follow the gnomic elegist Theognis and the Athenian politician Solon. Prose writers, on the other hand, do not receive the same recommendation, and this imbalance is not merely due to Basil's personal taste. Already in his discussion of the poets he does not show any interest in the stylistic and aesthetic qualities of their compositions; instead, emphasis is laid exclusively on the content of their verses. It is not hard to see the reason for this: Basil displays a sense of unease when it comes to the pleasure of reading. His reservations apply first and foremost to prose writings, and in particular to rhetoric; he suspects that writers of prose fabricate their tales primarily for the sake of entertainment and, even worse, that orators do not refrain from lying as long as they persuade their audience.[46]

The reason why entertainment may prove harmful is that Basil conceives of the task of literature in the same way as Chrysostom does: literary texts should be exploited for the moral lessons they offer to the reader. Homer's and Hesiod's lines provide countless models of blameless behaviour, which the student is admonished to absorb and imitate. In similar vein, philosophers have presented beacons of virtue, for instance Prodicus in his fable of the Choice of Heracles.[47] But since the classical writers also portrayed many villains and fools, the young must choose carefully whom to follow and whom to despise. So anything in the texts that is likely to divert from the good path has to be eliminated. As he assigns to literature essentially a protreptic function, Basil follows in the footsteps of ancient literary criticism. He decontextualises memorable sayings, especially maxims; readily identifies their meaning with the author's opinion; reduces entire works to simple messages; and is quick to harmonise the teachings of the great classics. This treatment of literature does not differ much from that in, say, Aristophanes' *Frogs*, Plato's *Republic* or Plutarch's *De audiendis poetis*.[48]

What is striking about Basil's approach, though, is that he refers to Christian writings only sparsely. For instance, when he puts forward the appropriate attitude to the physical needs, he draws on the authority of Paul:

> But, in a single word, the body in every part should be despised by everyone who does not care to be buried in its pleasures, as it were in filth; or we ought to cleave to it only in so far as we obtain from it service for the pursuit of wisdom, as Plato advises, speaking in a manner somewhat similar to Paul's when he admonishes us to make no provision for the body towards the arousing of lusts.[49]

Interestingly, it is not only Romans 13:14 that neatly encapsulates how the Christian ought to govern his body; but, as Basil highlights in this passage, the same rule is laid down in Plato's *Republic*. And this is no exception; quite

94   Jan R. Stenger

the contrary, Basil draws repeatedly a parallel between Christian teachings and the views of the classics, for example between David and Pythagoras. He gives the impression that the wise men of the Greek past and the authorities of the Scriptures all advocated the same ethical rules and standards.[50] Be it the pursuit of virtue, the divide between body and soul, the right attitude to material things or the harmony of words and deeds: nothing that Basil wants to engender in children's souls seems genuinely Christian.[51] It is all rooted in the mainstream of Greek popular morality and philosophy – all of which begs the question as to what is specifically religious about Basil's education policy.

Here the method that he proposes in several places comes into play. Most famously, it is captured in the simile of the bees:

> But we shall accept rather those passages of theirs [i.e. the prose writers] in which they have praised virtue or condemned vice. For just as in the case of other beings, enjoyment of flowers is limited to their fragrance and colour, but the bees, as we see, possess the power to get honey from them as well, so it is possible here also for those who are pursuing not merely what is sweet and pleasant in such writings to store away from them some benefit also for their souls. It is, therefore, in accordance of the whole similitude of the bees that we should participate in [pagan] literature. For these neither approach all flowers equally, nor in truth do they attempt to carry off whole those upon which they alight, but taking only so much of them as is suitable for their work, they let the rest go untouched. We ourselves too, if we are wise, having appropriated from it what is suitable to us and akin to the truth, will pass over the remainder. And just as in plucking the blooms of a rose-bush we avoid the thorns, so also in garnering from such writings whatever is useful, let us guard ourselves against what is harmful. At the very outset, therefore, we should examine each of the branches of knowledge and adapt it to our end, according to the Doric proverb, 'bringing the stone to the line'.[52]

Since pagan literature contains, intertwined with the beneficial elements, many ingredients that exert an unwholesome influence upon the soul, it is imperative to select only what is useful. As the bees do not visit all blossoms indiscriminately, so Basil's nephews and every Christian student ought to pick up from the classical works only lessons which are conducive to the aim of virtue.[53] This strategy, however, presupposes a clear criterion of selection. Keeping a close eye on the overall goal of the life to come, the fledgling student must adopt from Greek literature what is congruent with Christian morality and truth. By this guideline will he be able to distinguish the essentials in the texts from accessory and potentially harmful elements, such as the pagan gods.[54] In other words, discerning the essential core of a literary text from its dispensable elements requires an independent yardstick, that of Christian dogma. A fine illustration of Basil's principle is Moses, who is reported to have borrowed from the knowledge of the Egyptians on the basis of the affinity between the two bodies of teaching.[55]

More importantly, Moses did not stop with the Egyptian teachings but proceeded to gaining insight into the nature of God. Transferred into the reality of the fourth century, this means that adolescent Christians should first become acquainted with the teachings of the Greek classics and make use of them as preliminary exercise until they go over to reading the Scriptures. With a reference to the Platonic notion of shadows and reflections, Basil suggests that the young first exercise their intellectual abilities on the pagan texts and afterwards, when they have attained the necessary level of understanding, turn to the sacred books of Christianity.[56] In this central passage, Basil puts special emphasis on the two-tiered model of education by expanding upon it through three comparisons: the ontological hierarchy of mirrors and the true light, the sequence of gymnastic exercise and military engagement, and the two-stage work flow of dyers all drive home the point that before you enter the path to the aim proper you ought to make provisions and ensure that you master the required skills.[57] The reason why such a preparatory training in pagan literature is needed is the nature of the sacred mysteries which lies way beyond the capacities of children.[58]

When compared with Chrysostom's attempt, Basil's approach looks more realistic and feasible because it acknowledges the status quo in cultural matters at the time. It was outright delusional to expect that affluent Christians would willingly desert the traditional culture, which had long been part and parcel of their self-definition. Furthermore, his model accounts for the fluid identities that were characteristic of Late Antiquity.[59] For a cultivated Greek, it was unthinkable to neatly separate his Hellenic selfhood from his Christian belief, not to mention further overlapping identities. The Cappadocian Fathers themselves by their very lives bear witness to the impossibility of disentangling Christianity from Greek philosophy and literature. Yet, Basil creates serious problems with this conciliatory move. First, he is only able to claim the classics for his pedagogical purpose because he is rather vague on the point of virtue: what Christian virtue is and how it relates to philosophical conceptions is nowhere discussed. Thus, the core subject of teaching is a catch-all at the cost of specificity. (Needless to say, pagan philosophers also frequently shunned this challenge.) Second, and connected to this issue, the content of teaching seems to be wanting in a religious stamp. Basil is convinced that all Greek authorities and the Scriptures hold the same ethical views and, consequently, he does not go as far as to posit a religious nature of these rules. What is genuinely Christian is left to the second stage of education when the idea of virtue has already secured a firm place. And third, the fundamental problem lurks exactly in Basil's two-tiered model. If it is essential to assess the value of pagan texts according to Christian wisdom and truth, you need to acquire knowledge of this goal and criterion beforehand.[60] The goal, however, cannot be reached unless your intellect is sufficiently equipped for this task. Basil himself betrays this weakness when he draws the analogy of gymnastic exercise: to choose the suitable preparatory training you need to know your aim; otherwise you will easily go astray.[61]

These problems severely damage Basil's pedagogical model. He is neither aware of this circularity nor does he address the question why Christian religion

96   *Jan R. Stenger*

is necessary at all to become a virtuous person. In essence, Basil retains the role and functions of the pagan schools in their entirety, including their aim, content and methods. Far from distancing himself from the classical tradition, he does not even form an idea of developing an originally Christian approach to education; nor does he call the basic tenets of traditional *paideia* into question.

Gains and Losses

We have analysed two divergent schemes of religious upbringing and attempts at resolving the problem of the Christian attitude towards traditional schooling. It is evident that both approaches to the didactic use of literary texts are informed by longstanding views on education and the role of literature in it. As Plato and Plutarch had led the way, so the two Church Fathers followed in judging the quality of literature by applying an external measure, morality and truth. This chapter has argued that their stance on literary works throws their conceptions of education into sharp relief. Chrysostom's vision is outspokenly Christian, as he is still entertaining the idealistic goal of the believer as a semi-monk; he seeks to tackle the fundamental problem of non-Christian elements in teaching through distinction and the erection of boundaries. In contrast, Basil's strategy is flexible, inclusive and down to earth.

The basic difference between Chrysostom's and Basil's approaches is that between what we might call 'idealism' and 'realism', or between aiming at the maximum and recognising the environmental constraints. The Antiochene preacher is determined to abolish entrenched elite habits with his rigid model of a religious upbringing in the household; however, he does so at the cost of turning a blind eye to the ethical impact of the classical curriculum. The Cappadocian Father, by comparison, presents himself as open-minded and ready for compromise for the sake of a marriage between Greek culture and Christian belief; he is, though, not perfectly clear on the nature of the relationship in this couple. In these inherent tensions, both authors reflect the uncertainty of a transitional period when the question of the dominant value system had not yet been settled. While Chrysostom promotes his ideal as if he could neatly divorce this couple and ignore the ethical repercussions of Greek schooling, Basil wholeheartedly embraces the classics without thinking through who comes first, the bride or the groom. In pointing out this contrast we must not forget the difference in the communicative setting. While Basil, as a representative of a Christianised *paideia*, addresses like-minded members of his family and his social milieu, Chrysostom, often facing recalcitrant parishioners with a penchant for mundane concerns, pursues the aim of converting Antioch into a Christian city for good. His was a comprehensive agenda that called for distinctiveness, whereas Basil set out to tackle one single educational issue.

The pedagogical programme of *On Vainglory* is meant to bring about a desecularisation of the core education and places the burden on the Christian family, whereas the *Address to the Young* accepts and defends the status quo, apart from superimposing a vague religious end onto secular teaching. Thereby, the

Athens and/or Jerusalem?   97

former underestimates the impact of traditional schooling on socialisation, and the latter runs into serious problems of consistency and priorities. To return to our initial question, we may say that both Chrysostom and Basil fail to conceive a completely novel model of religious education because they fall short of a conclusive position on traditional culture. The religious element remains a kind of supplement that is intended to amend or give finish to secular education, but it is not fully integrated in the pedagogical process. In the centuries to come, though, Basil's strategy would prove immensely successful. But that is another story.

Notes

1 Brown 1988. For an overview see Krawiec 2008. On attitudes towards children and upbringing in early Christianity see Bakke 2005.
2 Rapp 2005b.
3 For an instructive overview of education in the fourth century see Cameron 1997. On the cultural framework of _paideia_ shared by pagans and Christians see further Brown 1992, esp. 121–92.
4 Cf. the catalogue of criteria suggested by Tanaseanu-Döbler and Döbler 2012, 8–18.
5 Particular attention deserve in this respect Athanasius' _Life of Antony_ and Gregory of Nyssa's _Life of Macrina_.
6 Gärtner 1985; Horn and Martens 2009, 149–61.
7 Malingrey (1972, 46–7) suggests 393/94 as the date of composition. Cf. Gärtner 1985, 193 and Liebeschuetz 2011, 138.
8 What he says about a particular exhortation finds a parallel in the _Homily 10 on Ephesians_ (10.3, PG 62,80). See Malingrey 1972, 41–6; Gärtner 1985, 197–200.
9 On the intended audience see Horn and Martens 2009, 151; 158–9.
10 Chrysostom, _On Vainglory or the Education of Children_ 19.
11 On Chrysostom's use of the Platonic imagery of the city see Stenger 2015a.
12 Chrysostom, _On Vainglory or the Education of Children_ 18; 39.
13 That Chrysostom was a student of Libanius is reported by the Church historians Socrates (_Ecclesiastical History_ 6.3.1-5) and Sozomen (_Ecclesiastical History_ 8.2.5, 7). However, this information has been called into question by modern scholarship. Cf. Nesselrath 2012, 114–15.
14 Chrysostom, _Against those who oppose the Monastic Life_ 3.12; _Homilies on the Acts of the Apostles_ 60. See Stenger 2014.
15 In _On Vainglory or the Education of Children_, books 4–10, Chrysostom vigorously denounces the vainglory (_kenodoxia_) by which the euergetism of wealthy citizens was driven. In _Homilies on the Gospel of Saint Matthew_ 71.2 (PG 58,664) he discusses the adverse effects of vainglory on Christian values and practices. See Pasquato 1992, 262–3 for further references.
16 The father ought to instruct the entire household, with his wife and the children as pupils: Chrysostom, _Vidua eligatur_ 9 (PG 51,329). On the mutual obligations and respect within the family see also Chrysostom's _Homily 21 on Ephesians_. Chrysostom seems to envisage greater social contact between parents and their children in Christian families than was usual in a pagan context. See Bakke 2005, 221.
17 Cf. Maxwell 2006, 113–15.
18 'Christian philosophy' is the key concept used for the whole conduct and especially as opposed to pagan philosophy, i.e. reasoning. Chrysostom, _Against those who oppose the Monastic Life_ 1.2, 3.18; _On the Statues_ 18.4 etc. See Stenger 2014, 89, n. 20.
19 On the Christian use of paraenetic examples in teaching see Gärtner 1985, 88–96.
20 Chrysostom, _On Vainglory or the Education of Children_ 78.

98   Jan R. Stenger

21 Chrysostom, *On Vainglory or the Education of Children* 39: λέγε τοίνυν πρὸς αὐτὸν καὶ διηγοῦ ὅτι ᾽Ἦσαν παρὰ τὴν ἀρχὴν δύο τινὲς παῖδες πατρὸς ἑνός, ἀδελφοὶ δύο᾽. Εἶτα διαστήσας ἐπάγαγε· ᾽Καὶ τῆς αὐτῆς ἐξελθόντες γαστρός. Καὶ ὁ μὲν ἦν πρεσβύτερος, ὁ δὲ νεώτερος. Καὶ ὁ μὲν ἦν γεωργός, ὁ πρεσβύτερος, ὁ δὲ ποιμήν, ὁ νεώτερος. Κἀκεῖνος μὲν ἐξῆγε τὰ ποίμνια ἐπὶ νάπας καὶ λίμνας᾽. Καὶ καταγλύκαινε τὰ διηγήματα, ὥστε τινὰ εἶναι τῷ παιδὶ καὶ τερπνότητα καὶ μὴ ἀποκάμνειν αὐτῷ τὴν ψυχήν. Ὁ δὲ ἔσπειρεν καὶ ἐφύτευεν. Ἔδοξεν δή ποτε τούτοις τιμῆσαι τὸν Θεόν. Καὶ ὁ μὲν ποιμὴν τὰ πρωτεῖα τῶν ποιμνίων λαβὼν προσήνεγκε τῷ Θεῷ᾽. Οὐ πολλῷ μᾶλλον ἀντὶ τῶν χρυσομάλλων προβάτων καὶ τῆς τερατείας ἐκείνης ταῦτα διηγεῖσθαι καλόν; Εἶτα αὐτὸν καὶ διανάστησον – ἔχει γάρ τι καὶ ἡ διήγησις – μηδὲν ψευδὲς ἐπιφέρων, ἀλλὰ τὰ ἀπὸ τῆς Γραφῆς. The translations are based on Laistner 1951. Chrysostom here refers to the story of Cain and Abel in Genesis 4:1–2. His second illustration (in 43–51) is the story of Jacob and Esau in Genesis 25:24–33:16.

22 Chrysostom's attempt is similar to that of his contemporaries, the two Apollinarises of Laodicea, who set out to counter the pagan literature with a newly composed body of Christian writings. See Socrates, *Ecclesiastical History* 3.16–17. Nesselrath 1999, 80–86.

23 Chrysostom, *On Vainglory or the Education of Children* 39; 46.

24 This is brought out in *On Vainglory or the Education of Children* 43, where Chrysostom is speaking of the pleasure (*hedone*) that the story of Jacob and Esau can give when told in an attractive fashion. Here, he makes use of a term of literary criticism, *peripeteia*, the reversal typical of Greek tragedy.

25 Chrysostom, *On Vainglory or the Education of Children* 40.

26 Chrysostom, *On Vainglory or the Education of Children* 40: Ἄν τοῦτο μόνον τὸ δόγμα ἐγκατασπείρῃς τῷ παιδί, οὐ δεήσῃ τοῦ παιδαγωγοῦ, τοῦ φόβου τούτου τοῦ παρὰ τοῦ Θεοῦ παντὸς φόβου μᾶλλον ἐφεστῶτος τῷ παιδὶ καὶ κατασείοντος αὐτοῦ τὴν ψυχήν.

27 See also Chrysostom in the *Homilies on Ephesians* 12.1 (PG 62,87); 20.9 (PG 62,148). For fear as a pedagogical mechanism in Chrysostom's anthropology see Jacob 2010, 195–200.

28 See Webb 2008, 168–96 and Stenger (2015b) on the role of mimesis in Chrysostom's instruction.

29 Chrysostom, *On Vainglory or the Education of Children* 51: Τὰ περὶ τῆς νύμφης λοιπὸν διαλέγου καὶ τῆς ἐπανόδου καὶ πολλὰ κερδανεῖ κἀντεῦθεν. Ὅρα γὰρ πόσα μαθήσεται· εἰς Θεὸν ἐλπίζειν παιδευθήσεται, ἀπὸ εὐγενοῦς ὢν καταφρονεῖν μηδενός, μὴ ἐπαισχύνεσθαι τὴν εὐτέλειαν, φέρειν συμφορὰς γενναίως, τἆλλα δὴ πάντα.

30 Cf. Wilson 1975, 11–12. Pasquato 1992 notes further traditional motifs and allusions in *On Vainglory or the Education of Children* which show that Chrysostom's work, despite its anti-traditional stance, was deeply informed by the classical tradition.

31 Cf. Brown 1988, 309; 312–13.

32 Chrysostom, *On Vainglory or the Education of Children* 89: Ποιῶμεν δὲ αὐτὸν καὶ πραγμάτων ἅπτεσθαι πολιτικῶν τῶν κατὰ δύναμιν, τῶν οὐκ ἐχόντων ἁμαρτήματα. Ἄν τε γὰρ στρατεύηται, μαθέτω μὴ κερδαίνειν αἰσχρῶς· ἄν τε τοῖς ἀδικουμένοις συναγορεύῃ, ἄν τε ὁτιοῦν τοιοῦτον.

33 Chrysostom, *On Vainglory or the Education of Children* 84. Cf. also the use of 'men of old', pagan and Christian' as equally suitable models of self-restraint in 79 (καὶ τῶν πάλαι ἐπὶ σωφροσύνῃ λαμψάντων καὶ τῶν ἔξω καὶ τῶν παρ᾽ ἡμῖν).

34 On Chrysostom's conception of Christian wisdom see Stenger 2014.

35 Rousseau 1994, 27–36.

36 Nesselrath 2012, 112–13.

37 On the role of classical culture in the lives and personal relationships of the Cappadocians see Van Dam 2003, 145–50.

38 Greek text and commentary in Wilson 1975; Italian commentary in Naldini 1984. The date of the treatise cannot be established with certainty. See Bräutigam 2003, 154–5. Naldini 1984, 16 suggests a composition between 370 and 375. For the author's relationship to his audience see Lamberz 1979, 224–7.

39 This has been rightly pointed out by Lamberz 1979, 227.
40 On the composition see Naldini 1984, 21–3; Schwab 2012, 149–50.
41 Basil, *Address to the Young* 2.9–10; 9.35–6.
42 On Basil's use of the classical authors see Naldini 1984, 26–8.
43 Basil, *Address to the Young* 2.37; 4.4; 4.28–31; 5.3.
44 Basil's way of dealing with literature clearly indicates that his addressees are more advanced in age (about 15 years old) and intellectual abilities than the children Chrysostom envisages in *On Vainglory or the Education of Children*. Cf. Lamberz 1979, 227; Döring 2003, 553.
45 Basil, *Address to the Young* 5.25–42, probably with a reference to the rhetorician Libanius (Wilson 1975, 52; Naldini 1984, 174–5). On the use of, and judgement on, Homer in late antiquity see Lamberton 1986.
46 On Basil's misgivings about attractive style and entertainment see *Address to the Young* 4.12–15; 28–34.
47 Basil, *Address to the Young* 5.55–77. See *Xenophon, Memorabilia* 2.1.21–34.
48 It is also Plutarch's technique to take short passages out of context and attach meanings to them quite other than those which they originally carried. The cause for this distortion lies in the moralising and ethical bias of his whole educational programme. Hunter and Russell 2011, 16. For the view ancient critics had of literature see Hunter 2009.
49 Basil, *Address to the Young* 9.61–6: Ἑνὶ δὲ λόγῳ, παντὸς ὑπεροπτέον τοῦ σώματος τῷ μὴ ὡς ἐν βορβόρῳ ταῖς ἡδοναῖς αὐτοῦ κατορωρύχθαι μέλλοντι, ἢ τοσοῦτον ἀνθεκτέον αὐτοῦ ὅσον, φησὶ Πλάτων, ὑπηρεσίαν φιλοσοφίᾳ κτωμένους, ἐοικότα που λέγων τῷ Παύλῳ, ὃς παραινεῖ μηδεμίαν χρῆναι τοῦ σώματος πρόνοιαν ἔχειν εἰς ἐπιθυμιῶν ἀφορμήν. Cf. Plato, *Republic* 498b; 533d; Romans 13:14; Galatians 5:13. The translations are adapted from Deferrari 1934.
50 Basil, *Address to the Young* 6.1–4; 10.1–4.
51 E.g., Basil, *Address to the Young* 5.13–22; 6.8–11; 9.3–15. Cf. Rousseau 1994, 54.
52 Basil, *Address to the Young* 4.34–54: Ἀλλ' ἐκεῖνα αὐτῶν μᾶλλον ἀποδεξόμεθα, ἐν οἷς ἀρετὴν ἐπήνεσαν, ἢ πονηρίαν διέβαλον. Ὡς γὰρ τῶν ἀνθέων τοῖς μὲν λοιποῖς ἄχρι τῆς εὐωδίας ἢ τῆς χρόας ἐστὶν ἡ ἀπόλαυσις, ταῖς μελίτταις δ' ἄρα καὶ μέλι λαμβάνειν ἀπ' αὐτῶν ὑπάρχει, οὕτω δὴ κἀνταῦθα τοῖς μὴ τὸ ἡδὺ καὶ ἐπίχαρι μόνον τῶν τοιούτων λόγων διώκουσιν ἔστι τινὰ καὶ ὠφέλειαν ἀπ' αὐτῶν εἰς τὴν ψυχὴν ἀποθέσθαι. Κατὰ πᾶσαν δὴ οὖν τῶν μελιττῶν τὴν εἰκόνα τῶν λόγων ἡμῖν μεθεκτέον. Ἐκεῖναί τε γὰρ οὔτε ἅπασι τοῖς ἄνθεσι παραπλησίως ἐπέρχονται, οὔτε μὴν οἷς ἂν ἐπιπτῶσιν ὅλα φέρειν ἐπιχειροῦσιν, ἀλλ' ὅσον αὐτῶν ἐπιτήδειον πρὸς τὴν ἐργασίαν λαβοῦσαι, τὸ λοιπὸν χαίρειν ἀφῆκαν· ἡμεῖς τε, ἢν σωφρονῶμεν, ὅσον οἰκεῖον ἡμῖν καὶ συγγενὲς τῇ ἀληθείᾳ παρ' αὐτῶν κομισάμενοι, ὑπερβησόμεθα τὸ λειπόμενον. Καὶ καθάπερ τῆς ῥοδωνιᾶς τοῦ ἄνθους δρεψάμενοι τὰς ἀκάνθας ἐκκλίνομεν, οὕτω καὶ ἐπὶ τῶν τοιούτων λόγων ὅσον χρήσιμον καρπωσάμενοι, τὸ βλαβερὸν φυλαξώμεθα. Εὐθὺς οὖν ἐξ ἀρχῆς ἐπισκοπεῖν ἕκαστον τῶν μαθημάτων καὶ συναρμόζειν τῷ τέλει προσῆκε, κατὰ τὴν Δωρικὴν παροιμίαν, τὸν λίθον ποτὶ τὰν σπάρτον ἄγοντας. For classical parallels to the simile of the bees see the commentary by Naldini 1984, 166–7.
53 Cf. also Gregory of Nazianzus in his oration on the late Basil in ad 381: Gregory of Nazianzus, *Orations* 43.11; 13.
54 Strikingly, Basil seems to consider the outspoken pagan elements such as anthropomorphic gods as non-essential components of the texts. Basil, *Address to the Young* 5.27–8.
55 Basil, *Address to the Young* 3.11–18: Λέγεται τοίνυν καὶ Μωϋσῆς ἐκεῖνος ὁ πάνυ, οὗ μέγιστόν ἐστιν ἐπὶ σοφίᾳ παρὰ πᾶσιν ἀνθρώποις ὄνομα, τοῖς Αἰγυπτίων μαθήμασιν ἐγγυμνασάμενος τὴν διάνοιαν, οὕτω προσελθεῖν τῇ θεωρίᾳ Τοῦ ὄντος. Παραπλησίως δὲ τούτῳ, κἂν τοῖς κάτω χρόνοις, τὸν σοφὸν Δανιὴλ ἐπὶ Βαβυλῶνός φασι τὴν Χαλδαίων σοφίαν καταμαθόντα, τότε τῶν θείων ἅψασθαι παιδευμάτων. ('Now it is said that even Moses, that illustrious man whose name for wisdom is greatest among all mankind, first trained his mind in the learning of the Egyptians, and then proceeded to the

100 *Jan R. Stenger*

contemplation of Him who is. And like him, although in later times, they say that the wise Daniel at Babylon first learned the wisdom of the Chaldaeans and then applied himself to the divine teachings.') See Acts 7:22.

56 Basil, *Address to the Young* 2.26–47. Plato, *Republic* 515e–16b. For further Platonic reminiscences in this passage see the commentaries of Wilson 1975, 42–4 and Naldini 1984, 149–55. Döring 2003 highlights the indebtedness of Basil's thoughts on the use of literature to the Platonic tradition.

57 The simile of the dyers is again a Platonic allusion; cf. Plato, *Republic* 429d–30b.

58 In *Address to the Young* 8.54–6 Basil makes no secret of the fact that the ultimate goal of Christian education is a mystery that cannot be communicated through words.

59 See e.g. Johnson 2012, with further literature.

60 This is clearly pointed out by Rousseau 1994, 53.

61 Basil, *Address to the Young* 8.1–43, where Basil repeatedly highlights that in every serious effort you must have the attainment of the end in view.

Part III
Protreptic

7 Christian Hagiography and the Rhetorical Tradition

Victricius of Rouen, *In Praise of the Saints*

Peter Gemeinhardt*

Introduction: Should Rhetoric Be Applied to Saints and Holiness?

Late antique Christianity was deeply indebted to classical culture and education, as was already noted in Late Antiquity itself and later confirmed by modern research. From the very beginning, recognising this debt provoked the question whether this heritage may consciously and willingly be utilised by Christian writers, e.g., for preaching, exegesis or clarifying theological questions. I just mention in passing the outspokenly critical stance of Tertullian and the comprehensive educational programme of Origen's 'one-man university' in Alexandria and Caesarea as two extremes within a multitude of positions already in the second and third centuries AD. This debate, which was intensely conducted at the turn of the fourth to the fifth century by prominent theologians such as Basil and John Chrysostom as well as Augustine and Jerome,[1] involved a broad variety of literary genres, including hagiographical writing. While the relationship between hagiography and (literary) education has mostly been investigated with respect to the *Lives* of saints,[2] other (sub-)genres of hagiographical discourse have hitherto been widely neglected.[3]

Hagiography was an increasingly important part of late antique Christian literature, since the stories about early Christian martyrs and about contemporary ascetics, virgins and bishops contributed fundamentally to the construction and communication of role models for true Christian life. While most earlier martyr acts and passions – with notable exceptions such as the *Passion of Perpetua and Felicity* – do not betray significant literary ambitions, the so-called hagiographical discourse of Late Antiquity freely employed classical genres, topics and rhetorical strategies. Sometimes, this forced the hagiographers to reflect upon their practice; and in many cases – like, e.g., Sulpicius Severus in the preface to his *Life of Martin of Tours* – they rejected classical education as inadequate, or even dangerous when writing the life of a saint (in contrast to, e.g., depicting an ancient hero). Other authors, such as Prudentius, did not care for such issues of legitimacy and used their literary skills for the praise of the saints. The relationship between programmatic

104   *Peter Gemeinhardt*

prefaces and actual narratives of *Lives* of saints, which would sometimes turn out to be a real hiatus, deserves a systematic investigation. The result would most probably reflect the general observation that late antique writers more or less explicitly made use of what they had learned at school, whether they acknowledged this debt or not.[4] There are, however, qualifications which depend upon the concrete martyr or saint: The 'illiterate' Martin has to be praised without any rhetorical decorum, as Sulpicius Severus argues, while the eminently cultured bishop Hilary of Arles (d. 449) is honoured with a splendid biography which stresses his abilities as an orator and thus as a worthy spokesman for the Word of God.[5]

Writers such as Sulpicius have attracted much interest, and rightly so, since they are fine examples of what Averil Cameron has termed the Christian 'rhetoric of paradox'.[6] Yet, the many hagiographers who were not at all concerned with apologising for their manner of writing but consciously made use of their rhetorical skills equally deserve our attention. Among them, Victricius – bishop of Rouen from c. 380 or 386 – is an interesting case in point, though widely neglected by scholars of Late Antiquity. The exception in recent times has been David Hunter, author of an instructive paper on the debate about asceticism, celibacy and the cult of relics in late ancient Gaul, published in 1999.[7] It discusses Victricius and his relic piety as criticised by Vigilantius, who in turn was refuted by a very upset Jerome. While I agree with Hunter's account of the conflict over ascetic practice and the cult of relics in Gaul, I will not pursue this aspect further, since Vigilantius' criticism was not aimed at Victricius' literary skills but at his theology of relics.[8] It should, however, be mentioned that, if Hunter is right, Victricius appears as a figure as influential as he was controversial in Gaul around AD 400,[9] being one of the few bishops who were friends with Martin of Tours, as Paulinus of Nola and Sulpicius Severus report.[10]

Only one treatise of Victricius has been preserved, a sermon entitled (in modern research, though not in the manuscripts) *De laude sanctorum*, 'In Praise of the Saints', which is actually considered 'the earliest extant sermon from Gaul'.[11] This highly elaborate speech was delivered on the occasion of the translation of martyrs' relics from Milan to Rouen in the year 396. The main part of my chapter will be devoted to a close reading of this text in order to elucidate how classical rhetoric is employed for the praise of the saints arriving at Rouen.[12] After examining the use of topoi of imperial rhetoric for the sake of hagiography, I will turn to Victricius' demarcations of classical and Christian rhetorical discourse and then analyse how the church itself is depicted as a place of learning: the bishop not only praises the deceased saints but also exhorts the living Christians to imitate the saints. Summarising, I will briefly return to the more general question of how the rhetorical tradition became an integral part of Christian hagiographical panegyric, and thus situate Victricius' speech within the overarching question concerning the relationship of education and religion in Late Antiquity.[13]

Imperial Rhetoric in Christian Guise:
How to Welcome the Saints

As is well known, the practice of translating relics of martyrs from their graves outside the cities to new resting places in churches *intra muros* emerged in the middle of the fourth century AD. Despite imperial edicts forbidding such transfers of corpses (or parts of them), Ambrose of Milan introduced this practice to the West when he brought the relics of Gervasius and Protasius to the 'Basilica of the Apostles' in 386.[14] Apparently he soon started to equip other churches in the West with holy articles, sending relics also to Rouen in 396.[15] The veneration of the martyrs' bodily remains would now support the memory of their sufferings: 'The saints come a second time to the city of Rouen; long ago they entered our heart, now they frequent the church of the city.'[16]

In his sermon, Victricius made considerable efforts to point out how the saints can be present in heaven as well as in Rouen (and in many other places of the Christian world, too). The argument is quite sophisticated,[17] but in short it goes as follows: from Adam on, all people share the same human substance, thus there is 'one body of all human beings'.[18] Analogously, 'for those who live in Christ and the church there is one substance of flesh and blood and spirit, by the gift of adoption'.[19] Within this unity of baptism, constituted by the 'bond of a constant confession',[20] the apostles and martyrs undoubtedly have already earned 'perfect and absolute concord'.[21] Since they have already ascended to the throne of Christ (as had been believed since the time of Tertullian), they share not only blessing, knowledge and wisdom with the Saviour, but also concorporeality and consanguinity.[22] Though this proximity of the saints and the godhead may already be questionable, Victricius goes even one step further: since this consubstantiality with the Trinity can never be conceived of as divided or incomplete, it is present in every fragment of a martyr's body, that is, every relic is divine by adoption.[23] It is thus not the mimetic relationship to the very body of the martyr which renders a scattered fragment of a human being holy (as, e.g., in the second-century *Martyrdom of Polycarp*).[24] Instead, as Patricia Cox Miller has summarised Victricius' view:

> a dead body no longer functioned primarily as a record of human living but rather as a material artifact whose referent lay outside itself in a spirituality that demanded sensory expression for its abstract belief in conduits of divine presence.[25]

Therefore, it is not the single particle of a deceased human being that merits veneration – which would appear idolatrous (an accusation which Vigilantius introduced in the early fifth-century debate, earning him a polemical refutation by Jerome).[26] Victricius clarifies that the martyrs and apostles are 'bound to the relics by the bond of all eternity'.[27] They thus form together a community of participants in the salvific narrative, stretching out from Jesus Christ's death and resurrection to eternity, but being actually present in the life and worship of the church. In turn, it is not only the individual martyr with his specific merits who is to be welcomed in the city, but also the martyr as part of this communion and as participant in divine life.[28] This being so, Victricius concludes that 'our apostles and martyrs have come to us with their powers intact'.[29] Their acquired divinity is wholly present in Rouen.

This theological assessment of the divine power which is present in relics is unique in Late Antiquity and would deserve further discussion, especially with regard to later developments since Victricius has at times been called the 'father of the medieval relic cult'.[30] Be that as it may, what is of interest for the question of education and religion in Late Antiquity is the rhetorical shaping of the welcome address for the martyrs in Rouen. At the very beginning of his sermon, which was most likely given in the cathedral of Rouen with the receptacles containing the relics visible to the faithful, Victricius points out that the Christians of Rouen who have not experienced any persecution themselves will greatly benefit from having the saints with them as visitors and even fellow citizens of their city: 'See, a very great part of the heavenly army deigns to visit our city, so that we are now to live among throngs of saints and renowned celestial powers.'[31] In what follows, Victricius repeatedly applies elements of an imperial *adventus* to the relics arriving in Rouen.[32] The notion of *adventus* itself is employed several times: Victricius speaks of 'the arrival of your majesty'[33] and points out that 'a number of soldiers and kings have come to us from the camp of heaven'.[34]

Victricius had been a soldier himself, and the story of his attempt to leave the Roman army which brought him near to martyrdom is narrated by Paulinus of Nola, apparently modelled on the respective episode from the *Life of Martin of Tours*.[35] So Victricius knew well what was required of the participants in an *adventus* ceremony, when he himself included a panegyric addressed to the high-ranking guests.[36] Accordingly, he apologises for not having welcomed the saints outside the city but only 'at the fortieth milestone',[37] since he had been in Britain at the request of fellow bishops 'in order to make peace'.[38] Nothing more is known about this mission, but Victricius makes it clear that he is an obedient soldier of the saints and their *apparitor*, that is, 'a member of their official staff who is under their orders'.[39] The saints themselves have obtained their position like claimants to power from the emperor: 'Whoever raises the standard of the holy confession seizes from worthy givers the power which brings salvation.'[40]

Being a soldier of Christ under the command of the saints not only involves the bishop of course, but also his entire flock. The rhetorical setting of the imperial *adventus* assigns an important role to the many people who are said to participate in this ceremony: 'See, all ages pour out to serve you, each one strives to surpass the other in zeal for religion.'[41] Victricius himself compares the arrival of the relics to the visit of 'one of the princes of this world'.[42] Accordingly, as Clark points out, the saints are 'welcomed by an aristocracy of clergy and ascetics and then by the people as a whole'.[43] This distinction is also visible in the structure of Victricius' sermon: not all inhabitants of Rouen are equally prepared to welcome the saints, since not everyone is, in a spiritual sense, a 'known and veteran soldier' who has been 'tested over time in duty to you, purged of vices, proved by hard work and watchfulness'.[44] Only people who conduct an ascetic life are fully entitled to hasten to meet the martyrs. There is however an important qualification: while members of the imperial house would be adorned with clothes and jewellery in order to mark their secular rank,[45] ascetics do not display their spiritual rank by splendid clothes. 'Here no one's cloak emits a blaze of purple',[46] Victricius declares, alluding to a verse of Virgil's *Aeneid* that would have been familiar to everyone sharing in the literary culture of Late Antiquity.[47] And he continues: 'Human concerns are despised where divine concerns are taken into account.'[48] The ornaments of monks and virgins, celibate clergy and widows are spiritual ones. And thus 'the throng of the chaste is the joy of the saints'.[49] Only after them the crowd of the faithful appears: 'Hence, in short, is the one feeling of the entire people towards your majesty.'[50] All of them will 'prostrate on the ground' and 'bow down',[51] and they will do so according to their social and spiritual ranks, as it is mandatory at the arrival of an emperor, and by this *adventus* they will also make public their political and religious *consensus*.[52]

In sum, Victricius' rhetorical performance creates an imperial *adventus* for the saints. The victims of persecution become addressees of a panegyric. But, one might ask, is it actually legitimate to praise the saints in such a manner?

Orandum, non Perorandum: How to Praise the Saints

We are not well informed about Victricius' education, but his style, his knowledge of the discourse of imperial rhetoric and the few classical quotations and allusions with which he sprinkles his sermon indicate that he had received a similar education to that of Augustine.[53] He also participated, if only marginally, in another discourse of Late Antiquity, namely on the legitimacy of applying grammatical, rhetorical and dialectic methods to religious texts. Victricius therefore had to face the question whether imperial rhetoric should be employed at all when praising the saints. Obviously, Victricius did in fact adopt this very rhetoric, but only with several characteristics that mirror what Averil Cameron has termed the 'rhetoric of paradox' of Christianity in Late Antiquity.[54] In this section, I will take a close look at a few illuminative passages.

In his sermon, Victricius struggles with the question of the lasting presence of the deceased saints in their relics which are, as I mentioned above, consubstantial with mankind on the one hand and even with God on the other. The divinity of the relics is present as a whole in each part: 'They do not inflict loss upon themselves by their own dissemination, but being endowed with unity, they distribute benefactions.'[55] Thus, relics are media of divine presence within the world in a manner not unlike sunlight: 'Before the day of judgement, the radiance of the righteous pours into all basilicas, all churches, the hearts of all faithful.'[56] Victricius anticipates criticism of such comparisons, and points out that the sun is only an image of the 'heavenly principle'. The latter is 'taught, not compared; conveyed, not presented with rhetorical decorum'.[57] Now the sun as a classical image for God is nothing more than a hint of God's unlimited power. If He made the world from nothing, He would also be able to turn flesh and blood into divine substance. Ascending from the created to the creator by virtue of images from creation 'draws out the poison of the dialecticians'.[58] Victricius concludes, that is, that critics of comparisons of God with nature are silenced by what is evident to every believer.

Victricius advocates a 'realistic' view of relics, as it were: for him, relics were not merely signs but rather divine entities within the world. By calling blood and clay 'relics', they receive 'the seal of living language'. The word 'relic' represents a reality which is accessible to 'the eyes of the heart'.[59] Victricius postulates that 'the ambushes of language be removed, and thing war with thing, reason with reason' – an allusion to Cicero's *Pro Caelio*, quoted a few years before in Augustine's *De utilitate credendi*.[60] Language should no longer obscure the real difference between the statements 'This is a piece of bone' and 'This is the power of God'.[61] The faithful must resist the dialectician's claim that words constitute reality; it is just the other way round.

Victricius himself, however, does make use of dialectic when defining relics by *species* and *genus*: relics are not simply remains, but remains *of something* – that is, of human beings, conceived of as animate substances united with God by baptism. Since the notion of 'animate substance' includes 'sentient flesh and blood', relics are by definition 'remains of flesh and blood united with God'. God is always complete, and the whole is implicit in the parts; therefore the martyr's acquired divinity is present in any part of his body.[62] This theological argument is evidently based upon Porphyry's 'Introduction to Aristotle's *Categories*', which represents a classical piece of dialectic argumentation.[63] Despite Victricius' own claim that 'I am not tied to hypothetical and categorical syllogisms; the empty sophisms of philosophers do not deceive me',[64] one of the manuscripts of his sermon from the tenth century contains the following note from a later hand: 'He demonstrates by dialectics that the saints are entirely in the relics.'[65]

As mentioned above, David Hunter has identified the opponent with Vigilantius, a critic of such an account of relics. In any case, Victricius argues against people who are not ready to perceive more than merely 'blood and clay'. This, he complains, is not appropriate when dealing with holy matter: the latter requires fear, not knowledge.[66] It is clear what his opponents lack:

> The faithless malice of the doubter questions this [*sc.* that relics are identical with divinity in genus and species and number] – or perhaps not the doubter but the one who does not love. Indeed, when I grasp the whole matter by faith, I think superfluous questions should be dismissed for now: they require sight, not investigation![67]

It is thus not permitted to enquire into the mysteries of divinity. Instead, 'he who loves believes, and he who believes examines the faith of disputant and priest, not their words'.[68] Victricius does not deny the importance of *ratio* for theological inquiry, but he specifies it as a *ratio* guided by Scripture.[69] Insofar as dialectic help to elucidate Scripture, it is legitimate to use them; and it is obvious that Victricius refers to Porphyry's *Isagoge* in rejecting his opponent's claims to language and logic. But, in his own words, he argues 'by simple faith, not by words; by worship, not by arguments; by reverence, not by curiosity'.[70] With these demarcations, Victricius takes part in the over-arching debate concerning the possibility and legitimacy of pagan education for Christian theology, an observation that might add a new perspective to Hunter's account of the debate with Vigilantius: not only is the veneration of dead bodies as holy relics at stake, but the debate also touches upon the question whether a dialectic approach is appropriate for spiritual matters. By employing Aristotelian logic to clarify the case of the total presence of divine power in every fraction of the bone of a deceased saint while at the same time refuting an 'empiricist' approach based upon the logic of human language and on sober judgement from the visible, Victricius participates in the 'rhetoric of paradox' mentioned above: he makes use of non-Christian techniques of argumentation while claiming a special theo-logical *ratio* for matters of faith. In doing so, Victricius actually anticipates medieval debates on the Eucharist. His sermon concludes: 'It is not eloquence which is needed here, but the pure simplicity of happiness.'[71] Or, to put it even more briefly, 'what we need is prayer, not peroration'.[72]

Teaching Sanctity: How to Imitate the Saints

There is, however, something else that Christians urgently need besides prayer: they need a teacher. To the best of my knowledge, Victricius' sermon has not yet been scrutinised under the perspective of Christian education, although it is obvious that the bishop presents himself as the teacher of his flock.[73] And this might well offer another possibility of contextualising his treatise.

Victricius' lifetime is a period in which Christian homiletics flourished, at first in the Greek East – there are numerous homilies on biblical texts as well as on martyrs, e.g., by Basil of Caesarea and Gregory of Nyssa, not to mention the vast number of homilies and sermons delivered by John Chrysostom – and then in the Latin West as well. It should suffice to mention Ambrose of Milan and Augustine, but also less prominent figures like Gaudentius of Brescia or Zeno of Verona.[74] The history of late antique Latin preaching has still to be writ-ten. Many of these sermons have catechetical purposes, yet the aim of teach-ing is not definitive of this genre. Victricius' sermon, however, displays several textual signs that reveal the author's intention: 'for the sake of instruction' he employs an 'easy and familiar example' like the sun in order to elucidate the omnipresence of divine power in the relics.[75] This doctrine 'we proclaim with all our faith and authority';[76] thus the bishop claims to provide answers to the 'riot of questions' with which he has filled his book, i.e., his present sermon.[77] And when referring to his recent stay in Britain which caused the delay of

110   *Peter Gemeinhardt*

his welcome to the saints, Victricius describes the task he fulfilled in terms of missionary teaching:

> I instilled in the wise the love of peace, I lectured on it to the teachable, I instructed the ignorant, I constrained the unwilling, insisting, as the Apostle says, 'in season and out of season' (2 Tim 4:2); I reached their souls with teaching and touching.[78]

With these only superficially modest remarks Victricius posits himself as a successor to the Apostles, by referring not to his bishopric but to his duty as a teacher. Bishop and teacher are, however, not to be separated (unlike in previous centuries when both tasks were often conducted by different persons, as is visible in Rome as well as in Alexandria).[79] In his sermon, Victricius devotes a whole chapter to a central catechetical topic, that is, to the explanation of the belief in the triune God, based upon a creedal text of uncertain origin.[80] Strikingly, the quotations from this text do not include the *communio sanctorum* as in the contemporary formulas which Rufinus of Aquileia and Niceta of Remesiana refer to.[81] But precisely the notion of communion with the martyrs as fellow citizens in Rouen and as friends and advocates in heaven is central to Victricius' argument.

Hence, the martyrs are not only to be venerated but also to be imitated: they are themselves imitators of Christ[82] and, like Christ himself, 'brought death to death'.[83] But they also show the path of truth in an age that has not experienced persecutions and executions by emperors:[84] 'They teach reverence, faith, wisdom, righteousness, courage, concord, self-control, chastity';[85] and by doing so, they display not only mercy but also their 'concern for teaching'.[86] Therefore the saints are the actual teachers whom the bishop follows with his instruction, not only with words but also with deeds, as he had previously demanded from the dialecticians. His journey to Britain testifies that the bishop was ready to instruct and to suffer for his message, and the arrival of the saints provokes his teaching:

> If I could have been silent in so great a crowd of people rejoicing, I should have incurred a charge of sadness: the apostles and martyrs are coming, it is not proper for the bishop to be silent. The altars are being erected; let the people take the lead from the joy of their priest.[87]

Thus, teaching includes the communication of knowledge of the Creed and of the correct understanding of the martyrs' presence in their relics, as well as the exhortation to imitate them and to celebrate their coming. Victricius, who seizes the occasion of the martyrs' immigration into his city as an opportunity to instruct his flock about the martyrs' achievements, is himself acknowledged by his contemporaries not only as a priest but also as a 'living martyr' – that is, as Paulinus of Nola puts it, as a teacher (*magister*) by word and life.[88] Education is thus more than an intellectual reflection: it is an initiation to a Christian way of life, and in Victricius' sermon we can observe the continuity of the martyrs as role models as well as a significant transformation of this 'Leitbild'.

Conclusion: Christian Hagiography and the Tradition of Rhetoric

The present chapter has investigated Victricius' reception of classical and imperial rhetoric in order to praise the saints. The question of his significant and controversial theology of the relics, which Gillian Clark has termed a 'cultural translation' of what was really significant about the relics ('leftovers') and blood of the martyrs,[89] has been taken into account only insofar as Victricius applies his rhetorical abilities to it. Here we observed demarcations against rhetoric and thus a paradoxical stance.

This 'rhetoric of paradox' is, however, more than just a clever manoeuvre to win over pagans with their own weapons or to refute Christian heretics by allocating them within the pagan camp. As mentioned above, the question of how to praise the saints appropriately posed a real problem to late antique Christian writers (even if they were not charged with continuing the polytheistic Greco-Roman cult by venerating the dead).[90] When surveying the various attempts to justify the reception of school training for writing on holiness,[91] it becomes clear that Victricius must be counted among the authors who make use of their literary skills in a more or less outspoken way, e.g., by referring to the rhetoric of imperial *adventus*. This is certainly due to his audience, which consisted of the faithful of Rouen, not of critics of the Christians. He thus composed not an apologetic but an encomiastic speech, a protreptic piece urging its listeners to become imitators of the saints, therewith departing from his assessment of the efficacy of the martyrs' relics themselves.

In doing so, Victricius participated in the ongoing debate on the true imitation of Christ in an increasingly Christianised society. While his answer may appear conventional on a basic level – the imitation of the martyrs had already been recommended in the *Martyrdom of Polycarp* in the second century, and had most recently been applied to post-Constantinian Christianity by Athanasius in his *Life of Antony* – depicting the saints as fellow citizens and welcoming them rhetorically like emperors and princes was truly an innovation. The insistence on the bodily presence of the saints, which has dominated the references to Victricius in modern research – be it the survey of theological debates in Gaul by David Hunter, be it the history of the cult of relics as told by Arnold Angenendt[92] – has, however, to be modified according to the argument presented above: Victricius is not primarily interested in the relics themselves but in the martyrs as intercessors in heaven and role models on earth. He thus belongs in the hagiographical discourse of Late Antiquity and its, so to speak, 'semiotic' view of saints as signs of the presence of divine power within the world. If this is correct, then Victricius' definition of words as 'images of signs of things'[93] also justifies his employment of rhetoric, dialectic and quotations from Virgil: the

112 *Peter Gemeinhardt*

elements of pagan education, used in a conscious manner, are apt to describe the belief in the saints, and even in the triune God.

Notes

* The present chapter was written during my time as Associate Fellow of the Lichtenberg-Kolleg – the Göttingen Institute of Advanced Study. Its elaboration has greatly profited from discussions within the Kolleg, as well as from collaboration with my colleagues at the Courant Research Centre 'Education and Religion from Early Imperial Roman Times to the Classical Period of Islam' (EDRIS) at the University of Göttingen.

1 The following remarks equally apply to Greek and Latin Christian writers. In order to set the scene for the analysis of Victricius' speech, which is the focus of this chapter, I confine myself to examples from Latin literature and theology. For an introduction to the whole subject, see Gemeinhardt 2015.

2 See, e.g., Gemeinhardt 2007, 246–306.

3 To speak of a hagiographical *discourse* instead of a *genre* has been introduced by Van Uytfanghe 1988. The central issue in this terminological shift is the impossibility of defining such a genre with any precision. As Van Uytfanghe convincingly argues, there are many genres communicating hagiographical issues; moreover, there are similar discursive strategies in ancient paganism and Jewish religion. Thus, hagiographical discourse is a much more complex field than earlier debates about the applicability of classical biographical patterns to (Christian) lives of saints have suggested. Going beyond Van Uytfanghe's approach, one should also include questions of time, space and community in the investigation of constitution, construction and communication of holiness in Late Antiquity; see Gemeinhardt/Heyden 2012.

4 This is argued in detail in Gemeinhardt 2007.

5 See Gemeinhardt 2011, 93–4 (Martin) and 99–104 (Hilary); the latter's hagiographer is not known with certainty, though Honoratus of Marseille (fl. c. 480) has a considerable number of supporters in recent research.

6 Cameron 1991.

7 Hunter 1999, esp. 421–9.

8 Surprisingly, Victricius does not figure prominently in Hartmann 2010, who provides a survey of the employment of material remains for purposes of pious memory, ranging from classical Greece to Late Antiquity (cf. esp. ch. 6: 'Von Athen nach Jerusalem: neue Erinnerungen in alten Formen', 593–660). Victricius is only referred to as one of the protagonists of Hunter's article (Hartmann 2010, 263 n. 1300).

9 Cf. Clark 2001, 173: Victricius 'preached not only for a (perhaps puzzled) congregation in Rouen, but also to counter more widespread theological and secular opposition'.

10 Paulinus of Nola, *Epistula* 18.9; Sulpicius Severus, *Dialogi* 3.2.

11 Hunter 1999, 422; cf. Demeulenaere 1985, 57.

12 My analysis thus converges with the assessment of Clark 2001, 173: Victricius 'shared with his cleverer contemporaries, Ambrose and Augustine, a standard education in late-antique rhetoric and philosophy, and he used that training to make relic-cult intelligible and acceptable in a familiar discourse'. There are, however, more details to be discussed than Clark does; see especially my section below on the church as a place of learning.

13 I am indebted to the concise paper on Victricius' sermon by Clark 2001 (and also to her translation of this text, see below). Previous studies on Victricius' life and career include Andrieu-Guitrancourt 1970, Musset 1975 and Fontaine 1982, while the most elaborate accounts remain Vacandard 1903 and Mulders 1956/57. Victricius' relationship to Paulinus is referred to by Mratschek 2002, esp. pp. 167–8 (Victricius leaving the army), 541 and 577–8 (Paulinus, *Epistula* 37 where he complains that his correspondent did not visit Nola when travelling to Rome). A critical edition of *De laude sanctorum* is provided

by Demeulenaere in CCL 64, drawing upon Mulders' unpublished doctoral dissertation (Saint Victrice de Rouen, son *De Laude Sanctorum*. Texte et commentaire, Rome, Gregoriana, 1953). The translations into English follow Clark 1999, without indicating minor modifications. I have also compared the translation by Buc 2001.

14 For the invention and translation of the relics of Gervasius and Protasius to the newly erected 'Basilica of the Martyrs' (Basilica Ambrosiana) see Dassmann 2004, 150–54. The development of the relic cult since the second century and the state of legal issues in the fourth century are succinctly summarised by Clark 2001, 162–6.

15 Victricius seems to have been aware that Emperor Theodosius had forbidden any such translations in February 386 (*Codex Theodosianus* 9.7.17), and explicitly claims the 'right to move' relics (*ius translationis*): *De laude sanctorum* 9 (84.36).

16 *De laude sanctorum* 2 (72.16–17): *Bis ad Ratomagensem sancti ueniunt ciuitatem: dudum nostrum pectus intrarunt; modo celebrant ecclesiam ciuitatis.*

17 Cf. Clark 2001, 174: 'Its blend of dialectic and exegesis is typical of fourth-century theological debate, but it is both compressed and under-developed.'

18 *De laude sanctorum* 7 (79.13): *omnium hominum unum corpus.*

19 *De laude sanctorum* 7 (79.14–16): *sequitur ut in Christo et in ecclesia uiuentibus pari argumento unam beneficio adoptionis et carnis et sanguinis et spiritus credamus esse substantiam.*

20 *De laude sanctorum* 7 (80.24): *glutino perseuerantis confessionis.*

21 *De laude sanctorum* 7 (80.24–7).

22 *De laude sanctorum* 7 (80.40–41).

23 *De laude sanctorum* 9 (83.30–84.31): *Nos autem id tota fide et auctoritate clamamus, in reliquiis nihil esse non plenum.*

24 See *Martyrium Polycarpi* 18.3: The surviving fragments of the burnt body of the martyr-bishop which were collected by the Christians of Smyrna will from now on function to preserve and inspire the memory of Polycarp.

25 Miller 1998, 126.

26 Jerome, *Contra Vigilantium* 5 and *Epistula* 109.1. See Miller 1998, 125.

27 *De laude sanctorum* 11 (88.49–50): *In reliquiis igitur sunt totius uinculo aeternitatis adstricti.*

28 Cf. Miller 1998, 126.

29 *De laude sanctorum* 9 (84.34–35): *apostolos martyres que nostros integris ad nos uenisse uirtutibus.*

30 The uniqueness of Victricius' assessment of the theology of relics is also stressed by Clark 2001, 174. It is significant that Victricius does not address the cult of the deceased martyrs itself, which was highly controversial in Late Antiquity, since it attracted popular forms of piety which were in turn denounced by the bishops; for this issue see my recent paper on 'Volksfrömmigkeit' (Gemeinhardt 2013b).

31 *De laude sanctorum* 1 (69.11–13): *Ecce maxima pars caelestis militiae nostram dignatur uisere ciuitatem, ut iam nobis habitandum sit inter turbas sanctorum et inclitas caelitum potestates.* According to Bastiaensen 1996, 182–3, Victricius reckons the apostles and martyrs saint-like, since he adheres to the idea first attested in Tertullian that the deceased apostles and martyrs are not waiting for the Last Judgment in a kind of interim zone, but are already dwelling in heaven. For the emergence of this perception of the martyrs' fate see Gemeinhardt 2010.

32 For an analysis of *De laude sanctorum* in this respect see Gussone 1976, and for the reception of the imperial *adventus* in Latin hagiography Brown 1981, 95–101. For the late ancient *adventus* ceremony in general see MacCormack 1981, 17–61.

33 *De laude sanctorum* 5 (78.38): *aduentus uestrae maiestatis.*

34 *De laude sanctorum* 12 (90.49–50): *Cum igitur nobis e caelitum castris tantus militum et regum numerus aduenerit.*

35 Paulinus of Nola, *Epistula* 18.7; cf. Sulpicius Severus, *Vita Sancti Martini* 4.

36 See Fontaine 1982, 21.

37 *De laude sanctorum* 1 (70.30–31). See MacCormack 1981, 21; Gussone 1976, 128.

38 *De laude sanctorum* 1 (70.26–7).

39 *De laude sanctorum* 1 (71.51): *apparitor.* The quotation is found in Clark 1999, 371.

114 Peter Gemeinhardt

40 *De laude sanctorum* 7 (81.58–9): *Rapitur enim a dignis salutare imperium, quisquis extulerit sacrae confessionis insigne.* Cf. Clark 1999, 386 n. 114. The same image is alluded to in *De laude sanctorum* 12 (90.65).

41 *De laude sanctorum* 2 (72.17–19): *Ecce omnis aetas in uestrum funditur famulatum, alter alterum uincere studio religionis insistit.* See MacCormack 1981, 21.

42 *De laude sanctorum* 12 (89.15).

43 Clark 1999, 368.

44 *De laude sanctorum* 3 (73.1–5): *Huc accedit quod plus Dominum ueretur cognita et inueterata militia . . . Talis igitur, talis circa officium uestrum tempore exploratus, uitiis exantlatus, labore et uigiliis adprobatus miles occurrit.*

45 *De laude sanctorum* 12 (89.27–32).

46 *De laude sanctorum* 3 (74.29): *Nullius hinc indumentum tyrium uomit ardorem.*

47 Virgil, *Aeneid* 4.262: *Tyrioque ardebat murice laena*; see Clark 1999, 378 n. 65. The 'Tyrian purple' is also referred to in *De laude sanctorum* 12 (89.19), together with another allusion to Virgil's writings (*Georgica* 2.461–2).

48 *De laude sanctorum* 3 (74.31): *Sordent enim humana, ubi diuina pensantur.*

49 *De laude sanctorum* 3 (74.37–8): *Gaudium sanctorum est turba castorum.* In *De laude sanctorum* 5 (76.8–10), Victricius exhorts the 'holy and inviolable virgins' to chant and 'in your choirs dance on the paths which lead to heaven' (*Vos quoque, sacrae inuiolatae que uirgines, psallite, psallite, et choreis tramites quibus ad caelum ascenditur pede pulsate*). Dance and song belong to the imperial *adventus*, too (see MacCormack 1981, 51); but to view dancing as a legitimate liturgical practice is quite unusual in late ancient Christianity (see Gemeinhardt 2013c).

50 *De laude sanctorum* 3 (74.41–2): *Hinc denique totius populi circa maiestatem uestram unus affectus.*

51 *De laude sanctorum* 6 (77.27–8); 12 (88.2).

52 See Brown 1982, 247 (with n. 100 on Victricius).

53 Clark 1999, 370, who, however, remarks that 'Augustine, like Ambrose, expounds technical theology with far greater precision than Victricius'. Andrieu-Guitrancourt 1970, 16–19 reckons Victricius a highly competent theologian with respect to the Trinity, but (in my view) exaggerates his point.

54 Cameron 1991.

55 *De laude sanctorum* 9 (84.37–9): *non ipsos sibi inferre propria disseminatione iacturam, sed spargere beneficia unitate ditatos.*

56 *De laude sanctorum* 9 (82.1–3): *Haut aliter, carissimi, ante diem iudicii in cunctas basilicas, in omnes ecclesias, in omnium denique fidelium pectus iustorum splendor infunditur.*

57 *De laude sanctorum* 9 (83.9–10): *Caelestis ratio docetur, non conparatur; insinuatur, non ornatur.* Clark renders *ornatur* as 'elaborated', but this does not sufficiently express the aesthetic dimension of rhetorical decoration implied by *ornari* since Cicero's time. Cf. the translation by Buc 2001, 42, which is more a paraphrase of the short and concise Latin sentence: 'A concept of the celestial is not acquired by comparison; it is taught. It is a subject one suggests indirectly, not one which one adorns (with attributes).'

58 *De laude sanctorum* 9 (83.11–13): *unde saepe dialecticorum uirus eliditur.* See Clark's commentary on this difficult passage (Clark 1999, 389 n. 130).

59 *De laude sanctorum* 10 (84.3–6): *Id nos reliquiarum nomine, quia aliter non possumus, uelut uiuidi sermonis inpressione signamus. Sed nos nunc totum in parte dicendo non corporalium luminum obices, sed cordis oculos aperimus. Non enim res uerbis, sed uerba seruiunt rebus.*

60 *De laude sanctorum* 10 (84.6–85.7): *Vnde amotis sermonum insidiis, res cum re, ratio cum ratione confligat.* Cf. Cicero, *Pro Caelio* 22; Augustine, *De utilitate credendi* 3 (CSEL 25, 6 Zycha).

61 Cf. Clark 1999, 392 n. 142.

62 *De laude sanctorum* 10 (85.7–15). My rendering of Victricius' argument owes much to the subtle interpretation provided by Clark 1999, 392 nn. 142–4.

63 It is an exaggeration that Buc 2001, 31 states: 'Victricius makes heavy use of Christian Neoplatonism'.

64 *De laude sanctorum* 11 (87.23–4): *Non me hypothetici et categorici syllogismorum nodus intricat, non inania philosophorum sophismata decipiunt.*

65 Quoted in Clark 1999, 391 n. 140.

66 *De laude sanctorum* 11 (87.19–20): *Non enim scire prodest, sed timere.*

67 *De laude sanctorum* 11 (87.30–33): *De quo ambigit infida calumnia dubitantis, nec dubitantis fortasse, sed non amantis. At uero cum rem totam fide teneam, superuacaneis supersedendum interim reor: sed uidenda, non quaerenda!* Cf. already *De laude sanctorum* 2 (72.12): *Operari libet, non libet loqui.*

68 *De laude sanctorum* 11 (88.55–6): *Qui amat, credit. Qui credit, fidem in disputatore et sacerdote, non uerba rimatur.* See Andrieu-Guitrancourt 1970, 18.

69 *De laude sanctorum* 7 (79.1–4, 13–16). Cf. *De laude sanctorum* 10 (86.36–7).

70 *De laude sanctorum* 11 (88.57–9): *Siquidem nos uidebit librum simplici fide exarasse non uerbis, cultu non argumentis, ueneratione non curiositate.*

71 *De laude sanctorum* 12 (89.25): *Non hic eloquentia quaeritur, sed laetitiae pura simplicitas.*

72 *De laude sanctorum* 12 (90.43): *nobis orandum est, non perorandum.*

73 Andrieu-Guitrancourt 1970, 19 has at least drawn some general conclusions from the literary style of *De laude sanctorum*: 'Que Victrice a pu prononcer ce discours et le publier suppose qu'il avait devant lui des auditeurs assez cultivés pour l'entendre et des chrétiens assez fervents pour le comprendre; ce qui paraît obliger a penser que l'Église de Rouen possédait alors une élite assez nombreuse et, par conséquent, un enseignement régulièrement distribué et distribué avec compétence.'

74 For the latter, see the recent study of Dümler 2013.

75 *De laude sanctorum* 10 (85.22): *Docendi gratia in facili illo peruulgato que persistamus exemplo.*

76 *De laude sanctorum* 9 (83.30): *Nos autem id tota fide et auctoritate clamamus.*

77 *De laude sanctorum* 9 (83.16–18).

78 *De laude sanctorum* 1 (71.41–3): *Sapientibus amorem pacis infudi. Docilibus legi, nescientibus inculcaui, ingessi nolentibus, secundum apostolum, instans opportune, inportune; atque in eorum animas doctrina et palpatione perueni.* Victricius is also renowned as missionary of northern France (see Paulinus of Nola, *Epistula* 18.4; Mratschek 2002, 542–3).

79 See Kany 2009.

80 Westra 2002, 108 n. 27 excludes this text from his inquiry into the early forms and variants of the Apostles' Creed by classifying it as 'a personal formulation of faith which contains several traditional elements'; but see the critical remark of Vinzent 2006, 369 n. 143.

81 See Gemeinhardt 2012b, 398–401 (Rufinus and Niceta) and 405–11 (Victricius).

82 *De laude sanctorum* 6 (76.1); cf. *De laude sanctorum* 9 (84.47–48).

83 *De laude sanctorum* 6 (77.17–18): *Isti sunt uenerandi, isti sunt sancti, qui morti mortem intulere.*

84 Cf. the introductory passage in *De laude sanctorum* 1 (69.2–9).

85 *De laude sanctorum* 8 (82.26–8): *Docent reuerentiam, fidem, prudentiam iustitiam, fortitudinem, concordiam, continentiam, castitatem*; cf. *De laude sanctorum* 6 (77.9–10).

86 *De laude sanctorum* 8 (82.30): *docendi affectum.*

87 *De laude sanctorum* 12 (89.9–12): *Ego si tacere in tanta exultantium celebritate potuissem, crimen maeroris incurreram: apostoli ac martyres ueniunt, antistitem tacere non conuenit. Eriguntur altaria: de gaudio sacerdotis populus sumat exordium.*

88 Paulinus of Nola, *Epistula* 18.3 (*magister*) and 18.9 (*martyr vivus*). Apparently, this letter written c. 398 is the first reception of Victricius' sermon by other Latin writers.

89 Clark 2001, 175.

90 Cf. e.g., the accusations of the Manichaean Faustus against Augustine's parish (*Contra Faustum* 20.4, 21).

91 Cf. the provisional classification introduced in Gemeinhardt 2011, esp. 111–12.

92 Angenendt 2007, with numerous but unsystematic references to Victricius.

93 *De laude sanctorum* 10 (84.1–2).

8 Falsification as a Protreptic to Truth

The Force of the Forged Epistolary Exchange between Basil and Libanius

Lieve Van Hoof[1]

The topic of this chapter is the forged epistolary exchange between Basil of Caesarea (329/330–79) and Libanius of Antioch (314–93). The supposed epistolary exchange between both men consists, in modern editions, of 26 letters. Of these, the first 21 were transmitted together, and in a largely fixed order.[2] The last five letters, on the other hand, seem to have been added to this original corpus at a later stage,[3] and will therefore be of lesser concern to me here.

In modern scholarship on these letters, the focus has been almost exclusively on the question of the authenticity of individual letters. In 1730, Prudence Maran started the debate by questioning the authenticity of two letters,[4] and since then, doubts have been raised concerning the other letters as well.[5] The majority of scholars today, especially those working on Libanius, consider the whole epistolary exchange spurious. Some scholars – mainly, but not exclusively, working on Basil – disagree, and hold some, and by extension more or all of the letters, to be genuine. An excellent overview of the history of the debate and the arguments at play in it can be found in Nesselrath (2010). As a result of his analysis, Nesselrath comes to the conclusion that all of the 21 letters are spurious. Yet even if some of them were to be genuine, the collection as a whole – that is, the group of 21 letters taken together – is clearly a forgery.[6]

For many scholars, the observation that these are not genuine letters is the endpoint of research: if these letters are forgeries, then they cannot teach us anything about the historical figures of Basil and Libanius. The forgery as a whole can, however, teach us a lot about the reception of Basil and Libanius, as well as about the relation between education and religion in Late Antiquity. Richard Foerster and Heinz-Günther Nesselrath have already observed, for example, that these letters document a close relationship between Basil and Libanius, and suggested that the main point of the forgery is to sanction Basil's rhetorical superiority through an admission of defeat by Libanius.[7]

Taking my cue from these comments about the aim and point of the forgery, I leave aside the debate about authenticity and examine, instead, the techniques, contents and effects of the forgery.[8] In order to do so, I shall not limit myself to discussing individual letters, but read the collection as a literary composition in its own right.[9] In the first section of this chapter, I examine the origins of the forgery: when and how, and by what kind of person were these letters written?

Falsification as a Protreptic to Truth   117

After that, I turn to the contents of the forgery: how are Basil and Libanius characterised, and what point is thus being made? In the third section, I look at the effect generated by the forgery. We are, indeed, extremely fortunate in having a late antique witness to how this letter collection was being read. Finally, whilst education and religion will be implicitly present throughout the chapter, the conclusion will explicitly reflect upon what this forgery tells us about the topic of this book.

Searching for the Forger

Whilst forgeries by definition do not disclose their author's identity, the forgery itself as well as other late antique texts enables us to form a quite precise idea of the origins of this text. First, there are several indications as to the milieu in which this forgery originated. Of the 21 letters in the collection, 17 are forgeries *stricto sensu*:[10] they are texts written from scratch by a forger, but under the names of Basil and Libanius. In many of these cases, there are no specific references to any of the genuine letters of Basil or Libanius, and even several linguistic and conceptual errors that, upon careful examination, clearly show them to be forgeries.[11] In a few cases, however, the forger clearly did his best to make these letters look like real Basilian or Libanian letters,[12] for example by referring to specific people and situations that are familiar from Basil's or Libanius' epistolary collections.[13] An even more explicit reference to genuine letters of Libanius can be found in *Letters* 15 and 16, supposedly written by Libanius and Basil respectively, which start with the same words as the genuine Libanian letters 590 and 592.[14] At the same time, *Letter* 16 also contains a verbatim quotation from Basil's *Letter* 48, as well as from Gregory Nazianzen's *Letter* 4, which, incidentally, is addressed to Basil.[15] The forger was thus well acquainted with the letters of not only Libanius and Basil, but also of Basil's fellow Cappadocian Gregory of Nazianzus. This suggests that he was a well-read person, especially in the field of epistolography, and probably a Christian, given his interest in Christian letters alongside pagan ones.

This impression is confirmed in the four letters in the collection that are *falsifications* rather than forgeries in the sense that they re-use existing letters, with only some minor changes, and attribute them to Basil and Libanius.[16] *Letter* 9 is actually the first paragraph of a letter Libanius addressed to Julian, in which Libanius praises Julian for the exceptional rhetorical qualities of the letter he had received from him. By replacing the address to Julian with an address to Basil, the forger transfers Libanius' rhetorical praise from one of late antique Christianity's arch-enemies to one of its main proponents. Apart from the fact that the version to Basil is shorter than the one to Julian, the replacement of κρείττους with κρείσσους, whereas Libanius in all of his oeuvre prefers the former over the latter, clearly shows that the version found in the epistolary exchange is a falsification. Significantly, the forger, when re-addressing the letter to Basil, took over only its first half, thus leaving out the admiration for one of Libanius' speeches which Libanius referred to in the second half of his original letter to

118   *Lieve Van Hoof*

Julian. The three other falsifications, on the other hand, were taken not from the letters of Libanius or Basil, but from the epistolary collection of yet another Cappadocian,[17] Gregory of Nyssa: *Letter* 8, from Basil to Libanius, is Gregory's *Letter* 28.1–3 to an unknown recipient; and *Letters* 13 and 14, which belong together, are abbreviated versions of Gregory's *Letters* 26 and 27. In Gregory's collection, these letters are exchanged between Gregory as a bishop and the sophist Stagirius. If the parallel with the relation between the bishop Basil and the sophist Libanius is clear, the borrowing from Gregory confirms that our forger had an interest not only in Basil's and Libanius' letters, but also in those of Gregory of Nyssa.

This Cappadocian connection is all the more interesting as *Letters* 13 and 14 of Gregory of Nyssa are addressed to Libanius.[18] In *Letter* 13.4 Gregory claims that Basil was, at one point, Libanius' student.[19] It is not entirely certain whether this letter is genuine or a forgery too. If genuine and addressed to Libanius of Antioch, as most scholars seem to assume,[20] then it may have provided an important, maybe even the decisive, clue to our forger,[21] especially since the first letter of Libanius in our collection (*Letter* 2) explicitly refers to Basil's school days in Constantinople, by far the most probable place where a meeting between Basil and Libanius would have taken place.[22] If, on the other hand, Gregory's letter to Libanius was also forged, then what exactly is the relationship between both forgeries? Was the letter ascribed to Gregory based on the supposed epistolary exchange between Basil and Libanius, or was it the other way round? Or did one and the same person forge both?[23] The answer to these questions will probably never be known.[24] But we do know that in 439 Socrates of Constantinople states for a fact that Basil, as well as Gregory Nazianzen, studied with Libanius in Antioch. As a medieval scholiast already pointed out in the margins of Socrates' *Church History*, it cannot be in Antioch that Basil or, for that matter, Gregory studied with Libanius, so Socrates' account is not entirely trustworthy.[25] Nevertheless, given Socrates' historiographic methodology,[26] it seems unlikely that he invented the tradition of Basil as a student of Libanius out of the blue. This suggests that Gregory of Nyssa's letter to Libanius, whether genuine or not, and/or the forged epistolary exchange between Basil and Libanius, is likely to have been circulating by the 430s – that is, less than 50 years after Basil's and Libanius' deaths.[27] If Socrates based himself specifically on our forgery, then 439 is also its *terminus ante quem*; if not, then we have a secure *terminus ante quem* for our forgery in Zacharias Scholasticus' *Life of Severus*, which dates from the early sixth century and which will be discussed in the last section of this chapter.[28]

Yet whatever the precise dating of the forgery, our analysis thus far has shown that the forger was probably a well-read Christian with a particular interest in epistolography and the Cappadocian fathers. The fact that such a man could, in the early or late fifth century, write letters in the name and vein of Basil and Libanius shows that he had an excellent knowledge of both men's letters, as well as of other late antique epistolary authors. The fact that the forgery was not unmasked by his contemporaries might suggest, on the other hand, that not everybody had as thorough a knowledge of them. Yet given the fact that it was only in 1730 that the authenticity of the letters of our correspondence was first doubted, thanks to the application of rigorous philological analysis, and given the fact that some people even today doubt the forged nature of these letters, we should be careful to conclude from the lack of unmasking in antiquity that people had but scant knowledge of the genuine letters of Libanius and Basil. The very fact that our forger thought it worthwhile to write letters under the names of Basil and Libanius, and that he included in his forgery references to real Libanian and Basilian letters, suggests that these letters were widely known.

Forging the Characters

Now that we have an idea of the origin of the letters and the techniques of the forgery, let us turn to the contents of these letters: what point are they making, and how do they try to do this? The most dramatic moment in the correspondence occurs in *Letter* 4, where Libanius recounts how he received a letter from Basil, read it and cried out to his friends who were standing by: 'We have been defeated!' (νενικήμεθα). When his friends ask in what respect he has been beaten, and why he is not distressed about his defeat, he replies: 'I have been worsted in beauty of epistolary style (ἐν κάλλει . . . ἐπιστολῶν). And it is Basil who has gained the upper hand. But the man is dear (φίλος) to me, and on this account I am delighted.' Libanius is thus made to exclaim Basil's superiority in rhetoric.[29] Libanius' judgement is confirmed not only by the assent of his friends in *Letter* 4, who, after reading Basil's letter, agree that Libanius has indeed been defeated by Basil, but also through repeated appraisals of Basil's letters and orations in both comparative and absolute terms throughout the collection.[30] As such, then, the collection emphasises Basil's rhetorical superiority, as Nesselrath and Foerster already pointed out. But by extension, and at least as importantly, it makes the point that rhetoric is by no means the exclusive province of pagans: when it comes to rhetoric, Christians are as good as, or even better than, pagans. Rhetoric is, in other words, 'de-paganised': any intrinsic connections with paganism are denied. Yet the very fact that the forger introduces Libanius in order to sanction Basil's qualities, and thus to substantiate a religiously neutral view of rhetoric, shows how much the pagan rhetor Libanius was still considered the supreme authority in matters of rhetoric in the forger's own days.

As Libanius himself is also praised for his rhetorical qualities,[31] sometimes even in remarkably similar terms (ἔχω τὰ νικητήρια, *Letter* 20),[32] one could think that the forgery emphasises the similarities between both characters. Yet whilst it indeed confirms that Basil could have become a very successful rhetorician like Libanius, it highlights above all the fact that Basil chose to lead a different kind of life:

> For I . . . not only admired you long ago when you were young, when I saw you vying with the old men in sobriety (and that too in the famous city which teemed with pleasures! [*sc.* Constantinople]), and already possessing a

120 Lieve Van Hoof

great share of eloquence. . . . [Y]ou thought that you should see Athens also
. . . But when you returned and dwelt in your fatherland, I said to myself:
'What is our Basil doing now, and to what mode of life has he turned? Is he
frequenting the courts, emulating the orators of old? Or is he making orators
of the sons of wealthy fathers?' But when there came persons bearing the
tidings that you were traversing ways of life far better than these, and that
you were considering how you might become more pleasing to God rather
than how you could amass wealth, I congratulated both you and the Cappadocians, you for wishing to be a man of that kind, and them for being able
to produce such a citizen.' (transl. Deferrari 1934, vol. 4, 287–9, modified)

ἐγὼ γὰρ . . . καὶ πάλαι νέον ὄντα ἡδούμην σωφροσύνῃ τε πρὸς τοὺς
γέροντας ἁμιλλώμενον ὁρῶν, καὶ ταῦτα ἐν ἐκείνῃ τῇ πόλει τῇ ταῖς ἡδοναῖς
βρυούσῃ, καὶ λόγων ἤδη μοῖραν κεκτημένον μεγάλην. . . . ᾤήθης δεῖν καὶ
τὰς Ἀθήνας ἰδεῖν. . . . ἐπανήκοντος δέ σου καὶ ἔχοντος τὴν πατρίδα ἔλεγον
πρὸς ἐμαυτόν· τί νῦν ἡμῖν ὁ Βασίλειος δρᾷ καὶ πρὸς τίνα βίον ὥρμηκεν;
ἆρ' ἐν δικαστηρίοις στρέφεται τοὺς παλαιοὺς ῥήτορας ζηλῶν ἢ ῥήτορας
εὐδαιμόνων πατέρων ἀπεργάζεται παῖδας; ὡς δὲ ἧκόν τινες ἀπαγγέλλοντες
ἀμείνω σε πολλῷ τουτωνὶ τῶν ὁδῶν πορεύεσθαι καὶ σκοπεῖν, ὅπως ἂν
γένοιο θεῷ μᾶλλον φίλος ἢ συλλέξεις χρυσίον, εὐδαιμόνισα σέ τε καὶ
Καππαδόκας, σὲ μὲν τοιοῦτον βουλόμενον εἶναι, ἐκείνους δὲ τοιοῦτον
δυναμένους δεικνύναι πολίτην.

(*Letter 2*, Libanius to Basil)

In his youth, then, Basil got exactly the kind of rhetorical training that Libanius
had enjoyed himself as a student and subsequently provided to students as a
teacher. Whilst Libanius therefore expected Basil to make a successful career as
an advocate or a professor of rhetoric, Basil deliberately opted for a very different kind of life, trying to be more pleasing to God. Basil and Libanius thus
become exempla of different kinds of lives. On the one hand, they have different
professions: whereas Libanius was a sophist (σοφιστής, *Letters* 5 and 14),[33] Basil
became a bishop (ἐπίσκοπος, *Letter* 13). On the other hand, they are guided by
different values: whereas a career as an advocate promises wealth and fame,[34]
Basil is praised for his justice and sobriety.[35] Basil, in other words, converted from
a secular to a sacred life. I use the term 'sacred' in order to emphasise that the
point is not that Basil converted to Christianity – even though baptised only in
357 or 358,[36] he was, in fact, already a Christian – but that he chose to dedicate
his life no longer to rhetoric and its worldly values, but to God and the Church
instead. This conversion to a sacred of life is symbolised in his retreat from the
political (Constantinople) and cultural (Athens) centres of the Empire to his
native Cappadocia, a rather remote part of the Roman Empire, as is emphasised
in *Letters* 15 and 16,[37] but a central one in Christianity for being the birthplace
of the Cappadocian fathers.

Direct characterisation in individual letters, then, presents Basil and Libanius as
being similar in their rhetorical qualities but different in their choice of life: they

Falsification as a Protreptic to Truth   121

are exempla of a sacred Christian and a secular pagan life respectively. Indirect characterisation throughout the collection adds flesh to this skeleton.[38] In particular, it makes clear that although Basil and Libanius are equally good at rhetoric, the value they attach to rhetoric and the place they accord it in their respective lives are very different. Their respective reactions to the praise they receive from one another are illuminating in this respect. The most explicit praise Libanius gets from Basil occurs in *Letter* 19, where, upon reading Libanius' declamation *On the chattering wife*,[39] Basil admires it exceedingly and exclaims: 'O Muses, O Eloquence, O Athens!' Libanius' reaction to this appraisal in *Letter* 20 is telling:

> Now I know that I am what I am called. For since Basil has praised me, I hold the prize of victory over all![40] And now that I have received your vote it is permitted me to walk with swaggering gait, like a braggart who looks with contempt upon all.

This reaction shows two things. First, it shows that Libanius holds Basil's opinion in the highest esteem: whereas other people had apparently already called Libanius the best orator, Basil's judgement is apparently the one in which Libanius trusts most. Secondly, Libanius' reaction reveals how much importance he attaches to praise for his rhetoric: not only will Basil's praise change his behaviour in society – in that he shall henceforth, he jokingly says, walk around full of pride[41] – it is also only thanks to Basil's praise that Libanius knows *that he is what he is being called*, namely the best orator. For Libanius, praise for his oratory is, in other words, essential in the strongest possible sense of that word: Libanius' self-image stands or falls with Basil's praise for his rhetorical qualities.[42]

Very different is Basil's reaction to Libanius' exclamation, quoted above, that Basil has defeated him in beauty of epistolary style (*Letter* 4). Basil's response in *Letter* 5 is twofold. On the one hand, far from revelling in the appraisal, Basil explicitly unmasks Libanius' rhetoric by pointing out that such an exclamation is typical for sophists, who make small things big and big things small.[43] Rather than buying into Libanius' rhetoric, Basil thus takes a step back, questions it critically and spells out its emptiness. On the other hand, Basil confesses that he has turned away from the rhetoric he learned from Libanius a long time ago, and instead now associates with Moses and Elias, 'in meaning true, though in style unlearned' (νοῦν μὲν ἀληθῆ, λέξιν δὲ ἀμαθῆ, *Letter* 5). Libanius, in his response, allows Basil to stick to his new books, yet insists that 'of that which has always been ours and was formerly yours the roots not only remain but will remain as long as you live, and no lapse of time could ever excise them, not even if you should almost wholly neglect to water them'.[44] Whatever he does, then, Basil shall never lose his outstanding rhetorical abilities. This stands in strong contrast to Libanius' description of his own need for practice: in *Letter* 9, he admits that whereas Basil is fluent notwithstanding the fact that he does not exercise himself at rhetoric, he himself could not speak if he did not exercise on a daily basis.[45]

Taken together, then, the point made in these letters is not so much about Basil's rhetorical superiority, but about the value of rhetoric and the place of

122   *Lieve Van Hoof*

rhetoric in one's life.[46] Libanius fully believes in, and dedicates his whole life to, rhetoric. In Basil's 'sacred' life, rhetoric can still have a place; but as he unmasks its emptiness, he no longer considers it the primary aim or a very important aspect of life. The very art on which Libanius' life and esteem hinge is, in other words, merely one of Basil's many assets, and one that he esteems of inferior value at that.

The resulting hierarchical relation,[47] whereby Basil is not only Libanius' equal in rhetoric but also surpasses him in more important respects, becomes especially clear in *Letters* 7 and 8. In *Letter* 7, Libanius reproaches Basil for not writing to him. The cause, he supposes, is that Basil is angry with him. In order to convince Basil to resume his correspondence, Libanius tries to turn against Basil the famous biblical verse from Ephesians 4:26: 'Let not the sun go down upon your wrath.'[48] In the ensuing *Letter* 8, Basil compares Libanius' letter with a thorny rose, but ends by saying that he appreciates both the flower and the thorns, as the thorns make him only long more for Libanius' friendship. So whilst Libanius had tried to hit Basil below the belt by turning his own, biblical teachings against him, Basil responds with a beautiful, almost poetic metaphor – the very kind of metaphor he could have learned with a teacher of rhetoric such as Libanius. The juxtaposition of these letters shows the superiority of Basil over Libanius in two respects. First, it becomes clear that it is not Basil but Libanius who cannot control his anger, for whereas anger makes Libanius write a letter of reproach to Basil, the latter responds in a very polite way. Secondly, the juxtaposition of *Letters* 7 and 8 shows that whereas Basil lives up to both his own Christian and Libanius' rhetorical teachings, Libanius fails to meet the criteria of either: whereas Libanius verges on being impolite by ending his letter on a double imperative to its recipient,[49] Basil not only uses a rhetorical metaphor, but also turns his other cheek to Libanius by stating that the thorns of Libanius' letter only made him long more for his friendship – an implicit reference to the famous passage from Matthew 5:39 in response to Libanius' allusion to Ephesians. By the juxtaposition of *Letters* 7 and 8, then, the forger implicitly but clearly undermines Libanius' authority by having the intradiegetical facts,[50] which the reader can see for himself, contradict him: whereas Libanius reproaches Basil for being irritable, Basil is, in fact, seen to be polite and consistent, whereas Libanius himself appears to be rather irritable. By enabling as well as inviting the reader to draw this conclusion for himself on the basis of the facts he can see, the forger evokes the reader's sympathy for Basil, and antipathy for Libanius.

Reading the Forgery

Almost all scholars who have written on the epistolary exchange between Libanius and Basil quote a sentence from Zacharias Scholasticus' *Life of Severus*, written in the early sixth century, where Zacharias tells the reader that Severus of Antioch (ca. 465–538) praised the correspondence between Basil and Libanius, and especially Libanius' acknowledgement that Basil has defeated him. The aim of scholars in quoting this sentence is twofold. On the one hand, as stated earlier, the *Life*

Falsification as a Protreptic to Truth   123

of Severus provides a secure *terminus ante quem* for our forgery.[51] On the other hand, this sentence shores up the scholarly view that the point of the forgery is to posit Basil as the better rhetorician.

Yet if we expand our scope to include the context in which this sentence occurs, the *Life of Severus* offers, moreover, a unique chance to catch a glimpse of how our forgery was received in Late Antiquity, and what effect it generated. The sentence comes relatively early in the *Life*, at the point where Zacharias is telling how he met Severus when they both studied rhetoric with Sopater in Alexandria. At that point in time, as Zacharias tells us, Severus was completely fascinated with classical rhetoric, and had no eyes for anything but rhetoric. Then comes the passage in which the sentence occurs:

> We were worried at the time that such a sharp intelligence had not yet been held worthy of holy baptism, so we advised Severos to set the Discourses of Basil and Gregory, the renowned bishops, against those of the sophist Libanios whom he admired, along with the rhetoricians of old. Through the rhetorical art that he so loved he might in this way arrive at the views and philosophy of these two men. Having once tasted of writings such as these, he was completely won over: very soon he was praising openly Basil's letters to Libanios, and Libanios' reply to them where he acknowledges that he has been vanquished by Basil, according victory to the letters of the latter. As a result, from that moment on, he submerged himself in the images and thoughts of the famous Basil. My fellow student Menas, who was admired by everyone for his poetry, was led to say – prophetically, as it turned out – that Severos would shine out among bishops just like the holy John who had been entrusted with the helm of the holy Church of Constantinople.
>
> (Zacharias Scholasticus, *Life of Severus* 11
> Kugener; transl. Brock and Fitzgerald 2013, 36–7)

As we learn from this passage, written in the early sixth century, men who would become famous Christian bishops later in life tended to study rhetoric in their youth, just like Basil had done some 150 years earlier. Amongst the rhetoricians they would study, Libanius was likely to occupy pride of place.[52] Given their fascination and exclusive dedication to classical rhetoric, these young men needed – at least from a Christian point of view – to be turned away from rhetoric, towards Christian doctrine and philosophy, as Zacharias' motivations for his reading suggestions make clear ('Through the rhetorical art that he so loved he might in this way arrive at the views and philosophy of these two men').[53] In this process, the epistolary exchange between Basil and Libanius could function as a powerful catalyst. Indeed, *from the very moment* he has read these letters, and *as a result* of doing so, Severus starts reading Christian authors, and in doing so he sows the seeds of his conversion to a sacred and, in his case as well as in Basil's, clerical life, as Menas' comments make clear. Rather than just praising Basil's rhetoric, then, the forged epistolary exchange between Basil and Libanius could function, in Late Antiquity, as a protreptic to conversion from a life dedicated to

124   *Lieve Van Hoof*

rhetoric and worldly values to a sacred life in which rhetoric could have a place, yet would be subordinate to higher values.

How could the forgery fulfil this protreptic function? As we have seen above, the letters evoke the reader's sympathy for Basil. Given this sympathy, Basil could become an exemplum for the reader to follow: just like Basil, who converted from a secular life dedicated to rhetoric to a sacred life in which rhetoric was of lesser importance, the reader, who may be enthusiastic about rhetoric at the moment, can learn to see, through Basil's reactions to Libanius' praise, the hollowness of rhetoric, and choose to live a more sacred life instead, as happened to Severus. If he chooses to live a sacred life, the reader will not have to give up rhetoric completely, but will have to give it a new place and evaluation. Insofar as Basil's letters are instrumental in bringing about the reader's conversion, moreover, Basil is not just an exemplum, but becomes as it were an antitype of Moses and Elias: just as Basil's own conversion is intimately linked, in *Letter* 5, with his reading about Moses and Elias, so the reader's conversion, like Severus', may be brought about by reading about Basil. Far from being the final message of the forgery, then, Basil's excellence in rhetoric is used as a linchpin to turn people from pagan rhetoric over de-paganised and de facto Christian rhetoric to Christian doctrine and a sacred life.

Conclusion

What, then, can we learn about the relation of education and religion in Late Antiquity from the forged epistolary exchange between Basil and Libanius and its reception in Zacharias' *Life of Severus*? First of all, these texts overwhelmingly testify to the huge popularity which rhetoric in general, and Libanius in particular, enjoyed as part of the educational curriculum of pagans and Christians alike well into at least the early sixth century. Intradiegetically, we see the young Basil in the forgery and the young Severus in the *Life* passionately engaged in reading Libanius' rhetoric; extradiegetically, we have a fifth-century Christian who is so well read in the letters of Libanius (amongst others) that he can compose a forgery that will not be exposed until some 1,300 years later.

Secondly, the forgery *e contrario* shows that rhetoric often continued to be perceived as being pagan in character. Although many Christians, including Basil, had long adopted rhetoric and denied any exclusive connection between οἱ λόγοι and τὰ ἱερά, between rhetoric and paganism, the fact that the forger found it necessary to de-paganise rhetoric, and make the point that Christian orators could equal or even surpass their pagan counterparts, proves that many still considered rhetoric to be pagan, or thought that the best rhetorical models were pagans.

In order to counter this continuing attraction of the pagan word, the forgery and the *Life of Severus* show, last but not least, that what is necessary is the Christian word: Basil converts from a secular to a sacred life thanks to reading about Moses and Elias; Severus does the same after reading Basil's letters; and the

Falsification as a Protreptic to Truth   125

reader is invited to follow their examples whilst reading the forged epistolary exchange between Basil and Libanius. This forgery, so we can conclude, was one fifth-century Christian's reaction to the challenge of recruiting elite men, many of whom would have enjoyed a rhetorical education in their youth, for Christianity and the Church.

Notes

1 The main work for this chapter was done during my time as Fellow of the Lichtenberg-Kolleg – the Göttingen Institute of Advanced Study. I sincerely thank Peter Gemeinhardt, the Kolleg, Göttingen University and the German Research Foundation (DFG) for enabling this stimulating period of research. The final version of the chapter was written when I was already working as a postdoctoral researcher at Ghent University, receiving funding from the European Research Council under the European Union's Seventh Framework Programme (FP/2007–2013)/ERC Grant Agreement n. 313153.
2 Cf. Foerster 1927, 205–13. Noticeable exceptions are letters 13 and 14 in several manuscripts of Basil, and letter 7 in Paris. Gr. 1760 of Libanius.
3 Cf. Foerster 1927, 213–30.
4 Cf. Nesselrath 2010, 347.
5 For the popularity of letters as an object of forgeries, see Ehrman 2013, 82–3.
6 Letters acquire additional meanings in the context of their publication as part of a collection. If, however, the 21 letters were conceived together as one forgery, 'there is no question of collection changing the nature of the items collected, or the possible responses to them, for collection, and the collective impression of the whole set, is part of the plan from the outset'. Trapp 2006, 343.
7 Both Foerster and Nesselrath spend about a paragraph discussing the aims of the forger. Foerster (1927, 205) writes as follows: 'Ne consilium quidem, quo haec epistularum mutuarum sylloga (1–21) ficta est, latet. Auctor eius . . . ut eloquentiam christianam Basilii ab ethnica Libanii, si radices quaerantur, non diversam, sed parem, quin etiam superiorem esse ostenderet, non solum artam inter utrumque virum litterarum communionem amicitiamque fuisse, sed etiam a Libanio ipso palmam facundiae Basilio concessam esse fixit.' Nesselrath (2010, 351) is largely in agreement when stating the following: 'Ma se questo carteggio è un falso, perché fu scritto? . . . In primo luogo questo carteggio dovrebbe documentare un legame stretto fra i due autori protagonisti della cultura loro contemporanea; dalle lettere emerge ripetutamente l'alta considerazione che ciascuno di loro aveva della formazione culturale dell'altro. Nello stesso tempo, però, – e questo è il clou – ci si occupa abilmente del fatto che Basilio risulti generalmente un po' superiore, e sopratutto che Libanio riconosca ciò esplicitamente. Lo scopo del carteggio consiste quindi in questo, che il più grande rappresentante della retorica e della cultura greca tradizionale, non cristiana, riconosca formalmente, senza se e ma, la superiorità della nuova *Weltanschauung* rappresentata da Basilio.' Basil's superiority is mirrored in the titles which the collection has in some manuscripts, which invariably present Basil as more honourable than Libanius (τοῦ μεγάλου καὶ σοφοῦ vs. τοῦ σοφιστοῦ, τοῦ μεγάλου vs. no epithet). Cf. Foerster 1922, 572, critical apparatus. For the various motives at play in early Christian forgeries, see Ehrman 2013, 98–105: authorisation (pp. 98–9) and supplementing the tradition (pp. 104–5) are indeed key motives.
8 As stated by Hodkinson (2007, 286): 'For a study of letters as literature, the question of authenticity is not so important (although it would help us to date some letters precisely): far more important is to recognize that many later authors either treat such collections as genuine or do not consider the question of authenticity.'

126   Lieve Van Hoof

9   *Pace* Pouchet (1992, 154), who states that 'nous nous garderons de traiter ces vingt-cinq lettres en cause comme un bloc infrangible, comme si ce "bloc" avait été ainsi constitué depuis les origines, ce qui n'est pas du tout vraisemblable lorsque l'on considère la tradition basilienne de ces lettres'. His ensuing remarks about this Basilean manuscript tradition are based on Bessières' 1923 study of Basilean manuscripts. In his 1927 edition of Libanius' letters, however, Foerster clearly demonstrated the coherence of the original forgery of 21 letters in the Basilean as well as the Libanian tradition. Cf. above, n. 2.

10   For discussion of the terminology, see Ehrman 2013, 30.

11   Cf. Foerster 1927, 203–5.

12   A complete survey of parallels linking the epistolary exchange between Basil and Libanius with other fourth-century letters can be found in Foerster 1927, 199–203, on which this paragraph draws heavily. For various techniques used in processes of falsification, see Ehrman 2013, 121–3.

13   In *Letter* 11, for example, Libanius is made to say that he and Basil often visited Strategius (for a different reading of the text, see Deferrari 1934, vol. 4, 310, n. 2), and that there he asked Basil for lessons about Homer. Strategius is indeed frequently mentioned and addressed in Libanius' letter collection (cf. Bradbury 2004, 257–8), including in a letter where Libanius tells his best friend Aristaenetus how, together with their mutual friend Clematius, he visited Strategius who recited a bit of Homer (*Letter* 430.10). For verisimilitude as a technique of forgery, see Ehrman 2013, 122–3.

14   In itself, the identical but fairly regular opening words (οὐ παύσῃ) of Libanius, *Letter* 590 and the forged *Letter* 15 might well be a mere coincidence; but the fact that two shortly following letters – Libanius, *Letters* 592 and the forged *Letter* 16 – also start with an identical, and in this case less current, formula (λέλυταί σοι τὸ δύσθυμον) may suggest an intertextual allusion in the case of Libanius, *Letter* 590 and the forged *Letter* 15 too. In the case of these two letters in particular, it is interesting that the formula is transposed from a letter which Libanius addressed to the (actively) pagan priest Bacchius to the Christian bishop Basil.

15   Gregory Nazianzen published not only a collection of his own letters, but also of Basil's. Cf. Trapp 2003, 19–20. In Gregory's collection, *Letter* 236 is addressed to Libanius 'the sophist'; yet apart from the fact that the epithet may have been added at a later date, PLRE I 1971, 507 lists at least two persons called Libanius who busied themselves with rhetoric: besides Libanius of Antioch, there was also at least one Galatian rhetor called Libanius, to whom Gregory's letter may equally well have been addressed.

16   For a discussion of falsifications, see Ehrman 2013, 61–7.

17   On the basis of these links with the three Cappadocian fathers, Pouchet (1992, 168–9) concludes that 'la confection de ces cahiers n'a pu se faire, du moins pour la série initiale, que dans le milieu cappadocien le plus proche et de Basile et de Grégoire (*sc.* de Nysse)'. Genesis in a Cappadocian milieu is definitely possible, yet not necessary, especially given the popularity of the Cappadocian fathers in the fifth century. Cf. also Cassin 2012, 131.

18   Again, however, the identity of this addressee is unclear. In her introduction to *Letter* 13 (but not in her general introduction or in the introduction to *Letter* 14), Silvas (2007, 152) is quite cautious: 'This letter is written to an illustrious sophist who is not a Christian. F identifies him as Libanius, the famous master of rhetorical studies at Antioch, though no letter of Libanius to Gregory of Nyssa appears in the Libanian corpus.' Given that Gregory met Libanius in Antioch in 378–79 (cf. Maraval 1990, 194, n. 1 and Silvas 2007, 25 and 42), both men may well have corresponded, and the absence of letters to Gregory in Libanius' letter collection may be due to a deliberate choice on Libanius' part when editing his letters for publication as a collection (for Libanius' editing of his collection, see n. 21 and Van Hoof, forthcoming). As a result, this absence cannot be used as a decisive argument against the possibility that Gregory wrote to Libanius. Yet, on the other hand, it is striking that only the thirteenth-century codex Laurentianus Mediceus plut. LXXXVI (F) identifies the sophist addressed by Gregory as Libanius of Antioch.

19   It is possible that the other letter addressed by Gregory to Libanius (Gregory of Nyssa, *Letter* 14.2–4) may have provided inspiration for the forger concerning Libanius' account

Falsification as a Protreptic to Truth   127

of his receipt and public dissemination of a letter from Basil (*Letter* 4.2–4) – although it must be said that comments on the receipt of letters are a commonplace in ancient epistolography. Cf. Trapp 2003, 36.

20 Cf. Maraval 1990, 194 and Silvas 2007, 25, 42, 152 and 155; but see n. 18.

21 I see two other possible clues. First, there are two letters which Libanius addressed to a certain Basil, though probably not Basil the Great (cf. Foerster 1927, 197–9). Yet the fact that these two letters – which now go under numbers 24 (Libanius, *Letter* 501) and 25 (Libanius, *Letter* 647) of the epistolary exchange – were added to the original forgery only later, and only in a few manuscripts, pleads against their role as a source of inspiration for our forger. Better candidates for this role are therefore the two letters which Libanius addressed to the bishops Amphilochius and Optimus, which Foerster (1927, 188–91) holds to be genuine and which he locates at the end of the collection as numbers 1543 and 1544. In the manuscript tradition, however, these letters were not transmitted together with Libanius' letter collection – a clear indication for the fact that Libanius never intended these two letters to form part of his collection. Instead, they were transmitted separately (albeit sometimes in combination with the genuine letter 1214) and attached, mostly, to letters of Basil, Gregory Nazianzen, Gregory of Nyssa or, in three cases, the epistolary exchange between Libanius and Basil. If Foerster is right and these letters are genuine (as suggested also by Fatouros and Krischer 1980, 467–77), then they were probably found amongst the papers of Amphilochius and Optimus, and may have provided inspiration to our forger. Another possibility, however, is that they, too, were forged, in order to create links between famous fourth-century Christians on the one hand and the greatest contemporary rhetorician on the other.

22 Although *Letter* 2 does not state explicitly that Basil studied *with Libanius*, it strongly suggests as much not only through the stance of the elderly Libanius remembering how, a long time ago, he observed Basil's sobriety and eloquence (*Letter* 2.1–2), but also through his active personal interest in Basil's career after his education (τί νῦν ἡμῖν ὁ Βασίλειος δρᾷ, καὶ πρὸς τίνα βίον ὥρμηκεν, *Letter* 2.3) and through Basil's reference to what he has learned from Libanius (εἰ γάρ τι καὶ ἦμεν παρ' ὑμῶν διδαχθέντες, *Letter* 5.5). As for the location where Basil would have studied with Libanius, *Letter* 2 speaks about 'the famous city which teemed with pleasures' (ἐν ἐκείνῃ τῇ πόλει τῇ ταῖς ἡδοναῖς βρυούσῃ, transl. Deferrari 1934, vol. 4, 289) – in all probability a reference to the new capital Constantinople. See also Maraval 1990, 198, n. 2 and 2006, 109, n. 3. Nesselrath (2009, 13), following Petit (1957, 118 and 124–9), suggests that Basil and Libanius met in Nicomedia; yet whereas Libanius (340/41–42/3 and 348/9–53/4) and Basil (348 or 349) were both in Constantinople in 348/9, a stay in Nicomedia is attested for Libanius (ca. 344 to 349) but not for Basil. For a chronology of the life of Basil, see Fedwick 1981, 5–19, esp. 5–6; of Libanius, see Wintjes 2005, esp. 81–97.

23 The same or another forger also composed a letter addressed by Libanius to John Chrysostom, and, if not genuine, letters addressed by Libanius to the bishops Amphilochius and Optimus. On the letter to John, see Foerster 1927, 194–7; on the letters to Amphilochius and Optimus, see n. 21.

24 Another possibility, of course, is that Socrates, Gregory and/or the forger of the epistolary exchange between Basil and Libanius are based on a now unknown source; yet in any case, the tradition about Basil studying with Libanius must have been circulating by 439.

25 Cf. Maraval 2006, vol. 2, 109, n. 3.

26 On Socrates' methodology, see Van Nuffelen 2004, 223–42. This makes it unlikely that the letters discussed were forged in order to provide documentation for Socrates' statements – as was the case for several other late antique forgeries. Cf. Ehrman 2013, 104–5.

27 According to Speyer (1971, 105), the fact that the epistolary exchange between Basil and Libanius is an early forgery explains why it was so hard and took so long to discover it. As Ehrman (2013, 82–3) notes, some famous letter-writers were already the subject of

128 *Lieve Van Hoof*

forgeries during their own lifetime. Yet there are no arguments whatsoever that would suggest that this was the case with Basil or Libanius.

28 As all these examples illustrate, Libanius, no less than the Church Fathers, had a very rich *Nachleben*. On the reception of Libanius, see Nesselrath 2012, 118–35 and Nesselrath and Van Hoof 2014.

29 It should be noted, however, that Libanius' appraisal of Basil may be less unique or impressive than it may seem at first sight, as admissions of, and joy at, rhetorical defeats are a topos in Libanius' letters. See e.g. Libanius, *Letter* 1236. Also, in *Letter* 20 of our collection, Libanius will claim victory for himself.

30 Basil praised in comparison to others: *Letters* 6 (refutation of Basil's denial of his victory); 9 (Basil needs no training whereas Libanius does); 13 (Basil surpasses other bishops in eloquence); 18 (Basil so excellent at rhetoric that Libanius fears that his declamation will not be good enough for him). Basil's rhetorical skills praised in absolute terms: *Letters* 2 (Basil already showed great rhetorical skill at a young age); 7 ('your all-golden tongue', τῆς παγχρύσου σου γλώττης); 21 (praise for Basil's sermon 'Against Drunkenness').

31 Basil praises Libanius for his λόγοι ('eloquence', 19); λόγων καὶ παιδεύσεως ('eloquence and learning', 1); σου τὴν ἐν τοῖς λόγοις ἀρετήν ('excellence in eloquence', 17); τῆς σαυτοῦ δόξης, ἣν ἔχεις ἐν τοῖς λόγοις ('reputation in eloquence', 3); and characterises him as a σοφιστής ('a sophist', 5, 14) and τῆς ἀσκήσεως διδασκάλῳ ('a master of training', 1). Libanius thus appears as an excellent and famous orator and teacher of rhetoric. Thanks in part to the huge popularity which the epistolary exchange between Basil and Libanius enjoyed from the fifth to at least the eighteenth century, this is a familiar image of Libanius, which has recently been put in the spotlight again by Cribiore 2007b. Yet it is definitely not the only possible image of Libanius: Libanius himself – for example, in his *Autobiography* and other speeches – takes pride in his political activity in the face of various emperors and governors; and Eunapius, who is otherwise not always very positively disposed towards Libanius, confirms that Libanius 'had also a talent for administering public affairs' (ἱκανὸς δὲ ἦν καὶ πολιτικοῖς ὁμιλῆσαι πράγμασι, Eunapius, *VS* 496). Basil, however, limits himself to praising Libanius' rhetorical qualities. This strict focus of Basil's praise for Libanius is underlined in the very first letter, where Basil's praise for Libanius' 'eloquence and learning' is juxtaposed with his praise of another man as having 'won a great reputation among us for uprightness of life (βίου) and civic power'. Basil thus minimises Libanius' social impact and represents him instead as a teacher of rhetoric.

32 On this passage, see above, p. 121.

33 For Basil's characterisation and labelling of Libanius, see above, n. 31.

34 Wealth: *Letters* 2 and 14; fame: see above, p. 121.

35 Justice: *Letter* 11; sobriety: *Letters* 2 and 12.

36 Cf. Fedwick 1981, 6.

37 Whilst Libanius, in *Letter* 15, speaks disparagingly of the rustic character of the Cappadocians, albeit in jest, Basil, in *Letter* 16, takes pride in exaggerating the caricature.

38 For the difference between direct characterisation, i.e. the explicit mentioning of character traits, and indirect characterisation, whereby the reader is invited to infer character traits from deeds or words displaying it, see Rimmon-Kenan 1983, 59–67.

39 The fact that Basil praises Libanius for a school declamation rather than for any public oration again confirms the characterisation of Libanius as a teacher of rhetoric. Cf. above, n. 31.

40 With this exclamation, Libanius contradicts his earlier admission of defeat at the hands of Basil, which the wording here clearly calls to mind (νενικήμεθα – ἔχω τὰ νικητήρια).

41 Cf. already Basil's address to Libanius as 'you who make a parade (ἐμπομπεύοντι) of your declamations' in *Letter* 14.

42 It is telling, in this respect, that of the 20 instances in the letter collection where praise is explicitly mentioned, 17 occur in letters written by Libanius, against only three in

Falsification as a Protreptic to Truth 129

letters by Basil: praise is obviously an important issue for Libanius, but much less so for Basil.

43 *Letter* 5, Basil to Libanius: Τί οὐκ ἂν εἴποι σοφιστὴς ἀνὴρ καὶ σοφιστὴς τοιοῦτος, ᾧ γε ἴδιον εἶναι τῆς τέχνης ὁμολογεῖται καὶ τὰ μεγάλα μικρὰ ποιεῖν, ὅτε βούλοιτο, καὶ τοῖς μικροῖς περιτιθέναι μέγεθος. ('What would a sophist not say, and especially a sophist the peculiar quality of whose art is, as all men agree, the ability both to make great things small, whenever he so wishes, and to invest small things with greatness; I mean precisely the sort of ability that you have displayed in respect to us?' [transl. Deferrari 1934, vol. 4, 297]).

44 *Letter* 6.6, Libanius to Basil: βιβλίων μὲν οὖν ὧν φὴς εἶναι χείρω μὲν τὴν λέξιν, ἀμείνω δὲ τὴν διάνοιαν, ἔχου, καὶ οὐδεὶς κωλύσει· τῶν δὲ ἡμετέρων μὲν ἀεί, σῶν δὲ πρότερον αἱ ῥίζαι μένουσί τε καὶ μενοῦσιν, ἕως ἂν ᾖς, καὶ οὐδεὶς μήποτε αὐτὰς ἐκτέμῃ χρόνος οὐδ' ἂν ἥκιστα ἄρδῃς. ('Nay, rather stick to your books, whose style you say is inferior, though their substance is superior, and there is no one to prevent you. But of that which has always been ours and was formerly yours the roots not only remain but will remain as long as you live, and no lapse of time could ever excise them, not even if you should almost wholly neglect to water them.' [transl. Deferrari 1934, vol. 4, 303]).

45 *Letter* 9, Libanius to Basil: Εἰ ταῦτα γλώττης ἀργοτέρας, τίς ἂν εἴης αὐτὴν ἀκονῶν; σοὶ μὲν γὰρ ἐν τῷ στόματι λόγων οἰκοῦσι πηγαὶ κρείσσους ναμάτων ἐπιρροῆς· ἡμεῖς δὲ εἰ μὴ καθ' ἡμέραν ἀρδοίμεθα, λείπεται τὸ σιγᾶν. ('If this your letter comes from a tongue that has grown lazy, what would you be should you whet it? For in your mouth indeed dwell fountains of words, more powerful than the onrush of streams; if we, on the other hand, be not watered daily, naught is left but silence.' [transl. Deferrari 1934, vol. 4, 307]).

46 Basil's *Address to Young Men on Reading Greek Literature* addresses the different issue of how Christians should read classical, i.e. non-Christian literature, and is addressed at a public studying with the grammaticus rather than the rhetor. Cf. Kaster 1988, 77–8.

47 That Libanius needs Basil more than the other way round is also clear from the fact that whereas Libanius, in *Letter* 7, had requested that Basil write to him, Basil, in *Letter* 10, leaves Libanius the choice whether to write or not.

48 Libanius' reference to this passage from the Bible – πῶς ἄλλοις κηρύττων μὴ χρῆναι μέχρι δυσμῶν ἡλίου λύπην φυλάττειν αὐτὸς ἐν πολλοῖς ἡλίοις ἐφύλαξας ('how is it that you yourself, although you preach to others that they should not harbour their anger until the setting of the sun, have harboured yours for many suns?') – is one of the clearest indications that the letters are not genuine, as Libanius never alludes to the Bible.

49 *Letter* 7: γενοῦ πρᾷος καὶ δὸς ἀπολαῦσαι τῆς παγχρύσου σου γλώττης ('show yourself kindly, and permit me to enjoy your all-golden tongue').

50 Libanius is also made to contradict himself. In *Letter* 2, for example, he praises the Cappadocians, but in *Letter* 15 he disparages them. Or again, in *Letter* 2 Libanius congratulates Basil for not attaching importance to wealth, whilst in *Letter* 13 he reproaches him for being a grasping bishop – a fact that is, moreover, refuted by Basil's generosity in *Letter* 14.

51 Zacharias wrote his *Life of Severus* around 512 in order to counter accusations that Severus would have taken part in pagan sacrifices. These accusations were vented in a pamphlet that was circulated in the wake of the depositions of the pro-Chalcedonian patriarchs Macedonius II of Constantinople (in 511) and Flavian II of Antioch (in 512), for which Severus, who was made to succeed Flavian, had supported the Emperor Anastasius. Cf. Brock and Fitzgerald 2013, 1–26. Other early references and allusions to the text are listed by Foerster 1927, 197 and nn. 1–2. Foerster (1927, 212) also points out that the first and last letter of the collection are used as examples illustrating the letter of praise, respectively the recommendation letter in one manuscript of Ps-Demetrius' *Epistolary Types*.

52 In his biography of Libanius, written less than 10 years after the latter's death, Eunapius states that Libanius' works are widely in circulation (πλεῖστά γε αὐτοῦ περιφέρουσι βιβλία, *Lives of the Philosophers and Sophists* 496). Libanius, then, was a must-read, and, as such, was probably soon included in the educational curriculum in rhetorical schools all

130   Lieve Van Hoof

over the Eastern empire. As Eunapius shows, the letters were often considered to be the best part of Libanius' literary output. According to Eunapius, in his letters Libanius 'rises to the level of the ancient models' (περὶ δὲ ἐπιστολὰς καὶ συνουσίας ἑτέρας ἱκανῶς ἐπὶ τὸν ἀρχαῖον ἀναφέρει καὶ διεγείρεται τύπον, *Lives of the Philosophers and Sophists* 496). A clear indication for Libanius' fame as a letter-writer is the pseudonymous ascription of an epistolary handbook entitled *Epistolary Styles* (Ἐπιστολιμαῖοι χαρακτῆρες), possibly as early as AD 410. Thus Malosse (2004, 44), indicating, however, that this dating is a conjecture.

53 The fact that the correspondence between Basil and Libanius presents a de-paganised interpretation of rhetoric may also have helped Zacharias to do away with accusations that Severus was a pagan in his youth – a point for which several other arguments are adduced in the *Life of Severus*.

9 Scripture and Liturgy in the *Life of Mary of Egypt*

Derek Krueger

Two biblical citations, both fairly obscure, frame the introductory chapter of the *Life of Mary of Egypt*, a work composed in Palestine in the seventh century. The first quotation is from Tobit, the second from the Wisdom of Solomon; neither part of the emerging lectionary system in Jerusalem, and neither much commented upon in the patristic corpus (*Life of Mary of Egypt* 1).[1] The author supplies references: 'Such were the words of the angel to Tobit' and 'as Solomon taught with divine inspiration'. Most likely, his intended audience needed the citational help. By contrast, at the highpoint of the text, the two protagonists – the reformed harlot Mary and the monastic priest Zosimas – engage in a brief liturgical service. She asks him to recite the Nicene Creed ('the holy creed of our faith') and to lead her in the Lord's Prayer, of which the text quotes only the first two phrases. When the prayer comes to an end, they exchange a ritual kiss, and he provides her with reserve sacrament (35): 'And having received the life-giving sacraments, she raised her hands to heaven, sighed with tears in her eyes and cried aloud', the words of Luke 2:29, the prayer of the prophet Symeon upon seeing the infant Jesus in the temple. This prayer, known to Latin Christianity as the *Nunc Dimittis*, was chanted at Cathedral Vespers in the East since the fourth century and assimilated subsequently into the monastic office. Mary recites, accurately, 'Lord, you are now dismissing your servant in peace according to you word; for my eyes have seen your salvation.'[2] This scene, with its prayers, gestures and ritual action, needs no citations. All these elements were deeply familiar to any late ancient Christian who participated, even only occasionally, in the liturgy.[3]

Hagiography can reveal both the extent and the limits of the liturgy as a pedagogical environment in Late Antiquity. The use of biblical quotations, and authors' choices about what to tag with a source and what can be quoted as familiar, reflect authors' expectations about an audience's knowledge. While learned listeners might have intimate knowledge of the corpus of scripture through private study, the average lay Christian – and many monastics – absorbed the Bible primarily, and perhaps exclusively, through lections read out in church over the course of the liturgical year; through sermons that commented on them and applied them to moral formation; and through various prayers and hymns that quoted biblical passages and reworked biblical stories.[4]

Modern textual critics and translators fill the bottom of the pages of ancient and medieval Christian hagiography with biblical citations. Sometimes they supply those references in brackets within the running text, disrupting the visual flow of the text; at other times, their publishers require them to relegate these references to endnotes, a position that scholars generally regard as less desirable. Sometimes the biblical words are italicised or spaced differently from the non-citational text, offering typographical cues that an ancient author re-voices the older, sacred authority. The constant scholarly project of detecting and attesting quotations and echoes of biblical verses and phrases reinforces the generally accurate impression that saints' lives are filled with the language of the Bible and allusions to its stories.[5] Our modern practice both as scholars providing citations and as readers noting them is part of the history of the footnote, and derives in large part from modern, post-Reformation expectations about the centrality of the text of the Bible in Christian life and letters.[6] Late ancient practices, both literary and liturgical, reflect venues other than the Bible itself for the acquisition of biblical knowledge.

Late ancient and medieval Christians inhabited a culture of biblical reference, and indeed the Bible was the primary intertext in the composition of saints' lives, both as a source for quotation and for the typological figuration of later Christian heroes.[7] We assume that catching the reference was one of the *plaisirs du texte* for its premodern audience. Our editorial habit reflects more than the close relationship between hagiography and scripture. But *our* delight lies in detecting traces of a prooftext that we know in a rather different way – as a codex at hand, rather than primarily as a text encountered aurally. Because early Byzantine Christians absorbed their scripture in liturgical settings, when scripture shows up in Christian hagiography, it shows up more often than not untagged in the text itself. Authors seem to slip seamlessly from their own words into the language of scripture and back. The fabric of most hagiographical texts is woven with many biblical strands, likely detectable to many in the audience, but generally not cited. Yet if familiarity with scripture derived in large part from the liturgy, is it possible that hagiography should be seen not merely as participating in a culture of biblical reference, but also in a culture of *liturgical* reference? Is it the case that the primary and implicit intertext for hagiography might in fact be liturgical life itself?

The *Life of Mary of Egypt* provides a particularly useful place to investigate these issues, since in the middle of its narrative it engages again in an early Byzantine version of the footnote, a citation in the text calling attention to biblical quotations – but to rather different effect than in its opening paragraphs. Here, as we shall see presently, the author makes the acquisition of familiarity with the Bible a central theme. Because the text was composed in Palestine, it can be compared with surviving lectionary witnesses that attest late ancient liturgical reading practices in Jerusalem. The text also includes quotations of liturgical prayers and hymns which, while ultimately related to scripture, come to the author and his audience through liturgical participation and apparently need no introduction, including prayers of likely Palestinian

Scripture and Liturgy in the Life of Mary of Egypt   133

origin and a hymn with wide diffusion in the early Byzantine world. Such an investigation situates the rhetorical register of the text within the speech of liturgical life, a type of Byzantine prose that Ihor Ševčenko (1981) associated with the 'middle-style'; we might even say that the *Life of Mary of Egypt* has a churchy tone. The text's hagiographical style maintained continuity with the liturgical environment, and from this register acquired its own ability to teach and persuade.

Biblical Quotation and Biblical Knowledge

The *Life of Mary of Egypt*, ascribed erroneously in the manuscript tradition to Sophronios of Jerusalem, belongs to the wider early Byzantine tradition of stories of penitent harlots that includes the fifth-century *Life of Pelagia* and the sixth-century story of Mary, the niece of Abraham of Qidun.[8] While the authorship is uncertain, the text can be dated securely to the seventh century. In the eighth century, John of Damascus cited the work and Paul the Deacon translated it into Latin. The earliest manuscript dates from the ninth century. The work was very popular and survives in a great many copies.[9]

Within the text, Mary recounts her own story to a monk named Zosimas. She tells him about her 17 years of debauchery in Alexandria, and of her repentance and renunciation after a visit to the Church of the Anastasis in Jerusalem. She also explains how she crossed the River Jordan to spend the next 47 years wandering in the desert. With the exception of her moment of conversion in Jerusalem and a brief visit to pray at the Church of John the Baptist at the Jordan, Mary has spent no time at or near a house of worship. We would say, in modern parlance, that she is 'unchurched'. This point is crucial to the story, since the author wishes to contrast Zosimas's great learning and formation in the monastic life, and his unexamined arrogance, with Mary's simpler and humbler life of extreme ascetic penance.

Compared to other hagiographical works of the period, the *Life of Mary of Egypt* is relatively restrained in its use of biblical quotations. It contains approximately 20 quotations in just under 8,000 words, for a frequency of 2.5 quotations per 1,000, some of these only a few words in a row, many repeating language familiar from the liturgy. Such a pattern indicates a lay and non-elite audience, and not an exclusively monastic one. By contrast we might consider Eustratios the Presbyter's very learned *Life of Eutychios Patriarch of Constantinople*, composed in the capital in the 580s or 590s, with 9.2 quotations per 1,000 words; or Leontios of Neapolis's more colloquial *Life of John the Almsgiver*, Patriarch of Alexandria, composed on Cyprus in the early 640s with 3.9 quotations per 1,000 words.[10] A number of the biblical quotations in the *Life of Mary of Egypt* are embedded in the main characters' own prayers. Twelve of the *Life*'s quotations are from the Old Testament, with three from the Psalms; eight are from the New Testament; some of these are echoes and near quotations, not direct and accurate quotations of biblical verses. Nevertheless, in comparison with other hagiographical works of the period, there is not actually so much

134   *Derek Krueger*

Bible here, even though the author describes Zosimas early on as having 'one ceaseless task, which never ended, namely to sing psalms continuously and always study the scriptures' (*Life of Mary of Egypt* 2).

Imagine Zosimas's surprise when he discovers Mary's familiarity with the Bible! The author writes:

> When Zosimas heard her citing verses of Scripture, from Moses, Job, and the Book of Psalms, he asked her, 'Have you read the Psalms or other books, my lady?' When she heard this, she smiled gently and said to the monk, 'I have not seen another man since I crossed the Jordan . . . nor any beast. . . . So I never learned to read, nor have I heard anyone chant psalms or read [sacred] texts.'

(31)

Note that *our author*, and not Zosimas, has supplied the biblical references that underscore Mary's miraculous acquisition of biblical learning. He has provided his own sort of in-text citation. When one looks back in the text, one sees that Mary has in fact quoted these biblical writings. In her speech immediately preceding Zosimas's question about the source of her knowledge of the Bible, Mary has explained how she lived with very little food and without clothing. She adds prooftexts from the books of Deuteronomy (that is, Moses) and Job: 'For *man shall not live by bread alone* [Deut 8:3], and *because they had no shelter, those who have removed the covering of sin have embraced the rock* [Job 24:8]' (30). She does not note their sources; that is our author's task. Zosimas, of course, hears it as Bible, even if he does not name the specific books. The quotation from Deuteronomy falls in a passage that recalls the Israelites' 40 years of wandering in the desert (Deut 8:3) and is thus particularly apt to Mary's own arid journey. Significantly, Zosimas has asked her whether she needs food or clothing, for she is now naked and has apparently been eating only such wild plants as might be found in the desert. But she explains: 'I receive as inexhaustible food the hope of my salvation, for I feed and cover myself with the word of God [τρέφομαι γὰρ καὶ σκέπομαι τῷ ῥήματι τοῦ Θεοῦ] who governs the universe' (30). God has provided her with divine instruction as nourishment and garment.

The first of Mary's prooftexts, the one from Moses (Deut 8:2), is proverbial – 'man shall not live by bread alone' – and hardly remarkable at this distance. The pericope from Deuteronomy seems to have been assigned to Vespers for Friday of the second week of Lent in seventh-century Palestine.[11] If its biblical source was remembered at all, it may have been much more familiar from the Gospel of Matthew 4:4, where Jesus repeats it parrying the devil in the wilderness, another apt type for Mary's own life in the desert across the Jordan, although, surprisingly, this passage from Matthew does not occur in the extant Jerusalem lectionaries. That the author attributes the tag to Moses, however, as opposed to hearing it merely as a commonplace with a biblical ring to it, probably reflects knowledge available primarily through the monastic study of scripture, rather than a familiarity gained from liturgical readings.

In contrast to the familiar proverb, the passage from Job would ordinarily witness a higher level of book-learning. While the two principal late antique lectionary witnesses assign parts of Job to Lent, Job 24 does not occur in any reading cycle. Apparently the passage was rarely cited in patristic authors through the mid-fifth century.[12] Probably monks alone would have encountered Job 24 during a continuous reading of the text. Both the tag from Deuteronomy/Matthew and from Job reflect a monastic application of the biblical text to their own experience of asceticism in the wilderness.

One must look a fair bit further back in the text of the *Life of Mary* to find her quotation – or rather near quotation – from the Psalms. Four paragraphs previously (by the editor's reckoning), Mary explains what happened after she left Jerusalem and crossed the Jordan: 'So I came to this desert, and since then to this day *I have fled afar off and lodged in this* [desert], *waiting for* my God *Who delivers* those who return to him *from the soul's distress and tempest*' (26).[13] Standing behind this statement is Psalms 55:7–8 (LXX 54:8–9): 'Behold, I have fled far off and lodged in the desert. I await the one who will save me from the soul's distress and tempest.'[14] A comparison reveals that this sentence is more a melding of Mary's utterance with phrases from the psalm than a quotation. Her words exhibit the habituation of the language of the Psalms familiar throughout early Byzantine monastic literature, and perhaps reflect how monks and nuns actually spoke, at least some of the time.[15] Here we can be quite certain that for our author and for the character Zosimas, our male protagonist, knowledge of this psalm derived from regular recitation in the divine office. In various schemes it was also assigned as a fixed prayer to Sext, the mid-day monastic prayer office.[16] If Mary has not been around a church, she should not know it. But this is not evidence for bad characterisation on the part of the hagiographer.

Thus our author 'detects' three instances of Mary 'citing' scripture. One might regard obvious knowledge of three (and only three) biblical verses to be fairly minimal, but within the text it is cause for astonishment. As we have seen, it would suggest that Mary had miraculously acquired knowledge usually derived through study and liturgical prayer within monastic communities. The *Life of Mary* therefore confirms expectations of what one might – or might not – learn either in church or in the course of monastic life: the ability to quote scripture; the ability to meld scripture with one's speech; and the ability to hear such uses of scripture in the speech of others even without a citation in the text. The text plays on the varying levels of scriptural knowledge appropriate to an illiterate woman character who does not attend church; a learned monk who studies the Bible and performs the monastic liturgy; and a clerical authorial voice that not only quotes scripture but also instructs his audience to hear it. In this last instance, the author defines the level of biblical knowledge he expects of his audience – a congregation of listeners constructed to appreciate scripture, but also to need a cleric to alert them to it.

136 *Derek Krueger*

Biblical Echoes and the Classroom of Liturgy

In the *Life of Mary*, the author's citational gestures, his footnotes, do not indicate for the readers and listeners all the quotations in Mary's speech. Elsewhere, uncited by our author and unremarked by our characters, Mary quotes material that would have been familiar to a listening audience from the context of the liturgy. In the course of her narration, Mary tells Zosimas that she had run away from home at the age of 12 to the city of Alexandria: 'For more than seventeen years – please forgive me – I was a public temptation to licentiousness. Not for payment, I swear, since I did not accept anything although men often wished to pay me' (18). In her self-described rapacious lusts, she sought to seduce as many men as possible, 'turning my lust into a free gift' (18). One summer, she hopped on a boat bound for the Holy Land, full of pilgrims going to Jerusalem to celebrate the Feast of the Exaltation of the Cross on 14 September, offering, in her words, '[her] body in lieu of passage money' (19). In retrospect, she registers surprise that 'the sea endured [her] profligacy' and that the 'earth did not open its mouth to draw me alive down to Hell' (20). But as it seemed, 'God sought my repentance, for He *"does not desire the death of the sinner"*', but remains patient waiting for his [or her] conversion [ὁ θεὸς τὴν ἐμὴν ἐζήτει μετάνοιαν; οὐ γὰρ θέλει τὸν θάνατον τοῦ ἁμαρτωλοῦ, ἀλλὰ μένει μακροθυμῶν, τὴν ἐπιστροφὴν ἐκδεχόμενος]' (21; trans. modified). In citing a source for the phrase 'does not desire the death of a sinner', Maria Kouli's English translation invites the reader to compare Ezekiel 33:11.[17] In Rahlfs's edition of the Septuagint (1979), God declares: 'I do not wish the death of the impious, rather that the impious turn back from his way and he live [Οὐ βούλομαι τὸν θάνατον τοῦ ἀσεβοῦς ὡς τὸ ἀποστρέψαι τὸν ἀσεβῆ ἀπὸ τῆς ὁδοῦ αὐτοῦ καὶ ζῆν αὐτόν].' But Codex Alexandrinus contains a variant reading, supplying ἁμαρτωλοῦ ('of the sinner') instead of ἀσεβοῦς ('of the impious'), a reading also found in Theodoret of Cyrrhus's *Commentary on Ezekiel* and in the scriptural commentary tradition, or *Catena on Ezekiel*.[18] The variant would seem to have been influenced by the theological sentiment of 1 Timothy 1:15, that 'Christ Jesus came into the world to save sinners'.

It is quite possible – but uncertain – that the author of the *Life of Mary of Egypt* knows this version of the verse from Ezekiel, a common variant in Byzantine Late Antiquity: 'I do not desire the death of the sinner.' However and significantly, within the story, our author does *not* cite Mary's near quotation from Ezekiel; he cites only Moses, Job and the Psalms. Is it possible that our author does not hear this tag as a scriptural citation? Or, more precisely, is it possible that our author does not regard the phrase 'He does not desire the death . . . of a sinner' as biblical, but more properly as something else?

A more likely proximate source of the tag phrase may lie in liturgical practice. Wording close to Mary's can be found in two set prayers in the earliest surviving Byzantine prayer book, a manuscript known as the Barberini Euchologion (Barberini gr. 336), which dates from the second half of the eighth century, perhaps

Scripture and Liturgy in the Life of Mary of Egypt 137

around 790.[19] The first of these occurs in the rubrics for Vespers, in 'A Prayer of (or probably: over) the Catechumens' to be recited after the Trisagion:

> God, who knows all things hidden, who knows all things before they come into being, who does not desire the death of the sinner, as much as his conversion and life [ὁ μὴ βουλόμενος τὸν θάνατον τοῦ ἁμαρτωλοῦ, ὡς τὸ ἐπιστρέψαι καὶ ζῆν αὐτόν], look from your prepared habitation [Ex 15:17 (i.e. Odes 1:17); 1 Kgs 8:39, 43; cf. Ps 33:14 (LXX 32:14)] upon your servants the catechumens. Open the ears of their hearts to take in the mystery of your only-begotten Son and our God; regenerate them through water and the Spirit [Jn 3:5] to your eternal kingdom.[20]

The second instance of the phrase in the Euchologion occurs in a 'prayer for the soul undergoing judgement', that is, for the soul of someone recently departed.[21] One suspects that the Vespers prayer would have been the more familiar. Nevertheless the occurrence in two places in the prayer book suggests that this phrase 'does not desire the death of the sinner', in accord with the variant reading of Ezekiel 33:11, was a liturgical commonplace by the time of the production of the Barberini manuscript, and could show up in a variety of composed prayers.

Now, it is possible that both of these prayers derive their wording in part from the *Life of Mary of Egypt*, but this is unlikely. The reworking of the verse in Ezekiel (including God's desire for 'conversion' and 'life') is more complete in the Euchologion's examples. Moreover, the Barberini Euchologion should be seen as a single example of a prayer book type that would have been in relatively wide circulation. Miguel Arranz demonstrated that the Euchologion of this type originated in the Eastern Mediterranean, probably Palestine, not in Constantinople, and that many of the prayers in the Barberini Euchologion were composed and in use long before the manuscript's compilation, many in the sixth century.[22] These prayer forms most likely predate the *Life of Mary* and reflect the broader milieu in which the hagiographical text was written. (Indeed one might wonder how many catechumens there would have been to pray over in the eighth century, suggesting that these prayers survive from an earlier period.) It is not even necessary that the author of the *Life of Mary* quote either one of these prayers; only that he quotes this tagline familiar from liturgical practice. It is most likely this liturgical practice that the so-called Alexandrian version of Ezekiel has influenced or been influence by.[23] Here it is as liturgy and not as Bible in some modernist sense that the author slips in a quotation, and thus the author does not supply a biblical footnote. In that sense the tag 'does not desire the death of a sinner' works much as the quotation from the *Nunc Dimittis* that Mary also voices.

A more obviously liturgical borrowing occurs between the liturgical tag derived from the variant to Ezekiel and Mary's quotation of Psalms 55, and here we can be more confident of the chain of transmission. In the courtyard of the Church of the Anastasis in Jerusalem on the Feast of the Exaltation of the Cross, on 14 September, Mary found herself unable to enter the church: 'As soon as I

138   *Derek Krueger*

stepped on the threshold of the door, all the other people entered unhindered, while some kind of divine power held me back, not allowing me to pass through the entrance' (*Life of Mary of Egypt* 22).[24] At first, the source of this 'divine power' is vague; it is unclear what is preventing her entrance. The woman tried again:

> I mingled with other people and pushed with all possible strength, shoving my elbows and forcing myself inside. But I tried in vain . . . from the moment my wretched foot stepped on the threshold [φλιά], though the church received the others without any obstacle, it [the church?] refused entrance to me alone, miserable woman.
>
> (22)

Again, 'some kind of overwhelming power' held her back (22). After three or four attempts she retreated to the corner of the courtyard:

> Only then did I realize the cause which prevented me from laying eyes on the life-giving cross, for a salvific word [λόγος σωτήριος] touched the eyes of my heart, showing me that it was the filth of my deeds [ὁ βόρβορος τῶν ἔργων μου] that was barring the entrance to me.
>
> (23)

This phrase 'the filth of my deeds', is particularly striking. Βόρβορος is a strong word, indicating mud, slime and defilement. The onomatopoetic βορβορυγμός describes intestinal burbling. The single occurrence of βόρβορος in the New Testament signals associations with disgust; 2 Peter 2:22: 'Of them the proverb is true: "A dog returns to its own vomit, a washed sow to wallowing in filth [εἰς κυλισμὸν βορβόρου]"'.[25] Mary has also used the word βόρβορος a bit earlier when judging her life in Alexandria: 'The truth is that I had an insatiable passion and uncontrollable lust to wallow in filth [τῷ ἐν βορβόρῳ κυλίεσθαι]' (18). This may be a close echo of 2 Peter 2:22, or perhaps 'wallow' is just the verb that goes with 'filth'. Within the *Life*, in any case, 'filth' is an intensely negative term of self-directed moral assessment.

Mary's phrase 'the filth of my deeds' reveals more. It is in fact a quotation from Romanos the Melodist's hymn *On the Sinful Woman*, composed in the mid-sixth century and assigned in the manuscripts for performance on the Wednesday of Holy Week.[26] The poem's refrain is τοῦ βορβόρου τῶν ἔργων μου – 'of [or in] the filth of my deeds'. In this hymn, Romanos dramatises the encounter between Jesus and the woman who anointed him at the house of Simon the Leper. In a prelude and 18 stanzas, Romanos expands the narratives in Matthew 26:6–16 and Luke 7:36–50 to imagine the interior life of this biblical harlot and to recreate and enact the conversation among the story's characters. Each stanza ends with the refrain 'of [or in] the filth of my deeds'. Thus the phrase would have been the most familiar words of the hymn, easily memorised and repeated. Performance practice would have reinforced this. The stanzas were sung by the cantor, or *psaltēs*, but the congregation probably joined the choir in the refrain.

Scripture and Liturgy in the Life of Mary of Egypt   139

In his own voice, Romanos admires the sinful woman, who repented and 'with a sob, she said, "Lord, raise me up from/ *the filth of my deeds*"' (*On the Sinful Woman* 3), in contrast to himself: 'But I, though I quail, I remain in/ *the filth of my deeds*' (1). 'The filth of my deeds' thus shifts its voicing through the poem from the narrator to the harlot and back. Those joining in the refrain thus 'sang' alternately the words of the penitent harlot and the recalcitrant narrator, encouraging their own self-formation as sinners in need of divine forgiveness.

The hymns of Romanos apparently circulated widely within a few decades after his death. Papyrus fragments from the late sixth and early seventh century demonstrate the dissemination of his works in Egypt. The *Miracles of Artemios* (18) attests that the hymns of Romanos had become canonical in at least one church in Constantinople in the seventh century. The *Life of Mary of Egypt* should be included among other evidence for the dissemination and popularity of the hymns of Romanos.[27] The *Life* seems to expect the refrain to be familiar. The resonances of the sinful woman for the *Life of Mary of Egypt* are clear. Mary recapitulates the conversion of the sinful woman of the Bible; or, more precisely, Mary recapitulates the conversion of the sinful woman as experienced liturgically, both in the lectionary reading of the biblical narratives of the sinful woman and in the homiletic comment and interpretation of Romanos's hymn. The story of the sinful woman, invoked through liturgical quotation, identifies Mary of Egypt's conversion, repentance and ultimate salvation with a biblical type. Indeed, it was in the pedagogical environment of the liturgy that the *Life*'s audience had themselves learned to identify with the sinful woman.[28]

Conclusion

In the seventh-century *Life of Mary of Egypt*, while the harlot-turned-desert-recluse recounts her conversion from debauchery to renunciation, she quotes scripture, liturgical psalms, a prayer formula and a phrase from a hymn of Romanos the Melodist. These quotations illustrate the degree to which liturgy and hymnography, and not merely the biblical text, provided Christians with their culture of reference. The author and his audience can regard Mary's bookish and monastic quotations from Deuteronomy, Job and the Psalms as truly miraculous, while the tags from the liturgy remain unremarked because, for their seventh-century audience, they were unremarkable, even as they provide a critical intertextual context for understanding Mary of Egypt within a biblical and liturgical world. In contrast to his audience, the author – in his guise as the authorial voice – asserts a greater control over scripture, opening the work with obscure quotations and supplying references to demonstrate superior knowledge. He performs as a pedagogue, maintaining his authority while imparting information. In the process, he contributed a further element to the liturgical repertoire. Although we cannot know the original context for the reading of the work, the setting was likely liturgical as well, most probably on a day to which the commemoration of Saint Mary of Egypt was assigned, or perhaps the Feast of the Exaltation of the Cross.[29] From the eleventh century onwards,

140   Derek Krueger

manuscript evidence assigns the text to be read during the fifth week of Lent, coupled with the chanting of the massive penitential hymn, the *Great Kanon* of Andrew of Crete.[30] The hagiography itself, like much of its genre, functioned as an ecclesiastical teaching text, instilling compunction by example; inhabiting the linguistic register of the Bible and the prayers; and extending the language of the liturgy into the lives of the saints.

Notes

1 Tobias 12:7: 'It is good to keep close the secret of a king, but it is honourable to reveal the works of God.' Wisdom 7:27: '[Wisdom] in all ages enters into holy souls and makes them friends of God and prophets'; although here this action is attributed to 'the grace of the Spirit'. For the lectionary of Jerusalem in late antiquity, see the fifth-century Armenian witness (Armenian Lectionary 1969–71) and the Georgian witness dating to about 700 (Georgian Lectionary 1959–60).

2 *Life of Mary of Egypt* 35; Taft 1993, 45, 274.

3 The regular recitation of the Creed during the Divine Liturgy was introduced by the patriarch Theodore between 511 and 518. Theodore Lector, *Ecclesiastical History* 4.501; Taft 1978, 398–9.

4 Krueger 2014, 24–6, 66–105.

5 See Krueger 2016.

6 Grafton 1997.

7 Van Uytfanghe 1985, 1987; Krueger 2004, 15–32.

8 See Patlagean 1976; Burrus 2004, 128–59; Miller 2005. For the narrative's precursors and fictional character, see Flusin 2004.

9 P.B. Harvey 2004; Kouli in *Life of Mary of Egypt* 1996, 66–7.

10 Krueger 2016; Cameron 1990.

11 The Armenian lectionary, reflecting reading practices in the church in Jerusalem in the fifth century, assigns Deuteronomy 7:11–8:1 to Friday of the second week of Lent and Deuteronomy 8:11–9:11 to the following Friday, apparently skipping the passage with our quotation (Armenian Lectionary 1969–71 pp. 107, 109 [lections 24 and 26]). On the other hand, the Georgian Lectionary, reflecting usage in Jerusalem around 700, assigns Deuteronomy 8:1–9:6 to Vespers on Friday of the second week in Lent (Georgian Lectionary 1959–60 pp. 1, 55–6 [lection 387]). This practice is not observed in the Constantinopolitan lectionary synthesis of the late eighth century represented by the *Prophetologion* and reflected in the tenth-century *Typikon of the Great Church* ([Mateos] 1962–63), which has no readings from Deuteronomy at all during Lent.

12 A search of *Biblia Patristica Online* yields only Gregory of Nazianzus, *Orations* 26, 12.

13 Γέγονα τοίνυν κατὰ ταύτην τὴν ἔρημον, καὶ ἐξ ἐκείνου μέχρι τῆς σήμερον ἐμάκρυνα φυγαδεύουσα, καὶ ἐν ταύτῃ αὐλίζομαι, προσδεχομένη τὸν Θεόν μου, τὸν ἀπὸ ὀλιγοψυχίας καὶ καταιγίδος τοὺς ἐπιστρέφοντας πρὸς αὐτὸν διασώζοντα. *Life of Mary of Egypt* 26.

14 Ps 55:7–8 (LXX Ps 54:8–9): ἰδοὺ ἐμάκρυνα φυγαδεύων καὶ ηὐλίσθην ἐν τῇ ἐρήμῳ. προσεδεχόμην τὸν σῴζοντά με ἀπὸ ὀλιγοψυχίας καὶ καταιγίδος.

15 Burton-Christie 1993; Harmless 2004, 244–7; Krueger 2010; Rönnegård 2010.

16 Basil of Caesarea (*Longer Rules* 37.9) seems already to know the practice of reciting verses from Ps 54/55 at Sext, which later became standard Byzantine practice; Taft 1993, 85–7.

17 *Life of Mary of Egypt* 1996, 81 n. 47.

18 Ezechiel: Ziegler 1978, 1:247.

19 Barberini Euchologion 2000, 19–21.

20 Barberini Euchologion 2000, 9, Prayer 60; cf. Phenix and Horn 2008, 230–31.

Scripture and Liturgy in the Life of Mary of Egypt   141

21 Ibid., Prayer 214. Here the wording of the phase is nearly identical to that in the prayer from the Vespers liturgy (with a present participle βουλόμενος instead of an aorist). We note that this second prayer, for God to release the soul of his servant 'from every bond' and to free it 'from every curse', does not stand among the collection of prayers for the dead which occur later in the manuscript (Barberini Euchologion 2000, 264–9), and thus may not have been tied to a regular liturgy performed in the period after burial.

22 Arranz 1991, 90; cf. Phenix and Horn 2008, 29–30.

23 That said, it is reasonable to assume that the *Life of Mary*'s author would expect his audience to hear the echo of a Vespers liturgy at this point in the narrative. The penitential character of Vespers was already developed before the end of the fourth century, and it is precisely this invitation to penance and assurance of forgiveness that the author wishes to tag. See also Winkler 1975.

24 See also Krueger 2011.

25 See also the Septuagint version of Jeremiah 45:6 (corresponding to the Masoretic Jer 38:6): 'They let him [Jeremiah] down into the cistern. And there was no water in the cistern, but only filth and he was in the filth.' On the conception of filth in antiquity, see Aubineau 1974.

26 Romanos the Melodist [Maas and Trypanis] 1963, 73–9. Compare the anonymous *Akathistos Hymn* 9.13 (Trypanis 1968): χαῖρε, ἡ τοῦ βορβόρου ῥυομένη τῶν ἔργων, 'Hail, she who rescues from the filth of deeds.' The assignment to Wednesday of Holy Week is almost certainly original (Krueger 2014, 41–3; for further background see Barkhuizen 1990; S.A. Harvey 2002). The middle Byzantine Lectionary cycle for Constantinople, where Romanos had written, assigns Mt 26:6–16 to the Mass of the Presanctified Gifts on Wednesday of Holy Week (*Typikon of the Great Church* 1962–63, 2:71). The pericope begins with the story of the sinful woman (6–13) and ends with Judas's betrayal of Jesus to the Chief Priests (14–16). The next episode in the Gospel is the Last Supper (26:17–30); thus there is a certain logic to reading the story of the sinful woman at this point in the calendar. It seems highly likely that the story of the sinful woman was read at this moment of the year from an earlier date and also elsewhere. For Jerusalem, the Armenian Lectionary (fifth century) assigns Mt 26:3–16 to Wednesday of Holy Week (Armenian Lectionary 1969–71, 2:127, lection 37bis); as does the Georgian Lectionary (c. 700) (Georgian Lectionary 1959–60, 1:89, lection 632).

27 Koder 2003; Krueger 2014, 65.

28 For the liturgy's role in encouraging congregants to identify with biblical sinners, see Krueger 2014.

29 P.B. Harvey 2004, 496.

30 Lukashevich 2000; Diakovskij 1913, 167–9; Krueger 2014, 244–5.

Part IV

Secular and Religious Learning

10 How Shall We Plead?

The Conference of Carthage (411) on Styles of Argument

Peter Van Nuffelen[1]

The late ancient Church had a complex relationship with education. Culturally it was a part of the Greco-Roman world and therefore continued to value the forms and ideals of classical education. At the same time, in religious terms, Christianity saw itself in opposition to paganism, the religious outlook of the times that had produced classical education and the associated authoritative texts. It is hence impossible to describe Christianity's attitude to classical education in simple terms of rejection or adoption; depending on the context, the calibration between the two poles could shift and mutate. Moreover, late ancient Christianity was eminently concerned with protreptic and training, symbolised for ordinary believers by the institutions of catechesis and sermon. For that reason, as this volume illustrates, discussions about the right type and use of learning were not restricted to theoretical treatises but can be detected in almost all types of Christian writing. As a consequence, the use of forms of classical learning in Christian texts is often accompanied by a reflection on that use.

This chapter explores one particular instance of this combination of first-order use and second-order reflection: the styles of argumentation used in public debates. Public debates between members of different religious groups were ubiquitous in Late Antiquity.[2] In such a debate, the interlocutors exchanged arguments to determine who defended the truth. As I shall show in greater detail below, such debates were governed by expectations regarding the appropriate type of argument that could be deployed for a particular topic, expectations that, in turn, betray attitudes towards learning. As a starting point, I shall discuss the debate held at the Conference of Carthage (411), the state-sponsored disputation that was to put an end to the conflict between Donatists and Catholics. We shall see that the peculiar organisation of the Conference generated a high degree of ambiguity about the issue that was to be scrutinised, leading to extensive discussions of the way the possible case should be pleaded. Here we can follow in exceptional detail how a precise context generates a second-order reflection on what forms of learning can (indeed, should) be used on a particular occasion.

This chapter makes two general arguments. First, reflections on the appropriate style of argument are integral to late ancient debates and should not be

146   *Peter Van Nuffelen*

misconstrued as wholesale rejections of rhetoric, dialectic or, indeed, debate itself.[3] They are, in fact, one element of what I just called the second-order reflection that accompanies practice. Second, Christians accepted a multiplicity of styles of argument, each related to a particular topic, and which were valued differently depending on the context: one debated, for example, not in the same way with Jews as one did with heretics. Some of these were acknowledged to derive from classical learning, such as philosophical dialectic or forensic rhetoric, whereas others were seen as genuinely Christian. Even if the latter were generally esteemed more highly, these too were not universally applicable but only suited for particular issues. A multiplicity of styles and reflection on their appropriateness thus mark late ancient debates. Using late ancient debates as an example, this chapter suggests that to understand Christian attitudes towards learning in Late Antiquity we should complement models that see certain types of learning as pervasive cultural practices that unavoidably if grudgingly were adopted,[4] by restoring the normative reflections that accompany these practices to their rightful role as shapers of practice.

Ambiguities Exploited

The Conference of Carthage, which opened on 1 June 411, constitutes at least a symbolic end-point in the struggle between Donatists and Catholics in North Africa.[5] Since February 405 strict anti-Donatist legislation was in force.[6] After a brief relaxation, presumably in the spring of 410,[7] Honorius reconfirmed earlier measures in October 410 and accepted, 'moved by a care for peace and kindness' (*studio pacis et gratiae*), the proposition of Catholic bishops to hold a debate (*habitis disputationibus*) 'so that manifest reason can refute superstition' (*superstitionem ratio manifesta confutet*).[8] Such a debate had been often called for by Catholic bishops but studiously avoided by the Donatists, who, under increasing imperial pressure, saw no other option but to accept. A massive group of some 580 bishops gathered. For reasons of objectivity and propaganda, the debate was stenographed. We possess a version edited by a certain Marcellus, of which the end is lacking, which can, however, be reconstructed by having recourse to a summary published by Augustine (*Breviculus conlationis cum donatistis*).

Honorius' rescript created a profound ambiguity in the proceedings of the Conference of Carthage. It was going to be a debate, that is, a free exchange of argument; but, at the same time, it was called by the Roman state and hence organised within the legal framework of the later Roman Empire. In recent years, scholarship has tended to emphasise the legal nature of the Conference, identifying it as a trial according to Roman law.[9] Yet the participants were fully conscious of the ambiguous procedure they found themselves in and exploited the possibilities such a situation offered. Let us briefly look at the two faces of the Conference.

In the late ancient world, a *disputatio* was the normal and normative way to decide religious differences.[10] By normal I mean that public confrontations between members of different faiths were ubiquitous in Antiquity and ranged from disputations between philosophers in the Roman Empire to the confrontation between Christians and Muslims.[11] Their proliferation rests on the belief, also expressed by Honorius, that reason and thus truth will prevail – if the debate is allowed free flow. Debates took place on all levels of society: if disputations between high-profile bishops are best attested, Augustine alludes to debates between neighbours in small towns.[12] By normative I mean that it was seen as proper practice to settle differences first through disputations and not directly through punitive measures such as ecclesiastical excommunication and imperial decrees. So much is implicit in practices of mutual correction attested in the New Testament;[13] in the debate preceding Arius' excommunication by Alexander of Alexandria;[14] and in the striking role played by debates in Justinian's religious policies.[15] As such, disputations had a strongly public and, one could say, propagandistic value. They were often protocolled and circulated to demonstrate how one's opponents had been beaten by sound argument.

Disputations could be informal, in the sense that no consequences would be attached to them, except possible loss of face. This could be bad enough: narratives of debates indicate that the defeated party left the city.[16] As the example of the disputation between Arius and his opponents shows, they could also be part of a formal procedure, possibly leading to excommunication. At the Council of Aquileia (381), the 'Arian' Palladius seems to have expected a debate with Ambrose outside of a legal framework, whereas Ambrose turned the meeting into an ecclesiastical trial.[17] The Conference of Carthage represents, as it were, a next step: just as the Roman state started to criminalise heresies defined by the Church, and, on a less formal level, the emperor could decide to call councils, so disputations could be organised by imperial power and their outcomes subjected to legal consequences – that is, punishment beyond loss of face and excommunication. One should resist the idea that, at least in the fourth and fifth centuries, such state interventions were regulated by clear legal definitions of competences and mutual interaction.[18] So much becomes clear in the ambiguities that state intervention created at the Conference of Carthage.

The Conference of Carthage was not just a debate; its other face was shaped by the Roman legal framework within which it took place. Yet, as I shall argue, the convocation by Honorius and the procedure as implemented by its chairman, Marcellinus, created a specific legal space for a debate to take place without reducing it to a trial. Roman law was used to fence off a space for a supposedly free and fair debate and to implement punishments for the loser. This generated a series of ambiguities.

First of all, the legal form of the proceedings is unclear. Formally, it is usually defined as a *cognitio extraordinaria*, the normal procedure in civil cases in this period. Indeed, the emperor had appointed Marcellinus, *tribunus et notarius*,[19] as *iudex*, and attributed to him coercive powers to summon the participants. The possibility to judge *in absentia* if one side did not show up after three summons and the delay of a maximum of four months between summons and trial bear witness to this.[20] Throughout the protocolled acts, the Donatists raise issues that could occur within a *cognitio*; but precisely the fact that the initiative usually comes from them suggests that Marcellinus did not wish to impose procedural rigour. In fact, notwithstanding the legal similarities, the Conference was not a *cognitio*. Indeed, Marcellinus seems to do his best not to run the Conference as an ordinary trial. He admits that he does not have the capacity to judge bishops[21] and he offers the Donatists the chance to appoint a second judge of their own, an action that is reminiscent of procedure followed during disputations.[22] His summons calls the bishops to hold council, not to present themselves to a trial.[23] In a *cognitio* the judge was usually very active in fact-finding,[24] whereas Marcellinus actually rather holds back. In order to guarantee that all can follow the debates, he organises for a protocol of every session to be published, a protocol that is noted down and countersigned by both parties. Such publication and the desire to make it accessible to a wider public derive from practices in disputations.[25] Moreover, even if one wishes to assimilate the procedure to a *cognitio extraordinaria*, there remains considerable obscurity about what the procedure exactly was. The Donatists tried to present the Conference as a normal trial by suggesting that Marcellinus had not performed the proper *litis denuntiatio*. In this procedure of introduction of trial, the plaintiff addressed a *libellus* to the litigant, usually via the judge, who summoned the litigant by sending him the *libellus* and a summons. The litigant could then reply to the document of the plaintiff.[26] The Catholics had indeed sent a *libellus* to the emperor, who had then called the Conference, but this document had not been forwarded to the Donatists.[27] The latter repeatedly requested to see what they were accused of (and, if they could prove that the Catholics had used false arguments, the entire case should be dropped),[28] but Marcellinus refused, defining the act of the emperor as a *pragmatica rescriptio* to which the *preces* need not be attached.[29] Marcellinus and the emperor thus explicitly sought to avoid setting up the council as a normal legal procedure. Indeed, the reference to the supreme authority of the emperor through a pragmatic sanction, usually used to grant privileges to corporations,[30] seems designed to create a specific legal space for the debate without reducing it to a formal trial.

To add to the ambiguities, the imperial convocation did not hide its *parti pris* for the Catholics, vitiating the objectivity that was at least theoretically expected from a judge. Marcellinus' behaviour shows that he was aware of the peculiar situation he was in. He often referred to the terms of the convocation to indicate that, whilst it imposed certain procedural conditions, the bishops had the freedom to discuss the issue at hand in the way they wished. There clearly was ecclesiastical ground Marcellinus did not wish to step onto; a disputation normally was indeed self-regulating. Even if that ideal was seriously hampered by the mere fact of imperial convocation, Marcellinus strove to create a space where a proper debate could take place.[31]

Most strikingly, Marcellinus did not define what is going to be discussed, that is, what the issue at hand is. Was it a legal matter, namely the question whether Caecilian of Carthage had been ordained in a valid manner and hence whether the Donatists had been legally and properly condemned by previous emperors for crimes committed by their followers? Or was it a theological issue, namely which Church was the real one, living in accordance with the precepts of God? The distinction between both related causes had already been defined by the Catholics,[32] but the issue was raised very soon in the proceedings by the Donatists. It would not go away. Both parties gave priority to the second, ecclesiological issue.[33] The Catholics prioritised the second but refused to let the first drop, even when the Donatists requested that they choose one of either cause.[34] The Donatists, in turn, whilst explicitly expressing their wish to discuss the theological issue, tried to depict the Conference as a legal trial for tactical reasons.[35] They hinted at the Conference being a re-enactment of Christ's trial before Pilate,[36] and would later spread the rumour that the Catholics had bought the judge, as one could do in ordinary legal proceedings.[37] The Donatist argument was that the Conference was not a proper trial but also it served to undercut the anticipated Catholic claim that they had been beaten in a proper disputation. For the Donatists, the Conference was a secular legal procedure about a matter about which the state had no say, and therefore the outcome was rendered invalid.[38] The attempt by the Donatists to have the Catholics admit to being in a secular procedure dragged both Donatists and Catholics into a discussion of the *causa Caeciliani*, even though both desired to focus on the *causa ecclesiae*. Resoundingly beaten, the Donatists afterwards exploited the failure to discuss the *causa ecclesiae* in sufficient detail to question the fact of their defeat.

The seemingly dilatory tactics of the Donatists, who continually raised procedural matters, have sometimes been judged negatively.[39] Yet they exploited an ambiguity in the procedure to the best of their abilities and from a disadvantageous position. Whereas the Catholics wanted to enter the space for disputation granted by Marcellinus, the Donatists continued to draw attention to the fences that surrounded that space. It gave them the possibility to reject the disputation as anything but a staged, pre-judged trial. Such a tactic was only possible within the ambiguous context of the Conference, which was, in the end, a debate organised within a Roman legal framework. This ambiguity was constitutive for the development of the argument and for the strategies of both sides, and we should avoid reducing the Conference to either a debate or a trial.

'Forensic' and 'Legal' Argument

The difference between the two causes to be pleaded was not merely a matter of object, legal or theological: each presupposed a different style and argument. In two instances, the Donatist Emeritus makes the difference explicit:[40]

> But if, leaving aside these issues (which follow the habits of the forum and the ostentation of the debates that tribunals claim for themselves), we

150   *Peter Van Nuffelen*

always need to preserve the legal habit and speech, judge, o sublime man, in a Christian affair.[41]

Quod si, praetermissis istis − secundum forenses fasces iactantiamque illius controversiae quam tribunalia sibi vindicant − , semper legalis nobis ritus ac sermo servandus est, iudica, vir sublimis, in negotio christiano.

An objection to the cause are the words of the judge, namely that one should not follow among bishops forensic use and the habit of brawling and that the cunning of laws and legal debate should lessen when the discussion is about the faith and the whole of the church . . . so that the case can be heard not following the tricks of law and the knots of the oratory of each but according to the New and Old Testament that God created and Christ confirmed.

Causae praescriptio est iudicis sermo, servari forensem usum consuetudinemque iurgandi inter episcopos non oportere, nutare illam versutiamque legum iurisque controversiam, ubi de fidei statu et de totius sanctitatis disceptatione tractatur (. . .) ut non praestigiis iuris neque ligaminibus cuiusque facundiae, sed testamento novo ac veteri quod instituit Deus, quod sacravit dominus Christus, causa possit audiri.[42]

The distinction between the two procedures is described in various ways. Confusing to modern ears but common in patristic use[43] is that the primary way of expressing the distinction is that of opposing *forensis* and *legalis*. 'Forensic' refers to what is outside the Church, but also preserves the reference to the public character of legal proceedings. 'Legal' refers to divine law, not to human, Roman law (even though *lex* often refers to Roman law in the acts of the Conference). It is related to a *negotium christianum* or *negotium ecclesiae*. Tied up with this distinction is that of different types of proof material that can be brought: archival documents for the first, biblical proof texts for the second. In each procedure, different questions are asked: the date of an archival document, for example, is crucial in a forensic procedure but not in an ecclesiastical procedure.

If, so far, the distinction seems fairly factual, it rapidly becomes heavily charged with value judgement. Forensic procedure has a different style of argument: it is rhetorical,[44] cunning,[45] aggressive,[46] boastful;[47] interested in illusion[48] but not in truth.[49] This is contrasted with the honest revelation of the simple truth in an ecclesiastical procedure. Unsurprisingly, this moral valuation is most prominently articulated on the Donatist side. As I have argued, it was in their interest to create the impression that the Conference was a trial, so as to undercut its legitimacy.

Strikingly, for all the negative characterisation of forensic practice, both Donatists and Catholics present themselves as capable of pleading in both modes. The Donatist Petilian, at one point, requests that he is finally informed about the procedure he is in so that he can plead his cause appropriately:

So that I know the nature of the procedure, so that nobody accuses me in public, nobody considers that I am a weak defender of a good cause, nobody considers me devious, a deceitful and unrestrained adversary to whom all is

How Shall We Plead? 151

permitted, just as, when just and clear questions are being asked about these matters, it seems permitted to them in a subtle way to spread clouds and darkness in a way they want so that it impossible to get at the pivot of truth.

noverim genus actionis, nemo me reprehendat in publico, nemo causae bonae infirmum esse iudicet defensorem, nemo iudicet obliquum, nemo adversarium dolosum ac licentiosum cui omnia permittantur, ut, cum de his iusta atque evidentia requirantur, libeat illis delicate quomodo voluerint nebulas ac tenebras obtendere, ut veniri non possit ad cardinem veritatis.[50]

This passage implies that the audience would recognise the difference in mode and appreciate the actions of the pleaders in that context. In other words, it presupposes a high level of understanding of legal and ecclesiastical procedure among the wider Christian audience. Even more obviously, it implies that bishops had sufficient training and practice to be able to switch between the two modes of argument. Their knowledge of the forensic mode of pleading should not surprise us: many bishops, and certainly the ones selected to represent each Church at the Conference, would have had rhetorical training – and some indeed had practised at the bar.[51] Even if they had not received strictly legal training, many bishops would have acquired legal practice through the *audientia episcopalis*, during which secular law would be used. If bishops express themselves on the *audientia episcopalis*, it is often with a singular lack of enthusiasm, but there is no doubt that they spent quite some time engaged in judging cases.[52] The dual competence of the bishops at Carthage is, thus, a testimony to the depths of traditional learning that were still prevalent in this period among upper-level Christians and the extent to which the social role played by bishops in the later Roman Empire made such education unavoidable.

For all the emphasis put on the distinction between the two modes of pleading in the Acts of the Conference, we should not forget that it remains a polemical one: whilst generated by some deeply felt concerns about secular procedure, it cannot be seen as an accurate description of the real difference between a secular and an ecclesiastical trial.[53] So much becomes clear from considering just one aspect: the passages referred to above seem to suggest that the use of dated documents is typical for forensic practice. Yet, many of the cases brought at the councils of Ephesus (431) and Chalcedon (451) about ecclesiastical boundaries and illegitimate ordinations were judged with reference to documents and defended with what amounts to forensic arguments, but they were obviously not secular cases. The distinction made at Carthage was thus polemically charged, especially when used by the Donatists, who sought to undermine the framework within which the debate took place.

The Limits of Forensic Practice

Besides attesting to the multivalence of learning of late ancient bishops, the Acts of Carthage also allow us to reconsider the role played by legal training and practice in the late ancient Church. In several publications, Caroline Humfress

152   Peter Van Nuffelen

has emphasised the role played by forensic rhetoric in late ancient legal culture and in the formation of late ancient law. Her work is part of a salutary trend to shift attention away from a top-down perspective that interprets practice in light of the law to a bottom-up one that sees practice on the ground as a major engine of late ancient legal culture.[54] She has extended her argument also to legal practices of bishops, seeing them as engaging in forensic argument to settle disputes or to define heresy: 'The life of the late Roman church, at least as far as disputes were concerned, was dominated by a culture of forensic argumentation.'[55] Several chapters of her book trace the influence of forensic rhetoric on several aspects of the life of the Church, such as the formation of canon law, the settling of disputes and the definition of heresy. In her brief presentation of the Conference of Carthage, she emphasises the 'showcasing [of] forensic techniques of argument'.[56]

Whilst highlighting an important dimension, such a presentation disregards the explicit distinction that shapes the proceedings at Carthage. The bishops assembled at Carthage saw forensic practice as only part of their activity, and one that they thought about negatively. Even if that presentation is polemical, there remains the fact that there is a realm where forensic argument does not, or is not supposed to, penetrate: that of ecclesiological argument; and one could say, in a wide sense, that of theological argument. It seems that Humfress tends to define forensic argument rather broadly as the general denominator for a style of rhetorical argumentation, which could extend from matters of civil law to heresiological debate. It has already been suggested that this broad definition of forensic argument fails to distinguish usefully between broader rhetorical training and forensic practice,[57] for it is the case that many arguments produced in Late Antiquity are underpinned and driven by rhetorical training, but not all may be by forensic practice.

The Acts of Carthage demonstrate that we should introduce another distinction. It may be the case that all argument, even that based on the Bible, is rhetorical in nature; but it is significant that the bishops at Carthage insist on opposing 'legal' (i.e. biblical) and forensic argument. The distinction reveals, in fact, a more important point than the mere ubiquitous presence of rhetoric: certain styles of argument are thought to be suited for certain types of cause, and this distinction was known by practitioners and audiences alike. In other words, certain modes of argument and learning are appropriate for certain contexts. This diversified approach, caused by a reflection on traditional practices, seems to mark late ancient Christian attitudes towards *Bildung* in general.[58] Interestingly, it makes attitudes towards education part of the argument itself, allowing one to outlaw or stigmatise certain practices because they are perceived to be unsuited or morally inferior. This is, ultimately, a rhetorical move too, but it adds a level of complexity to the discourse that needs to be taken into account. Indeed, the idea that forensic argument spread into Christian circles obscures how the Church developed appropriate modes of argumentation for its own issues and consciously opposed these to 'secular' practice. But, interestingly, the Acts of Carthage show that bishops could use both modes of argument. Debates are, thus, also about identifying the appropriate type of argument for the issue at hand, and not just about finding the most convincing argument.

Disputations: Appropriate Argument and Sufficient Education

The distinctions made in the Acts of Carthage are not unique. The basic idea, that a certain style is suited for a certain type of cause, is a rhetorical precept already expressed by Cicero,[59] which returns in a modified form in Augustine's *De doctrina Christiana*.[60] The negative evaluation of (secular) trials and forensic practice among Christians goes back to 1 Cor 6:1–9, and is repeated in many later texts. As in the case of the Acts, it is often linked to negative judgements about the vain verbosity of the rhetoric practised there.[61] Yet Christian texts soon draw attention to more styles of argument than just the rhetorical one. Lactantius argues that when addressing Jews one should focus on biblical arguments, whereas in apologetic against the Hellenes one should use philosophical ones.[62] In an anonymous dialogue from the sixth century, the Jew is only persuaded to take part in the debate after having been assured by the Christian that the dialectical pyrotechnics of Plato and Aristotle will not be used in the debate. The Christian reassures him that these are only appropriate for debates among Christians, whereas discussions with the Jews are to be conducted on the basis of biblical exegesis.[63] This distinction accords rather well with observable differences between the type of argument used in *Contra Iudaeos* – texts and polemical tracts against heretics of this period.[64]

It was a sign of proper education to know when to employ what type of argument, as the following critique of Aetius, the supposed *maître à penser* of Eunomius, by the Church historian Socrates illustrates:

> Immediately he startled people with strange propositions. This he did by drawing on the *Categories* of Aristotle, and discussing on the basis of these he did not realise that he produced sophisms for himself; neither had he learned the purpose of Aristotle from scholars. For Aristotle wrote the work as an exercise for young people because of the sophists who poked fun at philosophy at that time and opposed dialectic to the sophists by way of sophisms. For the sceptic philosophers,[65] when setting out the doctrines of Plato and Plotinus, refute what was said craftily by Aristotle. But Aetius, not having had a sceptic teacher, remained at the sophisms of the *Categories*.
>
> Εὐθέως οὖν ἐξενοφώνει τοὺς ἐντυγχάνοντας· τοῦτο δὲ ἐποίει ταῖς Κατηγορίαις Ἀριστοτέλους πεισθείς, ἐξ αὐτῶν δὲ διαλεγόμενος {καὶ} ἑαυτῷ σοφίσματα ποιῶν οὐκ ἠσθάνετο, οὐδὲ παρὰ τῶν ἐπιστημόνων

154 *Peter Van Nuffelen*

ἔμαθεν τὸν Ἀριστοτέλους σκοπόν. Ἐκεῖνος γὰρ διὰ τοὺς σοφιστὰς τὴν φιλοσοφίαν τότε χλευάζοντας γυμνασίαν ταύτην συγγράψας τοῖς νέοις τὴν διαλεκτικὴν τοῖς σοφισταῖς διὰ τῶν σοφισμάτων ἀντέθηκεν. Οἱ γοῦν ἐφεκτικοὶ τῶν φιλοσόφων τὰ Πλάτωνος καὶ Πλωτίνου ἐκτιθεμένοι ἐξελέγχουσι τὰ τεχνικῶς παρὰ Ἀριστοτέλους λεγόμενα. Ἀλλὰ Ἀέτιος, ἐφεκτικοῦ μὴ τυχὼν διδασκάλου τοῖς ἐκ τῶν Κατηγοριῶν σοφίσμασιν ἐναπέμενε.[66]

Socrates makes two interrelated points about Aetius' use of Aristotle's *Categories*. First, Aetius is not properly educated, and hence misunderstands the nature of Aristotle's work. Its aim was to teach Aristotle's young students to undermine sophistry through sophistry (and thus to understand what sophistry is). Not having enjoyed advanced enough an education, Aetius took the *Categories* at face value, as a licence to use sophistry. Socrates thus does not argue that one should retract from education in response to the Eunomians, but rather that one should be properly educated. Second, Aristotle's *Categories* and the framework there developed serve a specific purpose; a style of argument thus needs to be suited for the purpose it sets itself.

At stake in discussions about the style of argument in a disputation is thus not a fundamental rejection of disputation but a quest for the right style of argument.[67] Rejections of Eunomian reliance on dialectic thus do not reject debates as such, but they argue that one should seek the most appropriate mode to discuss theological issues. The definition of an ecclesiastical mode by the bishops present at Carthage reflects the same preoccupation with using the correct − that is, suitable − way of arguing an ecclesiological case. In the normative discourse that accompanied these debates, it was not sufficient to have the necessary training to engage in rhetorical or forensic argument, one also needed to be properly trained to know when to deploy what style of argument.

Conclusion

In conclusion, I wish to make two final observations. First, the multiplicity of styles of argument and the expectation that one be able to use them appropriately presuppose a high level of learning on the part of Christian bishops (or, at least, the expectation thereof). One might expect all bishops to be able to argue in an 'ecclesiastical' mode, based on Scripture, but the ones speaking at Carthage seem to have been ambidextrous and able to switch to forensic argument without much trouble. In fact, this demonstrates not just the depth but also the variety of learning. Where did bishops acquire this learning? Often it is presupposed that many bishops had been rhetorically and legally trained before entering the Church. There is, undoubtedly, much truth in this. Yet we must also consider other possibilities. Education and training are not something that necessarily precedes one's career and can also be learned in practice. Bishops with little strictly legal training were likely to acquire a modicum of experience in this area through the *audientia episcopalis*. The proper 'ecclesiastical' mode of arguing would not be taught in any school, and is more likely to be acquired through assisting at theological debates and discussions. For all its debts to classical rhetoric, preaching a sermon was also a well-circumscribed social and literary act, the expectations about which would have been acquired by listening to predecessors and the act of preaching itself. In sum, social roles and social context can also be important channels of acquiring further training.

Second, I wish to emphasise that the Christian discourse on education was not a mere reflection on practices, traditional and new, that left these practices untouched. In fact, the examples in this chapter have shown that a reflection on appropriate styles of argument and the education related to them were part of the argument itself. The various distinctions between appropriate styles are exploited in debate to convict the other side of improper argument or, even, of relying on an inferior type of argument. In the examples surveyed, we are not dealing with a wholesale rejection of a particular form of education, but rather the creation of a hierarchy of forms and their topic-specific application. The idea of an ecclesiastical mode of argumentation was probably shaped by the contradistinction with 'secular' or 'pagan' forms, and thus was itself the product of a reflection on appropriate types of education in a Christian context. Reflection was thus shaped and sharpened by practice; and practice, in turn, regulated by reflection.

Notes

1 The research leading to these results has received funding from the European Research Council under the European Union's Seventh Framework Programme (FP/2007–2013)/ERC Grant Agreement n. 313153. The chapter was written when I was a fellow of the Lichtenberg-Kolleg – the Göttingen Institute of Advanced Study. I am grateful to Peter Gemeinhardt, the Lichtenberg-Kolleg and the DFG for making this stay possible.
2 See notes 10 and 11 below for references.
3 As does, in my view, Lim 1995.
4 Most obvious is the scholarly emphasis on the continuity in the field of rhetoric: for an overview, see Kinzig 1997. Humfress 2007 argues for the importance of continuity in the area of forensic rhetoric. Less systematically studied seems continuity in the area of philosophical dialectic and logic, which becomes particularly visible in the theological debates of the sixth century (Uthemann 1981 and 1985; see also King, Chapter 12 in this volume).
5 Context in Hogrefe 2009, 153–227; Brown 2000, 330–39; Lancel 1999, 404–29.
6 *Codex Theodosianus* 16.5.38, 16.3–5 (12/2/405) and 16.11.2 (5/3/415).
7 Alluded to in *Codex Theodosianus* 16.5.51 (25/8/410); 16.5.52 (30/1/415); Edict of Honorius in Marcellus, *Acts of Carthage* 1.4 1.20–5 (= *Codex Theodosianus* 16.11.3 [14/10/410]).
8 Marcellus, *Acts of Carthage* 1.4 ll. 28 and 33.
9 Tilley 1991; Humfress 2007, 177; Hogrefe 2009, 155–6; Shaw 2011, 555. See, however, Kussmaul 1981: 94: 'die Collatio cum Donatistis [war] nicht ein Prozess, sondern [wurde] nur nach dem Vorbild eines Prozesses abgehalten'. The traditional name, *collatio* (conference), is hence to be maintained.

156   *Peter Van Nuffelen*

10 I have argued for this view in Van Nuffelen 2014 and 2016, where further references can be found.
11 For orientation, see Griffith 2008; Cameron and Hoyland 2011; Cameron 2014.
12 Augustine, *Letter* 33, *Sermon* 131.10.
13 1 Thess 5.14; 2 Tim 4.2; Eph 6.4; Gal 2.
14 Sozomen, *Ecclesiastical history* 1.15.
15 Menze 2008.
16 Augustine, *Retractations* 1.16; Michael the Syrian, *Chronicle* 10.21.
17 Gryson 1980.
18 The German concept of *Reichskirche*, which presupposes a well-regulated interaction between Church and State, has now been subjected to penetrating criticism by Diefenbach 2012.
19 PLRE II, pp. 711–12 (10); Lancel 1972–75, vol. 1, 61–5.
20 Marcellus, *Acts of Carthage* 1.4 ll. 38–40. For further analysis on these lines, see Tilley 1991.
21 Marcellus, *Acts of Carthage* 1.3 ll. 9–10, 1.10 ll. 5–12.
22 See, e.g., *Gesta Episcoporum Aquileia* 51–2.
23 Marcellus, *Acts of Carthage* 1.5 l. 33: *concilii faciendi gratia*. This does not mean, in my view, that we are dealing with a Church council, as Hogrefe 2009, 188 suggests.
24 Kaser 1966, 485.
25 Van Nuffelen 2014, 163–7.
26 Kaser 1966, 456–60.
27 Marcellus, *Acts of Carthage* 3.38.
28 Marcellus, *Acts of Carthage* 3.85.
29 Marcellus, *Acts of Carthage* 3.38, ll.3–4.
30 Kussmaul 1981, 88–95. It is difficult to see why a pragmatic sanction would have to be used to call the Conference if it was to be an ordinary *cognitio*. If we understand the *pragmatica sanctio* as attributing a privilege to the Catholic Church to hold a disputation with the Donatists, it starts to make sense.
31 The interpretation of the role of Marcellinus by Hogrefe 2009, 194 is to be preferred to that by Shaw 2011, 555–6.
32 For the distinction, see already Augustine, *Epistula ad Catholicos de secta donatistarum* 3.6 (CSEL 51).
33 Lancel 1972–75, vol. 1, 68–9.
34 Marcellus, *Acts of Carthage* 1.40, 1.47, 3.155, 3.187–8.
35 Hogrefe 2009, 177. See, e.g, 3.201, 214, 222.
36 Graumann 2011.
37 Augustine, *Contra Emeritum* 2, *Ad donatistas post collationem* 1.
38 Marcellus, *Acts of Carthage* 3.295–302.
39 Frend 1952, 279; Grasmück 1959, 224; Lancel 1972–75, vol. 1, 74. More nuanced is Hogrefe 2009, 180–82.
40 The opposition recurs very often in the extant acts and is made by all sides: Marcellus, *Acts of Carthage* 1.30 ll. 11–12: *magis forensis est quam episcopalis obiectio* (Marcellinus); 1.40: *ut utrum a iure publico recedi velitis et totum divinis legibus agitari vestris professionibus demonstretis* (Marcellinus); 1.47: *fidei causa est quae . . . ipso iure agi potest . . . ut, si forensis altercatio iurisque conflictus in medio mittitur, proponatur; sin autem simplex illa veritas qua datur vita . . . in hoc iudicio spirituali altercatione conquiritur* (Emeritus, Donatist); 1.53 *sine praeiudicio nostro legat, saluo eo quia haec causatio forensis est, non legalis* (Petilian, Donatist); 1.70: *quoniam igitur et iacturam fecerunt earum rerum quas forensibus cancellis ac legibus uti poterant et recitaverunt mandatum quod non magis forense sit quam legale, hinc agnosco debere me illis lege divina conpetenter respondere* (Petilian, Donatist); 3.74: *catholicam monstramus ecclesiam de lege, de prophetis, de evangeliis, de psalmis, de omnibus divinis testimoniis; contra hoc a vobis profertur mandatum: publica. tecum ad ecclesiam demonstrandam evangelium proferamus*

How Shall We Plead? 157

(Fortunatianus, Catholic); 3.155: *ut autem leges, vel gesta, vel quaecumque de archivis prolata offeramus in hac conlatione recitanda, ipsi cogunt qui talibus agunt. Nam si, remotis huiuscemodi omnibus chartis, nollent ecclesim nisi in scripturis adverti, nihil vellemus, nihil aliud optaremus. . . . itaque pervidet prudentia tua distinguendas esse causas, quando cogamur publicis legibus agere, quando autem velimus et optemus negotium ecclesiae non nisi divinis eloquiis terminare* (Augustine, Catholic); 3.181: *si in forensem conflictum revertimur, constat eos legis divinae fecisse iacturam* (Petilian, Donatist); 3.183: *si forensis est actio, huius temporis causam audire praeceptus es, vir nobilis. Si simpliciter et ecclesiastico more res geritur, adquiescam in ea quae lege divina proferentur vel a me, vel a parte diversa* (Petilian, Donatist); 3.187: *non obiciant crimina hominibus et chartae cessabunt; sola divina loquetur auctoritas* (Augustine, Catholic); 3.190: *ut, utrum pars catholica . . . iure publico agi vellet an certe divinis testimoniis, evidenter ostenderet. . . . si crimina non obicerentur a documentis publicis discedendum . . . si vero cause ecclesiae tractaretur, legalia tantum testimonia proferrentur* (Marcellinus); 3.191: *utrum disceptationem legis divinae tenere cupiant, an publicas leges* (Petilian, Donatist); 3.193: *noverim genus actionis, nemo me reprehendat in publico, nemo causae bonae infirmum esse iudicet defensorem, nemo iudicet obliquum, nemo adversarium dolosum ac licentiosum cui omni permittantur, ut, cui de his iusta atque evidentia requirantur, libeat illis delicate quomodo voluerint nebulas ac tenebras obtendere, ut veniri non possit ad cardinem veritatis* (Petilian, Donatist); 3.249: *ut . . . spiritualiter peragamus* (Emeritus, Donatist); 3.253: *in mandato suo legalia quaeque se posuisse dixerunt. Haec eadem legalia nos scripturis legalibus convincimus* (Emeritus, Donatist).

41 Marcellus, *Acts of Carthage* 2.20. Cf. 1.30, 1.53, 1.70, 3.74, 3.156, 3.181–93, 3.249, 3.253, 3.193.
42 Marcellus, *Acts of Carthage* 1.31.
43 See, e.g., Augustine, *Contra litteras Petiliani* 2.56.127; Pseudo-Vigilius, *Contra Varimadum* pr.
44 Marcellus, *Acts of Carthage* 1.31: *praestigiis iuris neque ligaminibus cuiusque facundiae.*
45 Marcellus, *Acts of Carthage* 1.31: *versutiamque legum iurisque controversiam.*
46 Marcellus, *Acts of Carthage* 1.31: *consuetudinemque iurgandi.*
47 Marcellus, *Acts of Carthage* 2.20: *iactantiamque illius controversiae.*
48 Marcellus, *Acts of Carthage* 1.31: *praestigiis iuris neque ligaminibus cuiusque facundiae.*
49 Marcellus, *Acts of Carthage* 3.193: *libeat illis delicate quomodo voluerint nebulas ac tenebras obtendere.*
50 Marcellus, *Acts of Carthage* 3.193.
51 Humfress 2007, 188–9, 203. According to Humfress 2007, 188 the Donatist Primian excused himself for lack of forensic expertise, but this seems to be a misinterpretation. More accurate is the appreciation of Hogrefe 2009, 187 n. 164. For education in North Africa later in the fifth century, see Chapter 11 by Vössing.
52 See John Chrysostom, *De sacerdotio* 3.18; Augustine, *Letter* 24★.1. See Humfress 2007, 202.
53 Hogrefe 2009, 162–3.
54 For a synthesis, see Harries 1999.
55 Humfress 2007, 6.
56 Humfress 2007, 264.
57 Arjava 2009.
58 Gemeinhardt 2007.
59 Cicero, *De oratore* 21.72.
60 Augustine, *De doctrina Christiana* 4.19.38.
61 Minucius Felix, *Octavius* 14.7; Commodianus, *Apologia* 583–600; Augustine, *Confessions* 3.3.6; Jerome, *Commentary on Galatians* 2.11. See Gemeinhardt 2007, 125–6, 421.
62 Lactantius, *Divine Institutes* 5.4.4.
63 Anonymus Declerk, I.74–113 (CCG 30).
64 For an overview of the *Adversus Iudaeos* tradition, see Schreckenberg 1995 and the useful introduction of Fields 2012.

158   *Peter Van Nuffelen*

65 *Ephektikoi* designates philosophers who practise the *epoche* (Diogenes Laertius, *Lives of Philosophers* 1.16), and often more explicitly the followers of Pyrrho (John Philoponus, *In Aristotelis Categorias commentarium* vol. 13.1, p. 2 l. 4 (ed. Busse 1898)).
66 Socrates, *Ecclesiastical History* 2.35.6–9. Of course, there also exist principled rejections of dialectic: Hippolytus, *Refutation of all heresies* 7.19.9; Ephrem, *Hymn on Julian Saba* 1.8.
67 *Pace* Lim 1995, 158–77.

11 Victor of Vita and Secular Education

Konrad Vössing

The so-called *Passio Marculi*, written in Africa during the late fourth century, praises its hero for abandoning the slanderous practice of secular rhetoric (he was a lawyer) and instead applying himself to the holy 'school of the Church' and its teacher, Christ: 'As soon as he [Marculus] began to take in the rudiments of the blessed faith, he immediately rejected worldly education . . . he began to despise the false dignity of secular knowledge'.[1] Here, we are concerned more specifically with the lawyer's profession relinquished by Marculus; this profession – the culmination of rhetorical education – stands for pagan education as a whole.[2] Accordingly, Marculus's renunciation of the worldly school is represented as a transition to the *sanctissima ecclesiae schola* and a different, new teacher: Christ.[3]

This contrast between the two *scholae* is quite commonly found in Christian sermons. Characteristically, no comparison is drawn between institutions, as there was no counterpart to Christian children and adolescents in the worldly school.[4] Rather, the 'students of Christ' learn according to a completely different principle: neither the poor, nor women, nor the ignorant are excluded – as was the case in schools of grammar and rhetoric – and the aim is neither (directly) the ability to produce rhetorical evidence nor (indirectly) the social prominence that can be gained in this manner.[5] These aims are represented as the art of deception and as the result of unhealthy ambition.

This perspective is quite typical of the first centuries of Christianity in Africa. The relation between secular and religious education is often described as a harsh contradiction that calls for equally harsh decisions.[6] In reality, the relationship of Christians to the *studia saecularia* was very different, depending on their social status, for instance, as well as on their level of education, their role in their community and so on.[7] Even without actually rejecting the world of traditional education, there seems to have been an obligation to verbally emphasise this boundary. One need only recall Augustine's famous devaluation of traditional rhetoric and rhetorical education: 'In those years I taught the art of rhetoric, and being vanquished by greed, I sold a skill at speech designed for victories in court.' Later he speaks of the market of loquaciousness, where youths are equipped with the weapons needed for sick, dishonest battles in the forum.[8] Similarly to other Christians

160   *Konrad Vössing*

who turned away from the system of traditional educational culture, these statements of Augustine do not mean that he rejected the use of the *litterae saeculares* in principle; however, in order for them to be able to do good, they need to be completely cleansed of false content based on myths, the cult of gods and poetry, on the one hand; and of misleading aims, that is, of ambition, competitiveness and so on, on the other.[9] To what extent the proponents of this separation were aware of its artificiality can be left open. In practice, there were of course numerous compromises and combinations, which did not alter the fact that the principal lines of separation were kept very clear. The present contribution wants to propose that this contrast disintegrated in Africa during the time of the Vandals, and that this process can be seen particularly clearly in the works of Victor of Vita.

In manuscripts of his work he is referred to as *episcopus patriae Vitensis*, a bishop from the 'Vitensian home town'.[10] His home town is usually referred to as 'Vita' (other options would include Vite, for example); this town in the province of Byzacena is otherwise unknown.[11] Victor was very likely a Carthaginian cleric,[12] which fits in well with his close relationship to Bishop Eugenius of Carthage.[13] He probably went into exile with Eugenius when the Vandal king Huneric drove him out in AD 484, as the king did with all other bishops in his sphere of power who would not convert.[14] When Eugenius was allowed to return to his episcopal town in 487, this permission surely also applied to those in his circle. Back in Carthage (and with access to the city's Church archives), Victor made a start on the final editing of his work. Later he became bishop of an African town, the name of which we do not know.

The work's title is not transmitted exactly; possibly it was called *Historia persecutionis africanae provinciae temporum Geiserici et Hunerici regum Wandalorum* – 'The history of the persecution in Africa at the time of the Vandal kings Genseric and Huneric'.[15] Its topic is the persecution to which the Catholic Church was subjected under the Vandal king Genseric, and above all under his successor Huneric (477–84); and in its opening chapters it also covers the conquest of Africa by the Vandals.

The work's structure is simple: the prologue is followed by the chapters on King Genseric (1,1–51), which make up a quarter of the total work, and half of the text deals with the reign of Genseric's successor Huneric (2,1–55; 3,1–60); a kind of final appeal follows at the end (3,61–70). All extant manuscripts also include the *Liber Fidei Catholicae* (2,56–2,100), which again constitutes a quarter of the total work. This was not written by Victor but is a stand-alone work transmitted independently of Victor's text, a theological treatise on the Trinity written by the Catholic bishops during the doctrinal disputes with their opponents.

Overall, the author was not concerned with producing a comprehensive history of the Vandals' reign in Africa, or even with a history of their Church politics. His real aim was to criticise the Vandals from the point of view of those directly affected and damaged by them; the steadfastness of the oppressed is praised. How little he was interested in the historical context of the events reported is evident in the fact that this played no role where Huneric's motivation was concerned, for example. This motivation was quite simply evil, and if the king's politics were not evil from the beginning, then only because he was feigning or something prevented him from expressing his malice.[16]

However, Victor not only wants to level accusations, he also wants to document events. In his text he thus quotes the wording of a number of original documents that he probably found in the Carthaginian Church archives – a principle first introduced to historiography by Eusebius's Church history. Valuable archive material is thereby made available to us, such as the decrees of King Huneric (with the king's title, date, closing formula etc.) and a letter from Eugenius to the king.[17] What the author's precise intention was in representing the Catholics' martyrdom and willingness to be martyred and the Vandal methods of persecution is disputable and not of further interest here. Probably he was trying to gain the support of (or make the case for an intervention by) the Byzantine imperial court.[18] During his last years, Huneric had in fact given free rein to an outright persecution of the Church,[19] but ultimately failed in his aim to establish his son Hilderic as his successor. When he died in 484, his nephew Gunthamund (484–96) became king, the very person Huneric had hoped to prevent. While Gunthamund did not continue Huneric's violent politics, he failed to establish an understanding with the opposing Church. The bishops of the *Proconsularis* remained in exile (except for Eugenius; see above); the Church's property remained in the hands of its Arian opponent; and in the main areas of the Vandal settlements the Catholic Church was forced to remain invisible, regardless of the population's confession. Victor completed his work in the late 480s. Its uncompromising stance shows how entrenched the fronts still were at that time.

The following will be less concerned with Victor's actual education, with an analysis of his Latin, for example. Research has already shown that he enjoyed a literary education, albeit a fairly superficial one. His Latin is correct, but shows traits typical of the end of Antiquity;[20] he has clearly internalised the rules of correct language taught by the *grammaticus*, but it is not possible to detect any strong influence by 'classical' authors. He only really seems at home with Church writers[21] and the Bible, which is extensively quoted (both directly and indirectly). The work's overall structure shows that the author – regardless of the remoteness of the text's content to the genre of historiography – wanted to follow the rules of sophisticated historical works. The prologue is marked by the typical *topos* of humility (due to the author's poor literary skills) on the one hand,[22] and by its aspiration to an elevated style on the other, even though the result – measured by the standards of classical rhetoric – is not very convincing. This demonstratively erudite prologue is followed by a linguistically continuous main section with inserted speeches (by the author)[23] and a rhetorically rousing conclusion reminiscent of a *peroratio*.

However, for our purposes the actual level of Victor's literary education is less important than how this education is regarded and evaluated. It should be

162   *Konrad Vössing*

highlighted here – and research has been less surprised by this than it ought to have been – that this evaluation is exclusively positive, and in part emphatically so. In the prologue a distinction is already drawn between the historians *in saeculo* and the addressee, but this refers only to their motivation: ambition not 'in this world' but in the world to come is the deciding factor for the Christian author (*prol.* 2). Otherwise, the aim of the 'old' historians remains unchanged: 'to bring those unacquainted with the flower baskets of history the sweet-smelling blossoms of instruction (*magisterium*) as gifts donated free of any charge'. Although he is here referring to pagan historians, Victor is using the same metaphor as Eusebius does in his Church history.[24]

The preconditions for the historian's successful practice of his *magisterium* are referred to using characteristically mixed wording: on the one hand, a 'heavenly gift' is needed (James 1,17), while on the other the guidance of a teacher is required, whose *doctrina* (which can be seen in his taught works) plays a decisive role.[25] The relationship of these two preconditions is not discussed further. In fact, they effectively overlap. The education by a teacher passing on his knowledge (however this may take place specifically) is of equal importance to the commission and vocation from above.[26] Interestingly, here we can find a regard for technical instruction similarly high to that which existed for many centuries in education in the pagan context, albeit with a different orientation. While in the traditional value system *studia* were more or less equivalent to *mores*, and education was thus equated with character and accordingly went from a technical level directly to a 'moral' one,[27] we can observe a similar transition here to the religious level: the *doctrina* passed on by the teacher becomes a gift from God.

The appreciation of literary education – without any distinction between its traditional and Christian forms – then becomes clear in two passages. In the description of Augustine's death, which famously took place on 28 August 430 during the Vandals' siege of Hippo Regius,[28] the Church Father is characterised in a way that stresses only his literary production. He is introduced as the 'author of many books' (1,10), and his obituary reveals nothing of the Church Father's own reserve towards literary rhetoric but is rather reminiscent of a Christian Cicero:

> Then that river of eloquence, which flowed richly over all the fields of the church, dried up in the midst of its course, and the pleasant sweetness, so sweetly provided, was turned to bitter absinth, in accordance with the cry of David: 'When the sinner stood against me I became dumb and was abased, and kept silent even from good' [Ps 38.2–3. Vulg.]. Until that time he had written 232 books, not including his letters, which are beyond counting, his exposition of the entire psalter and the gospels, and his sermons to the people which the Greeks call 'homilies', the number of which it is quite impossible to establish.[29]
>
> *Tunc illud eloquentiae, quod ubertim per omnes campos ecclesiae decurrebat, ipso meatu siccatum est flumen, atque dulcedo suavitatis dulcius propinata in*

amaritudinem absinthii versa est . . . . Usque ad illud tempus ducentos iam triginta et duos confecerat libros, exceptis innumerabilibus epistulis vel expositione totius psalterii et evangeliorum atque tractatibus popularibus, quos Graeci homelias vocant, quorum numerum comprehendere satis inpossibile est.

(1,11)

Even more striking is a passage in which Victor, right before beginning his passionate final appeal, humbly draws attention to the poor literary tools available to him, which are insufficient to describe the suffering caused by the great famine of 484:

> But why do I linger over a topic I lack the ability to give an account of? For if they were still alive and it were proper for them to speak of such things, the river of Cicero's eloquence would be dried up, and Sallust would remain wholly speechless. And, to pass over strangers unworthy of so great a subject, if Eusebius of Caesarea, a man suitable for this task, were to rise up, or Rufinus, his translator, a man of Greek language skills and adorned with Latin flowers . . . but why go on? Not Ambrose, not Jerome, not our Augustine himself would suffice.[30]
>
> *Sed quid ego iam iam inmoror in hoc quod explicare non queo? Nam si nunc superessent vel eis fari de talibus rebus licuisset, et Tullianae eloquentiae fluvius siccaretur et Sallustius elinguis omnimodis remaneret. Et, ut alienos indignos rei tantae praeteream, si Caesariensis surgeret Eusebius ad hoc opus idoneus, aut eius translator Graecae facundiae Latinisque floribus Rufinus ornatus – et quid multa? – non Ambrosius, non Hieronimus, nec ipse noster sufficeret Augustinus.*

(3,61)

Given the emphasis on education, the brief description of Sallust and Cicero (the two most important Latin prose authors used in school lessons in Late Antiquity, including in Africa)[31] as 'foreign' compared to the Church authors seems mere lip service. The classical authors are 'peacefully united' with the Christians Eusebius, Rufinus, Ambrose, Jerome and Augustine through their rhetorical skill. Victor's selection of the authors mentioned here is not arbitrary; he was familiar with them from the secular tradition of education and his Christian studies. Among the four Christian writers, Eusebius falls out of line as a Greek author. As we have no evidence that Victor used Eusebius directly, or that he possessed any substantial knowledge of Greek,[32] the naming of Eusebius here is probably due to the fact that he was the recognised 'father' of Church historiography and served as a model for Rufinus's *Historia* – which Victor used heavily.[33] However, he would never have considered quoting pagan authors, or even listing them as models.[34]

If we now ask ourselves what has changed since the time of Augustine, who would never have tolerated this kind of comparison,[35] then it seems obvious to point to the Vandal reign. The establishment and consolidation of the *regn Vandalorum* in Africa went hand in hand with a cultural break that cannot be described in detail here. Research of recent years has been reluctant to acknowledge its severity, as a number of works surviving from this time – including a collection of Latin epigrams from the final stages of the Vandal Empire known as *Anthologia Salmasiana* – seem to attest an unbroken, continuous literary culture in Carthage. However, this deduction ignores that the break did not come about through the elimination of the provincial Roman upper class and its culture, but through the fact that it lost the significance it had held up until this time: it lost its link to power, which now followed a completely different set of rules.[36] This does not mean that the old elites in Africa gave up their education, which was an important constituent of their identity; but they were no longer able to instrumentalise it in the same way as before. The Vandal king saw and referred to himself as a *rex barbarus*.[37] On the other hand, the literary production of the later years must be seen against the background of the 'revolution' of King Hilderic, who repositioned the Vandal Empire after the death of his predecessor Thrasamund (496–523). In terms of foreign policy he brought his empire closer to Constantinople (and separated it completely from the Ostrogoth Empire), while on the domestic front he emphasised the complete integration of the Romans of Africa and their Church.[38] This went hand in hand with a cultural reorientation. Not only Hilderic, but also a number of important Vandal figures became more open to Roman literature.[39] This new phase, which only lasted seven years before coming to an end with Gelimer's deposition of Hilderic in 530, was based on a marked change of course and thus cannot be seen as representative of cultural conditions in the Vandal Empire.

Little of this was evident at the time Victor was writing his text. While schools teaching literary education certainly existed, for example in Carthage,[40] the Roman upper classes were not prevented from engaging in their traditional rhetorical battles in court cases before the proconsul. However, these were purely Roman events, separated from the centre of power.[41] It was not necessary to hold speeches in order to achieve success with the Vandal king; rather, one had to demonstrate a clear change of sides, breaking off connections to the *Imperium Romanum* and entering the service of the barbarian king, which also meant joining the Arian Church.[42]

We thus come to the situation of the Church. The old (Catholic) Church elite had a similar, but even harsher experience: it was expropriated, disempowered and marginalised completely, particularly in the main areas of Vandal occupation (that is, the *sortes Vandalorum*). Those who expected help from the outside were forced to look East, as the Roman West was no longer capable of intervening following the failure of Emperor Maiorianus's campaign against the Vandals (AD 460).[43] This was an unsettling situation, and not only for the Catholic Church in Africa, which was strongly rooted in the Western tradition.

In the time of Augustine, Christianity had not been victorious throughout the African upper classes by any means, and powerful pagan patrons continued to be supported by considerable parts of the populace, which repeatedly led to conflict.[44] After the conquest of Carthage by the Vandals (AD 439) we hear no more of this opposition. It would appear that the new front changed both sides' perspective, that of both the traditional elite and the formerly dominant Catholic hierarchy (now oppressed by the Arian Church). They stood united against the 'barbarian' invaders, and this conflict led to a new symbiosis between the two parties on the losing side.[45]

Seen against this background, it is completely consistent that under Vandal rule the earlier contrast between *studia divina* and *studia saecularia* was largely levelled from the point of view of the old (Church and secular) elites, even though it did not disappear completely. Victor's work attests this clearly, as do other works, including the oeuvre of the poet Dracontius and the writer Fabius Planciades Fulgentius. Both were Christians, but wrote for an audience interested in traditional literature and addressed Romans almost exclusively.[46]

Dracontius, a contemporary of Victor, not only authored a work titled *De laudibus Dei*, in which he praises God's blessings on human beings in flawless hexameters, but also wrote a number of traditional poems[47] that could also have been written by an educated pagan.[48] The author Fabius Fulgentius (the so-called mythographer), who was also classically educated, probably wrote his *Mitologiae* during the early years of Gunthamund's reign.[49] His allegorical explanations of classical myths are by no means specifically Christian,[50] although they are dedicated to a Carthaginian priest named Catus.[51] The author subsequently applies this same allegorical method to Virgil in his *Expositio Virgilianae continentiae*. This poet, who plays a central role in Latin grammar lessons, even makes an appearance himself as a wise authority the author must look up to.[52] His *Aeneid*, against which Augustine had explicitly warned because of its teachings of gods and political principles,[53] is here allegorised as a whole and thus 'saved' – and not in front of a pagan audience as with Macrobius, but for educated Christians and by a Christian who dedicates his work to a cleric.[54]

While these works have deep roots in the literary tradition of the pre-Christian world but nonetheless target a Christian audience (which would hardly have been conceivable in Augustine's time), the opposite is the case in the description of Victor's namesake, the monk and bishop of Ruspe (468–533).[55] His biography (probably written by the deacon Ferrandus) describes his literary education (by a home tutor and with a *grammaticus*) closely, praising it explicitly.[56] Upon joining a monastic order the need to bid the *saeculares deliciae* farewell is thematised;[57] but this refers first and foremost to good clothing, rich food, extensive visits to the baths and so on, while the *litterae saeculares* are not mentioned at all. Instead, the bishop's eloquence is praised throughout the entire Vita, starting with the prologue. Under King Thrasamund (496–523) he was the spiritual leader of the Catholics in Africa; and as a bishop, too, he was praised especially for his *doctrina*, which surpassed that of all others, but particularly the Arians.[58] This fact is linked to the culture of public theological debate, which still remained vibrant.[59] These kinds of disputation had already existed under Huneric, even though at that time they were a royal coercive measure and amounted to mere farce. Victor had also described his party's skill in disputation using the concepts of educational

166   *Konrad Vössing*

culture: Huneric prevented the opponents he regarded as particularly threatening (*episcopi eruditi* and *doctissimi*) from taking part.[60] Fulgentius also played an important role in this 'game' in his own time, under other political conditions.[61] His supporters celebrate his competence in a way that no longer draws any distinction between traditional and Christian rhetoric.

Of course, we cannot ignore the marked differences between the literary worlds of the bishops Victor of Vita and Fulgentius, or that of Victor's biographer on the one hand and that of Dracontius, Fabius Fulgentius and the authors of the African anthology on the other hand. On the one side we have the urban upper class and its erudite communication, which used traditional themes and forms of literature, and on the other we have specifically Christian instruction and controversy. However, adopting the point of view of the fourth century, we can see how these two spheres draw closer to one another, indeed partly overlapping, if not in terms of content then at least in terms of the persons involved. The double-sided value judgements, or rather judgements on worthlessness from earlier times, had obviously lost much of their validity.

Accordingly, Victor of Vita is not alone in the re-evaluation of secular education that can be observed in his works. That the confrontation between the old municipal elite and the Vandals played a significant role in this development immediately suggests itself. The speed of this change[62] is best explained in this way. However, this is not to say that the situation in Africa was the sole reason for the shift in values. On this level, too, there was no style typical only of Africa, no 'Africitas'.[63] A brief glance at contemporary Spain, Gaul or Italy serves to show this.[64]

Rather, this shift was informed by two supra-regional and long-term processes that can be seen as complementary, or even as identical and only possible to distinguish in perspective; at least they tend in the same direction. On the one hand, pagan education remained omnipresent, but increasingly lost its quality as a vital, independent system with a place in the life of an elite founded completely on traditional (and thus autonomous as compared to Christianity) qualifications. The loss of this position meant that the challenge or even the threat posed to Christians by the *litterae saeculares* increasingly vanished. Not only individual representatives, but also the vast majority of the late Roman upper classes made their peace with the Christian religion. This meant that the municipal and Church elites merged more and more. The transition from one sphere to the other lost its character of a rejection of old values, which on the one hand exonerated the traditional *litterae*, but on the other hand also robbed them of an important – and in the long run, vital – function.

However, the general climate of this educational history does not alter the fact that the specific conditions of the situation in Africa under Vandal reign need to be taken into account when evaluating Victor's attitude to secular education. Victor's work reflects the new conflicts and alliances of a time in which old certainties were dissolving. In the end, we find a relationship with proportions inverse to those of earlier times (such as the world of Augustine): familiarity with traditional classical culture had decreased, and this culture itself had lost its earlier position as a marker of social dominance. At the same time, however, its acceptance within the old elite had increased.

Notes

1 Maier 1987, 278: ch. 2: *Ille . . . ubi primum beatae fidei rudimenta suscepit, statim mundanas litteras respuens . . . falsam saecularis scientiae dignitatem calcavit.* On Marculus cf. PAC, p. 696s. Questions regarding the character of this 'martyrium' or the origins and genre of this Donatist *passio* can be left aside here; it exhibits a typical relationship to the *saecularis scientia.*

2 Vössing 1997, 384–91.

3 Maier 1987, 278: ch. 2: [Marculus] *sanctissimam ecclesiae transiens scholam, dum verum magistrum elegit Christum, sic inter principales Christi discipulos meruit honorari.* On the Church as the better school, cf. e.g. Augustine, Sermons. 292.1: *animo tenentes nostrae officium servitutis, ut loquamur, non tanquam magistri, sed tanquam ministri; non discipulis, sed condiscipulis; quia nec servis, sed conservis. Magister autem unus est nobis, cuius schola in terra est, et cathedra in caelo;* on this, cf. Studer 1999.

4 On the 'lack' of a Christian school in the sense of an institutionalised and compulsory education for young people, cf. Pack 1989; Markschies 2002; Gemeinhardt 2007, 19–20; Georges 2012.

5 Cf. Augustine's praise (*epist.* 138) of Christian instruction, which did not exclude the poor, the ignorant and women – unlike the traditional *schola;* significantly, its place is that of the sermon in church (not a Christian school). However, the contrast between (erroneous) pagan and (salutary) Christian schools is older: e.g. Lact. *inst.* 3.25, who criticises the exclusion of the masses from philosophical teachings.

6 Tertullian, *De idolatria* 10 goes particularly far in his rejection (on this, cf. Vössing 1997, 304–15), but only had a deeper influence on Christians' literary debate (not necessarily on their practice).

7 On this, cf. Gemeinhardt 2007.

8 Augustine, *Confessiones* 4.2.2: *Docebam in illis annis artem rhetoricam, et victoriosam loquacitatem victus cupiditate vendebam;* 9.2.2: *nundinae loquacitatis – insaniae mendaces – bella forensia – arma furori suo;* he refers to his own rhetorical teachings (in Milan) as *sedere in cathedra mendacii.* Once again, the common use of the rhetoric learnt in court forms the background here: see Chapter 10 by Van Nuffelen.

9 There is a vast amount of research on this topic – especially since Marrou 1938/95; cf. C. Mayer: 'doctrina'; 'eruditio'; in AugL II (1994–2002) 534–51; 1098–114.

10 Editions: Halm 1879; Petschenig 1881; Lancel 2002; Vössing 2011; translations: Costanza 1981; Moorhead 1992; Lancel 2002; Vössing 2011; Martyn 2008; commentaries: Costanza 1981; Moorhead 1992; Lancel 2002; Vössing 2011; also cf. Courtois 1954; Howe 2007; Merrills 2011.

11 It only appears in the *Notitia provinciarum et civitatum Africae* (Lancel 2002, 261), again only in adjective form; the bishop of the town in Byzacena (*Byz.* 44) referred to here again has the common African name Victor, but is probably not identical to the author (cf. Vössing 2011, 13).

12 That he was educated accordingly is evident in the great number of Bible quotes and the great significance accorded to sacramental acts in his work: cf. e.g. 1.18; 2.34; 3.29; also cf. 2.28.

13 Victor of Vita 2.18, 40. He is obviously familiar with the town's topography, its streets (3.31; cf. Lancel 1989), and is personally acquainted with many of the Catholics employed in Huneric's palace (2.9). On Eugenius, cf. PAC, 362–5.

14 Victor of Vita 3.20, 34, 43.

15 The title varies in the different manuscripts. 'African *provincia*' is used here (as in 1.3) in the general sense of a large geographical unit.

168   *Konrad Vössing*

16 Victor of Vita 2.17. Elsewhere I have proposed a reconstruction of the events in which I emphasise the succession politics of Huneric as the decisive factor: he needed allies, particularly within the Arian hierarchy, in order to bring his son to the throne.

17 Huneric's decrees: Victor of Vita 2.39, 3.3–14; also (perhaps paraphrased) 2.3–5, 3.19, 3.20. Eugenius's letter to Huneric: 2.41s.

18 This is evident in the work's final section in particular, which is characterised by pleas for assistance, not by a defence of his own behaviour.

19 Victor of Vita 3.45s.; 3.12–14; 3.20s. This was to give the Arian Church the chance to establish itself as the only Church in the Vandal heartlands.

20 Ferrère 1898; Ghedini 1927; Capello 1937; Pitkäranta 1978; also cf. Vössing 2011, n. 11; 16 and 324 of the commentary.

21 Of these, Rufinus merits particular mention; see below n. 33. In 3.62s. the most important Latin poet read in school is quoted: Virgil (e.g. *Aeneis* 6.853: *parcere subiectis*; see below n. 53). The expression *arx capitis* (1.7; also cf. 3.31) could be taken from Cicero, *Disputationes Tusculanae* 1.10.20, but probably reached Victor via Lactantius, *De opificio mundi*. 1.1 or other Christian intermediaries; 3.53 clearly alludes to Cicero's *O tempora, o mores* (*Oratio in Catilinam*. 1.2) – however, it is rather clumsily adapted to its new context. The description of the famine in 3.57 shows the author's aim to match classical descriptions of catastrophes.

22 The work's addressee is unknown; it cannot be Eugenius of Carthage (as claimed by Courtois 1954, 20–22; cf. Vössing 2011, 15). Victor claims that his writing is to serve as a collection of material for a larger work of the addressee (prol. 4), although this may be yet another expression of humility.

23 E.g. 1.19s., 31, 49s.; 2.34; 3.26, 27, 36s., 53.

24 Victor of Vita prol. 1: *redolentes magisterii flores ignaris historiae calathorum offerrent gratuito munere propinatos*. Cf. Eus. H.E. 1,1,4: ἀναλεξάμενοι καὶ ὡς ἂν ἐκ λογικῶν λειμώνων τὰς ἐπιτηδείους αὐτῶν τῶν πάλαι συγγραφέων ἀπανθισάμενοι φωνάς. In Rufinus's translation (Mommsen 1903, 9): *ex his . . . eligentes ac velut e rationabilibus campis doctorum flosculos decerpentes*. If Victor had Rufinus's formulation in mind here, then he wanted to differentiate himself from it by consciously using a *variatio*. It seems more likely however that he needed no model for the common literary metaphor of gathering flowers.

25 Prol. 2: *cuius ut astra lucentia extant quam plurima catholici dogmatis monumenta dictorum*. Here the addressee's teacher, Diadochus, is referred to. Of the known persons with this name, the only one who comes into question is the bishop of the Epirotic city of Photike (Marrou 1978; Ware 1981). Marrou posits that Diadochus could have been taken prisoner during Genseric's plundering and raids (Victor of Vita 1.51; Procop. *Vand.* 1.5.22s.) and abducted to Carthage. While this is a possibility, we should not ignore the fact that even the identification of the person named in Victor with the Epirotic bishop is a hypothesis.

26 Matthew 10.24–5. is reinterpreted somewhat forcibly in order to provide a written source for the significance of this discipleship: *quia satis est discipulo, ut sit quomodo magister eius*. Also cf. Luke 6.40. Subsequently the student–teacher relationship between Paul (the *magister gentium*, cf. 3.64, 69) and Timothy and Luke is evoked.

27 Cf. most recently Vössing 2014b.

28 However, the city only passed into Vandal possession years later; cf. Vössing 2012.

29 Translation by Moorhead 1992. The numbering of the books is taken from Augustine, *Retractationes* 2.93; also cf. Augustine, *Epistulae* 224.2.

30 Translation by Moorhead 1992 with one exception: see n. 32 below. Rufinus of Aquileia translated not only many works by Origen, but also (AD 401) Eusebius's Church history, which he continued until AD 395 (H.E. 10–11); see n. 33 below.

31 Vössing 1997, 377–80.

32 Victor's praise of Rufinus's *graeca facundia* is aimed at the latter's translation skills, given that Rufinus wrote no Greek works of his own. Moorhead's translation is misleading (1992, 89: 'The translator of his [*sc.* Eusebius's] Greek eloquence'); *Graecae facundiae* is (as *Latinisque*

floribus ornatus) clearly a quality of Rufinus, not of Eusebius. Victor's admiration suggests that he himself had no in-depth knowledge of Greek.

33 On this, cf. Wynn 1990. Wynn was able to show Rufinus's influence particularly on dramatic passages (esp. in 1.7; 1.36; 3.48; 3.55) of Victor's *Historia*; also cf. Vössing 2011 and above n. 24.

34 The topical reference to great literary figures, whose eloquence nevertheless was not great enough to describe terrible events, was widespread. Cf. *Epistula* 29 (to Apellion) of the Church historian Theodoret: even the great tragedians Aeschylus and Sophocles would have been unable to describe the suffering of Carthage after its conquest in 439.

35 Cf. e.g. his correspondence with the student of rhetoric Dioscurus (*Epistulae* 117 and 118); on this, cf. Vössing 1997, 300–302.

36 There is only a single (isolated) source that could be taken as evidence of Genseric's interest in Latin education (as claimed e.g. by Howe 2007, 167): one of his eight grandchildren is described as *magnis litteris institutus* in Victor of Vita 2.13. Whatever this education included, Victor describes it as an exception. Huneric had the prince killed as he stood in the way of his own son's succession.

37 Fulgentius of Ruspe, *Ad Trasamundum regem* 1.2.2; also cf. Ps.-Augustine, *Collatio Augustini cum Pascentio* 15.101.

38 Vössing, forthcoming.

39 Anthologia Latina 18 Riese (R.); 82 R. = 70 Shackleton Bailey (Sh.B.); 304–5 R. (= 299–300 Sh.B.); 320 (R.) = 315 (Sh.B.); 326 R (= 321 Sh.B.); 332 R. (= 327 Sh.B.); 345 R. (= 340 Sh.B.); 369 R. (= 364 Sh.B.); cf. Vössing, forthcoming, n.26 and 79–82

40 The Vandals also learnt Latin in school under certain circumstances, as shown by Dracontius, *Romulea* 1, *praef.* 12–14. However, this passage does not constitute evidence for shared lessons or for a particular regard of the Vandals for literary education; cf. Vössing 2014a, 100–101.

41 Cf. the subscriptio of Dracontius, *Romulea* 5 on his own function at the court of the Roman proconsul (also cf. Victor of Vita 3.27), who was not permitted however to decide on any cases in which Vandals were involved.

42 Victor of Vita 1.19–20; cf. also 2.8–10. The Vandals' deep-rooted suspicion that the Roman provincial elite was still cleaving to the Imperium and its emperors was confirmed not only by the latters' many attempts at intervention but also through many contacts (cf. Victor of Vita 3.19).

43 Vössing 2014a, 60–63. The Byzantine emperor was also forced to make peace with Genseric in 474 (ibid. 67–74), but remained an authority that sometimes advocated the Catholic cause in Africa (cf. e.g. Victor of Vita 2.3).

44 Cf. esp. Augustine, *Epistulae* 50 (for Sufes), 90–91 and 103–4. (for Calama); Quodvultdeus, *Liber de promissionibus* 3.38.44 (for Carthage).

45 Their defeats and losses differed: the old municipal upper classes were still needed in the Vandal Empire (unlike the Catholic hierarchy), even if to a much lesser extent than before, for the municipal administration outside the *sortes Vandalorum*, especially for the collection of taxes.

46 Exceptions are Dracontius's *Satisfactio* (Moussy 1988; Schetter 1990) – Dracontius had fallen out of favour with King Gunthamund and this work is an (unsuccessful) attempt to ask for mercy – as well as his eulogy of King Thrasamund (cf. Schetter 1990, 116–17), who probably released him from prison. As Dracontius wanted to be able to influence the kings, this literary way was his best option. Nevertheless, this indicates nothing about his success.

47 Bouquet and Wolff 1995; Wolff 1996; Moussy and Camus 1985; Moussy 1988. An overview of recent research can be found in Selent 2011, 8–12; also cf. Wasyl 2011.

48 Moussy and Camus 1985; Moussy 1988. The emphasis laid on Nicene orthodoxy, for example in *laud.* 2.60–110, shows that he was not targeting a Vandal audience.

170   *Konrad Vössing*

49 A likely date for Fulgentius's *Mitologiae* can be derived from the combination of *prol.* 5.13–16 Helm (a king fights successfully against invading *gentes*) and *Expositio Virgilianae continentiae* p. 83.4–5 Helm (the next work, as shown by *Expositio Virgilianae continentiae* 98.23–4), in which a particular *caritas* is attributed to the new (king's) reign. Taken together, both only really fit Gunthamund's reign, who fought against Moorish tribes but did not continue Huneric's harsh persecution (that is, if one does not take a purely imaginary setting as the work's starting point, for which there is no indication). G. Hays (who is preparing a new edition of Fulgentius) suggests dating this to the Byzantine period; however, it is difficult to link *Mitologiae* p. 5.14 Helm to the Byzantine emperor (Hays 2003, 243–4).

50 Hays 2003.

51 Wolff and Dain 2013, 135, n. 4.

52 Fulgentius, *Expositio Virgilianae continentiae* p. 86, 96, 97 Helm.

53 Cf. most recently Hübner 2007, 55. The very verse that Augustine had criticised several times in which Virgil justifies Roman claims to power (*Aeneis* 6.853, on this e.g. Augustine, *De civitate Dei* 1 praef.; 1.6; 5.1) is quoted in Victor of Vita 3.62 as a mere educational asset.

54 Fulgentius, *Expositio Virgilianae continentiae* p. 83.1 Helm; Wolff and Graziani 2009, 167, n. 2. On Fulgentius's Christian perspective, cf. e.g. *Expositio Virgilianae continentiae* p. 87, 89, 96, 102, 103.

55 PAC, 507–13; Tommasi Moreschini 2013.

56 *Vita Fulgentii Ruspensis* 1 (Lapeyre 1929, 11–13); on this, cf. Vössing 1997, 176–83. It is hardly convincing that this passage can be a decisive argument for the identity of the two Fulgentii (as stated by Isola 2010); for their differentiation cf. Vössing 2006.

57 *Vita Fulgentii Ruspensis* 2–3.

58 Chap. 5: When Fulgentius visits Abbot Felix's monastery, the abbot wants to give his office to Fulgentius as he far outshines him in *scientia*; chap. 12: F. is also honoured as the most educated man in the monastery of Junca and is thus made speaker of the bishops, who have been exiled to Sardinia, and advocate of the Catholic doctrine before Thrasamund, who expressly praises the *eloquentia* of the *vir doctissimus* (chap. 17, 20, 21).

59 Van Nuffelen 2014, 149–72.

60 Victor of Vita 2.45, 52; on the disputation cf. Victor of Vita 2.52–5; on this cf. Vössing 2011, 177–9.

61 The situation under Thrasamund had changed markedly, something which is often overlooked. While there were no non-hierarchical, 'power-free' discussions during this time, King Thrasamund (who was himself theologically active) seems to have been interested in an exchange of ideas. This was probably because in the meantime an opposing Vandal party had emerged with Thrasamund's presumptive successor Hilderic (and his supporters); cf. Vössing, forthcoming.

62 Genseric's conquest of Africa in the early 430s had still been interpreted in an anti-Christian way by some of the educated elite: Quodvultdeus, *De tempore barbarico II* 3.2–4.1.

63 Vössing 1997, 578–85; most recently Schmitt 2003.

64 Cf. e.g. recently Wasyl 2011.

12 Education in the Syriac World of Late Antiquity

Daniel King

The 'Shifting Frontiers' of Late Antiquity have become a scholarly sound bite: whether the frontiers in question be the *limes* that defined the edges of the empire, or the equally permeable frontiers between multiple religious identities; frontiers that (in both cases) seclude, con/preserve, define and control; frontiers that seep, leak; that remain open to negotiation and definition; that offer a variety of paths into a still undefined future. The Syriac-speaking peoples who inhabited provinces on both sides of the Euphrates were familiar with living near the military *limes*, and even with finding themselves suddenly in a different empire as the result of diplomacy or of being forcibly removed to a distant new home. Their religious *limes* were equally porous, however. Only very gradually did the doctrinal conflicts of the fifth century take on the concrete form of denominations, and for much of Late Antiquity their long-term futures were uncertainly dependent upon the vigorous persecutions of emperors and shahs; the tenacity of the monks; and the political and theological acumen of the bishops. Meanwhile the linguistic frontiers of deeper history continued to criss-cross both the religious and the political frontiers. And that is to say nothing of social or economic frontiers and how these might interact with, and influence, all those others. The Syriac-speaking peoples of those regions thus faced any number of intersecting identity issues. To which religion do I belong? To which denomination? To which empire and government? To which language group? To which social group?

It hardly comes as any surprise that amongst these questions of identity-formation, education must have held a significant place. One of the editors of this volume has argued that previous accounts of late ancient education have hardly grappled with the real issue, viz. 'the importance of education for the interplay of seclusion and permeability regarding those shifting frontiers. The precise impact of education for initiation into religions and conversion between religions still has to be explored in detail.'[1] The same agenda-setting essay sets out a number of more specific questions:

- whether certain ways of dealing with sacred writings are informed by non-religious education;
- the importance of historiography for the formation of worldviews;

172   *Daniel King*

- the role of educational theories and institutions (here we must consider what types of institution existed and how they related to/interacted with their 'pagan' equivalents and how theologians theorised about this relationship); and
- the effect of religious elites, or 'wise men', upon the presuppositions of educational policy and practice – which means in our case specifically the authoritative role of monasteries and of the ascetic mentality of Syriac Christianity upon educational ideas and practices.

The remainder of this chapter will thus explore the following broad areas of concern: the use of Greek and Syriac as the languages of education and the relative prestige of each; the question of pagan education in a Christianised environment; and the question of how identity (religious, ethnic, linguistic) may have affected, or been affected by, educational practices and expectations.

Setting the Scene

In his epoch-setting study of *The World of Late Antiquity*, Peter Brown set up a divide between classical literary culture on the one hand, and those aspects of classical learning which were successfully carried over into the Syro-Arabic world on the other:[2]

> Christian clergymen eventually passed Aristotle, Plato and Galen on to the Arabs; but in the mediaeval Near East, Christian and Muslim alike chose to remain ignorant of Homer, of Thucydides, of Sophocles. It was the end of a millennium of literary culture.

There are some vital points and claims lurking behind this assertion. It reminds us, for example, that the geographical regions in which these particular 'Christians and Muslims' became dominant were those very same regions in which (Greek) literary culture had previously flourished. It therefore follows that if the educational system of the late empire, so much of which was built around the reading of Greek literature, did not survive into the 'Arab' era, then this must have been in some sense a deliberate 'choice', a rejection of a central aspect of existing culture in favour of a new and fresh vision of what constituted education. In fact, in view of the realisation that the cities of the eastern empire did not, on the whole, undergo major population changes in Late Antiquity or even in the Umayyad era, Brown's view assumes a substantial shift in cultural outlooks and expectations, in the identity markers of the educated. Is this assumption warranted? Did the educational expectations of the elites of the easternmost parts of the empire undergo a major transformation? And, conversely, in what ways did they retain the old standards of a classical *paideia*? Hence a basic question of continuity and discontinuity presents itself to the modern interpreter. And whatever sort of shift did occur, was it uncontested?

Or was there among the Syrians just the same type of debate (explicit or otherwise) about the clash of religious cultures that we may witness in the writings of Basil or Jerome?

Education as a Desirable Elite Activity in Church and State

Biography, as many scholars have rightly noted, was a key weapon in the battle for the formation of borders and frontiers. By depicting and setting forth ideal behaviours for imitation by readers and hearers their authors hoped to mould and control a sense of identity within the target communities. Hagiographies set before us ideals already deeply cherished by significant portions of the wider community to which the author, and his monastery, belonged. Their significance is enhanced for historians by the very contradictions and differences that may be found among them, not least in the field of education. For every hagiography that emphasises its hero's educational background and knowledge, there will be a companion piece which insists that its subject was all the more powerful as a holy man for his lack of the very same education, for his purity from its polluting, urbanising, paganising effects. Syriac literature is well endowed with hagiographical collections, potted biographies which fill the pages of the monastic histories such as the *Book of Chastity* and Thomas of Marga's *Book of Governors* (c.840), as well as wider-scale propagandistic works such as John of Ephesus' *Lives of the Eastern Saints* (c.580), all works aimed at (re)forming the cultural, social and religious expectations of their readers.[3]

> As formerly everyone who wished to learn and to become master of the foreign/pagan (*baraytha*) philosophy of the Greeks went to Athens, the famous city of philosophers, so in this case, everyone who desired to be instructed in spiritual philosophy went to the monastery of Rabban Mar Abraham, and inscribed himself in sonship to him.[4]

So said Thomas of Marga in relation to the great founder of the East Syrian monastic reform movement. No doubt Thomas would have us develop his logic: to seek an education elsewhere is to seek an unspiritual philosophy. Yet the desire for a spiritual philosophy hardly precluded the acquisition of a less transcendent learning, and many other lives of saints stress the significance and value of a traditional education. The renowned East Syrian theologian Babai the Great (seventh century) experienced what would have been a typical upbringing for any member of the Persian aristocracy, being educated in Persian literature (or science) and then progressing to medicine, studying for a total of 15 years, before being converted to a life of asceticism and moving to Mar Abraham's monastery.[5] The level of his education is admirably borne out by the quality of his extensive literary work. A 'proper' education of this type was clearly of great value in Abraham's monastery, despite Thomas' dictum about spiritual philosophy, for another monastic leader of the same era, Babai of Nisibis, sent

174   *Daniel King*

his pupils to receive just such an education before becoming ascetics themselves, even though he himself seems to have entered the monastic life without any such propaedeutic.[6]

It is hardly a matter for surprise that attitudes to education should vary widely and often clash. An option that must have appealed to many wealthier families is represented for us by the lady Aphtonia. Her husband having been known for his excellence in secular learning (a reference to his attainment of *paideia* and civic office), she ensured after his death that her children received a similar education, herself even acting as *grammatikos* to her youngest. While his brothers acquired imperial appointments, this youngest was introduced to the monastery of St Thomas in Seleuceia near Antioch, not so that his secular learning might be replaced by an alternative, but rather that his literary and rhetorical skills might be honed to perfection. This John bar Aphtonia (d.538) was to become a composer of eloquent prose literature in both Greek and Syriac, and the founder of a Graecophone monastery on the Euphrates.[7] It is perhaps ironic that it was the monasteries that both inherited the early Christian ascetic's protest against traditional, urban, Hellenistic values, and at the same time found themselves increasingly dominant in social life as the traditional functions of the cities gradually gave way. They took upon themselves the burden of providing the literary and rhetorical education to which wealthy parents still aspired.

Another John (he of Tella) who was also brought up and educated by his own mother had a comparable but slightly different experience – he had to flee 'the Roman walls' (i.e. the urban environment) to pursue his ascetic calling in defiance of his mother's attempts to push him into a civil career. He is praised for avidly but secretly reading the Psalms while his more traditionally minded mother believed him to be studying classical literature; and yet his biographer still praises his mother for having in effect prepared her son for a great ecclesiastical career by training him in this very Greek literature and wisdom.[8] The biographer thus shows a somewhat uncertain stance towards the real value of the old *paideia*. It remained crucial because it enabled its fortunate recipients to interact with the highest in the land on an equal footing, and it was a sign that the church-grouping to which the hero belonged (in this case the emerging Miaphysites) was not the social inferior of the imperial church in Constantinople.

In John's biography, then, the issue of sectarian identity takes centre stage. Elias' account of his master's life was written as a piece of propaganda for the anti-Chalcedonian cause in those years in the middle of the sixth century when the schism between the 'Jacobite' church and the imperial church was fast becoming irrecoverable. Elias' panegyric is a monument of carefully crafted invective against the imperial agents of religious persecution, and yet in no way is Elias prepared to leave 'Greek' learning and education to the opposing camp. On the contrary, his hero's being armed with an aristocratic education serves rather to complement and strengthen his principal weapons, ascetic virtue and devotion to true doctrine. Yet despite the admitted importance of this *paideia*,

John's biographer leaves us in no doubt that the Syriac Psalm book, at least theoretically, is of infinitely greater import.

The sources offer us many examples of both intra-group and inter-group contests over education. The particular patterns of reading adopted in the different schools were used as identity markers, ways in which children, and future monks and church leaders, could be provided with a form of *paideia* that was specific to their in-group.[9] The claim that the monastery of Rabban Mar Abraham was the source of spiritual philosophical learning should be heard as a conflict on multiple fronts. It confronts 'Syriac' ascetic practice with 'Greek' cerebral vanities; it serves as a challenge to the West Syrian ('Jacobite') church with its own educational system; and it sets spiritual against secular learning at a time when the compatibility of the two was still very much a matter for cultural negotiation. Thus the 'spiritual philosophy' of Rabban Mar Abraham is unlikely to have involved much, if any, reading of Aristotle or Plato. Nor is much, if any, in the way of rhetoric likely to have been in view. Abraham's 'philosophy' is in fact on a par with the 'new philosophy' declared by Athanasius and others in the Hellenophone world to have replaced the 'old', by which they meant that the unlearned wisdom of the desert fathers had replaced the sophistical reasonings of the old learned philosophers. The polemical debate between those who valued a higher education in (necessarily Greek) philosophy and those for whom it was a path leading nowhere which should be abandoned at the earliest opportunity for the pursuit of ascetic purity was just as much a live one in the Syriophone as in the Hellenophone world.

The Question of Language in Education

It is hardly surprising that this perennial question which dogged many church leaders in the Greek-speaking world – how to navigate between Christian religion and 'pagan' learning, and especially the *paideia* which was the inheritance of every wealthy landowning family – was transferred also to the Syriac-speaking realm. One must not lose sight of the fact that the 'Syriac world' developed always in the shadow of Greek culture and language and was never wholly divorced from it until long after the arrival of Islam. Teaching and learning the wisdom of the Greeks *in Greek*, as we shall see shortly, remained an important feature of Syriac church culture at least until the ninth century.

The question of the persistence of Greek *paideia* thus interleaves closely with the question of language(s) and their distribution and usage patterns. The data at our disposal – literary, epigraphic, palaeographic – all points clearly enough towards significant changes in the status of the Syriac language. In the earliest period of its emergence as a more-than-local dialect, its literary use was confined to the provinces of Osrhoene and Mesopotamia, while to the west of the Euphrates Syriac remained the spoken language of the rural population. The first signs of literary Syriac west of the river come from the fifth century, although even then the records of the church councils leave us in no doubt that Greek

176   *Daniel King*

was still the predominant language of education and authority, both religious and secular, on both sides of the river.[10] Paradoxically, the rise in the status and usage of Syriac did not really coincide with a decline in the use or status of Greek; at least among the wealthier classes and those seeking position in church or state, a Greek education was still the ultimate goal, and the highest church authorities of the emergent Miaphysite movement looked to Greek theology, rather than to the indigenous religious heritage, for guidance in the construction of those specific doctrines which would become their hallmark.

There is good evidence in the histories of John of Ephesus for the spread of Syriophone education even amongst the lower end of the literacy spectrum and its being increasingly assigned a prestige equal to that of Greek.[11] This rise in status coordinated with the gradual spread in the use of Syriac as a language of church inscriptions and in ecclesiastical discourse, and in the increasing confidence shown by Syriophone poets and theologians of the century following Ephrem. Very rarely, however, is this set in any contrast to Hellenophone education. Even Ephrem did not reject Greek philosophy or educational forms as such. His famous barb regarding the 'venom of the wisdom of the Greeks' was an attack upon sectarianism and disputatiousness (seen as a 'Greek' vice) rather than upon Greek philosophy as contrasted with the philosophy of some other language.[12]

Ephrem himself deployed a quite distinctive *form* of educational policy, training choirs of women (daughters of the covenant) to sing his didactic hymns around the streets and churches of Edessa. We are told by the church historian Sozomen that, in using this approach, Ephrem was merely aping the practices of his opponents, the Bardesanites, who had been training their own choirs in these techniques. The hymns which the latter wrote sprang not from indigenous cultural forms, but from 'Greek learning'.[13] Ephrem beat them at their own game, and it is his hymns that have survived to tell what Syriac theology was (meant to look) like, but this should not lead one to imagine that he represented a 'native' movement which launched itself against Hellenism *per se*; nor should it blind us to the varieties of pedagogical traditions that may well have been commonplace in cities such as Edessa. That city had its more formal structures of imperially sanctioned *grammatici* and *rhetores*, and also seems to have kept up a lively trade in lower-level forms of 'popular' education. In this mix of approaches, it was a typical city of the late ancient Empire, and the question of language nuances, rather than alters, this observation.

The Question of Paganism in Syriac Christian Education

In all sorts of ways, the changes and developments that may be observed in the Greek-speaking world were simply carried over into the Syriac. For example, while it is quite true, as Brown noted above, that the classics of Greek epic and tragedy were never translated into Syriac, in fact by the era of Justinian[14] the proliferation of handbooks of grammar and rhetoric testify to a shift in

Education in the Syriac World of Late Antiquity   177

educational practice away from the direct reading of these classics even in Greek circles. These now 'Christian' rhetorical handbooks are suffused with quotations from the Scriptures and the Church Fathers as well as, or instead of, the Greek classics.[15] Things had moved on from the days of Basil of Caesarea, when elite Christian parents seemed to face a choice between a regular pagan rhetorical education, on the one hand, and the monastic alternative on the other. By Justinian's day, a new *oikoumene* had developed, and new 'Christian classics' were beginning to take the place of the pagan classics of traditional education.

The inmates of many Syriac monasteries studied (the Syriac versions of) Gregory Nazianzen or of the Psalms not as a way to avoid a Greek *paideia*, but rather as a Christianised form of that same course of rhetoric and literature that remained as desirable as ever.[16] A basic educational textbook such as (pseudo-)Dionysius Thrax's *Grammar* was, in its translated version, Christianised insofar as the examples were taken now from Scripture rather than from the Greek classics; yet it hardly alters the basic fact that the work is a piece of Greek pedagogy.[17] The translator of Dionysius Thrax states his aim as being the 'the instruction (διατριβή = *durasha*) and education (παιδεία = *mardutha*) of future readers'. By teaching the structure of the Syriac language through a Greek-based medium, it witnesses to that amalgamation of both languages and cultures that was perceived as constituting an ideal education for those Syrians wealthy enough to afford it.

In the sixth century, not long after their original composition in Greek, the scholia to Gregory Nazianzen's orations were translated and disseminated in a Syriac version. So popular were they that they were even revised a century later. The scholia contain a wealth of information on the background to Gregory's many classical allusions, discussing in sometimes great depth matters of pagan religion, often quite ephemeral issues that might on a superficial reading seem to have been of no interest to the (supposedly) ascetically minded and schismatic churches of the east. Yet copies of these scholia abound, most copies deriving from the ninth century, traditionally seen as rather a barren period in the history of Syriac church literature.[18] If the ninth century was the era in which knowledge of the Greek language was gradually seeping from the Syriac mind, then the multiple copying of these scholia suggest at least that a decrease in knowledge of the language did not in any way entail a decrease in the Syrians' interest in matters pertaining to Greek paganism. At least, those who produced and read these manuscripts seem to have felt no greater compunction about using and studying them than did those who originally composed them.

The observation is not limited to the West Syrian, and usually more Graecophile, church. The early translation of these scholia is known especially through its use by seventh-century Church of the East luminaries Babai and Sahdona.[19] The scholia themselves were said to be 'formed according to the ability of their authors by the training of the schools', a training which was given them in the Justinianic era, and which remained an active tradition in the Syriac monasteries some two–three centuries later. One of the best copies of the Syriac revision of the earlier, sixth-century, translation was produced in a monastery overseen at that time by Athanasius of Balad, a future patriarch of the Syrian Orthodox Church who had already received a thorough training in Greek philosophy at Qenneshre, and by a monk who came from another monastery, Mar Zakkai, renowned for its scholarship on Gregory's orations as ideals of rhetorical form. A network and system of monastic schools preserving, copying and propagating a form of Greek *paideia* was still thriving in the eighth and most likely in the ninth century in the former lands of the Roman Empire, and its bosses did not share Tertullian's dread that a lecturer in Greek poetry could not avoid speaking about Greek gods every time he opened his mouth.[20]

The Syriac-speaking churches were not faced only, however, with the problem of the *Greek* pagan past, but also with the parallel difficulty of *their* pagan past. The cities of the eastern provinces had by no means been entirely 'hellenised' before they began the process of becoming 'Christianised', and many are the polemics that were launched against traditional religious practices. Texts such as pseudo-Melito's *Apology*, which describes and attacks the astrological religious practices of Mabbug (Hierapolis, in Euphratense), and Jacob of Serug's *Homily on the Fall of the Idols*, which does the same for Harran, testify to the persistence of many of these pre-Christian religious practices far into Late Antiquity. When the former of these works utilises the *paideia* of Greek rhetoric to fight pre-Christian religious and cultural traditions, this is not a case of using the enemy's weapons against him, as it was when western theologians wrote rhetorically sophisticated tracts against Graeco-Roman gods.[21] Rather the author is introducing an already Christianised *hellenismos* in order to battle against his own past. While it was often possible for the 'wisdom of the Greeks' to be viewed as some sort of shadow prefiguring the true revelation of the Christian faith, it was rather more difficult to think of the pre-Christian culture of the Aramaeans in the same light, though in fact some Syriac thinkers may well have felt just this way about *their* past.[22]

Education may well have been a battleground of sorts between those with different visions of how the religio-cultural (Syrian) past should fuse with a religio-cultural (Hellenised) present. There are hints in the patchy evidence: for example, that the school of Bardaisan, which incorporated many elements of Syriac traditional practice with a form of Stoic philosophy, continued to function in at least some urban centres long after the supposed triumph of episcopal orthodoxy;[23] and the aristocratic faction that opposed Ephrem in Edessa was not at all far removed from the families who not long before had been decorating that city with mosaics depicting Syro-Greek pagan myths, and whose educational aspirations are likely still to have been closer to those of a traditional civic elite than of the emergent authorities of Nicene orthodoxy.[24] There may have been different versions of a rhetorical education propagated among different groups, different specifically as to just how much Hellenistic and how much 'Aramaic' culture ought to be incorporated within a basically Christian education.[25] At the same time, we might instructively compare the poems produced in Syriac in Late Antiquity with the output of the Egyptian lawyer-poet Dioscorus of Aphrodito.[26] Dioscorus freely mixes his official Christian religion with allusions and elements from the 'pagan past' into a new cultural mix that may have been typical of his particular social position in late antique Egypt; it is difficult to find parallels in Syriac.

Institutions of Syriac Education

In contrast to the western parts of the empire, the cities of Syria, and even those east of the river, did not undergo any major decline during the sixth century despite invasion and plague.[27] The government in Constantinople continued to invest heavily in the Hellenised lives of the administrative cities of the empire. Expensive buildings and churches, mosaics and inscriptions, were built under patronage as they long had been, in many cases in unbroken continuity until the ʿAbbāssid takeover in the eighth century. The villages too expanded rather than contracted during this period, both in terms of population and wealth. All is suggestive of a vigorous and persistent aristocracy confidently maintaining their by then ancient traditions of Hellenic life and culture. Although educational practice is largely invisible archaeologically (outside of Alexandria, schools are rather harder to identify than are churches and basilicas), we have no reason to doubt that the urban institutions of education were strongly preserved and propagated in the interests of the governing classes. Only gradually did a Syriac-only, purely monastic-based education displace the primarily Greek urban-based one as the old forms of Roman government eventually slipped away in the course of the eighth–ninth centuries. Even as it did so, strong links indeed remained with the old world.

The written sources add only slivers of data here and there. There are, in reality, very few 'schools' about which we know anything more than their names and locations. The School of Nisibis, of course, offers the parade example and much is known about it, at least for a limited cross-section of its existence.[28] Others we know only hazily, such as the monasteries which tutored the likes of Abū Bishr Mattā, the Baghdad Aristotelian philosopher who in turn tutored al-Fārābī. We can guess at what Mattā learned there only through the content of his own learning and from what little al-Fārābī tells us (or as often tries to prevent us from understanding). Among the West Syrians we know of some key monasteries, Qenneshre and Mar Zakkai in particular; but even of these our knowledge comes not from narratives or historical sources but from the manuscripts produced in these monasteries or the works of those who taught or trained there. Almost the only extended account of Qenneshre we have from a historical source is concerned entirely with an invasion of rather unsavoury demons and the means by which they were exorcised[29] – if that were all we knew we could hardly imagine that the same monastery at the same time was producing translations and commentaries on Aristotelian logic in the mould of the School of Ammonius.

180 *Daniel King*

There is no reason to believe that, at least prior to the Arab invasions and the withdrawal of Roman power from the cities of the eastern provinces, the patterns of urban schooling had changed much from the early period of Romanisation in the second/third centuries. What is true for the empire as a whole was most likely true for cities such as Edessa and Harran, and probably even border cities such as Nisibis. A synod of the Persian church in 486 speaks of monks causing trouble in urban schools, though whether these are schools attached to churches or not (and the difference may have been significant in the Persian realm) is unclear. In any case, as the monastic reforms developed over the two following centuries, both east and west of the border, monasteries became increasingly urban phenomena (where before they had been heavily rural and rooted in the old anchoretic ideals of early eastern Christianity) and central parts of the church authority structure.[30]

The 'School of Nisibis' was only the most noteworthy of such monastically associated foundations. Its close association with the monastic life and the ecclesiastically focused nature of its curriculum have been analysed as thoroughly as the sources will permit.[31] It represented what the pinnacle of a church-based education might achieve, a sophisticated version of what was available in the many village schools that both denominations were building even in the remotest areas for the sake of propagating their sectarian peculiarities and establishing on a firm footing the authority of their hierarchies; for there can be no doubt that education, at all levels, formed a key element in the identity-forming processes that are so notable a feature of the emergence of both West and East Syrian denominations in the course of the sixth/seventh centuries.[32] They fought fiercely too, through literary constructions, over the founding of the great School of Nisibis itself.[33]

This is certainly true for the School of Nisibis, so closely associated with the Great Monastery at Izla and treated as guardian of the special theological teachings of the Church of the East, a theoretical association between monastery and school that is only strengthened and confirmed by the events by which the Great Monastery appears to have switched its support to new and more loyal schools after the supposed 'apostasy' of the School of Nisibis itself under Ḥenana.[34] It was in the context of this struggle for pedagogical authority that we find the reference quoted above about Mar Abraham's school becoming the new Athens — what is meant is simply that orthodox families ought no longer to send their children to heretical Nisibis, but rather to one of the new foundations more directly under the control of the monastic reform movement.

This association between the growth and development of educational institutions and the monastic reform movements is vital. They enjoyed a symbiotic relationship which marks both off from the more anti-intellectual form of asceticism which was common in Syria up to that point in the sixth century when both West and East Syrians began to form themselves into distinct communities. As doctrinal dispute increasingly forced these churches apart from the imperial centre, a crystallisation of social and political structures began to take

Education in the Syriac World of Late Antiquity   181

place, of which both the monastic reform movement and the emerging educational institutions are only facets.[35]

Ḥenana's educational changes at the School of Nisibis have been the subject of much debate,[36] and we can hardly be sure in what they consisted; yet it would be a mistake to assume, because the monastic leaders perceived it as deeply unorthodox, that it therefore consisted in a greater freedom given to the study of pagan traditions. It is true that there always was, among both West and East Syrians, a tradition of conflict between learned and unlearned monks, just as indeed had been the case in Hellenophone regions; a conflict between monks seeking theological acumen and bookish learning against those for whom such things were only a distraction from the true aim of the ascetic life. There are plenty of polemics from the latter camp, while the former position was, on the whole, that of the synods, governed as they were by often wealthy and well-educated ecclesiastical authorities.[37] It does not follow, however, that those who argued in favour of literacy and learning were wedded to a more 'Greek' or 'pagan' style of education, either in form or content. The principal mission of the schools was always the doctrinally orthodox formation of the clergy. Both theological reflection and biblical exegesis supported this general aim. This is indeed why those great learned manuscripts of the Bible traditionally (but misleadingly) called the Syriac Masora attribute so much detailed work of exegesis to 'the schools', the great masters of which were above all experts in the different reading traditions of the biblical text: men who wrote lists of difficult words and expressions found in Scripture, or who wrote summaries of systems of accentuation whose purpose was to facilitate the public reading, and thus also dissemination, of Scripture.

It is in this context (albeit not exclusively) that the forms and content of the old Greek systems of education did impact the pedagogy of the Syriac church. The authoring, for instance, of a tract on accentuation, which was such an important stage in the Syrians' analysis of their own linguistic structures, inevitably led to more developed grammatical reflection and writing which took its point of departure from the well-developed traditions of Greek grammar.[38] The already mentioned translation of Dionysius Thrax is a case in point – reoriented towards a new set of aims and a new world, yet also with a sure backward gaze to the achievements of Greek learning. Nor was it an isolated case, for in fact all Syriac grammatical writing, for the period of Late Antiquity at least, was based on Dionysius Thrax, the Theodosian canons and a few other Greek sources which were well known in the grammatical-rhetorical schools still wedded to the structures of the Byzantine Empire and its ideal of *Romanitas*.

This type of formal continuity has been especially noted in the case of certain texts relating to the curriculum used at Nisibis.[39] For instance, the propaedeutic outlines used in the *Instituta Regularia Divinae Legis*, the rhetorical structures of Barḥadbeshabba's *Cause of the Foundation of the Schools* and the Syriac translation of Nestorius' *Bazaar of Heracleides* all draw on the same outlines that were used in philosophical commentaries, and indeed all sorts of works of a pedagogical nature, emanating from the School of Ammonius in Alexandria. Such parallels are fascinating for the light they shed on the perceived value of these forms of Greek education and the aspirations of the Syriac masters and students; yet they should not be taken as a sign that the content of the teaching was therefore comparable. The use of this well-known isagogic structure in theologically conditioned texts in Syriac is not evidence for the inclusion of Aristotelian studies, for instance, in the School of Nisibis, or indeed anywhere else in the Syriophone realm.[40]

Evidence for the implementation of a genuine philosophical curriculum in the schools, which can only ever have been for an elite within an elite in any case, and which never formed a central part of the curriculum, awaits a rather later period and a rather different route.[41] Among the West Syrians, Sergius of Reshaina was without doubt the most significant proponent of Aristotelian learning, along the lines of the Alexandrian schools. He worked closely with an East Syrian bishop, with whom he was fond of discussing matters both philosophical and medical, and there are suggestions that his own ecclesiastical background was neither monastic nor particularly 'orthodox' – accusations of Origenism and the association of some of his writings with Bardaisan place him quite apart from the traditions of the School of Nisibis. Paul the Persian famously summarised Aristotelian logic for the East, but in fact did so for the Persian court, not the Syriac church from which he had absconded, and his writings were only much later adopted into a more general curriculum, in the West Syrian monastery at Qenneshre.

Since none of the Syriac philosophical authors of the sixth century can be shown to have had any links with the establishment or with any known educational institutions, it is very likely that there was no interest in Greek philosophy within the curricula of the schools before at least the beginning of the seventh century, if even then. When it did make its appearance, it did so in full Greek dress, a Syriac adoption of the late Platonist interpretation of Aristotelian logic as taught in the schools of Alexandria. It was also much more closely associated with medicine than it was with theology (again this is true of the Greek schools too), and Sergius' evidence suggests to us that it was the traditional Syriac interest in medicine which served as the incentive and the conduit for the arrival of Aristotle. Such a curriculum was known not just in West Syria, where it was much expounded upon at Qenneshre and doubtless elsewhere to a lesser level, but also in the East where authors such as Sylvanus of Qardu (probably seventh century) show a very close knowledge of some of the Greek commentaries. Once established in this pedagogical context, philosophy was not perceived as a threat to ecclesiastical authority; nor was it pursued primarily for the purpose of theological polemics, but was rather seen as a first, but thus all the more indispensable, step on the path to that immediate vision of God which was the aim of every ascetic. It seems only to have been in the context of the awakening of learned Muslims to the benefits of Greek philosophy in the ninth century that Syrians too began to study logic as the art of refuting contrary doctrine, a

Education in the Syriac World of Late Antiquity   183

pursuit that was to have a long, though not always profitable, afterlife in Christian–Muslim relations for centuries to come.[42]

Continuities in Philosophy and Rhetoric

To return now to Late Antiquity before the rise of the 'Abbāssid caliphate and to the question of the continuities in educational form, if not content, between Hellenophone and Syriophone educational structures. We have seen that grammar was an important part of Syriac education, and to that extent mirrored its Greek counterpart and drew freely upon it. We have seen also the ways in which, at the other end of the scale almost, philosophy gradually but eventually followed a like path. What of rhetoric, the middle stage of the classical curriculum? The question has been repeatedly researched and discussed by Watt,[43] whose work leaves little doubt, despite the apparent paucity of the extant evidence, that the Syriac schools were from an early stage quite accustomed to the teaching of rhetoric and that in this they were again, therefore, showing a continuity of form with the Greek schools which were almost certainly still active in all urban centres throughout the period of Byzantine control and beyond.[44] The principal testimony is the work of Antony of Tagrit, a ninth-century (most likely) rhetorical theorist whose extensive work on the topic draws heavily upon Greek rhetorical theory as it was taught in the Aphthonius-Hermogenes corpus of rhetorical handbooks that were available in the Hellenophone schools of the empire.[45] We cannot be certain how these were mediated to Antony, but the fact that he seems not to have been literate in Greek suggests strongly that Syriac handbooks of the same sort already existed. Antony presupposes the *trivium* of grammar, rhetoric and poetics, imitating thereby a Greek structure which is almost unknown among his Arabic contemporaries or successors. Barhebraeus in the thirteenth century was harking back to these old and distinctive Syriac traditions when he proposed that students should read Antony's rhetoric as a propaedeutic to the higher matters of philosophy and mathematics. In Antony's own day, however, he complains of those who opposed his rhetorical theories, who say that 'it is an abomination that the church should engage in such things', reminding us that there always was a strong tradition of opposition to such forms of education and that Syriophone pedagogy was anything but homogeneous through all its stages.

We do have enough, however, to be sure that the Greek educational structures that were alive and well in the urban centres of empire in the fourth and fifth centuries maintained their value, and therefore their existence, within the newly forming church-based social structures of the Syriac population. Mothers still wanted their children to receive the formal education of the grammarian and the rhetor, very often in Greek while that was still possible, but otherwise in Syriac, which gradually supplanted Greek in the seventh and eighth centuries but which had always been dominant east of the Euphrates and in the Persian Empire. Battles over education – over its value for the true Christian ascetic, over its particular form and content – were as rife as perhaps they always are in

184 Daniel King

most cultures and at most times. There were battles over how deep and far the literary-theological education of future monks and clergy ought to proceed, and also battles (not necessarily connected) over the extent to which Greek learning (either in form or in content) was appropriate in the church. There were those for whom the mythical allusions in Gregory of Nazianzen's orations were part and parcel of a proper rhetorical education, and those for whom anything from Homer was only so much corrupting pollution. There were those for whom some of the old forms of Syriac religion, such as an astrological understanding of the universe, were compatible with both philosophy and theology, and those for whom Aristotle and the Bible were the only possible guides to cosmology. Education forms a path to identity, and that is precisely why it always was, and always will be, such a very contentious issue.

Notes

1 Gemeinhardt 2012c, 57.
2 Brown 1971, 186.
3 For the general import of hagiography for the history of late ancient Christianity, Cameron 1991, 141–51.
4 Thomas of Marga, *Book of Governors* (Wallis Budge 1893, 23, 20–24, 1; English trans., vol. II, 41).
5 Kitchen 2012.
6 Bettiolo 2007, 301–3 on the two Babais.
7 On John bar Aphtonia, Watt 1999.
8 The biography was written by his pupil Elias: *Vita Iohannis Episcopi Tellae* (Brooks 1907, 29–95 text, 21–60 trans).
9 Tannous 2013.
10 Millar 1998.
11 Ashbrook Harvey 1990, 40–42.
12 As the immediately following words make clear: 'Blessed is he that has not let slip the simplicity of the apostle' (Ephrem, *On the Faith* II, 1, trans. Morris 1847, 112). As he says elsewhere, 'envy is from Satan . . . accursed disputation is from the Greeks' (*The Pearl, Hymns on Faith* VII, trans. Morris 1847, 102), essentially repeating a commonplace found equally among Hellenophone authors as among Syriophone ones.
13 Sozomen, *Ecclesiastical History* III, 16.
14 For the reception of the Troy cycle, see now Hilkens 2013.
15 For another aspect of this process, see Chapter 5 by Alberto Rigolio in this volume.
16 The best-known Syriac rhetorician, Antony of Tagrit, calls him the 'prince of sophists'.
17 King 2012.
18 Brock 1971, 7–12.
19 On the texts and their traditions, see the introduction to Brock 1971.
20 Tertullian, *On Idolatry*, 10.
21 Rappe 2001, 409–10.
22 The Syriac philosopher Sergius of Reshaina may have seen elements of local astrological religion as being worthy of incorporation into Christian philosophy. See King 2010, 199–208.
23 King 2010, 204–8.
24 Brock 1992, 228. See also Drijvers 1982.
25 The Syrians themselves often used the term 'Aramaic' to refer specifically to the pagan past of the Aramaic-speaking people.
26 MacCoull 1988; Fournet 1999.

27 The seminal study is Foss 1997.
28 Most of what is known may be extracted from Becker 2006.
29 Penn 2013.
30 As argued cogently in Camplani 2007.
31 Bibliography in Becker 2006.
32 Tannous 2013.
33 Wood 2010, 115.
34 Camplani 2007, 283–4.
35 Wood 2010, 57ff., for one example. Ascetics such as Adelphius of Antioch, in clear contrast to Mar Abraham, would never have attempted the founding of a school.
36 Reinink 1995.
37 Camplani 2007, 290.
38 The tract was studied grammatically by Segal 1953; for its significance and context, King 2012.
39 Riad 1988; Becker 2006.
40 Contra, for example, Vööbus 1965, esp. 212.
41 King 2013.
42 See King 2013 and King 2015.
43 Various articles reprinted in Watt 2010.
44 Greek grammars were still being written in Edessa in the ninth century: Donnet 1982.
45 For what follows, we follow the findings of Watt 2009 and other articles on the subject found in Watt 2010.

Bibliography

Editions

Acts of the Conference of Carthage (411 AD)

Lancel, S., 1972–75. *Actes de la Conférence de Carthage en 411*, 3 vols (SChr 194, 195, 224). Paris: Cerf.

Akathistos Hymn

Trypanis, C.A., 1968. *Fourteen Early Byzantine Cantica.* Vienna: Böhlau.

Armenian Codex Jerusalem 121

Renoux, A., 1969–71. *Le codex arménien Jérusalem 121*, 2 vols (Patrologia Orientalis 163, 168). Turnhout: Brepols.

Athanasius

Gregg, R., 1980. *Athanasius: Life of Antony and the Letter to Marcellinus.* New York: Paulist Press.

Barberini Euchologion

Parenti, S. and Velkovska, E., 2000. *L'Eucologio Barberini Gr. 336.* Rome: Edizioni Liturgiche (2nd edition).

Basil of Caesarea

Clarke, W.K.L., 1925. *The Ascetic Works of Saint Basil.* London: SPCK.
Deferrari, R.J., 1934. *Basil: Letters*, 4 vols (Loeb Classical Library). Cambridge, MA: Harvard University Press.
Naldini, M., 1984. *Basilio di Cesarea: Discorso ai giovani, Oratio ad Adolescentes.* Florence: Nardini.
Wilson, N.G., 1975. *Saint Basil on the Value of Greek Literature.* London: Duckworth.

Besa

Bell, D., 1983. *The Life of Shenoute* (Cistercian Studies 73). Kalamazoo, MI: Cistercian Publications.

188 *Bibliography*

Kuhn, K.H., 1956. *Letters and Sermons of Besa* (CSCO 157, 158). Louvain: Imprimerie orientaliste.

Book of Paradise

Wallis Budge, E.A., 1904. *The* Book of Paradise, *being the histories and sayings of the monks and ascetics of the Egyptian desert by Palladius, Hieronymus and others: The Syriac text, according to recension of 'Anân-Îshô' of Bêth 'Âbhê.* London: Drugulin.

Caesarius of Arles

Klingshirn, W., 1994. *Caesarius of Arles: Life, Testament, Letters* (Translated Texts for Historians 19). Liverpool: Liverpool University Press.

Dialogue with Jews

Declerk, J.H., 1994. *Anonymus Dialogus cum Iudaeis saeculi ut videtur sexti* (CCG 30). Turnhout: Brepols.

Fields, L.M., 2012. *An Anonymous Dialogue with a Jew.* Turnhout: Brepols.

Dracontius

Bouquet, J. and Wolff, E., 1995. *Dracontius: Œuvres*, Volume 3: *La tragédie d'Oreste, Poèmes profanes I – V.* Paris: Les Belles Lettres.

Moussy, C., 1988. *Dracontius: Œuvres*, Volume 2: *Louanges de Dieu, Livre III–Réparation.* Paris: Les Belles Lettres.

———— and Camus, C., 1985. *Dracontius, Œuvres*, Volume 1: *Louanges de Dieu, Livre I–II.* Paris: Les Belles Lettres.

Wolff, É., 1996. *Dracontius, Œuvres*, Volume 4: *Poèmes profanes VI–X; Fragments.* Paris: Les Belles Lettres.

Ephrem the Syrian

Morris, J.B., 1847. *Select Works of Ephrem the Syrian.* Oxford: J.H. Parker.

Epictetus

Boter, G., 1999. *The* Encheiridion *of Epictetus and Its Three Christian Adaptations.* Leiden: Brill.

Eusebius of Caesarea

Schwartz, E., 1903–09. *Die Kirchengeschichte* (Die griechischen christlichen Schriftsteller der ersten drei Jahrhunderte 9). Leipzig: J.C. Hinrichs'sche Buchhandlung.

Ferrandus

Lapeyre, G.G., 1929. *Ferrand, Diacre de Carthage, Vie de Saint Fulgence de Ruspe.* Paris: Lethielleux.

Fulgentius

Helm, R., 1970. *Fabii Planciadis Fulgentii V. C. Opera* (Bibliotheca Scriptorum Graecorum et Romanorum Teubneriana). Leipzig: Teubner.

Wolff, É. and Dain, Ph., 2013. *Fulgence: Mythologies*. Villeneuve d'Ascq: Presses universitaires du Septentrion.

Wolff, É. and Graziani, F., 2009. *Fulgence: Virgile dévoilé*. Villeneuve d'Ascq: Presses universitaires du Septentrion.

Georgian Lectionary of Jerusalem

Tarchnischvili, M., 1959–60. *Le grand lectionnaire de l'Église de Jérusalem, Ve–VIIIe siècle*, 4 vols (CSCO 188, 189, 204, 205). Louvain: Secrétariat du CSCO.

Gregory of Nyssa

Maraval, P., 1990. *Grégoire de Nysse: Lettres* (SChr 363). Paris: Cerf.

Jerome

Wright, F.A., 1933. *Jerome: Select Letters* (Loeb Classical Library). London: Heinemann.

John Chrysostom

Laistner, M.L.W., 1951. *Christianity and Pagan Culture in the Later Roman Empire: Together with an English Translation of John Chrysostom's Address on Vainglory and the Right Way for Parents to Bring Up Their Children*. Ithaca, NY: Cornell University Press (reprint 1967).

Malingrey, A.-M., 1972. *Jean Chrysostome: Sur la vaine gloire et l'éducation des enfants* (SChr 188). Paris: Cerf.

John of Apamea

Dedering, S., 1936. *Johannes von Lykopolis, ein Dialog über die Seele und die Affekte des Menschen*. Leiden: Brill.

Lavenant, R., 1984. *Jean d'Apamée: Dialogues et traités* (SChr 311). Paris: Cerf.

Strothmann, W., 1972. *Johannes von Apamea*. Berlin: De Gruyter.

John Philoponus

Busse, A., 1898, *Philoponi (olim Ammonii) in Aristotelis categorias commentarium* (Commentaria in Aristotelem Graeca 13.1). Berlin: Reimer.

Libanius

Bradbury, S., 2004. *Selected Letters of Libanius from the Age of Constantius and Julian* (Translated Texts for Historians 41). Liverpool: Liverpool University Press.

Fatouros, G. and Krischer, T., 1980. *Libanios: Briefe*. Munich: Heimeran.

Foerster, R., 1922. *Libanius: Opera*, Volume 11 (Bibliotheca Scriptorum Graecorum et Romanorum Teubneriana). Leipzig: Teubner.

Foerster, R., 1927. *Libanius: Opera*, Volume 9 (Bibliotheca Scriptorum Graecorum et Romanorum Teubneriana). Leipzig: Teubner.

Norman, A.F., 1992. *Libanius: Autobiography and Selected Letters*, 2 vols (Loeb Classical Library). Cambridge, MA: Harvard University Press.

190   *Bibliography*

Life of Eutychius

Laga, C., 1992. *Eustratii Presbyteri: Vita Eutychii patriarchae Constantinopolitani* (CCG 25). Turnhout: Brepols.

Life of Saint Mary of Egypt

Kouli, M., 1996. *Life of St. Mary of Egypt*. In Talbot, A.-M. ed. *Holy Women of Byzantium: Ten Saints' Lives in English Translation*. Washington, DC: Dumbarton Oaks, pp. 65–93.

Life of Simon the Fool

Festugière, A. J. and Rydén, L., 1974. *Vie de Syméon le Fou et Vie de Jean de Chypre*. Paris: Geuthner.

Lucian

Bompaire, J., 1998. *Lucien, Œuvres, Tome II opuscules 11–20*. Paris: Les Belles Lettres.
Sachau, E., 1870. Inedita Syriaca. Vienna: Hof & Staatsdruckerei.

Marinus of Naples

Masullo, R., 1985. *Marino di Neapoli: Vita di Proclo* (Speculum, Contributi di Filologia Classica). Naples: M. D'Auria.

Michael Syncellus

Donnet, D., 1982. *Le traité de la construction de la phrase de Michael Syncelle de Jérusalem* (Études de Philologie, d'Archéologie et d'Histoire anciennes 22). Brussels: Institut historique belge de Rome.

Miracles of Saint Artemius

Crisafulli, V. and Nesbitt, J., 1997. *The Miracles of Saint Artemios: A Collection of Miracle Stories by an Anonymous Author of Seventh-Century Byzantium*. Leiden: Brill.

Monophysites

Brooks, E. W., 1907. *Vitae virorum apud Monophysitas celeberrimorum* (CSCO 7, 8). Paris: Typographeo Reipublicae.

Pachomius

Boon, A., 1932. *Pachomiana Latina*. Louvain: Universiteitbibliotheek.
Lefort, L. Th., 1933–34. *Sancti Pachomii vitae Sahidice scripta*, 2 vols (CSCO 99, 100). Louvain: Durbecq.
———, 1953. *Sancti Pachomii vitae Bohairice scripta* (CSCO 90). Louvain: Durbecq.
———, 1956. *Oeuvres de S. Pachôme et de ses disciples*, 2 vols (CSCO 159, 160). Louvain: Imprimerie orientaliste.
Veilleux, A., 1980. *Pachomian Koinonia*, 3 vols. Kalamazoo: Cistercian Press.

Palladius

Bartelink, G. J. M., 1974. *Palladio: La storia Lausiaca* (Scrittori Greci e Latini; Vite dei Santi 2). Milan: Fondazione Lorenzo Valla.

Bibliography   191

Philostratus

Kayser, C.L., 1870–71. *Flavii Philostrati opera*, 2 vols (Bibliotheca Scriptorum Graecorum et Romanorum Teubneriana). Leipzig: Teubner.

Wright, W.C., 1921. *Philostratus: Lives of the Sophists; Eunapius: Lives of Philosophers* (Loeb Classical Library). Cambridge MA: Harvard University Press.

Plato

Burnet, J., 1903. *Platonis opera*, 3 vols. Oxford: Clarendon (reprint 1968).

Plutarch

De Lagarde, P., 1858. Analecta Syriaca. Leipzig: Teubner.

Hunter, R. and Russell, D., 2011. *Plutarch: How to Study Poetry (De audiendis poetis)*. Cambridge: Cambridge University Press.

Nestle, E., 1894. A Tract of Plutarch: On the Advantage to be Derived from One s Enemies (Studia Sinaitica 4). Cambridge: Cambridge University Press.

Pohlenz, M., et al., eds, 1929. Plutarchi moralia (Bibliotheca Scriptorum Graecorum et Romanorum Teubneriana). Leipzig: Teubner.

Pseudo-John of Lycopolis

Hausherr, I., 1939. *Jean le Solitaire (Pseudo-Jean de Lycopolis): Dialogue sur l'âme et les passions des hommes* (OCA 120). Rome: Pontificio Istituto Orientale.

Pseudo-Nonnos

Brock, S.P., 1971. *The Syriac Version of the Pseudo-Nonnos Mythological Scholia*. Cambridge: Cambridge University Press.

Pseudo-Plutarch

De Lagarde, P., 1858. Analecta Syriaca. Leipzig: Teubner.

Rohlfs, W., 1968. *Pseudo-Plutarch, Peri askeseos*. In Dörries, H. ed. *Paul de Lagarde und die syrische Kirchengeschichte*. Göttingen: Lagarde-Haus, pp. 176–84.

Quintilian

Russell, D.A., 2001. *The Orator's Education* (Loeb Classical Library). Cambridge, MA: Harvard University Press.

Romanos the Melodist

Maas, P. and Trypanis, C.A., 1963. *Sancti Romani Melodi Cantica: Cantica Genuina*. Oxford: Clarendon.

Sayings of the Fathers

Ward, B., 1975. *The Sayings of the Desert Fathers: The Alphabetical Collection*. Kalamazoo, MI: Cistercian Press.

192   Bibliography

————, 2003. *The Desert Fathers: Sayings of the Early Christian Monks*. London: Penguin.

Scholia on the Council of Aquileia

Gryson, R., 1980. *Scolies ariennes sur le concile d'Aquilée* (SChr 267). Paris: Cerf.

Septuagint

Rahlfs, A., 1979. *Septuaginta: Editio Altera*. Stuttgart: Deutsche Bibelgesellschaft.
Ziegler, J., 1978. *Septuaginta:Vetus Testamentum Graecum*, Volume 16. Göttingen: Vandenhoeck & Ruprecht.

Sextus

Wilson, W.T., 2012. *The Sentences of Sextus*. Atlanta: Society of Biblical Literature.

Shenoute

Boud'hors, A., 2013. *Le Canon 8 de Chénouté*, 2 vols Cairo: Institut français d'archéologie orientale.
Emmel, S., 2004a. *Shenoute's Literary Corpus*, 2 vols (CSCO 599, 600). Leuven: Peeters.
Layton, B., 2014. *The Canons of Our Fathers: Monastic Rules of Shenoute*. Oxford: Oxford University Press.
Leipoldt, J., 1906–13. *Sinuthii Archimandritae Vita et Opera Omnia*, 3 vols (CSCO 41, 42, 73). Paris: Imprimerie nationale.
Lubomierski, N., 2007. *Die Vita Sinuthii*. Tübingen: Mohr Siebeck.
Moussa, M., 2010. I Have Been Reading the Holy Gospels *by Shenoute of Atripe (Discourses 8, Work 1): Coptic Text, Translation, and Commentary*. PhD diss. Catholic University of America.

Socrates of Constantinople

Maraval, P., 2004–07. *Socrate de Constantinople: Histoire Écclesiastique*, 3 vols (SChr 477, 493, 505). Paris: Cerf.

Themistius

Downey, G. and Norman, A.F., 1971. *Themistii orationes quae supersunt* (Bibliotheca Scriptorum Graecorum et Romanorum Teubneriana). Leipzig: Teubner.
Sachau, E., 1870. Inedita Syriaca. Vienna: Hof & Staatsdruckerei.

Theodore Lector

Hansen, G.C., 1995. *Theodoros Anagnostes: Kirchengeschichte* (Die griechischen christlichen Schriftsteller der ersten Jahrhunderte, N.F. 3). Berlin: Akademie Verlag (2nd edition).

Thomas of Marga

Wallis Budge, E.A., 1893. *The Book of Governors: The Historia Monastica of Thomas Bishop of Marga*, 2 vols. London: Kegan Paul, Trench, Trübner.

Typikon of the Great Church

Mateos, J., 1962–63. *Le typicon de la Grande Église*, 2 vols. Rome: Pontificium Institutum Orientalium Studiorum.

Victor of Vita

Costanza, S., 1981. *Vittore di Vita: Storia della persecuzione vandalica in Africa.* Rome: Città Nuova.

Halm, K., 1879. *Victor Vitensis: Historia persecutionis africanae provinciae sub Geiserico et Hunirico regibus Wandalorum* (Monumenta Germaniae Historica, Auctores Antiquissimi III 1). Berlin: Weidmann.

Helm, R. 2002. *Victor de Vita: Histoire de la persécution vandale en Afrique; La passion des sept martyrs.* Paris: Les Belles Lettres.

Martyn, J.R.C., 2008. Victor of Vita (Historia Persecutionis Africanae Provinciae). In Martyn, J.R.C., *Arians and Vandals of the 4th–6th Centuries.* Newcastle upon Tyne: Cambridge Scholars, pp. 1–129.

Moorhead, J., 1992. *Victor of Vita: History of the Vandal Persecution.* Liverpool: Liverpool University Press.

Petschenig, M., 1881. *Victoris episcopi Vitensis Historia persecutionis africanae provinciae; accedit incerti autoris Passio septem monachorum et notitia quae vocatur* (CSEL 7). Vienna: Gerold.

Vössing, K., 2011. *Victor von Vita: Kirchenkampf und Verfolgung unter den Vandalen in Africa.* Darmstadt: Wissenschaftliche Buchgesellschaft.

Victricius of Rouen

Buc, Ph., 2001. *Victricius of Rouen: In Praise of the Saints.* In Head, T. ed. *Medieval Hagiography: An Anthology.* New York: Routledge, pp. 31–51.

Mulders, J. and Demeulenaere, R., 1985. *Uictricius Rotomagensis: De laude sanctorum* (CCL 64). Turnhout: Brepols.

Zacharias Scholasticus

Brock, S. and Fitzgerald, B., 2013. *Two Early Lives of Severos, Patriarch of Antioch* (Translated Texts for Historians 59). Liverpool: Liverpool University Press.

Secondary Literature

Albarrán Martínez, M., 2012. Women Reading Books in Egyptian Monastic Circles. In Montferrer-Sala, J., Teule, H. and Torallas Tovar, S. eds. *Eastern Christians and Their Written Heritage.* Leuven: Peeters.

Andrieu-Guitrancourt, P., 1970. Notes, remarques et réflexions sur la vie ecclésiastique et religieuse à Rouen sous le pontificat de saint Victrice. In Lobin, Z. ed. *Études offertes à Jean Macqueron.* Aix-en-Provence: Faculté de Droit et de Science Politique, pp. 7–20.

Angenendt, A., 2007. *Heilige und Reliquien: Die Geschichte ihres Kultes vom frühen Christentum bis zur Gegenwart.* Munich: Beck (2nd edition).

Arjava, A., 2009. Review of Humfress 2007. *Classical Review*, 59, pp. 570–72.

Arranz, M., 1991. Les prières pénitentielles de la tradition byzantine: Les sacrements de la restauration de l'ancien Euchologie Constantinopolitain. *Orientalia Christiana Periodica*, 57, pp. 87–143.

Arzhanov, Y. 2013. The Arabis version of the Syriac Gnomologies "On the Soul" by Mubaššir b. Fātik. *Kristianskij Vostok*, n.s. 6 (XII), pp. 312–322.

Ashbrook Harvey, S., 1990. *Asceticism and Society in Crisis: John of Ephesus and the Lives of the Eastern Saints* (Transformation of the Classical Heritage 18). Berkeley: University of California Press.

194   Bibliography

Aubineau, M., 1974. Le theme du 'Bourbier' dans la literature grecque profane et chrétiennes. In Aubineau, M. ed. *Recherches patristiques: enquêtes sur des manuscripts, texts inédits, études.* Amsterdam: Hakkert, pp. 225–54.

Bagnall, R., 1993. *Egypt in Late Antiquity.* Princeton, NJ: Princeton University Press.

Bakke, O.M., 2005. *When Children Became People: The Birth of Childhood in Early Christianity.* Minneapolis: Fortress.

Bardy, G., 1936. Antiochus. *Dictionnaire de Spiritualité,* 1. Paris: Beauchesne, pp. 701–2.

Barkhuizen, J.H., 1990. Romanos Melodos, *Kontakion 10* (Oxf.): 'On the Sinful Woman'. *Acta Classica,* 33, pp. 33–52.

Bastiaensen, A.A.R., 1996. Les martyrs esprits célestes selon Victricius de Rouen. In Nip, R.I.A. ed. *Media latinitas: A Collection of Essays to Mark the Occasion of the Retirement of Lodewijk J. Engels* (Instrumenta Patristica 28). Steenbrügge: Brepols, pp. 181–5.

Baumstark, A., 1894. Lucubrationes Syro-Graecae. *Jahrbücher für classische Philologie,* Suppl. 21, pp. 353–524.

Becker, A., 2006. *Fear of God and the Beginning of Wisdom: The School of Nisibis and the Development of Christian Scholastic Culture in Late Antique Mesopotamia.* Philadelphia: University of Pennsylvania Press.

Bellet, P., 1982. *Anthologia Palatina* 9.538: The Alphabet and the Calligraphic Examination in the Coptic Scriptorium. *Bulletin of the American Society of Papyrologists,* 19, pp. 1–6.

Bessières, M., 1923. *La tradition manuscrite de la correspondance de S. Basile.* Oxford: Oxford University Press.

Bettiolo, P., 2007. Contrasting Styles of Ecclesiastical Authority and Monastic Life in the Church of the East at the Beginning of the Seventh Century. In Camplani, A. and Filoramo, G. eds. *Foundations of Power and Conflicts of Authority in Late-Antique Monasticism: Proceedings of the International Seminar, Turin, December 2–4, 2004.* Leuven: Peeters, pp. 297–331.

Biblia Patristica Online. http://www.biblindex.mom.fr.

Biedenkopf-Ziehner, A., 2000. *Koptische Ostraka aus dem Ashmolean Museum in Oxford,* 2 vols. Wiesbaden: Harrassowitz.

Binggeli, A., 2008. Fragments du Pandecte d'Antiochus de Saint-Sabas dans le fonds du Supplément grec de la Bibiothèque Nationale de France. *Scriptorium,* 62/2, pp. 278–82.

Blair, A., 2010. *Too Much to Know: Managing Scholarly Information before the Modern Age.* New Haven, CT: Yale University Press.

Booth, P., 2014. *Crisis of Empire: Doctrine and Dissent at the End of Late Antiquity* (Transformation of the Classical Heritage 52). Berkeley: University of California Press.

Boter, G., 1999. *The Encheiridion of Epictetus and Its Three Christian Adaptations.* Leiden: Brill.

Bowersock, G.W., 2012. *Empires in Collision in Late Antiquity.* Waltham, MA: Brandeis University Press.

Brakke, D., 1995. *Athanasius and Asceticism.* Baltimore, MD: Johns Hopkins University Press.

Bräutigam, F., 2003. *Basileios der Große und die heidnische Bildung: Eine Interpretation seiner Schrift 'Ad adolescentes'.* PhD thesis, Jena.

Brock, S., 1980. Towards a History of Syriac Translation Technique. In Lavenant, R. ed. *III Symposium Syriacum, Goslar 7–11 Sept. 1980: Les contacts du monde syriaque avec les autres cultures* (OCA 221). Rome: Pontificium Institutum Orientalium Studiorum, pp. 1–14.

———, 1982. From Antagonism to Assimilation: Syriac Attitudes to Greek Learning. In Garsoïan, N.G., Mathews, T.F. and Thomson, R.W., eds. *East of Byzantium: Syria and Armenia in the Formative Period.* Washington, DC: Dumbarton Oaks, pp. 17–34.

———, 1990. Diachronic Aspects of Syriac Word Formation: An Aid for Dating Anonymous Texts. In Lavenant, R., ed. *V Symposium Syriacum: Katholieke Universiteit, Leuven, 29–31 août 1988* (OCA 234). Rome: Pontificium Institutum Orientalium Studiorum, pp. 321–30.

Bibliography 195

———, 1992. Eusebius and Syriac Christianity. In Attridge, H.W. and Hata, G. eds. *Eusebius, Christianity, and Judaism* (Studia Post-Biblica 42). Leiden: Brill, pp. 212–34.

———, 2003. Syriac Translations of Greek Popular Philosophy. In Bruns, P. ed. *Von Athen nach Bagdad* (Hereditas 22). Bonn: Borengässer, pp. 9–28.

———, 2005. The Instructions of Anton, Plato's Physician. *Journal of Semitic Studies*, Suppl. 16, pp. 129–38.

———, 2012. Some Syriac Pseudo-Platonic Curiosities. In al-Akiti, M.A., Burnett, C. and Hansberger, R. eds. *Medieval Arabic Thought: Essays in Honour of Fritz Zimmermann*. London: Warburg Institute, pp. 19–26.

Brown, P., 1971. *The World of Late Antiquity: From Marcus Aurelius to Muhammad*. London: Thames and Hudson.

———, 1981. *The Cult of the Saints: Its Rise and Function in Latin Christianity*. Chicago: University of Chicago Press.

———, 1982. *Society and the Holy in Late Antiquity*. Berkeley: University of California Press.

———, 1988. *The Body and Society: Men, Women and Sexual Renunciation in Early Christianity*. New York: Columbia University Press.

———, 1992. *Power and Persuasion in Late Antiquity: Towards a Christian Empire*. Madison: University of Wisconsin Press.

Bucking, S., 1999. Review of R. Cribiore, *Writing, Teachers and Students in Graeco-Roman Egypt*. *Bulletin of the American Society of Papyrologists*, 36, pp. 191–202.

———, 2007. Scribes and Schoolmasters: On Contextualizing Coptic and Greek Ostraca Excavated at the Monastery of Epiphanius. *Journal of Coptic Studies*, 9, pp. 21–47.

Burrus, V., 2004. *The Sex Lives of Saints: An Erotics of Ancient Hagiography*. Philadelphia: University of Pennsylvania Press.

Burton-Christie, D., 1993. *The Word in the Desert: Scripture and the Quest for Holiness in Early Christian Monasticism*. New York: Oxford University Press.

Cabouret, B., 2004. *Libanios: Lettres aux hommes de son temps*. Paris: Les Belles Lettres.

Cadiou, R., 1966. Le problème des relations scolaires entre Saint Basile et Libanios. *Revue des Etudes Grecques*, 79, pp. 89–98.

Cameron, Al., 2007. Poets and Pagans in Byzantine Egypt. In Bagnall, R., ed. *Egypt in the Byzantine World 300–700*. Cambridge: Cambridge University Press, pp. 21–46.

Cameron, Av., 1990. Models of the Past in the Late Sixth Century: The Life of the Patriarch Eutychius. In Clarke, G.W., ed. *Reading the Past in Late Antiquity*, pp. 205–23. Canberra: Australian National University Press. (Reprinted in Cameron, A., *Changing Cultures in Byzantium*. Aldershot: Variorum, 1996, n. II).

———, 1991. *Christianity and the Rhetoric of Empire: The Development of Christian Discourse* (Sather Classical Lectures 55). Berkeley: University of California Press.

———, 1997. Education and Literary Culture. In Cameron, A. and Garnsey, P. eds. *The Late Empire, AD 337–425* (Cambridge Ancient History 13). Cambridge: Cambridge University Press, pp. 665–707.

———, 2014. *Dialoguing in Late Antiquity*. Cambridge, MA: Centre for Hellenic Studies.

———and Hoyland, R., 2011. *Doctrine and Debate in the East Christian World, 300–1500*. Farnham: Ashgate.

Camplani, A., 2007. The Revival of Persian Monasticism: Church Structures, Theological Academy, and Reformed Monks. In Camplani, A., and Filoramo, G. eds. *Foundations of Power and Conflicts of Authority in Late-Antique Monasticism*. Leuven: Peeters, pp. 277–95.

Capello, G., 1937. Il latino di Vittore di Vita. In *Atti della Società Italiana per il Progresso delle Scienze, Riunione* 25, pp. 74–108.

196   Bibliography

Carr, D., 2005. *Writing on the Tablet of the Heart: Origins of Scripture and Literature*. New York: Oxford University Press.

Cassin, M., 2012. *L'écriture de la controverse chez Grégoire de Nysse: Polémique littéraire et exégèse dans le* Contre Eunome (Collection des Études augustiniennes, Série Antiquité 193). Paris: Institut d'Études Augustiniennes.

Champollion, J.F., 1889. *Monuments de l'Égypte et de la Nubie*. Paris: Didot.

Chase, M., Clark, S.R.L. and McGhee, M., eds. 2013. *Philosophy as a Way of Life: Ancients and Moderns. Essays in Honor of Pierre Hadot*. Chichester: Wiley-Blackwell.

Clark, G. 1999. Victricius of Rouen: *Praising the Saints. Journal of Early Christian Studies*, 7, pp. 365–99 (repr. ead. 2011, no. 12).

———, 2001. Translating Relics: Victricius of Rouen and the Fourth Century Debate. *Early Medieval Europe*, 10, pp. 161–76 (repr. ead. 2011, no. 13).

———, 2011. *Body and Gender, Soul and Reason in Late Antiquity* (Collected Studies Series 978). Farnham: Ashgate.

Conterno, M., 2010. Retorica pagana e cristianesimo orientale: la traduzione siriaca dell'orazione 'Peri philias' di Temistio. *Annali di Scienze Religiose*, 3, pp. 161–88.

———, 2014. *Temistio orientale: Orazioni temistiane nella tradizione siriaca ed araba*. Brescia: Paideia.

Cotterill, J.M., 1884. *Modern Criticism and Clement's Epistles to Virgins, or their Greek Version newly Discovered in Antiochus Palaestinensis, with Appendix Containing Newly Found Versions of Fragments Attributed to Melito*. Edinburgh: T&T Clark.

Courtois, Chr., 1954. *Victor de Vita son œuvre: Étude critique*. Algiers: Imprimerie officielle du Gouvernement Général de l'Algérie.

Cribiore, R., 1996. *Writing, Teachers and Students in Graeco-Roman Egypt*. Atlanta, GA: Scholars Press.

———, 1999. Greek and Coptic Education in Late Antique Egypt. In Emmel, S., ed. *Ägypten und Nubien in spätantiker und christlicher Zeit*. Wiesbaden: Reichert, pp. 279–86.

———, 2001. *Gymnastics of the Mind: Greek Education in Hellenistic and Roman Egypt*. Princeton, NJ: Princeton University Press.

———, 2007a. Higher Education in Early Byzantine Egypt: Rhetoric, Latin, and the Law. In Bagnall, R., ed. *Egypt in the Byzantine World 300–700*. Cambridge: Cambridge University Press, pp. 47–66.

———, 2007b. *The School of Libanius in Late Antique Antioch*. Princeton, NJ: Princeton University Press.

———, 2009. Education in the Papyri. In Bagnall, R., ed. *The Oxford Handbook of Papyrology*. Oxford: Oxford University Press, pp. 320–37.

———, Davoli, P. and Ratzan, D., 2008. A Teacher's Dipinto from Trimithis (Dakhlah Oasis). *Journal of Roman Archaeology*, 21, pp. 170–91.

Cristea, H.-J., 2011. *Schenute: Contra Origenistas: Edition des koptischen Textes mit annotierter Übersetzung und Indizes einschließlich einer Übersetzung des 16. Osterfestbriefs des Theophilus in der Fassung des Hieronymus (ep. 96)* (Studien zu Antike und Christentum 60). Tübingen: Mohr Siebeck.

Dahlman, B., 2013. The *Collectio Scorialensis Parva*: An Alphabetical Collection of Old Apophthegmatic and Hagiographic Material. *Studia Patristica*, 55.3, pp. 23–34.

Dassmann, E., 2004. *Ambrosius von Mailand: Leben und Werk*. Stuttgart: Kohlhammer.

De Halleux, A. 1983. Le milieu historique de Jean le Solitair: une hypothèse. In Lavenant, R. ed. IIIo Symposium Syriacum: Les contacts du monde syriaque avec les autres cultures (Goslar 7-11 Septembre 1980) (Orientalia Christiana Analecta 221). Rome: Pontificium Institutum Orientalium Studiorum, pp. 299–305.

Demeulenaere, R., 1985. Préface. In Mulders, J. and Demeulenaere, R. eds. *Uictricius Rotomagensis: De laude sanctorum* (CCL 64). Turnhout: Brepols, pp. 55–65.

Bibliography 197

Diakovskij, E.P., 1913. *Posledovanie časov i izobrazitel'nyx: Istoričeskoe issledovanie* [The Rite of the Hours and the 'Typika': An Historical Inquiry]. Kiev: Mejnander.

Diefenbach, S., 2012. Constantius II. und die 'Reichskirche' – ein Beitrag zum Verhältnis von kaiserlicher Kirchenpolitik und politischer Integration im 4. Jh. *Millenium*, 9, pp. 59–122.

Dieleman, J., 2005. *Priests, Tongues, and Rites: The London-Leiden Magical Manuscripts and Translation in Egyptian Ritual (100–300 CE)*. Leiden: Brill.

Döring, K., 2003. Vom Nutzen der heidnischen Literatur für eine christliche Erziehung: Die Schrift *Ad adolescentes de legendis libris gentilium* des Basilius von Caesarea. *Gymnasium*, 110, pp. 551–67.

Drijvers, H.J.W., 1982. Facts and Problems in Early Syriac-Speaking Christianity. *Second Century*, 2, pp. 157–75.

Dümler, B., 2013. *Zeno von Verona zu heidnischer Kultur und christlicher Bildung* (Studien und Texte zu Antike und Christentum 75). Tübingen: Mohr Siebeck.

Egberts, A., Muhs, B.P. and van der Vliet, J., 2002. *Perspectives on Panopolis*. Leiden: Brill.

Ehrman, B.D., 2013. *Forgery and Counterforgery: The Use of Literary Deceit in Early Christian Polemics*. Oxford: Oxford University Press.

Emmel, S., 1995. Theophilus's Festal Letter of 401 as Quoted by Shenute. In Fluck, C., ed. *Divitiae Aegypti: Koptologische und verwandte Studien zu Ehren von Martin Krause*. Wiesbaden: Reichert, pp. 93–8.

———, 2004a. *Shenoute's Literary Corpus*, 2 vols (CSCO 599, 600). Leuven: Peeters.

———, 2004b. Shenoute the Monk: The Early Monastic Career of Shenoute the Archimandrite. In Bielawski, M. and Hombergen, D. eds. *Il monachesimo tra eredità e aperture*. Rome: Pontifio Ateneo S. Anselmo, pp. 151–74.

———, 2007. Coptic Literature in the Byzantine and Early Islamic World. In Bagnall, R., ed. *Egypt in the Byzantine World 300–700*. Cambridge: Cambridge University Press, pp. 83–102.

Faraggiana, C., 1997. *Apophthegmata Patrum:* Some Crucial Points of their Textual Transmission and the Problem of a Critical Edition, *Studia Patristica*, 29, pp. 455–67.

Fedwick, P.J., ed. 1981. *Basil of Caesarea: Christian, Humanist, Ascetic*, 2 vols. Toronto: Pontifical Institute of Mediaeval Studies.

Ferrère, F., 1898. *De Victoris Vitensis libro qui inscribitur: Historia persecutionis Africanae provinciae historica et philologica commentatio*. Paris: Klincksieck.

Flusin, B., 2004. Le serviteur caché ou le saint sans existence. In Odorico, P. and Agapitos, P. eds. *Les vies de saints à Byzance: Genre littéraire ou biographie historique?* Paris: Centre d'études byzantines, neo-helleniques et sud-européennes, pp. 59–71.

Fontaine, J., 1982. Victrice de Rouen et les origines du monachisme dans l'ouest de la Gaule (IVe–VIe s.). In Musset, L., ed. *Aspects du monachisme en Normandie (IVe–XVIIIe s.)*. Paris: Vrin, pp. 9–29.

Formisano, M. and Fuhrer, T., eds. 2014. *Décadence: 'Decline and Fall' or 'Other Antiquity'?* Heidelberg: Universitätsverlag Winter.

Foss, C., 1997. Syria in Transition, AD 550–750: An Archaeological Approach. *Dumbarton Oaks Papers*, 51, pp. 189–269.

Fournet, J.-L., 1999. *Hellénisme dans l'Egypte du VIe siècle: la bibliothèque et l'œuvre de Dioscore d'Aphrodité*. Cairo: Institut français d'archéologie orientale.

———, 2009. The Multilingual Environment of Late Antique Egypt: Greek, Latin, Coptic, and Persian Documentation. In Bagnall, R., ed. *The Oxford Handbook of Papyrology*. Oxford: Oxford University Press, pp. 418–51.

Frend, W.H.C., 1952. *The Donatist Church: A Movement of Protest in Roman North Africa*. Oxford: Clarendon.

Gane, J.H., 2012. *Fourth Century Christian Education: An Analysis of Basil's Ad Adolescentes*. PhD thesis, Newcastle.

198   Bibliography

Gärtner, M., 1985. *Die Familienerziehung in der Alten Kirche: Eine Untersuchung über die ersten vier Jahrhunderte des Christentums mit einer Übersetzung und einem Kommentar zu der Schrift des Johannes Chrysostomus über Geltungssucht und Kindererziehung* (Kölner Veröffentlichungen zur Religionsgeschichte 7). Cologne: Böhlau.

Géhin, P., 2013. Les collections de *kephalaia* monastiques: naissance et succès d'un genre entre création originale, plagiat et florilège. In Rigo, A., Ermilov, P. and Trizio, M. eds. *Theologica Minora: the Minor Genres of Byzantine Theological Literature.* Turnhout: Brepols, pp. 1–50.

Gemeinhardt, P., 2007. *Das lateinische Christentum und die antike pagane Bildung* (Studien und Texte zu Antike und Christentum 41). Tübingen: Mohr Siebeck.

———, 2010. 'Tota paradisi clauis tuus sanguis est'. Die Blutzeugen und ihre Auferstehung in der frühchristlichen Märtyrerliteratur. In Nicklas, T., Merkt, A. and Verheyden, J. eds. *Gelitten – Gestorben – Auferstanden: Passions- und Ostertraditionen im frühen Christentum* (Wissenschaftliche Untersuchungen zum Neuen Testament 2, 273). Tübingen: Mohr Siebeck, pp. 97–122 (reprint id. 2014, pp. 193–218).

———, 2011. Sancta simplicitas? Bildung als Thema der spätantiken lateinischen Hagiographie. In Suchla, B.R. ed. *Von Homer bis Landino: Beiträge zur Antike und Spätantike sowie zu deren Rezeptions- und Wirkungsgeschichte. Festschrift für Antonie Wlosok.* Berlin: Pro Business, pp. 85–113 (reprint id. 2014, pp. 239–58).

———, 2012a. In Search of Christian Paideia: Education and Conversion in Early Christian Biography. *Zeitschrift für Antikes Christentum*, 16, pp. 88–98 (reprint id. 2014, pp. 221–31).

———, 2012b. Die Heiligen der Kirche: die Gemeinschaft der Heiligen. In Gemeinhardt, P. and Heyden, K. eds. *Heilige, Heiliges und Heiligkeit in spätantiken Religionskulturen* (Religionsgeschichtliche Versuche und Vorarbeiten 61). Berlin: de Gruyter, pp. 385–414 (reprint id. 2014, pp. 71–98).

———, 2012c. Education and Religion: A New Research Centre at Göttingen. *Zeitschrift für Antikes Christentum*, 16, pp. 56–61.

———, 2013a. *Antonius: Der erste Mönch: Leben, Lehre, Legende.* Munich: Beck.

———, 2013b. Volksfrömmigkeit in der spätantiken Hagiographie: Potential und Grenzen eines umstrittenen Konzepts. *Zeitschrift für Theologie und Kirche*, 110, pp. 410–38 (reprint id. 2014, pp. 259–87).

———, 2013c. Art. Dance: Early Christian Attitudes. *Encyclopedia of the Bible and Its Reception*, 6. Berlin: de Gruyter, cols. 72–3.

———, 2014. *Die Kirche und ihre Heiligen: Studien zu Ekklesiologie und Hagiographie in der Spätantike* (Studien zu Antike und Christentum 90). Tübingen: Mohr Siebeck.

———, 2015. Art. Hagiography. Greek and Latin Patristics. *Encyclopedia of the Bible and Its Reception*, 10. Berlin: de Gruyter, cols. 1153–9.

———and Günther, S. eds., 2013. *Von Rom nach Bagdad: Bildung und Religion von der römischen Kaiserzeit bis zum klassischen Islam.* Tübingen: Mohr Siebeck.

———and Heyden, K., 2012. Heilige: Heiliges und Heiligkeit in spätantiken Religionskulturen. In Gemeinhardt, P. and Heyden, K. eds. 2012. *Heilige, Heiliges und Heiligkeit in spätantiken Religionskulturen* (Religionsgeschichtliche Versuche und Vorarbeiten 61). Berlin: de Gruyter, pp. 417–38.

Georges, T., 2012. Justin's School in Rome: Reflections on Early Christian 'Schools'. *Zeitschrift für Antikes Christentum*, 16, pp. 75–87.

Ghedini, G., 1927. *Le clausole ritmiche della* Historia persecutionis Africanae provinciae *di Victor de Vita.* Milan: Vita e Pensiero.

Gibbon, E., 1807. *The History of the Decline and Fall of the Roman Empire*, vol. 8. London: Cadell & Davies.

Bibliography   199

Gildemeister, J. and Bücheler, F., 1872a. Pseudo-Plutarchos, *Peri askeseos*. *Rheinisches Museum für Philologie*, 27, pp. 520–38.

———, 1872b. Themistios, *Peri aretes*. *Rheinisches Museum für Philologie*, 27, pp. 438–62.

Goehring, J., 1986a. *The Letter of Ammon and Pachomian Monasticism*. Berlin: de Gruyter.

———, 1986b. New Frontiers in Pachomian Studies. In Pierson, B.A. and Goehring, J. eds. *The Roots of Egyptian Christianity*. Philadelphia: Fortress, pp. 236–57.

Grafton, A., 1997. *The Footnote: A Curious History*. Cambridge, MA: Harvard University Press.

Grasmück, E.L., 1959. *Coercitio, Staat und Kirche im Donatistenstreit* (Bonner historische Forschungen 22). Bonn: Röhrscheid.

Graumann, T., 2011. Upstanding Donatists: Symbolic Communication at the Conference of Carthage (411). *Zeitschrift für antikes Christentum*, 15, pp. 329–55.

Grenzmann, W., 1976. Probleme des Aphorismus. In Neumann, G. ed. *Der Aphorismus: zur Geschichte, zu den Formen und Möglichkeiten einer literarischen Gattung*. Darmstadt: Wissenschaftliche Buchgesellschaft, pp. 177–208.

Griffith, S.H., 2008. *The Church in the Shadow of the Mosque: Christians and Muslims in the World of Islam*. Princeton, NJ: Princeton University Press.

Gussone, N., 1976. Adventus-Zeremoniell und Translation von Reliquien: Victricius von Rouen, De laude sanctorum. *Frühmittelalterliche Studien*, 10, pp. 125–33.

Gutilla, G., 2003. La presenza di Vittricio di Rouen nell'opera di Paolino di Nola dal *De laude sanctorum* all'*Epist*. 18 e ai *Carmm*. 27 e 19. *Augustinianum*, 43, pp. 453–71.

Guy, J.-C., 1974. Educational Innovation in the Desert Fathers. *Eastern Churches Review*, 6, pp. 44–51.

Hadot, P., 1981. *Exercices spirituels et philosophie antique*. Paris: Etudes augustiniennes.

———, 1995. *Philosophy as a Way of Life: Spiritual Exercises from Socrates to Foucault*. Oxford: Blackwell.

Haidacher, S., 1905. Nilus-Exzerpte im Pandectes des Antiochus. *Revue Bénédictine*, 22, pp. 244–50.

Hall, H.R., 1905. *Coptic and Greek Texts of the Christian Period in the British Museum*. London: British Museum.

Harmless, W., 2004. *Desert Christians: An Introduction to the Literature of Early Monasticism*. New York: Oxford University Press.

Harries, J., 1999. *Law and Empire in Late Antiquity*. Cambridge: Cambridge University Press.

———, 2013. Encyclopaedias and Autocracy: Justinian's *Encyclopaedia* of Roman Law. In König, J. and Woolf, G. eds. *Encyclopaedism from Antiquity to the Renaissance*. Cambridge: Cambridge University Press, pp. 178–96.

Hartmann, A., 2010. *Zwischen Relikt und Reliquie: Objektbezogene Erinnerungspraktiken in antiken Gesellschaften* (Studien zur Alten Geschichte 11). Berlin: Antike.

Harvey, P.B., 2004. 'A Traveler from and Antique Land': Sources, Context, and Dissemination of the Hagiography of Mary the Egyptian. In Knoppers, G.N. and Hirsch, A. eds. *Egypt, Israel, and the Ancient Mediterranean World: Studies in Honor of Donald B. Redford*. Leiden: Brill, pp. 479–99.

Harvey, S.A., 2002. Why the Perfume Mattered: The Sinful Woman in Syriac Exegetical Tradition. In Blowers, P.M., Christman, A.R., Hunter, D.G. and Young, R.D. eds. *In Dominico Eloquio / In Lordly Eloquence: Essays on Patristic Exegesis in Honor of Robert Louis Wilken*. Grand Rapids, MI: Eerdmans, pp. 69–89.

Hasitzka, M. ed., 1990. *Neue Texte und Dokumentation zum Koptisch-Unterricht* (Mitteilungen aus der Papyrussammlung der Österreichischen Nationalbibliothek (Papyrus Erzherzog Rainer) 18), 2 vols. Vienna: Nationalbibliothek.

200   Bibliography

Hatlie, P., 2002. A Rough Guide to Byzantine Monasticism in the Early Seventh Century. In Reinink, G. J. and Stolte, B.H. eds. *The Reign of Heraclius (610–641): Crisis and Confrontation* (Groningen Studies in Cultural Change 2), Leuven: Peeters, pp. 205–26.

Hays, G., 2003. The Date and Identity of the Mythographer Fulgentius. *Journal of Medieval Latin*, 13, pp. 163–252.

Hilkens, A., 2013. The Fall of Troy in Syriac Historiography. *Le Muséon*, 126, pp. 285–317.

Hock, R.F. and O'Neil, E.N., 1986. *The Chreia in Ancient Rhetoric: The Progymnasmata*. Atlanta, GA: Scholars Press.

———, 2002. *The Chreia and Ancient Rhetoric: Classroom Exercises*. Atlanta, GA: Scholars Press.

Hodkinson, O., 2007. Better than Speech: Some Advantages of the Letter in the Second Sophistic. In Morello, R. and Morrison, A.D. eds. *Ancient Letters: Classical and Late Antique Epistolography*. Oxford: Oxford University Press, pp. 283–300.

Hogrefe, A., 2009. *Umstrittene Vergangenheit: Historische Argumente in der Auseinandersetzung Augustins mit den Donatisten* (Millenium-Studien 24). Berlin: de Gruyter.

Holmberg, B., 2013. The Syriac Collection of *Apophthegmata Patrum* in MS Sin. syr. 46. *Studia Patristica*, 55.3, pp. 35–58.

Horn, C.B. and Martens, J.W., 2009. *'Let the Little Children Come to Me': Childhood and Children in Early Christianity*. Washington, DC: Catholic University of America Press.

Horster, M. and Reitz, C. eds, 2010. *Condensing Texts, Condensed Texts* (Palingenesia 98). Stuttgart: Steiner.

Howe, T., 2007. *Vandalen, Barbaren und Arianer bei Victor von Vita* (Studien zur Alten Geschichte 7). Frankfurt: Antike.

Hübner, W., 2007. Klassische lateinische Literatur und Rhetorik. In Drecoll, V.H. ed. *Augustin Handbuch*. Tübingen: Mohr Siebeck, pp. 49–60.

Humfress, C., 2007. *Orthodoxy and the Courts in Late Antiquity*. Oxford: Oxford University Press.

———, 2011. Bishops and Law Courts in Late Antiquity: How (Not) to Make Sense of the Legal Evidence. *Journal of Early Christian Studies*, 19, pp. 375–400.

Hunter, D.G., 1999. Vigilantius of Calagurris and Victricius of Rouen: Ascetics, Relics, and Clerics in Late Roman Gaul. *Journal of Early Christian Studies*, 7, pp. 401–30.

Hunter, R., 2009. *Critical Moments in Classical Literature: Studies in the Ancient View of Literature and Its Uses*. Cambridge: Cambridge University Press.

Isola, A., 2010. Sul problema dei due Fulgenzi: un contributo della *Vita Fulgentii*. In Piras, A. ed. *Lingua et ingenium: Studi su Fulgenzio di Ruspe e il suo contesto*. Cagliari: Sandhi, pp. 147–64.

Jacob, C., 1997. The Library and the Book: Forms of Alexandrian Encyclopedism. *Diogenes*, 45/2, pp. 63–82.

———, 2002. Gathering Memory: Thoughts on the History of Libraries. *Diogenes*, 49, pp. 41–57.

———, 2010. *Das geistige Theater: Ästhetik und Moral bei Johannes Chrysostomus*. Münster: Aschendorff.

Johnson, A.P., 2012. Hellenism and Its Discontents. In Johnson, S.F. ed. *The Oxford Handbook of Late Antiquity*. Oxford: Oxford University Press, pp. 437–66.

Kalvesmaki, J., 2013. Pachomius and the Mystery of the Letters. In Leyerle, B. and Young, R.D. eds. *Ascetic Culture: Essays in Honor of Philip Rousseau*. Notre Dame, IN: University of Notre Dame Press, pp. 11–28.

Kany, R., 2009. Art. Lehrer. In *Reallexikon für Antike und Christentum*, vol. 22. Stuttgart: Hiersemann, pp. 1091–132.

Kaser, M., 1966. *Das Römische Zivilprozessrecht* (Handbuch der Altertumswissenschaften. Rechtsgeschichte des Altertums 3.4). Munich: Beck.

Bibliography 201

Kaster, R., 1988. *Guardians of Language: The Grammarian and Society in Late Antiquity* (Transformation of the Classical Heritage 11). Berkeley: University of California Press.

Kennedy, G. ed., 2003. *Progymnasmata: Greek Textbooks of Prose Composition and Rhetoric* (Writings from the Greco-Roman World 10). Atlanta, GA: Scholars Press.

King, D., 2008. *The Syriac Versions of the Writings of Cyril of Alexandria: A Study in Translation Techniques.* Louvain: Peeters.

———, 2010. Origenism in Sixth Century Syria: The Case of a Syriac Manuscript of the Pagan Philosophers. In Fürst, A. ed. *Origenes und seine Bedeutung für die Theologie- und Geistesgeschichte Europas und des Vorderen Orients* (Adamantiana. Texte und Studien zu Origenes und seinem Erbe 1). Münster: Aschendorff, pp. 179–212.

———, 2012. Elements of the Syriac Grammatical Tradition as These Relate to the Origins of Arabic Grammar. In Marogy, A. ed. *The Foundations of Arabic Linguistics: Sibawayhi and the Earliest Arabic Grammatical Theory.* Leiden: Brill, pp. 189–209.

———, 2013. Why Were the Syrians Interested in Greek Philosophy? In Wood, P. ed. *History and Identity in the Late Antique Near East.* Oxford: Oxford University Press, pp. 61–82.

———, 2015. Logic in the Service of Ancient Eastern Christianity: An Exploration of Motives. *Archiv für Geschichte der Philosophie*, 97/1, pp. 1–33.

Kinzig, W., 1997. The Greek Christian Writers. In Porter, S.E, ed. *Handbook of Classical Rhetoric in the Hellenistic Period 330 B.C.–A.D. 400.* Leiden: Brill, pp. 631–70.

Kirk, A.K., 1998. *The Composition of the Sayings Source: Genre, Synchrony, and Wisdom Redaction in Q.* Leiden: Brill.

Kitchen, R., 2012. Babai the Great. In Casiday, A. ed. *The Orthodox Christian World.* London: Routledge, pp. 237–43.

Koder, J., 2003. Romanos der Melode: Der Dichter hymnischer Bibelpredigten in Dokumenten seiner Zeit. In Froschauer, H., Gastgeber, C. and Harrauer, H. eds. *Ein Buch verändert die Welt: Älteste Zeugnisse der Heiligen Schrift aus der Zeit des frühen Christentums in Ägypten.* Vienna: Phoibos, pp. 59–71.

Konstan, D., 2011. Excerpting as a Reading Practice. In Reydams-Schils, G.J. ed. *Thinking Through Excerpts: Studies on Stobaeus.* Turnhout: Brepols, pp. 9–22.

Kotsifou, C., 2007. Books and Book Production in the Monastic Communities of Byzantine Egypt. In Klingshirn, W.E. and Safran, L. eds. *The Early Christian Book.* Washington, DC: Catholic University of America Press, pp. 48–66.

Krawiec, R., 2002. *Shenoute and the Women of the White Monastery.* Oxford: Oxford University Press.

———, 2008. Asceticism. In Harvey, S.A. and Hunter, D.G. eds. *The Oxford Handbook of Early Christian Studies.* Oxford: Oxford University Press, pp. 764–85.

———, 2012. Monastic Literacy in John Cassian: Towards a New Sublimity. *Church History*, 81, pp. 765–95.

Krueger, D., 2004. *Writing and Holiness: The Practice of Authorship in the Early Christian East.* Philadelphia: University of Pennsylvania Press.

———, 2009. The Unbounded Body in the Age of Liturgical Reproduction. *Journal of Early Christian Studies*, 17, pp. 267–79.

———, 2010. The Old Testament in Monasticism. In Magdalino, P. and Nelson, R. eds. *The Old Testament in Byzantium.* Washington, DC: Dumbarton Oaks, pp. 199–221.

———, 2011. Mary at the Threshold: The Mother of God as Guardian in Seventh-Century Palestinian Miracle Accounts. In Brubaker, L. and Cunningham, M. eds. *The Cult of the Mother of God in Byzantium: Texts and Images.* Farnham: Ashgate, pp. 31–8.

———, 2014. *Liturgical Subjects: Christian Ritual, Biblical Narrative, and the Formation of the Self in Byzantium.* Philadelphia: University of Pennsylvania Press.

202 Bibliography

———, 2016. The Hagiographers' Bible: Intertextuality and Scriptural Culture in the Late Sixth and Early Seventh Centuries. In Krueger, D. and Nelson, R. eds. *The New Testament in Byzantium*. Washington, DC: Dumbarton Oaks.

Kussmaul, P., 1981, *Pragmaticum und Lex: Formen spätrömischer Gesetzgebung* (Hypomnemata 67). Göttingen: Vandenhoeck & Ruprecht.

Lamberton, R., 1986. *Homer the Theologian: Neoplatonist Allegorical Reading and the Growth of the Epic Tradition* (Transformation of the Classical Heritage 9). Berkeley: University of California Press.

Lamberz, E., 1979. Zum Verständnis von Basileios' Schrift 'Ad adolescentes'. *Zeitschrift für Kirchengeschichte*, 90, pp. 221–41.

Lancel, S., 1989. Victor de Vita et la Carthage vandale. In Mastino, A. ed. *L'Africa romana 6: Atti del VI convegno di studio Sassari, 16–18 dicembre 1988*. Sassari: Gallizzi, pp. 649–61.

———, 1999. *Augustin*. Paris: Fayard.

———, 2002. *Histoire de la persécution vandale en Afrique: suivie de la passion des sept martyrs*. Paris: Les Belles Lettres.

Larsen, L.I., 2006. *Pedagogical Parallels: Re-Reading the* Apophthegmata Patrum. PhD thesis, Columbia University.

———, 2008. The *Apophthegmata Patrum*: Rustic Rumination or Rhetorical Recitation? *Meddelanden från Collegium Patristicum Lundense*, 22, pp. 21–31.

———, 2012a. Monastic Meals: Resisting a Reclining Culture. In Smith, D.E. and Taussig, H.E. eds. *Meals in the Early Christian World: Social Formation, Experimentation, and Conflict at the Table*. New York: Palgrave Macmillan, pp. 245–60.

———, 2012b. Meals and Monastic Identity. In Klinghardt, M. and Taussig, H. eds. *Mahl und religiöse Identität* (Texte und Arbeiten zum neutestamentlichen Zeitalter 56). Tübingen: Francke, pp. 307–28.

———, 2013a. 'On Learning a New Alphabet': The Sayings of the Desert Fathers and the Monostichs of Menander. *Studia Patristica*, 55/3, pp. 59–77.

———, 2013b. Redrawing the Interpretive Map: Monastic Education as Civic Formation in the *Apophthegmata Patrum*. *Coptica*, 12, pp. 1–34.

———, forthcoming. Excavating the Excavations: Examining the Material Record of Monastic Education. In Larsen, L.I. and Rubenson, S. eds. *Rethinking Monastic Education*. Cambridge: Cambridge University Press.

Laube, A., 1913. *De litterarum Libanii et Basilii commercio*. Diss., Breslau.

Layton, B., 2002. Social Structure and Food Consumption in an Early Christian Monastery: The Evidence of Shenoute's *Canons* and the White Monastery Federation A.D. 385–465. *Le Muséon*, 115, pp. 25–55.

———, 2007. Rules, Patterns, and the Exercise of Power in Shenoute's Monastery: The Problem of World Replacement and Identity Maintenance. *Journal of Early Christian Studies*, 15, pp. 45–73.

Liebeschuetz, J.H.W.G., 2011. *Ambrose and John Chrysostom: Clerics between Desert and Empire*. Oxford: Oxford University Press.

Lim, R., 1995. *Public Disputation, Power, and Social Order in Late Antiquity* (Transformation of the Classical Heritage 23). Berkeley: University of California Press.

Lukashevich, A., 2000. Velikij Kanon. *Pravoslavnaja Encyklopedia*, 7, pp. 453–4.

Luisier, P., 2009. Chénouté, Victor, Jean de Lycopolis et Nestorius: Quand l'archimandrite d'Atripé en Haute-Égypte est-il mort? *Orientalia*, 78, pp. 258–81.

MacCormack, S., 1981. *Art and Ceremony in Late Antiquity* (Transformation of the Classical Heritage 1). Berkeley: University of California Press.

Bibliography   203

MacCoull, L.S.B., 1988. *Dioscorus of Aphrodito: His Work and His World* (Transformation of the Classical Heritage 16). Berkeley: University of California Press.

Macleod, M.D. and Wickham, L.R., 1970. The Syriac Version of Lucian *De Calumnia*. *Classical Quarterly*, 20, pp. 297–9.

Maier, J.-L., 1987–89. *Le dossier du donatisme*, 2 vols (Texte und Untersuchungen 134, 135). Berlin: Akademie Verlag.

Malosse, P.-L., 2004. *Lettres pour toutes circonstances*. Paris: Les Belles Lettres.

Markowski, H., 1913. Zum Briefwechsel zwischen Basileios und Libanios. *Berliner Philologische Wochenschrift*, 33, pp. 1150–52.

Markschies, Ch., 2002. Lehrer, Schüler, Schule: Zur Bedeutung einer Institution für das antike Christentum. In Schäfer, A. and Egelhaaf-Gaiser, U. eds. *Religiöse Vereine in der römischen Antike: Untersuchungen zu Organisation, Ritual und Raumordnung* (Studien und Texte zu Antike und Christentum 13). Tübingen: Mohr Siebeck, pp. 97–120.

Marrou, H.-I., 1938. *Saint Augustin et la fin de la culture antique*. Paris: De Boccard.

———, 1956. *A History of Education in Antiquity*. Translated by George Lamb. Madison: University of Wisconsin Press.

———, 1978. Diadoque de Photikè et Victor de Vita. In Marrou, H.-I., *Christiana Tempora: Mélanges d'histoire, d'archéologie, d'épigraphie et de patristique*. Paris: Ecole française de Rome, pp. 373–80.

———, 1982. *Augustinus und das Ende der antiken Bildung*. Paderborn: Schöningh.

Martínez, J. ed., 2011. *Fakes and Forgers of Classical Literature/Falsificaciones y falsarios de la Literatura Clásica*. Madrid: Ediciones Clásicas.

Maxwell, J.L., 2006. *Christianization and Communication in Late Antiquity: John Chrysostom and His Congregation in Antioch*. Cambridge: Cambridge University Press.

Mayerson, P., 1984. Antiochus Monachus' Homily on Dreams: An Historical Note. *Journal of Jewish Studies*, 35, pp. 51–6.

McVey, K., 1998. *Chreia* in the Desert: Rhetoric and the Bible in the *Apophthegmata Patrum*. In Malherbe, A.J., Norris, F.W. and Thompson, J.W. eds. *The Early Church in its Context: Essays in Honor of Everett Ferguson*. Leiden: Brill, pp. 246–57.

Menze, V. 2008. *Justinian and the Making of the Syrian Orthodox Church* (Oxford Early Christian Studies). Oxford: Oxford University Press.

Merrills, A.H. ed., 2004. *Vandals, Romans and Berbers: New Perspectives on Late Antique North Africa*. Aldershot: Ashgate.

———, 2011. Totum subuertere uoluerunt: 'Social Martyrdom' in the Historia Persecutionis of Victor of Vita. In Kelly, Ch., Flower, R. and Williams, M.S. eds. *Unclassical Traditions*, Volume 2: *Perspectives from East and West in Late Antiquity*. Cambridge: Cambridge Philological Society, pp. 102–15.

Millar, F., 1998. Ethnic Identity in the Roman Near East, 325–450: Language, Religion, and Culture. *Mediterranean Archaeology*, 11, pp. 159–76.

Miller, P.C., 1998. Differential Networks: Relics and Other Fragments in Late Antiquity. *Journal of Early Christian Studies*, 6, pp. 113–38.

———, 2005. Is There a Harlot in This Text? Hagiography and the Grotesque. In Martin, D.B. and Miller, P.C. eds. *The Cultural Turn in Late Ancient Studies: Gender, Asceticism, and Historiography*. Durham, NC: Duke University Press, pp. 87–102.

Modéran, Y., 2003. Une guerre de religion: Les deux Eglises d'Afrique à l'époque vandale. *Antiquité Tardive*, 11, pp. 21–44.

Morgan, T., 1998. *Literate Education in the Hellenistic and Roman Worlds*. Cambridge: Cambridge University Press.

———, 2007. *Popular Morality in the Early Roman Empire*. Cambridge: Cambridge University Press.

204   Bibliography

Moss, A., 2001. Commonplaces and Commonplace Books. In Sloane, T.O. ed. *Encyclopedia of Rhetoric*. Oxford: Oxford University Press, pp. 119–24.

———, 2011. Power and Persuasion: Commonplace Culture in Early Modern Europe. In Cowling, D. and Bruun, M.B. eds. *Commonplace Culture in Western Europe in the Early Modern Period*, vol. 1: *Reformation, Counter-Reformation and Revolt* (Groningen Studies in Cultural Change 39). Leuven: Peeters, pp. 1–17.

Mratschek, S., 2002. *Der Briefwechsel des Paulinus von Nola: Kommunikation und soziale Kontakte zwischen christlichen Intellektuellen* (Hypomnemata 134). Göttingen: Vandenhoeck & Ruprecht.

Mulders, J., 1956–57. Victricius van Rouaan: Leven en Leer. *Bijdragen*, 17, pp. 1–25; 18, pp. 19–40 and 270–89.

Musset, L., 1975. De saint Victrice à saint Ouen: La christianisation de la province de Rouen d'après l'hagiographie. *Revue d'histoire de l'Église de France*, 62, pp. 141–52.

Nau, F., 1906. Notes sur les mss. de Paris qui renferment la notice biographique d'Antiochus moine de S. Sabba. *Revue de l'Orient Chrétien*, 11, pp. 327–30.

Nesselrath, H.-G., 1999. Die Christen und die heidnische Bildung: Das Beispiel des Sokrates Scholastikos (*hist. eccl.* 3,16). In Dummer, J. and Vielberg, M. eds. *Leitbilder in der Spätantike: Eliten und Leitbilder*. Stuttgart: Steiner, pp. 79–100.

———, 2009. Der heidnische Rhetor und der christliche Bischof: Libanios und Basileios der Große in einer spätantiken Basileios-Vita. *Jahresheft der Göttinger Freunde der antiken Literatur*, 8, pp. 11–25.

———, 2010. Libanio e Basilio di Cesarea: Un dialogo interreligioso? *Adamantius*, 16, pp. 338–52.

———, 2012. *Libanios: Zeuge einer schwindenden Welt* (Standorte in Antike und Christentum 4). Stuttgart: Hiersemann.

———and Van Hoof, L., 2014. The Reception of Libanius: From Pagan Friend of Julian to (Almost) Christian Saint and Back. In Van Hoof, L. ed. *Libanius: A Critical Introduction*. Cambridge: Cambridge University Press, pp. 160–83.

Newberry, P.E., 1893. *Beni Hasan* 2. London: Archaeological Survey of Egypt.

Nodar, A., 2012. Christianity at School: Early Christian Schooltexts on Papyri. In Montferrer-Sala, J., Teule, H.J.B. and Torallas Tovar, S. eds. *Eastern Christians and Their Written Heritage:* Manuscripts, Scribes and Context (Eastern Christian Studies 14). Leuven: Peeters, pp. 183–97.

Odorico, P., 1988. La sanzione del poeta: Antiocho di S. Saba e un nuovo carme di Arsenio di Pantelleria. *Byzantinoslavica*, 49, pp. 1–22.

———, 1990. La cultura della συλλογή. 1. cosiddetto Enciclopedismo Bizantino, 2. Le Tavole del Sapere di Giovanni Damasceno. *Byzantinische Zeitschrift*, 83, pp. 1–21.

———, 2004. Gli gnomologi greci sacro-profani: Una presentazione. In Funghi M.S. ed. *Aspetti di letteratura gnomica nel mondo antico*, vol. 2 (Accademia Toscana di Scienze e Lettere 'La Colombaria' Studi 225). Florence: Olschki, pp. 61–96.

Olster, D. 1994. *Roman Defeat, Christian Response, and the Literary Construction of the Jew*. Philadelphia: University of Pennsylvania Press.

O'Neil, E.N., 1981. The Chreia in Greco-Roman Literature and Education. In Meyer, M. ed. *The Institute for Antiquity and Christianity Report: 1972–1980*. Claremont, CA: Claremont Graduate School.

Orlandi, T., 2002. The Library of the Monastery of Saint Shenute at Atripe. In Egberts, A., Muhs, B.P. and van der Vliet, J. eds. *Perspectives on Panopolis*. Leiden: Brill, pp. 211–31.

Bibliography   205

Pack, E., 1989. Sozialgeschichtliche Aspekte des Fehlens einer christlichen Schule in der römischen Kaiserzeit. In Eck, W. ed. *Religion und Gesellschaft in der römischen Kaiserzeit: Kolloquium zu Ehren von F. Vittinghoff.* Cologne: Böhlau, pp. 185–263.

Papadogiannakis, Y., 2012. *Christianity and Hellenism in the Fifth-Century Greek East: Theodoret's Apologetics against the Greeks in Context.* Cambridge, MA: Center for Hellenic Studies, Trustees for Harvard University.

Pasquato, O., 1992. Forme della tradizione classica nel 'De inani gloria et de educandis liberis' di Giovanni Crisostomo. *Orientalia Christiana Periodica*, 58, pp. 253–64.

Patlagean, E., 1976. L'histoire de la femme déguisée en moine et l'évolution de la sainteté féminine à Byzance. *Studi Medievali*, ser. 3, 17, pp. 597–623.

Penn, M., 2013. Demons Gone Wild: An Introduction, and Translation of the Syriac Qenneshre Fragment. *Orientalia Christiana Periodica*, 79, pp. 367–99.

Pernot, L., 1986. Lieu et lieu commun dans la rhetorique antique. *Bulletin de l'Association Guillaume Budé*, pp. 253–84.

Petit, P., 1957. *Les étudiants de Libanius.* Paris: Nouvelles Editions Latines.

Pevarello, D. 2013. The Sentences of Sextus and the Origins of Christian Asceticism (Studien und Texte zu Antike und Christentum 78), Tübingen: Mohr Siebeck.

Phenix, R.R. Jr and Horn, C.B., 2008. Prayer and Penance in Early and Middle Byzantine Christianity: Some Trajectories from the Greek- and Syriac-Speaking Realms. In Boda, M. J., Falk, D.K. and Werline, R.A. eds. *Seeking the Favor of God*, Volume 3: *The Impact of Penitential Prayer Beyond Second Temple Judaism.* Atlanta, GA: Society of Biblical Literature, pp. 225–54.

Piccione, R. M. and Perkams, M. eds, 2003. *Selecta Colligere*, 2 vols. Alessandria: Edizioni dell'Orso.

Pitkäranta, R., 1978. *Studien zum Latein des Victor Vitensis.* Helsinki: Societas Scientiarum Fennica.

Pollmann, K. and Otten, W. eds, 2013. *The Oxford Guide to the Historical Reception of Augustine*, 3 vols. Oxford: Oxford University Press.

Possekel, U., 1998. Der *Rat der Theano*: Eine pythagoreische Spruchsammlung in syrischer Übersetzung. *Le Muséon*, 111, pp. 7–36.

Pouchet, R., 1992. *Basile le Grand et son univers d'amis d'après sa correspondence: Une stratégie de communion* (Studia Ephemeridis 'Augustinianum' 36). Rome: Institutum Patristicum Augustinianum.

Rapp, C., 2005a. The Antiochos Manuscript at Keio University: A Preliminary Description. In Matsuda, T. ed. *Codices Keioenses: Essays on Western Manuscripts and Early Printed Books in Keio University Library.* Tokyo: Keio University Press, pp. 11–29.

————, 2005b. *Holy Bishops in Late Antiquity: The Nature of Christian Leadership in an Age of Transition* (Transformation of the Classical Heritage 37). Berkeley: University of California Press.

Rappe, S., 2001. The New Math: How to Add and to Subtract Pagan Elements in Christian Education. In Too, Y.L. ed. *Education in Greek and Roman Antiquity.* Leiden: Brill, pp. 405–32.

Reinink, G. J., 1995. 'Edessa grew dim and Nisibis shone forth': The School of Nisibis at the Transition of the Sixth–Seventh Century. In Drijvers, J.W. and MacDonald, A.A. eds. *Centres of Learning: Learning and Location in Pre-Modern Europe and the Near East* (Brill's Studies in Intellectual History 61). Leiden: Brill, pp. 77–89.

Riad, E., 1988. *Studies in the Syriac Preface* (Studia Semitica Upsaliensia 11). Uppsala: Acta Universitatis Upsaliensis.

206 Bibliography

Rigolio, A., 2013, From *Sacrifice to the Gods* to the *Fear of God*: Omissions, Additions and Changes in the Syriac Translations of Plutarch, Lucian and Themistius. *Studia Patristica*, 64, pp. 133–44.

———, forthcoming. The Syriac *De exercitatione*: A Lost Edifying Piece Attributed to Plutarch. In Mack, P. and North, J. eds. *The Afterlife of Plutarch* (*Bulletin of the Institute of Classical Studies* Suppl.).

Rimmon-Kenan, S., 1983. *Narrative Fiction: Contemporary Poetics*. London: Routledge.

Rodríguez, R., 2009. Reading and Hearing in Ancient Contexts. *Journal for the Study of the New Testament*, 32, pp. 151–78.

Rönnegård, P., 2010. *Threads and Images: The Use of Scripture in* Apophthegmata Patrum. Seattle: Eisenbrauns.

Rousseau, P., 1994. *Basil of Caesarea* (Transformation of the Classical Heritage 20). Berkeley: University of California Press.

———, 1999a. *Pachomius: The Making of a Community in Fourth-Century Egypt* (Transformation of the Classical Heritage 6). Berkeley: University of California Press (2nd edition).

———, 1999b. Pachomius. In Bowersock, G.W., Brown, P. and Graber, O. eds. *Late Antiquity: A Guide to the Post-Classical World*. Cambridge, MA: Harvard University Press, pp. 624–5.

———, 2007. The Successors of Pachomius and the Nag Hammadi Codices: Exegetical Themes and Literary Structures. In Goehring, J. and Timbie, J. eds. *The World of Early Egyptian Christianity*. Washington, DC: Catholic University of America Press, pp. 140–57.

Rubenson, S., 1995. *The Letters of St. Antony: Monasticism and the Making of a Saint*. Minneapolis: Fortress.

Ryssel, V., 1880. *Über den textkritischen Werth der syrischen Übersetzungen griechischer Klassiker*. Leipzig: Fernau.

Schenkeveld, D., 1997. Philosophical Prose. In Porter, S. ed. *Handbook of Classical Rhetoric in the Hellenistic Period, 330 B.C.–A.D. 400*. Leiden: Brill, pp. 195–264.

Schetter, W., 1990. Zur 'Satisfactio' des Dracontius. *Hermes*, 118, pp. 90–117.

Schick, R., 1995. *The Christian Communities of Palestine from Byzantine to Islamic Rule: A Historical and Archaeological Study*. Princeton, NJ: Darwin.

Schmitt, Chr., 2003. Die verlorene Romanität in Afrika: Afrolatein/Afroromanisch. In Ernst, G. ed. *Romanische Sprachgeschichte*. Berlin: de Gruyter, pp. 668–75.

Schreckenberg, H., 1995. *Die christlichen Adversus-Judaeos-Texte und ihr literarisches und historisches Umfeld (1.–11.Jh.)* (Europäische Hochschulschriften. Reihe 23: Theologie 172). Frankfurt: Lang.

Schroeder, C.T., 2014. An Early Monastic Rule Fragment from the Monastery of Shenoute. *Le Muséon*, 127, pp. 19–39.

Schwab, A., 2012. From a Way of Reading to a Way of Life: Basil of Caesarea and Gregory of Nazianzus about Poetry in Christian Education. In Tanaseanu-Döbler, I. and Döbler, M. eds. *Religious Education in Pre-Modern Europe* (Numen Book Series 140). Leiden: Brill. pp. 147–62.

Segal, J.B., 1953. *The Diacritical Point and the Accents in Syriac*. London: Oxford University Press.

Selent, D., 2011. *Allegorische Mythenerklärung in der Spätantike: Wege zum Werk des Dracontius*. Rahden: Leidorf.

Ševčenko, I., 1981. Levels of Style in Byzantine Prose. *Jahrbuch der österreichischen Byzantinistik*, 31, pp. 289–312.

Shaw, B.D. 2011. *Sacred Violence: African Christians and Sectarian Hatred in the Age of Augustine*. Cambridge: Cambridge University Press.

Bibliography 207

Sheridan, M., 2007. Rhetorical Structure in Coptic Sermons. In Goehring, J. and Timbie, J. eds. *The World of Early Egyptian Christianity*. Washington, DC: Catholic University of America Press, pp. 25–48.

Siegert, F., 1997. Homily and Panegyrical Sermon. In Porter, S. ed. *Handbook of Classical Rhetoric in the Hellenistic Period, 330 B.C.–A.D. 400*. Leiden: Brill, pp. 421–43.

Silvas, A.M., 2007. *Gregory of Nyssa, the Letters: Introduction, Translation and Commentary* (Supplements to Vigiliae Christianae 83). Leiden: Brill.

Snyder, G.H., 2000. *Teachers and Texts in the Ancient World: Philosophers, Jews and Christians*. London: Routledge.

Speyer, W., 1971. *Die literarische Fälschung im heidnischen und christlichen Altertum: Ein Versuch ihrer Deutung* (Handbuch der Altertumswissenschaft 1.2). Munich: Beck.

Stenger, J.R., 2014. On the Use and Abuse of Philosophy for Life: John Chrysostom's Paradoxical View of Knowledge. In Geus, K. and Geller, M. eds. *Esoteric Knowledge in Antiquity* (Preprints TOPOI 454). Berlin: Max Planck Institut für Wissenschaftsgeschichte, pp. 85–105.

———, 2015. The Soul and the City: John Chrysostom's Modelling of Urban Space. In Fuhrer, T., Mundt, F. and Stenger, J.R. eds. *Cityscaping: Constructing and Modelling Images of the City*. Berlin: de Gruyter, pp. 133–54.

———, 2015b. John Chrysostom and the Power of Literary Imagination. In Stenger, J.R. ed. *Spätantike Konzeptionen von Literatur*. Heidelberg: Winter, pp. 207–26.

Studer, B., 1999. Die Kirche als Schule des Herrn bei Augustinus von Hippo. In Studer, B. *Mysterium Caritatis* (Studia Anselmiana 127). Rome: Centro Studi S. Anselmo.

Taft, R.F., 1978. *The Great Entrance: A History of the Transfer of Gifts and other Preanaphoral Rites of the Liturgy of St. John Chrysostom*. Rome: Pontificium Institutum Studiorum Orientalium (2nd edition).

———, 1993. *The Liturgy of the Hours in East and West: The Origins of the Divine Office and Its Meaning for Today*. Collegeville, MI: Liturgical Press (2nd edition).

Tanaseanu-Döbler, I. and Döbler, M., 2012. Towards a Theoretical Frame for the Study of Religious Education: An Introduction. In Tanaseanu-Döbler, I. and Döbler, M. eds. *Religious Education in Pre-Modern Europe* (Numen Book Series 140). Leiden: Brill, pp. 1–37.

Tannous, J., 2013. You Are What You Read: Qenneshre and the Miaphysite Church in the Seventh Century. In Wood, P. ed. *History and Identity in the Late Antique Near East*. Oxford: Oxford University Press, pp. 83–102.

Thompson, H., 1909. Coptic Inscriptions. In Quibell, J.E. ed. *Excavations at Saqqara 3*. Cairo: Institut français d'archéologie orientale, pp. 27–77.

Tilley, M.A., 1991. Dilatory Donatists or Procrastinating Catholics: The Trial at the Conference of Carthage. *Church History*, 60, pp. 7–19.

Timbie, J., forthcoming a. Shenoute Addresses the Misplaced Confidence of Monks and Other Christians: Interpretation of Romans 9 and 11 in *Discourses*, Book 8. In Aufrère, S. et al. eds. *Festschrift for Ariel Shisha-Halevy*. Leuven: Peeters.

———, forthcoming b. *Meleta* and Monastic Formation. *Coptica*.

Tommasi Moreschini, C.O., 2013. Fulgentius of Ruspe. In Pollmann, K. and Otten, W. eds. *The Oxford Guide to the Historical Reception of Augustine*, vol. 2. Oxford: Oxford University Press, pp. 1022–4.

Too, Y.L. ed., 2001. *Education in Greek and Roman Antiquity*. Leiden: Brill.

Torallas Tovar, S., 2013. What is Greek and What is Coptic? School Texts as a Window into the Perception of Greek Loanwords in Coptic. In Feder, F. and Lohwasser, A. eds. *Ägypten und sein Umfeld in der Spätantike*. Wiesbaden: Harrassowitz, pp. 109–17.

Trapp, M., 1997. Philosophical Sermons: The 'Dialexeis' of Maximus of Tyre. *Aufstieg und Niedergang der römischen Welt 2*, 34/3, pp. 1945–76.

208   *Bibliography*

————, ed., 2003. *Greek and Latin Letters: An Anthology*. Cambridge: Cambridge University Press.

————, 2006. Biography in Letters, Biography and Letters. In McGing, B. and Mossman, J. eds. *The Limits of Ancient Biography*. Swansea: Classical Press of Wales, pp. 335–50.

Treucker, B., 1961. *Politische und sozialgeschichtliche Studien zu den Basilius-Briefen*. Diss., Frankfurt am Main.

Uthemann, K.-H., 1981. Syllogistik im Dienst der Orthodoxie: Zwei unedierte Texte byzantinischer Kontroverstheologie des 6. Jahrhunderts. *Jahrbuch der österreichischen Byzantinistik*, 30, pp. 103–12.

————, 1985. Stephanos von Alexandrien und die Konversion des Jakobiten Probos, des späteren Metropoliten von Chalkedon: Ein Beitrag zur Rolle der Philosophie in der Kontroverstheologie des 6. Jahrhunderts. In Laga, C., Munitiz, J.A. and Van Rompay, L. eds. *After Chalcedon: Studies in Theology and Church History Offered to Professor Albert Van Roey for His Seventieth Birthday* (Orientalia Lovaniensia Analecta 18). Leuven: Peeters, pp. 381–99.

Vacandard, E., 1903. Saint Victrice, évêque de Rouen (IVe–Ve s.). *Revue des questions historiques*, 37/n.s. 29, pp. 379–441.

Van Dam, R., 2003. *Families and Friends in Late Roman Cappadocia*. Philadelphia: University of Pennsylvania Press.

Van Deun, P., 2013. Exploration du genre byzantine des *kephalaia*: la collection attribuée à Theognoste. In Rigo, A., Ermilov, P. and Trizio, M. eds. *Theologica Minora: The Minor Genres of Byzantine Theological Literature*. Turnhout: Brepols, pp. 51–66.

Van Hoof, L., forthcoming. The Letter Collection of Libanius of Antioch. In Sogno, C., Storin, B. and Watts, E. eds. *A Critical Introduction and Reference Guide to Letter Collections in Late Antiquity*. Berkeley: University of California Press.

Van Minnen, P., 2002. The Letter (and Other Papers) of Ammon: Panopolis in the Fourth Century A.D. In Egberts, A., Muhs, B.P. and van der Vliet, J. eds. *Perspectives on Panopolis*. Leiden: Brill, pp. 177–200.

Van Nuffelen, P., 2004. *Un héritage de paix et de piété: Etude sur les Histoires Ecclésiastiques de Socrate et de Sozomène* (Orientalia Lovaniensia Analecta 142). Leuven: Peeters.

————, 2014. The End of Open Competition? Religious Disputations in Late Antiquity. In Engels, D. and Van Nuffelen, P. eds. *Competition and Religion in Antiquity* (Collection Latomus 343). Brussels: Latomus, pp. 148–71.

————, 2016. *Penser la tolérance durant l'Antiquité tardive*. Paris: Cerf.

Van Uytfanghe, M., 1985. L'empreinte biblique sure la plus ancienne hagiographie occidental. In Fontaine, J. and Pietri, C. eds. *Le monde latin antique et la Bible*. Paris: Beauchesne, pp. 565–611.

————, 1987. *Stylisation biblique et condition humaine dans l'hagiographie mérovingienne (600–750)*. Brussels: Paleis der Academiën.

————, 1988. Art. Heiligenverehrung II (Hagiographie). *Reallexikon für Antike und Christentum*, vol. 14. Stuttgart: Hiersemann, pp. 150–83.

Veilleux, A., 1980. *Pachomian Koinonia: The Life of Saint Pachomius* (Cistercian Studies 45). Kalamazoo, MI: Cistercian Publications.

————, 1981. *Pachomian Koinonia: Pachomian Chronicles and Rules* (Cistercian Studies 46). Kalamazoo, MI: Cistercian Publications.

————, 1982. *Pachomian Koinonia: Instructions, Letters, and Other Writings of Saint Pachomius and His Disciples* (Cistercian Studies 47). Kalamazoo, MI: Cistercian Publications.

Vinzent, M., 2006. *Der Ursprung des Apostolikums im Urteil der kritischen Forschung* (Forschungen zur Kirchen- und Dogmengeschichte 89). Göttingen: Vandenhoeck & Ruprecht.

Von Ivánka, E., 1954. Κεφάλαια: Eine byzantinische Literaturform und ihre antiken Wurzeln. *Byzantinische Zeitschrift*, 47, pp. 285–91.

Vööbus, A., 1965. Abraham de-Bet Rabban and His Role in the Hermeneutic Traditions of the School of Nisibis. *Harvard Theological Review*, 58, pp. 203–14.

Vössing, K., 1997. *Schule und Bildung im Nordafrika der römischen Kaiserzeit* (Collection Latomus 238). Brussels: Latomus.

———, 2006. Notes on the Biographies of the Two African Fulgentii. In Young, F.M., Edwards, M.J. and Parvis, P.M. eds. *Papers Presented at the Fourteenth International Conference on Patristic Studies held in Oxford 2003*. Leuven: Peeters, pp. 523–9.

———, 2012. Hippo Regius, die Vandalen und das Schicksal des toten Augustinus: Datierungen und Hypothesen. *Hermes*, 140, pp. 202–29.

———, 2013. Victor of Vita. In Pollmann, K. and Otten, W. eds. *The Oxford Guide to the Historical Reception of Augustine*, Oxford: Oxford University Press, pp. 1857–8.

———, 2014a. *Das Königreich der Vandalen: Geiserichs Herrschaft und Imperium Romanum*. Darmstadt: Von Zabern.

———, 2014b. Bildung und Charakterbildung in Julians Schulgesetzgebung. In Iliescu, V., Nedu, D. and Barboş, A.-R. eds. *Graecia, Roma, Barbaricum: In memoriam Vasile Lica*. Galati: Muzeului de Istorie 'Paul Păltănea', pp. 329–40.

———, forthcoming. Das Vandalenreich unter Hilderich Gelimer: Neuanfang, Kontinuität and Untergang In Gauly, B.M. and Zimmerman, M. eds. *Dialoge mit dem Altertum*, Heidelberg: Winter.

Ware, K., 1981. Art. Diadochus von Photice. In Theologische Realenzyklopädie, 8. Berlin: de Gruyter, pp. 617–20.

Wasyl, A.M., 2011. *Genres Rediscovered: Studies in Latin Miniature Epic, Love Elegy, and Epigram of the Romano-Barbaric Age*. Kraków: Jagiellonian University Press.

Watt, J.W., 1999. A Portrait of John Bar Aphtonia, Founder of the Monastery of Qenneshre. In Drijvers, J.W. and Watt, J.W. eds. *Portraits of Spiritual Authority: Religious Power in Early Christianity, Byzantium, and the Christian Orient*. Leiden: Brill, pp. 155–69.

———, 2009. Literary and Philosophical Rhetoric in Syriac. In Woerther, F. ed. *Literary and Philosophical Rhetoric in the Greek, Roman, Syriac, and Arabic Worlds*. Hildesheim: Olms, 141–54.

———, 2010. *Rhetoric and Philosophy from Greek into Syriac* (Variorum Collected Studies Series 960). Farnham: Ashgate.

Watts, E.J., 2005. Orality and Community Identity in Eunapius' *Lives of the Sophists and Philosophers*. *Byzantion*, 75, pp. 334–61.

———, 2007. Creating the Academy: Historical Discourse and the Shape of Community in the Old Academy. *Journal of Hellenic Studies*, 127, pp. 106–22.

———, 2010. *Riot in Alexandria: Tradition and Group Dynamics in Late Antique Pagan and Christian Communities* (Transformation of the Classical Heritage 46). Berkeley: University of California Press.

———, 2011. Doctrine, Anecdote, and Action: Reconsidering the Social History of the Last Platonists (c. 430–c. 550 AD). *Classical Philology*, 106, pp. 226–44.

Webb, R., 2008. *Demons and Dancers: Performance in Late Antiquity*. Cambridge, MA: Harvard University Press.

Westra, L.H., 2002. *The Apostles' Creed: Origin, History, and Some Early Commentaries* (Instrumenta Patristica et Mediaevalia 43). Turnhout: Brepols.

Wilken, R.L., 2013. *The First Thousand Years: A Global History of Christianity*. New Haven: Yale University Press.

Williams, J.G., 1980. The Power of Form: A Study of Biblical Proverbs. In Crossan, J.D. ed. *Gnomic Wisdom* (Semeia 17). Chico, CA: Scholars Press, pp. 35–58.

210   Bibliography

Wimbush, V.L., 1997. Interpreting Resistance, Resisting Interpretation. *Semeia*, 79, pp. 1–10.

Winkler, G., 1975. L'aspect pénitentiel dans les Offices du soir en Orient et en Occident. In *Liturgie et rémission des péchés. Atti (Parigi 1973)*. Rome: Edizioni liturgiche, pp. 273–93.

Winlock, H.E. and Crum, W.E., 1926. *The Monastery of Epiphanius at Thebes*, 2 vols. New York: Metropolitan Museum of Art.

Wintjes, J., 2005. *Das Leben des Libanius* (Historische Studien der Universität Würzburg 2). Rahden: Leidorf.

Wipszycka, E., 1996a. *Études sur le christianisme dans l'Égypte de l'antiquité tardive*. Rome: Institutum Patristicum Augustinianum.

———, 1996b. Contribution à l'étude de l'économie de la congrégation Pachômienne. *Journal of Juristic Papyrology*, 26, pp. 167–210.

Wire, A., 1990. *The Corinthian Women Prophets: A Reconstruction through Paul's Rhetoric*. Minneapolis: Fortress.

Wood, P., 2010. *We Have No King but Christ: Christian Political Thought in Greater Syria on the Eve of the Arab Conquest*. Oxford: Oxford University Press.

Wynn, Ph., 1990. Rufinus of Aquileia's Ecclesiastical History and Victor of Vita's History of the Vandal Persecution. *Classica et Mediaevalia*, 41, pp. 187–98.

Zeegers-Vander Vorst, N., 1978. Une *gnomologie* d'auteurs grecs en traduction syriaque. *Symposium Syriacum*, 205, pp. 163–77.

Index

Authors and Persons

Abū Bishr Mattā 179
Adelphius of Antioch 185
Aeschylus 169
Aetius (of Antioch) 153–4
Agathon, Abba 22–3, 31
Alexander of Alexandria 147
Alexander (the Great) 16, 32
Ambrose of Milan 105, 109, 112, 114, 147, 163
Amphilochius of Iconium 127
Anacharsis 32
Anastasius I (Emperor) 129
Andrew of Crete 140
Antiochus 6, 61–7, 71
Antony of Tagrit 183–4
Antony the Great 13–16, 26–7, 47, 56
Aphthonius 30–1, 33
Aphtonia 174
Apollinaris of Laodicea (Father and Son) 98
Apollonius of Tyana 47, 56
Aristaenetus 126
Aristophanes 93
Aristotle 16, 64–5, 84–5, 108, 153–4, 172, 175, 182, 184
Arius 147
Arsenius, Abba 13–16, 24, 26–7
Athanasius of Alexandria 13–14, 27, 43, 97, 111, 175
Athanasius of Balad 178
Augustine of Hippo 4, 8, 103, 107–9, 112, 114–15, 146–7, 153, 156–7, 159–60, 162–70
Augustine, Ps.- 169

Babai of Nisibis 173, 184
Babai the Great 173, 177, 184
Babrius 31
Bacchius 126

Bardaisan 178, 182
Barhadbeshabba 181
Barhebraeus 183
Basil of Caeserea 4, 6–7, 15–17, 21, 29–30, 43, 84, 87, 91–7, 99–100, 103, 109, 116–30, 140, 173, 177
Benjamin, Abba 23
Besa 34, 36, 42

Caecilian of Carthage 149
Caesarius of Arles 1–2
Catus 165
Chrestus of Byzantium 57
Cicero 1–2, 9, 108, 114, 153, 157, 162–3, 168
Clematius 126
Clement of Alexandria 62, 84
Clement, Ps.- 62
Commodianus 157

Demetrius, Ps.- 129
Diadochus of Photike 64, 168
Diogenes 32
Diogenes Laertius 63, 158
Dionysius the Areopagite 62
Dionysius Thrax 177, 181
Dioscurus 169
Dorotheus of Gaza 64
Dracontius 165–6, 169

Ebonh 42
Elias 174, 184
Emeritus (Donatist) 149, 156–7
Ephrem 158, 176, 178, 184
Epictetus 82, 85
Epiphanius, Abba 24
Eugenius of Carthage 160–1, 167–8
Eunapius of Sardis 128–30
Eunomius 153
Eusebius of Caesarea 81–2, 161–3, 168–9

212   Index

Eustathius (Abbot) 61, 67
Eustochium 1–2, 16
Eustratios the Presbyter 133
Eutropius 81–2
Euxenus 56
Evagrius Ponticus 13–16, 26–7, 62

al-Fārābī 179
Faustus 115
Flavian II of Antioch 129
Fulgentius, Fabius Planciades 165–6, 170
Fulgentius of Ruspe 165–6, 170

Galen 66, 172
Gaudentius of Brescia 109
Gelimer 164
Genseric 160, 168–9
Gervasius 105, 113
Gregory of Nazianzus 85, 99, 117–18, 123,
    126–7, 140, 177–8, 184
Gregory of Nyssa 28, 97, 109, 118, 126–7
Gregory Thaumaturgus 9
Gunthamund 161, 165, 169–70

Henana of Adiabene 180–1
Hermogenes 30
Hesiod 31, 92–3
Hieronymus of Rhodes 77
Hilary of Arles 104, 112
Hilderic 161, 164, 170
Hippocrates 74–5
Hippolytus 158
Homer 19, 93, 99, 126, 172, 184
Honoratus of Marseille 112
Honorius (Emperor) 8, 146–7, 155
Horace 1–2
Horsiesius 34, 41–2, 56–7
Huneric 160, 161, 165–70

Ignatius of Antioch 62
Irenaeus of Lyons 62
Isocrates 72, 84

Jacob of Serug 178
Jerome 1–3, 9, 15–17, 19, 21, 28–30, 34–5,
    54, 103–5, 113, 157, 163, 173
John, Abba 23
John bar Aphtonia 174–5, 184
John Chrysostom 6, 29, 87, 103, 109,
    127, 157
John of Apamea ('the Solitary') 6, 80–5
John of Damascus 133
John of Ephesus 173, 176
John of Tella 174

John Philoponus 158
Julian (Emperor) 117–18
Julianus Pomerius 1
Justinian (Emperor) 61, 147, 176–7

Lactantius 153, 157, 168
Leontios of Neapolis 133
Libanius of Antioch 7, 38–9, 57, 87, 91, 97,
    99, 116–30
Lucian of Samosata 6, 73–4, 79–80, 81,
    83–4

Macedonius II of Constantinople 129
Macrobius 165
Maiorianus 164
Mar Abraham 173, 175, 180, 185
Marcellinus 147–9, 156–7
Marcellus 146, 155–7
Marcus Aurelius (Emperor) 63
Mark, Abba 24
Martin of Tours 104, 112
Mary of Egypt 7, 131, 133–9
Maximus of Tyre 64, 72
Melito, Ps.- 178
Menander 22
Menas 123
Michael the Syrian 156
Minucius Felix 157
Moses, Abba 22

Nestorius 43, 181
Niceta of Remesiana 110, 115
Nicolaus 30
Nilus 62
Nonnus 38

Olympiodorus 56
Optimus 127
Origen 2, 9, 103, 168

Pachomius 16–17, 21, 30, 34–7, 39–41, 46,
    48–51, 53–7
Palladius of Helenopolis 56–7, 147
Pambo, Abba 24
Pamprepius 38
Paul the Deacon 133
Paul the Persian 182
Paulinus of Nola 104, 106, 110,
    112–13, 115
Petilian (Donatist) 150, 156–7
Petronius 37, 49
Philostratus 56–7
Pittacus of Mytilene 32
Plato 32, 93, 96, 99–100, 153, 172, 175

Index 213

Plotinus 153
Plutarch 6, 33, 73–4, 77, 79–81, 83–5, 93, 96, 99
Plutarch, Ps.- 73
Polycarp 62, 113
Porphyry 63, 108–9
Primian 157
Proclus 47, 56
Prodicus of Ceos 93
Protasius 105, 113
Prudentius 103
Pyrrho 158
Pythagoras 31, 66, 94

Quintilian 28–30, 64

Romanos the Melodist 7, 138–9, 141
Rufinus of Aquileia 2, 80, 110, 115, 163, 168–9

Sahdona 177
Sallust 163
Sara, Amma 25, 32
Sergius of Reshaina 182, 184
Shenoute of Atripe 34–46, 54
Socrates 32
Socrates of Constantinople 36, 44, 97, 98, 118, 127, 153–4, 158
Solon 92–3
Sopater 123
Sophocles 169, 172
Sophronios of Jerusalem 133
Sozomen 97, 156, 176, 184
Stobaeus 62
Strategius 126
Sulpicius Severus 103–4, 112–13
Sylvanus of Qardu 182

Tertullian 6, 103, 105, 113, 167, 178, 184
Theano 32
Themistius 6, 73–4, 78–81, 83–4
Theodore (Pachomian Abbot) 34, 37–8, 40–2, 45–8, 50–1, 53–8
Theodore, Abba 25
Theodore Lector 140
Theodore of Constantinople 140
Theodore the Alexandrian 40
Theodoret of Cyrrhus 64, 136, 169
Theodosius I (Emperor) 113
Theognis 92–3
Theon 24, 30–3
Theophilus 43
Thomas 81–2, 85

Thomas of Marga 29, 173, 184
Thrasamund 164, 165, 169–70
Thucydides 172

Victor of Vita 8, 160–70
Victricius of Rouen 7, 103–15
Vigilantius 104–5, 108–9
Vigilius, Ps.- 157
Virgil 1–2, 107, 111, 114, 165, 168, 170

Xenophon 84

Zacharias Scholasticus 118, 122–4, 129–30
Zeno of Verona 109

Places

Alexandria 2, 35, 39, 42, 82, 85, 103, 110, 123, 133, 136, 138, 179, 182
Ancyra 61
Antioch 7, 38, 87, 91, 96, 118, 126, 174
Arles 1
Athens 6, 120–1, 173, 180

Beni Hasan 29
Bethlehem 16

Caesarea in Cappadocia 15
Caesarea in Palestine 2, 103
Carthage 8, 151–2, 154, 160, 164, 168–70
Constantinople 118–20, 127, 137, 139, 141, 164, 174, 179
Cyprus 133

Dakhleh Oasis 38
Deir el Bahri 30
Diospolis Magna (Thebes) 37
Diospolis Parva 37

Edessa 176, 178, 180, 185
Ephesus 42

Harran 178, 180
Hippo Regius 162

Izla 180

Jerusalem 6, 61, 67, 131–7, 140–1
Junca 170

Kedron 61
Kom el-Dikka 39

214   *Index*

Lérins 1

Mabbug 39
Mar Zakkai 178–9
Milan 104, 167

Nicomedia 127
Nisibis 179–82
Nitria 24

Oxyrhynchus 30

Panopolis 37–8, 42, 45–6
Pbow 37, 40, 42, 49, 56
Photike 168

Qenneshre 178–9, 182

Rome 2, 16, 110, 112
Rouen 7, 104–6, 110–12, 115
Ruspe 165

Sakkara 30
Scetis 22
Seleuceia 174
Smyrna 113

Tabennisi 56
Thbew 37, 49
Thebes 19, 37
Thmoušons 49, 56
Trimithis 38–9

Vita 160

Subjects

adventus 7, 106–7, 111, 113–4
a-literacy 13–14, 17, 25–6, 45; *see also*
    illiteracy
allegory 165
alphabet 14, 17, 19, 26, 29, 37–41
anchoretic life 13, 25, 81–2, 180
anthology 62, 64–5, 92, 166
aphorism 6, 64, 67, 72, 74–5, 80, 83
apology, apologetics 104, 106, 111, 153
apophthegma 5, 13–14, 26, 30–1, 57, 63,
    65–6, 85; *see also* saying
apostle, apostolic 1, 6, 16, 19, 21, 35, 50–1,
    105–6, 110, 113, 184, 189
Apostles' Creed 115
Arians 8, 165
Aristotelian tradition 56, 109, 179, 182
arithmetic 42

artes liberales 2
ascetics, asceticism 1, 4, 5, 7, 27, 37, 48–50,
    52–6, 64, 80–2, 86–7, 92, 103–4, 106–7,
    133, 135, 172–5, 177, 180–3, 185
audientia episcopalis 151, 155
authority: biblical 132; ecclesiastical 109,
    180, 182; imperial 148, 169, 176;
    monastic 6, 47–50, 52–6; personal
    authority (of a teacher) 6, 47–8, 52, 55,
    122, 139; spiritual 55

Bible 4, 6, 8, 19, 61–2, 64–6, 129, 131–2,
    134–5, 137, 139–40, 152, 161, 167, 184;
    in Coptic 34, 40–1, 43; reading 36, 41–3;
    in Syriac 181; *see also* scripture
bilingualism 8, 34, 39, 45
biography 53, 56, 104, 112, 129, 165–6,
    173–5

catechesis 56, 109–10, 145
catechumenate 137
celibacy 104, 107
cenobitic life 34, 36–41
Chreia 22, 23, 25, 26, 30–3
classical: authors 8, 38, 53, 84, 92–4, 161,
    163; culture 86, 91–2, 96, 98, 103, 166,
    172; education 1–5, 7–8, 40, 91, 96, 103,
    145–6, 165, 172, 177, 183; literature 2–3,
    38, 40, 42–3, 92, 95–6, 107, 129, 174,
    176–7; rhetoric 3, 5, 21, 104, 111, 123,
    155, 161
classroom 17, 21, 30–1, 33, 37, 39, 55, 136
cognitio extraordinaria 147–8, 156
commentary 62, 136, 179, 182
commonplaces 65, 72, 127, 134, 137, 184
conversion 120, 123–4, 133, 136–7, 139, 171

declamation 21, 41, 121, 128
de-paganisation 119, 124, 130
dialectic 81–3, 107–9, 111, 113, 146,
    153–5, 158
dialectician 108, 110
dialexis 63–4, 72
dialogue 6, 57, 80–3, 153
diatribe 34, 40, 42, 177
didactic 6–7, 63, 67, 78, 80–3, 92–3, 96, 176
didaskalos see teacher
disciple, discipleship 47, 52, 55, 57, 85,
    92, 168
discourse: didactic 67; hagiographical 2,
    103, 111–12; inner-Christian 2–4, 92,
    107, 112, 155, 176; rhetorical 3, 21, 26,
    104, 107, 152, 154; totalising 54
disputation 145–9, 154, 156, 165

Index 215

dogma 66, 86, 94
Donatists 8, 145–6, 148–51, 156–7, 167

education (monastic) *see* monastic education
educational institutions *see* institutions of education
elite 4, 7–8, 37, 72, 86–8, 90–2, 96, 115, 125, 164–7, 169–70, 172, 177–8, 182
eloquence 38, 109, 120–1, 127–8, 162–3, 165, 169, 174
encomium, encomiastic 37, 40–2, 111
epic 93, 176
epigram 38, 164
epistles 2, 4, 7, 25, 34, 36, 41–3, 57, 85, 92, 125; epistolary collections 117–18, 126; epistolary exchange 116–18, 122–8; epistolary style 2, 92, 119, 121; epistolography 2, 40, 117–18, 127
erotapokriseis 24, 25, 30, 63
ethics 88, 90–6, 99
exegesis 6, 48, 103, 113, 115, 153, 181
exempla 31, 65–6, 74, 79–80, 82–3, 88, 90, 120–1, 124
exhortation 64, 66, 97, 104, 110, 114

festal letters 42–3
forensic rhetoric 8, 40, 146, 150–5, 157

genre 2, 4, 7, 15, 21, 26, 33, 63, 80, 103, 109, 112, 140, 161, 167
gnome, gnomic sayings 5, 6, 19, 21, 26, 30, 33, 62–5, 72–8, 80, 82–5, 93
grammar 4, 8, 21, 26, 31, 38, 40–3, 107, 159, 165, 176, 181, 183, 185
gymnastic exercise 95

hagiography, hagiographical discourse 2, 4, 15, 103–4, 111–12, 131–3, 135, 137, 140, 173, 184
hellenism, hellenistic 3, 30, 95, 153, 174–6, 178–9, 181, 183–4
heresy, heretics 111, 146–7, 152–3, 180
hermit *see* anchoretic life
historiography 4, 118, 161, 163, 171
holiness 7, 111–12
homily 6, 40, 61–4, 109, 139, 162
hymn 7, 81, 131–3, 138–40, 176

identity-formation 171, 180; Pachomians 6, 50; Roman-African 164; Syriac 171–3, 180, 184; Vandals 8
illiteracy, illiterate 13, 16, 35–6, 44, 86, 104, 135; *see also* a-literacy

imitation of Christ and of the saints 7, 90, 104, 110–11
inclusio 74, 77, 80, 83
initiation 56–7, 111, 171
institutions of education 2, 5, 8, 86, 88, 90, 145, 159, 167, 172, 179–82
instruction: ascetic/monastic 2, 5–6, 14–16, 26, 35, 39, 47, 49, 53–5, 57, 173; biblical 50–1, 135; of children 15, 29, 92; Christian 88–90, 109–10, 166–7; divine 134; elementary 25, 35, 38, 42; ethical 92; in the liberal arts 2, 80, 162, 177; rhetorical 25, 31
intellectual training 8, 27, 65, 91, 95, 99
intellectual vs. moral 14, 29, 88, 91, 110
interpreter 40, 47

kephalaia 61–7
Koinonia see Pachomian Koinonia

learning: biblical 134–5; Christian/ecclesiastical 4, 8, 14, 36, 57, 146, 173, 181; classical/secular 3–4, 7–8, 16, 34, 145–6, 151, 154, 172–6, 184; philosophical 173, 175, 182
lectionary 131–2, 134–5, 139–41
library 36, 45, 85; portable 65
literacy, literate 5, 13–15, 22, 25–7, 36, 39–42, 80, 183
literature: Christian 3–4, 6, 26, 37, 40, 64, 66, 80, 103, 132, 135, 173–4, 177; secular 6, 38, 41, 83, 92–6, 98–9, 129, 164–6, 172, 174, 177
litterae saeculares 13
liturgical prayer 132, 135, 139, 141
liturgical reading 132, 135, 139
liturgy 4, 7, 114, 131–3, 135–7, 139

magisterium 162
martyr, martyrdom 7, 61, 103–11, 113, 161, 167
master (ascetic/monastic) 47–8, 52–4, 174
maxim 5, 15, 19, 21–3, 26, 30, 33, 63–5, 72, 80, 84–5, 93
meditation 6, 36, 38, 43, 63, 66
memorisation 6, 17, 35–6, 38, 63, 65–6, 83, 138
mentor (ascetic) 6, 47, 52, 55
metaphor 61, 122, 162, 168
Miaphysites 174, 176
monastery 5, 16, 34–6, 38, 40–4, 48–9, 51–4, 61, 87, 91, 173–5, 178–80
monastic education 5–6, 13–17, 21–2, 26, 30, 34–5, 81, 179

216   *Index*

morals 6–7, 14, 26, 29, 64–7, 77–83, 88–94, 96, 99, 131, 138, 150, 152, 162
multilingualism 39
multiliteracy 39
myth, mythology 15, 73–4, 89–90, 160, 165, 178, 184

Neoplatonism 3, 114
Nicene Creed 131, 178

oral transmission of teaching 6, 17, 36, 40, 43–5, 47–9, 53–5, 57
orator, oratory 1, 64, 66, 93, 104, 120–1, 124, 128, 150

Pachomian Koinonia 6, 34–5, 37, 41, 46–57
pagans, paganism 1, 3, 7, 39, 46, 73–4, 81, 86, 89–90, 92, 94–9, 109, 111–12, 117, 119, 121, 124, 126, 129–30, 145, 155, 159, 162–7, 172–3, 175, 177–9, 181, 184
paideia 7, 87–8, 91, 96–7, 172, 174–5, 177–8
panegyric 7, 104, 106–7, 174
pedagogy 4–5, 14–15, 21, 25–7, 30, 39, 86, 88–91, 95–8, 131, 139, 176–7, 180–3
peroratio 109, 161
philosopher 43, 46, 52, 55, 64, 74, 79, 82, 93, 95, 108, 147, 153, 158, 173, 175, 179, 184
philosophy 3, 8, 66, 72, 83, 90, 93–5, 97, 112, 123, 153, 173, 175–6, 178, 182–4
Platonism 45, 100, 182
poetry 14, 92, 123, 160, 178
preacher, preaching 1, 4, 6–7, 38, 43, 87–8, 91–2, 96, 103, 109, 155
progymnasmata 21–2, 31, 41
protreptic 3–5, 7, 93, 111, 123–4, 145

questions and answers *see erotapokriseis*

recitation 33, 36, 38, 65, 135, 140
relics 7, 104–13
rewriting 65
rhetoric 2, 4–8, 21, 26–7, 30–1, 33, 40, 42–4, 64–6, 84, 87, 93, 103–4, 106–8, 111–12, 116–17, 119, 120–6, 128–30, 133, 146, 150–5, 159, 161–4, 166–7, 174–8, 181, 183–4; *see also* classical rhetoric; forensic rhetoric; instruction, rhetorical
rhetoric of paradox 3, 104, 107, 109, 111

sacred and secular 120, 121, 123, 124
saints 7, 50, 103–12, 132, 140, 173
saying 4, 15, 19, 21, 23–6, 33, 37, 64–5, 92–3; *see also apophthegma*; gnomic saying

school, schooling 2–4, 19, 26, 38, 40–2, 55, 87–8, 90–2, 96–7, 104, 111, 155, 159, 163, 175, 179–80; the church as school 104, 159; elementary school 37; grammar school 1, 159, 181; monastic school 14, 38, 178, 180–1; philosophical school 46, 55, 90, 178, 182; rhetorical school 1, 129, 159, 181
school texts 1, 30, 37–8, 40, 42, 45
scribal training 38
scripture 7, 14–16, 21, 28, 33, 35, 38–40, 43–4, 50–1, 53–4, 61, 66, 89–90, 94–5, 109, 131–2, 134–5, 139, 154, 177, 181
self-education 34, 43
self-formation 91, 139
sententia 5–6, 16, 21–2, 26, 63, 66, 80, 83; *see also* gnomic sayings
sermon 4, 34, 39–42, 104–11, 131, 145, 155, 159, 162, 167
socialisation 86, 97
sophist, sophism 87, 92, 108, 118, 120–1, 123, 126, 153–4, 184
spiritual: exercise 66; family 52; leader 165; master 29; philosophy 173, 175
Stoicism, stoic 90, 178
studia divina 165
studia saecularia 159, 162, 165
syllable, syllabary 16–17, 19, 21, 26, 29, 35, 37–8, 40–1
syllogism 108
synaxis 35, 44, 51–2

teacher 19, 39, 42, 47–8, 52, 54–5, 57, 65, 88–90, 92, 162, 168; the bishop as teacher 7, 110; Christ as teacher 159; elementary (*didaskalos*) 41–2; of grammar (*grammatikos, grammaticus*) 38, 41–2, 129, 161, 165, 174, 176, 183; monastic 39, 48, 55, 65, 81; of philosophy 55–6, 153; of rhetoric (*rhetor*) 1, 4, 7, 38, 99, 119–20, 122–3, 127–8, 184
tragedy 98, 169, 176
translation 4, 6, 34–5, 40, 43, 66, 73–84, 87–9, 133, 163, 168, 176–9, 181; cultural translation 111; of relics 104–5, 113
Trisagion 137
typology 132

vainglory 64, 87, 90–1, 97
virgin, virginity 1, 64, 103, 107
virtue 5, 7, 21, 26, 64, 72, 81–3, 85, 88, 90–5, 174

wisdom 2, 14, 62, 91, 93, 95, 98–100, 105, 110, 174–6, 178
wisdom literature 6, 73–4, 78, 80, 83–5